The Mind–Body Problem

A Guide to the Current Debate

Edited by Richard Warner and
Tadeusz Szubka

BLACKWELL
Oxford UK & Cambridge USA

Copyright © Basil Blackwell Ltd 1994
(Full copyright details for previously published essays can be found in the
Acknowledgments.)

First published 1994

Blackwell Publishers
238 Main Street
Cambridge, Massachusetts 02142
USA

108 Cowley Road
Oxford OX4 1JF
UK

Library of Congress Cataloging-in-Publication Data
The mind–body problem: a guide to the current debate / edited by Richard Warner and
Tadeusz Szubka.
     p. cm.
   Includes bibliographical references and index.
   ISBN 0–631–19085–6 (alk. paper). – ISBN 0–631–19086–4 (pbk.: alk. paper)
  1. Mind and body. I. Warner, Richard. II. Szubka, Tadeusz.
BF161.M554 1994 128'.2–dc20 93-31975
                        CIP

British Library Cataloguing in Publication Data
A CIP catalogue record for this book is available from the British Library.

Typeset in 10.5 on 12 pt Ehrhardt by Pure Tech Corporation, India
Printed in Great Britain by Hartnolls Ltd, Bodmin
This book is printed on acid-free paper

Contents

Notes on the Contributors

George Bealer is Professor of Philosophy at the University of Colorado, Boulder. His research interests include intensional logic, epistemology, metaphysics, philosophy of language and philosophy of mind. He is the author of *Quality and Concept* (1982), and is currently working on a book entitled *Philosophical Limits of Science*.

Patricia S. Churchland is Professor of Philosophy at the University of California, San Diego, and Adjunct Professor at the Salk Institute. She is the author of *Neurophilosophy* (1986) and co-author (with T. J. Sejnowski) of *The Computational Brain* (1992).

Paul M. Churchland is Professor of Philosophy at the University of California, San Diego. He is the author of *Scientific Realism and the Plasticity of Mind* (1979), *Matter and Consciousness* (1984, rev. edn 1988), and *A Neurocomputational Perspective: the Nature of Mind and the Structure of Science* (1989).

Fred Dretske is Professor of Philosophy at Stanford University. He has published articles in epistemology and philosophy of mind, and is the author of three books: *Seeing and Knowing* (1969), *Knowledge and the Flow of Information* (1981), *Explaining Behavior* (1988).

Jerry A. Fodor is Professor of Philosophy at Rutgers University and at the City University of New York Graduate Center. He is the author of numerous books, including *Representations* (1981), *The Modularity of Mind* (1983), *Psychosemantics* (1987), and *A Theory of Content and Other Essays* (1990).

John Foster is a Fellow and Tutor in Philosophy at Brasenose College, Oxford. He is the author of three books – *The Case for Idealism* (1982), *Ayer* (1985), *The Immaterial Self: a Defence of the Cartesian Dualist Conception of the Mind* (1991) – and a number of articles in epistemology, philosophical logic, metaphysics and philosophy of mind.

John J. Haldane is Reader in Moral Philosophy, and Director of the Centre for Philosophy and Public Affairs, at the University of St Andrews. He has written on a wide range of topics, and has co-edited three collections of essays, including (with C. Wright) *Realism, Reason, and Projection* (1993).

John Heil is Professor of Philosophy at Davidson College. He is the author of a number of publications, including *The Nature of True Minds* (1992), and a co-editor (with A. Mele) of *Mental Causation* (1993).

Ted Honderich is the Grote Professor of the Philosophy of Mind and Logic. He has published widely in political philosophy, metaphysics, and philosophy of mind. His recent publications include *A Theory of Determinism: the Mind, Neuroscience, and Life-Hopes* (1988) and *How Free Are You? The Determinism Problem* (1993).

Terence Horgan is Professor of Philosophy at Memphis State University. He has published widely in metaphysics, philosophy of mind, and philosophy of language, and co-edited (with J. Tienson) *Connectionism and the Philosophy of Mind* (1991).

Jaegwon Kim is Professor of Philosophy at Brown University, and has published numerous papers in metaphysics, philosophy of mind, and theory of knowledge. He is the author of *Supervenience and Mind: Selected Philosophical Essays* (1993).

Ernest LePore is Professor of Philosophy at Rutgers University. He has published numerous articles in philosophy of language and mind, and is co-author (with J. A. Fodor) of *Holism: a Shopper's Guide* (1992). He has edited or co-edited a few collections.

Barry Loewer is Professor of Philosophy at Rutgers University. He has published a number of articles on issues in philosophy of language and mind.

John Macnamara is Professor of Psychology at McGill University and the author of *A Border Dispute: the Place of Logic in Psychology* (1986). He works on the foundations of psychology and cognitive science.

Colin McGinn is Professor of Philosophy at Rutgers University. He is the author of several philosophical books, including *Mental Content* (1989) and *The Problem of Consciousness* (1991). He has also published a novel, *The Space Trap* (1992).

George Myro was, until his death in 1987, Professor of Philosophy at University of California, Berkeley. He worked primarily in metaphysics, epistemology, philosophy of mind, and philosophical logic.

Thomas Nagel is Professor of Philosophy and Law at New York University. He is the author of many publications in ethics, epistemology, philosophy of mind, and political philosophy, including *The Possibility of Altruism* (1970), *Mortal Questions* (1979), *The View from Nowhere* (1986), and *Equality and Partiality* (1991).

Brian O'Shaughnessy is Emeritus Reader in Philosophy at King's College London. He has held different visiting professorships at UCLA and University of California at Berkeley. His major work is *The Will: a Dual Aspect Theory* in two volumes (1980).

Joseph Owens is Professor of Philosophy at University of Minnesota. He is the author of a number of papers in philosophy of language and mind, and co-editor (with C. A. Anderson) of *Propositional Attitudes* (1990).

Richard Rorty is University Professor of Humanities at the University of Virginia. He is the author of *Philosophy and the Mirror of Nature* (1979) and *Contingency, Irony, and Solidarity* (1989). Some of his numerous articles have been collected in *Consequences of Pragmatism* (1982), *Objectivity, Relativism and Truth* (1991), and *Essays on Heidegger and Others* (1991).

John Searle is the Mills Professor of the Philosophy of Mind and Language at University of California, Berkeley. He is the author of *Speech Acts* (1969), *Expressions and Meaning* (1979), *Intentionality* (1983), *Minds, Brains and Science* (1984), and *The Rediscovery of the Mind* (1992).

Sydney Shoemaker is Susan Linn Sage Professor of Philosophy at Cornell University. He is the author of *Self-Knowledge and Self-Identity* (1963), *Identity, Cause, and Mind* (1984), and co-author (with R. Swinburne) of *Personal Identity* (1984).

Jack J. C. Smart is Emeritus Professor of Philosophy in the Research School of Social Sciences at the Australian National University. He is the author of *An Outline of a System of Utilitarian Ethics* (1961), *Philosophy and Scientific Realism* (1963), *Between Science and Philosophy* (1968), *Ethics, Persuasion and Truth* (1984), and *Essays Metaphysical and Moral* (1987).

Stephen P. Stich is Professor of Philosophy at the Department of Philosophy and Center for Cognitive Science at Rutgers University. He is the author of *From Folk Psychology to Cognitive Science* (1983) and *The*

Fragmentation of Reason (1990), and numerous papers in philosophy of mind and language.

Galen Strawson is Fellow and Tutor in Philosophy at Jesus College, Oxford. He is the author of *Freedom and Belief* (1986), *The Secret Connexion: Causation, Realism and David Hume* (1989). His book *Mental Reality* is due to be published by the MIT Press in 1994.

Richard Swinburne is the Nolloth Professor of the Philosophy of Christian Religion at Oxford University. He is the author of many books, including *The Coherence of Theism* (1977, rev. edn 1993); *The Existence of God* (1979, rev. edn 1991); *Faith and Reason* (1981); *The Evolution of the Soul* (1986); *Responsibility and Atonement* (1989); *Revelation: from Metaphor to Analogy* (1992).

Zeno Vendler is Emeritus Professor of Philosophy at University of California, San Diego, and the author of a number of publications, mainly in philosophy of language and philosophy of mind, including *Res Cogitans* (1972) and *The Matter of Minds* (1984).

Steven J. Wagner is Professor of Philosophy at the University of Illinois, Urbana-Champaign. He has published in philosophy of language, philosophy of mathematics, and philosophy of mind. He is completing a book-length manuscript *Truth, Pragmatism, and Ultimate Theory*.

Richard Warner is Professor of Law at the Chicago-Kent College of Law. His fields of research in philosophy include ethics, philosophy of mind, and philosophy of law. He is the author of *Freedom, Enjoyment, and Happiness* (1987).

Preface

Recent Anglo-American philosophy has vigorously pursued the philosophy of mind, to the extent that philosophy of mind may claim to have replaced philosophy of language as "first philosophy." The reasons for this change are various. Some are internal to philosophy itself: many contemporary philosophers share the conviction that any adequate theory of language must be grounded in an adequate philosophy of mind. Other – external – reasons come from the rapid development of cognitive science and neuroscience. These "external" developments may account in part for the renewed interest in the mind–body problem, traditionally the most central problem in the philosophy of mind.

This collection provides an accessible introduction and guide to the main themes in the contemporary debate about the mind–body problem. The contributions cover a wide range of views, from eliminative materialism to strong dualism. The anthology begins with J. J. C. Smart's essay as a way of giving pride of place to a philosopher whose work on the identity theory gave new impetus in the 1960s to the mind–body debate. Apart from this, the essays are arranged conceptually, with thematically related essays placed together. The order of the essays does not reflect the way in which the contemporary debate evolved. Readers completely unfamiliar with the mind–body problem may do well to begin with Fodor's essay.

Richard Warner
Tadeusz Szubka

Acknowledgments

The editors gratefully acknowledge the editorial expertise – and patience – of Steve Smith at Blackwell. We also wish to thank the contributors, in particular John Heil, for their patient co-operation and their editorial suggestions.

We are grateful to the original publishers for permission to reprint papers by the following authors:

Jerry A. Fodor: originally published in *Scientific American* 244 (1981), no. 1 (January), pp. 114–23; © 1980 Scientific American, Inc.; reprinted with permission of the author and the journal. Paul M. and Patricia S. Churchland: reprinted, with permission of the authors and the publisher, from *The Neurosciences* 2 (1990), pp. 249–56; © 1990 W. B. Saunders Co. Colin McGinn: reprinted, with permission of the author and the publisher, from *Mind* 98 (1989), pp. 349–66; © 1989 Oxford University Press. Stephen P. Stich: reprinted, with permission of the author and the publisher, from *Mind* 101 (1992), pp. 243–61; © 1992 Oxford University Press. Jaegwon Kim: Presidential Address delivered before the Eighty-seventh Annual Central Division Meeting of the American Philosophical Association in Chicago, Illinois, April 28, 1989; reprinted, with permission of the author and APA, from *Proceedings and Addresses of the American Philosophical Association* 63 (3) (1989), pp. 31–47. Ernest LePore and Barry Loewer: reprinted, with permission of the authors and the editor, from *Journal of Philosophy* 84 (1987), pp. 630–42; © 1987 The Journal of Philosophy, Inc. John Searle: This the first chapter of John R. Searle's book *The Rediscovery of the Mind*, Cambridge, Mass. Bradford Books/MIT Press, 1992, pp. 1–26; © 1992 Massachusetts Institute of Technology; reprinted with permission of the author and the publisher.

Introduction
The Mind–Body Debate

Richard Warner

Are mental states – pain, belief, anger, and so on – nothing over and above physical states? Some philosophers think so; others do not; others reject the question as ill-conceived. Even if not ill-conceived, the question does demand explanation. What, for example, does "nothing over and above" mean? The contributions discuss the possibilities: type-identity theories, token-identity theories, functionalism, supervenience, anomalous monism, eliminativism. Let us put these possibilities aside, however, and let us do the same with another obvious issue, the meanings of the crucial terms, "mental" and "physical." The contributions treat these concerns in detail. We will treat them, not *in* detail, but *as* details, details of interpretation concerning the basic question, "Is the mental just the physical?" Our focus is on motivation: why ask the question at all? To understand the debate one has to understand *why* the debaters are debating.

1 The Explanatory Adequacy of Physics

The "why" lies in the divergent attitudes contemporary philosophers take toward science. Many philosophers share the attitude of David Lewis, who accepts the thesis of the explanatory adequacy of physics. This is

> the plausible hypothesis that there is some unified body of scientific theories, of the sort we now accept, which together provide a true and exhaustive account of all physical phenomena (i.e. all phenomena describable in physical terms). They are unified in the sense that they are cumulative: the theory governing any physical phenomenon is explained by

theories governing phenomena out of which that phenomenon is composed and by the way it is composed out of them. The same is true of the latter phenomena, and so on down to the fundamental particles or fields governed by a few simple laws, more or less as conceived of in present-day theoretical physics. (Lewis, 1971, p. 169)

Post-World-War-II Anglo-American philosophy saw the ever-increasing acceptance of the explanatory adequacy of physics, and – in various weaker and stronger versions – the thesis remains widely accepted today.[1]

The explanatory adequacy of physics leads directly to the conclusion that mental states are physical states (as Lewis points out). Take pain. Pain has physical effects: it can cause you to take aspirin, or hold your hand to your head, for example. According to the explanatory adequacy of physics, physical effects have physical explanations; more precisely: *all* physical phenomena are in principle ultimately explainable in terms of "fundamental particles or fields governed by a few simple laws, more or less as conceived of in present-day theoretical physics" (Lewis, 1971, p. 169) It follows trivially that the physical effects of pain are so explainable. Of course, *pain* is what explains these effects; consequently, pain itself is ultimately completely described and explained in terms of fundamental physics.[2] So pain is physical – in the sense that it is *completely* describable and explainable by physics.[3] This does not mean that we will ever actually produce the explanation. Chemistry, for example, reduces to quantum mechanics, but actually constructing the quantum mechanical explanations of chemical phenomena is generally beyond human capabilities.

2 Naturalism

These considerations compel many to conclude that mental phenomena are just a variety of physical phenomena. Indeed, the prevailing view in Anglo-American analytic philosophy today is naturalism. Naturalism is the view that everything is, in principle, completely describable and explainable in the terms of the physical sciences. This is, we should note, not quite the same thesis as the explanatory adequacy of physics. The latter asserts ultimate explanability in terms of fundamental physics; naturalism asserts explanability in terms of the physical – or, if one likes, the natural – sciences. What counts as natural science is controversial, of course. If we count as "natural" only physics and the theories reducible (in some sense of "reducible") to physics, naturalism is just the explanatory adequacy of physics in different dress. But many are more liberal, counting, for example, chemistry and biology as natural, whether or not these reduce to physics; and more liberally still, others add other disciplines, for example, economics, psychology, and sociology. These details do not matter for us, and we will talk interchangeably of naturalism and the explanatory adequacy of physics. We will also use "physicalism" and "naturalism" interchangeably. Many contributors use the term "materialism" in approximately the same sense as we are using "physicalism" and "naturalism."[4] We will use the term sparingly; this is simply a matter of expositional convenience and reflects no philosophical commitment.

Those who accept naturalism place considerable confidence in the ultimate explanatory power of science. Smart, Fodor, Shoemaker, and the Churchlands evince such confidence in their contributions. For Fodor, science defines the task for the philosopher concerned with mind–body issues: the appropriate philosophical project is articulating a conception of the mental that is consistent with, and an aid to, scientific investigation of the mental. Smart, Shoemaker, and the Churchlands provide paradigms of such a philosophical orientation: Smart, as he defends the identity theory he originally championed as a leader in naturalism's post-World-War-II rise to hegemony; Shoemaker, as he defends functionalism, perhaps the most favored view of the mental among naturalists today; and the Churchlands as they defend physicalism (in the form of eliminative materialism) against various objections. The Churchlands are supremely confident that science will succeed in explaining the mental, although they acknowledge that it will "surely be a long and difficult business."

3 Doubts about Naturalism

Not all philosophers share this confidence. Thomas Nagel, for example, writes in his contribution that

> We have increasing knowledge of a fascinating character about the physical conditions of particular types of conscious states, but these correlations, even if substantially multiplied, do not amount to a general explanatory theory. In order to achieve a real understanding of these matters, we would have to make progress of a fundamental kind with the mind–body problem: progress which constituted a conceptual advance, rather than merely more empirically ascertainable information, however interesting. A theory which succeeded in explaining the relation between behavior, consciousness, and the brain would have to be of a fundamentally different kind from theories about other things: It cannot be generated by the application of already existing methods of explanation.

This denies the explanatory adequacy of physics as understood by Lewis. Lewis contends that "there is some unified body of scientific theories, *of the sort we now accept*, which together provide a true and exhaustive account of all physical phenomena." The "of the sort we now accept" qualification is essential. It is an almost entirely empty thesis to assert that the present-day physical sciences will evolve into something – still called "physical science" – that explains the mental. Nagel does not deny this. He claims that the evolution will lead to a theory of "a fundamentally different kind from theories about other things." Lewis thinks the theory will *not* be of a fundamentally different kind.

An example highlights the disagreement. Suppose twenty-fifth century psychophysiology contains basic, undefined terms for sensations (like pain, pleasure, and seeing red). If this theory evolved in appropriate ways out of our current *fin de siècle* psychophysiology, we might well regard it as a physical science.[5] However, Lewis would – as would virtually any naturalist – regard our imagined future psychophysiology as fundamentally different in kind from our contemporary theories.

Smart, Fodor, Shoemaker, and the Churchlands should be interpreted as thinking that theories *not too different from our current theories* will explain the mental. Otherwise, they have advanced no substantive thesis. The "long and difficult business" (to use the Churchlands' phrase) of explaining the mental does not lead to too much change in our theories. But is it reasonable to expect that the explanation of the mental will not lead to too much change? It is very difficult to say. Nagel is indisputably correct when he observes that present-day psychology and neuroscience provide us with no "general explanatory theory," no "real understanding," of the relation between the mind and the brain. To take just one example, we have fascinating and relatively detailed knowledge of the psychophysiology of pain, but we still have no explanation at all of how electro-chemical events produce the *feeling* of pain.[6] Correlations are not explanations, as Nagel points out. But lacking even a proto-account of how the feeling is physical, how can we assess the likelihood that science – science not too different from our own – will succeed? How can we be in a position either to assert or to deny that contemporary science, or its not too distant progeny, will provide an account of the mental?[7] The explanatory adequacy of physics is not an obvious truth; it is a substantive *empirical* claim about the future course of science, and it is not at all clear that the claim is true.

But aren't there alternatives here? Can't we drop "of the sort we now accept" qualification and replace it with something else? This is the point at which Strawson, Wagner, and McGinn enter the debate. They do not deny, to use Wagner's words, that "brains consist of physical particles whose particular structures and motions are our thinking [using thinking as a stand-in for mental phenomena generally]." They differ, however, in their attitude toward the explanatory adequacy of physics. We can start with Strawson. In agreement with Nagel, he notes that "when we consider the brain as current physics and neurobiology present it to us, we have to admit that we do not know how experience as such – experiential 'what-it-is-likeness' as such – is or even could be based in the brain," and he contends that "[i]t is the descriptive scheme of physics that will have to change dramatically if there is to be an acceptable theoretical unification with the mental." This clearly rejects the explanatory adequacy of physics, understood in terms of the "of the sort we now accept" qualification. Strawson replaces that qualification with the requirement that the ultimate scientific account of the mind must be "theoretically satisfying," a requirement he persuasively defends as a substantive constraint. Wagner shares Strawson's assessment of current science; he regards it as an open question whether "thought can be brought into an explanatory fold that includes physics, chemistry, and biology," and he counsels us that "we can rarely know what future science will explain and where it will fail." Wagner, however, does not think we should worry much about replacing the "of the sort we now accept" qualification; rather, he simply notes that we are not "in any position to evaluate [the possibility that the mental is not physical], since there is no good existing concept of nonphysical reality." McGinn is more extreme. While he does not doubt that the mental is the physical, he argues that we may be "precluded from *ever* understanding [the relation between mind and body] given the way we have to form our concepts and develop our theories." This is a radical rejection of the explanatory adequacy of physics. Science – be it "of the sort we now accept" or fundamentally of a different kind – may *never* explain the mental. McGinn contends that accepting the epistemological limitation does not bar us from embracing the ontological claim that everything is physical.

4 Saying Something Substantive

McGinn's radical road does not beckon to those philosophers who, quite unlike Nagel, Strawson, Wagner (to some extent), and McGinn, think that philosophy can say something substantive about how the mental is the physical. A number of the contributions belong to this genre. There is no need for a detailed discussion of these essays, but a general overview is certainly in order. Like photos in a family album, the following snapshot descriptions of the essays reveal a range of similarities and differences characteristic of family resemblances.

Dretske, Owens, Heil, Macnamara, and Stich are concerned with the way in which the mind represents reality. Thus Dretske: "We must . . . try to say . . . what representation is and how it is realized in living systems." Take belief by way of illustration. Beliefs are *about* things; they are *representational*, or, equivalently, *intentional* (we will use these expressions interchangeably). Dretske explains representation in terms of information and history: "the important relations are informational [in the non-intentional sense of mathematical information theory] and historical – facts having to do with the way an organism developed (during learning) to more efficiently service its own needs." Dretske's ambition is to explain intentionality in a way that shows it to be a physical property of physical organisms. Many share this ambition. One center of attention among this group is the thesis of externalism, the thesis that two individuals exactly alike in their "internal" states (the states "inside" the skin, so to speak) may, because of different external environments, nonetheless differ in their psychological states. As Owens points out, current models of mental representation ignore externalism by assuming that representation is entirely a matter of internal properties, and he concludes that externalism "casts into doubt some central elements in the contemporary model of the mental." Heil also raises such doubts; he worries that externalism may lead to the unpalatable conclusion that the intentional properties of mental states play no causal role in the production of behavior; Heil, however, sees externalism as a definite sign of progress, as a philosophical advance in our understanding of the mind.

Dretske, Owens, and Heil may give the impression that intentionality is a central topic of contemporary psychology, but, Macnamara – a psychologist – contends that contemporary cognitive psychology does not in fact come to grips with that topic. He points out that our ability to refer to things in the world essentially involves an ability to classify individuals into kinds, and he argues that psychology simply ignores this latter ability. Intentionality, it would seem, fascinates philosophers, not psychologists. This suggests the attractive image of philosophers as trail-breakers, carving out a path for the science to follow. But is it the right path? Stich argues that the trail-breakers are hopelessly lost. Discussing the work on mental representation, Stich argues that "the projects I will sketch cannot readily be pursued by philosophers using the familiar techniques of philosophical analysis that predominate in the literature. Rather they are intrinsically interdisciplinary projects in which the construction and testing of empirical theories play a central role . . . [W]ith few exceptions . . . [such] work . . . is notably absent in the literature . . . This . . . might be taken as an indication that . . . people are actually pursuing . . . different projects . . . I am inclined to draw a darker conclusion: it is my contention that most of the players in this very crowded field have *no* coherent project that could possibly be pursued successfully with the methods they are using." Stich argues forcefully for his "darker conclusion."

Stich confines his dark vision to work on mental representation, but many think that, in general, work on the mind–body problem has reached a dead end, and that the time has come to seek new avenues. This negative assessment forms the background for the contributions from Haldane, O'Shaughnessy, Honderich, Horgan, Kim, and LePore and Loewer. Haldane characterizes work on the mind–body problem as a philosophical failure. He suggests a return to an Aristotelian–Thomistic framework that would exploit the form–matter distinction to recast the mind–body problem in a way that would dispel philosophical puzzlement. The form–matter distinction echoes distinctly, if implicitly, through O'Shaughnessy's contribution. He emphasizes form – matter-like relations of nonidentity-with-essential-dependence as he argues that "the animal body is that material object whose sole and primary function is to support the life and existence of the enmattered living entity with psychological characteristics to which it belongs." O'Shaughnessy devotes his contribution to a sketch of his positive program. Honderich, on the other hand, like Haldane, sharply criticizes current theory before proposing his own solution: union theory. Among the virtues Honderich finds in union theory is its recognition of psychophysical causation: the theory regards mental events as the physical effects of neural events while still assigning to the mental a genuine causal role in the production of thought and behavior. Horgan's position has affinities with Honderich's. Horgan's "nonreductive materialism" sees the physical as determining what happens on the mental level while still allowing the mental level to be genuinely explanatory and not reducible to the physical. Kim attacks nonreductive naturalism as a myth. Kim argues that "If nonreductive physicalists accept the [explanatory adequacy of physics (as Horgan and Honderich do)] . . . they have no visible way of accounting for the possibility of psychophysical causation." Finally – this is the last snapshot in the album – LePore and Loewer dispute the criticism that nonreductive naturalism is open to this objection as they explain and defend Donald Davidson's anomalous monism.

5 A Perspective on the Mind–Body Debate

An unsympathetic observer leafing through the family album of this debate might cast the participants in the role of alchemists arguing over whether lead can be transmuted into gold. Science settled that question, and the alchemical debate now has minor historical significance as one of the intellectual antecedents of modern chemistry. Aren't mind–body philosophers in much the same situation? Whether and how to give a scientific account of the mind would seem to be a *scientific* question to be settled by science; moreover, the work of philosophers has hardly marked out a clear direction for science to take. Disagreement characterizes the mind–body debate, not unanimity. The alchemical analogy is, however, *too* unsympathetic. Philosophical speculation about how mind and brain interrelate may play a useful scientific role; indeed the analogy with alchemy works the opposite way here. Alchemy did play a role in the development of chemistry, and it is not unreasonable to think that scientifically minded philosophers with the self-conscious aim of aiding science might do considerably more for psychology and psychophysiology than alchemy did for chemistry.

But these considerations might still leave our unsympathetic observer mostly unmoved. The mind–body debate still looks like a squabble among possibly helpful underlaborers hoping to prepare the way for future serious science. Intellectual historians looking back from a one-or-two-hundred-year vantage point may find the current debate quite significant in the account of how the by-then-successful science of psychophysiology arose, but it would seem that *we* can at best only regard it as providing possible answers to possible future scientific questions. After all, not knowing what future science will look like, how do we know what answers to what questions will be relevant? Fortunately, a more flattering portrait is possible.

The problem is that we have centered the mind–body debate on an empirical claim about the future of science, the claim that physical sciences, "of the sort we now accept," can in principle explain the mental; however, present-day science has made little progress on explaining the mental; to repeat Nagel's assessment: "We have increasing knowledge of a fascinating character about the physical conditions of particular types of conscious states, but these correlations, even if substantially multiplied, do not amount to a general explanatory theory." The current state of physical science provides little assurance that sciences "of the sort we now accept" will ultimately explain the mental. Removing the "of the sort we now accept" restriction, however, seems problematic, for – unless McGinn is right – it is a relatively trivial claim that some day something we will call "physical science" will explain the mental. We can, however, recast the terms of the debate to sidestep this difficulty.

The relevant historical context shows the way. The relevant history is the rise of science. A *very* brief summary (adapted from Taylor, 1985): seventeenth century "moderns" rebelled against the Aristotelian view of the universe as a meaningful order of final causes. The vision of final causes yielded to a Pythagorean vision of a mathematically ordered world (Bruno, Kepler, and Galileo), and finally to the contemporary vision of the world as a complex of contingent correlations delineated by empirical observation. From the modern point of view, Aristotelian science projected on nature what people wanted to find there: a meaningful order of final causes. Nature, however, reveals its truths only to those who avoid such projection: the discovery of truth requires a constant struggle against what Bacon called the "idols of the human mind." The reason is that science aims at representing the world as it is in itself, not as it merely appears to this or that observer, or kind of observer. To achieve this goal we must guard against various distorting influences, not just wish fulfillment and prejudice, but even a particular location in time and space, and our own innate sensory constitution. We must correct for the influence of *any* factor that makes the world appear different than it really is. Science so conceived involves a practice of adjudication that corrects for the illusions of mere appearance and leads to a conception of the world as it really is. Israel Scheffler nicely captures the conception in his comments on scientific objectivity:

> A fundamental feature of science is its ideal of objectivity, an ideal that subjects all scientific statements to the test of independent and impartial criteria, recognizing no authority of persons in the realm of cognition. The claimant to scientific knowledge is responsible for what he says, acknowledging the relevance of considerations beyond his wish or advocacy to the judgment of his assertions. In assertion . . . he is trying to meet independent standards, to satisfy factual requirements whose fulfillment cannot be guaranteed in advance. (Scheffler, 1967, p. 1)

The "criteria" need not, of course, be precisely formulable; they may range from explicit methodological injunctions to vague and unformulated problem-solving procedures.

Reflection on the role of such criteria shows the way to recast the mind–body debate. The first step is to give more content to the terms "independent and impartial." We can do so by noting that objectivity comes in degrees. Nagel makes this point:

> At one end is the point of view of a particular individual, having a specific constitution, situation, and relation to the rest of the world. From here the direction of movement toward greater objectivity involves first, abstraction from the individual's specific spatial, temporal, and personal position in the world, then from the features that distinguish him from other humans, then gradually from the forms of perception and action characteristic of humans, then gradually away from the narrow range of a human scale in space, time, and quantity, toward a conception of the world which as far as possible is not the view from anywhere within it. (Nagel, 1979, p. 00)

Science aims at objectivity in the highest degree; it abstracts "from the forms of perception and action characteristic of humans, then gradually away from the narrow range of a human scale in space, time, and quantity."

The crucial point about "independent and impartial criteria" is that they effect the abstraction; this is what makes them independent and impartial. A simple example: suppose I assert that apples are red, i.e., not just red for humans, but red *simpliciter*. My sole reason is that apples appear red to humans; thus, my criterion of acceptability is "appearing red to humans." This criterion is not "independent and impartial." To accept that apples are red on this ground is to recognize the authority of certain persons – humans – in the realm of cognition; apples, after all, might normally appear green to the people from Alpha Centauri, and the strictures of objectivity prevent us from favoring the human perspective over the Alpha Centaurian. Of course, apples might really be red *simpliciter*; perhaps, as some have suggested, redness is a microstructural property of the surface of objects, a structural property that makes objects that have it appear red to humans (but green to Alpha Centaurians). The point is that "appearing red to humans" does not provide an "independent and impartial" ground for thinking that apples are red *simpliciter*.

The key to recasting the mind–body debate is to see that, in correcting in this way for distortions in our view of the world, independent and impartial criteria yield a picture of the world as a complex of *mind-independent* items. Mind-independence is the concept we need. An item is mind-independent just in case it's being the way it is does not, in any essential way, depend either on our beliefs about it, or on the way in which we form those beliefs (see, e.g. Scheffler, 1967). For example, redness as a microstructural property of surfaces is a mind-independent feature of objects; objects with that property *appear* red to beings with a certain sensory constitution, and appear in others ways to beings with other sensory constitutions. To see how to recast the mind–body debate, consider that to mistake the way nature *appears* to us for the way it *is* would be to commit an error similar to the error of Aristotelian science, which projected on to nature a meaningful order of final causes. It would be to lose the Baconian struggle against "idols of the human mind" by projecting on to nature the ways that it merely seems to us: to see the world as it is in itself, we must correct all distorting influences that make the world appear to be different than it really is. One can apply these points to the mental. Pain, for example, *feels* a certain way; indeed, it is natural to think that to be, for example, a pain *just is* an experience with a certain characteristic feel. But if everything has a mind-independent nature, we cannot assume that the way pain feels to us reveals the way it is *in itself*. This is to be revealed by scientific investigation, by developing a theory of the central nervous system.

We can generalize these remarks into a version of naturalism that makes no reference to physical science *of the sort we now accept*. We can interpret naturalism as the claim that everything can be completely described and explained as entirely mind-independent. To endorse this naturalism is of course still to make an empirical claim about the future of science. It is to claim that science, operating under the strictures imposed by appropriate independent and impartial criteria, can in principle completely describe and explain everything.[8] As an example of a theory that would not meet these strictures, recall our imagined twenty-fifth century psychophysiology; it contains undefined terms for sensations such as pain, pleasure, seeing red, and so on. If we are to understand these terms just from *our* experience of what they designate, from the way the states appear to us, then the theory fails to provide a mind-independent account of the mind.

6 Is the Mind Mind-independent?

With the exception of Nagel and McGinn, all of the contributors discussed so far can be interpreted as thinking that a mind-independent account of the mental is in principle possible. Strawson and Wagner would, however, agree with Nagel and McGinn that we lack any real understanding of what a mind-independent account of the mental would be like. Others, as we have seen are more ambitious. Dretske, Owens, Heil, Stich, LePore and Loewer, Haldane, O'Shaughnessy, Honderich, Horgan, and Kim are all – in one or another way – concerned with the possibility of articulating a consistent conception of the mental as mind-independent. It is worth remarking that their concern takes the form of a traditional philosophical activity: they survey our thought about a subject matter and provide a general characterization of it that reveals fundamental features of how we do, or should, conceive of ourselves. So understood, these essays – even if that is not always their intention – speak as much to *self* as to science. We need not see these essays exclusively as proto-science; we can see them more humanistically as responding to the need to have a coherent self-conception. The question, "Am I an object fully describable and explainable by science?" is as much a concern of self as of science, and it is certainly a concern of self to which the mind–body debate speaks.

The prevailing answer is that one is indeed an object fully describable and explainable by science. But there is a significant dissent. Nagel, Searle, Foster, Swinburne, Vendler, Myro, Warner, and Bealer comprise the contributions of the dissenting minority, with Rorty dissenting in part and concurring in part with the naturalist majority. The dissenters, with the exception of Rorty, all contend that the mental is not mind-independent. They make this contention in a variety of different vocabularies: the mental is subjective; private; that to which we have privileged access, and so on. The common thread through this diversity is that the mental (or more carefully, at least some mental phenomena) cannot be completely described and explained in the mind-independent terms of science.

Searle sees a certain attitude toward science as a fundamental mistake of naturalism. Searle objects to the persistent objectifying tendency in contemporary philosophy, science, and intellectual life generally. We have the conviction that if something is real, it must be equally accessible to all competent observers. Since the seventeenth century, educated people in the West have come to accept an absolutely basic metaphysical presupposition: *reality is objective.*

Searle regards the assumption as "obviously false, as a moment's reflection on one's own subjective states reveals . . . The actual ontology of mental states is a first-person ontology." Searle insists that mental states are nonetheless open to scientific study. Nagel and Searle take quite similar positions in their contributions. Nagel:

> We at present lack the conception of a complete analysis of the subjective, phenomenological features of mental reality in terms of an objective physical basis, and there is no reason to believe that such a thing is possible . . . The limits of the classical methods of objective science are not surprising, since those methods were developed to deal with a definite, though universal, type of subject matter. If we are to take the next great step, to a truly theoretical understanding of the mental, we must proceed by regarding this limitation as a challenge to develop a new form of understanding appropriate to a subject whose exclusion from physical science was essential to its progress.

Searle and Nagel dissent from the naturalist majority. Both receive criticism from Rorty, who characterizes their views as "pre-Galilean obscurantism." The root of the obscurantism lies in thinking that science has, so far, aimed at representing a mind-independent reality, and that the issue is whether such a representation of the mental is also possible. Rorty rejects the idea that science, and thought generally, represent reality at all. Of course, this point counts against the naturalists as well as anti-naturalists such as Searle and Nagel.[9] So it would be a mistake to place Rorty in the camp of the naturalist majority; however, he does concur with the majority in contending that we should think of ourselves as physical organisms in a physical world.

Several contributors – Foster, Swinburne, Vendler, Myro, Warner, and Bealer – think they can *prove* we are not fully physical (in the appropriate sense of "physical", i.e. fully describable and explainable in terms of the fundamental physical science). Foster begins with the "strong intuition" that any sensation that we correctly count as pain must feel like pain (more precisely, the feeling is a *de re* necessary property of any pain sensation). He notes that, if the strong intuition is true, a currently popular physicalist position – the token-identity theory – is false, and he defends the strong intuition against various objections to reach a dualist position. As Foster explains, he argues that certain mental *properties* are not physical properties, but he points out that he also believes that there are nonphysical *substances*. Swinburne argues explicitly for this latter claim on the ground that it is logically possible that I should exist after my body is destroyed. Unlike Swinburne and Foster, Vendler explicitly rejects the existence of nonphysical substances. The issue for Vendler is "whether anything exceeds the explanatory power of a 'unified' science," and, drawing on Wittgenstein and Aquinas, he argues that subjective experiences do lie outside science's explanatory power: "They exist only for the subject that has them . . . they are not in the publicly observable, interpersonal domain."

Arguments of the Foster–Swinburne–Vendler sort have a common pattern. They assert that a mental state (e.g. pain) *necessarily* has a certain feature (feeling a certain way); they contend that nothing physical has, or can have, this feature, and conclude that the state in question cannot be a physical state. Naturalists standardly reject the first premise, or argue that any sense in which it is true is a sense consistent with the state's being physical. Myro, Warner, and Bealer concern themselves with the first premise.

Myro argues that we have privileged access to (at least some) mental phenomena and no privileged access to any physical phenomena. This is not a new claim, but Myro's explanation and defense of this traditional position is both novel and (typically) ingenious. Warner and Myro share the same basic approach and intuitions, but differ in execution and vocabulary. Warner argues that certain beliefs about mental states enjoy a necessary, if qualified, immunity to error, and he argues that beliefs about physical items – i.e. the mind-independent items – enjoy no such immunity. He infers that mental states that enjoy such qualified incorrigibility cannot be mind-independent. Warner emphasizes that such qualified incorrigibility is not confined to the mental; rather, the incorrigibility of the mental is an instance of a more general phenomenon. Myro and Warner give an a priori defense of the claim that mental states necessarily have a feature that physical states lack. Some will appeal to a Kripke–Putnam scientific essentialism to argue that we cannot have such a priori knowledge. Bealer explains and responds to this objection in a careful consideration of the arguments of Kripke, Nagel, and Jackson. Linking traditional Cartesian intuitions to contemporary discussions, Bealer argues persuasively for the coherence and truth of the claim to know a priori that mental states necessarily have features that physical states lack. Bealer lays down an essential line of defense in the Myro–Warner–Bealer position.

7 Conclusion

The contributions typify the vigorous mind–body debate that occupies center stage in contemporary philosophy. The issue is whether the scientific program of a fully mind-independent description and explanation of nature extends without fundamental modification to the description and explanation of the mind. It is difficult to imagine a philosophical issue more fundamental to our understanding of science and self.

Notes

1 One way to weaken the thesis is to substitute a weaker requirement for Lewis's requirement that the micro-level theory explain the macro-level theory. One may still call the relation "explanation" but weaken Lewis's requirement that "the theory governing any physical phenomenon [the macro-theory] is explained by theories governing phenomena out of which that phenomenon is composed [the micro-theories] and by the way it is composed out of them." One could also be more liberal about what micro-theory does the explaining. One might not insist that it be physics, but allow it to be any one of the physical sciences.

2 Strictly speaking, this does not follow. What follows is that pain is physical, or it does not really explain the behavior we currently think it causes. Lewis considers this possibility in detail. We will not.

3 This is the usual – although certainly not universal – sense in the literature, although many would define the physical, not by reference to physics, but by reference to the physical sciences. Physical things are the sorts of things that the predicate expressions of the physical sciences are true of; and physical properties are the sorts of properties denoted by such predicates.

4 Some use "materialism" for the position that all substances are physical but have nonphysical, mental *properties*. This form of materialism rejects the explanatory adequacy of physics and is, to that extent, a form of dualism.

5 Imagine that we are forced to the theory after theories without such terms fail to yield the right predictions, while the theory with such terms does. Some may object that such a theory would not count as a *physical* theory. This objection has little force, however. Physical theories are theories relevantly like current theories to which we give the title "physical." The boundaries of relevant likeness are hardly clear; it is largely a matter of developing in appropriate ways from a theory recognized as physical, and the "appropriate ways" allow for a great deal of change. Quantum mechanics, after all, is still physics even though it differs from Newtonian mechanics in ways that would stun a Newtonian physicist.

6 Another example from the work on the psychophysiology of fear and stress: "Exactly how the neurons in the opiate and benzodiazepine pathways function and how they might cooperate is unclear. But one plausible scenario goes like this: when a young monkey is separated from its mother, opiate-releasing and, consequently, opiate-sensitive, neurons become inhibited. Such inhibition gives rise to a yearning for the mother and a generalized sense of vulnerability" (Kalin, 1993, p. 99). There is no explanation of how "such inhibition" produces the *feeling* of a yearning for the mother, or the *feeling* of a generalized sense of vulnerability. What we know is the inhibition correlates with the feeling.

7 It is a truism about reduction that the question of whether one theory reduces to another cannot be fruitfully raised unless the macro-theory and the micro-theory involved are both well-developed, mature theories. What is obvious in the philosophy of science seems easily overlooked in the philosophy of mind.

8 Whether a fully mind-independent description and explanation of nature is possible is very much a live issue in contemporary physics. Consider Steven Weinberg's reflections on quantum theory:

> The orthodox Copenhagen interpretation [of quantum mechanics] . . . is based on a sharp separation between the physical system, generated by the rules of quantum mechanics, and the apparatus used to study it, which is described classically, that is according to the prequantum rules of physics. . . . [T]his difference of treatment between the system being observed and the measuring apparatus is surely a fiction. We believe that quantum mechanics governs everything in the universe, not only individual electrons and atoms and molecules, but also the experimental apparatus and the physicists who use it. If the wave function describes everything the measuring apparatus as well as the system being observed, and evolves *deterministically* according to the rules of quantum mechanics, even during a measurement, then . . . where do the probabilities come from? (Weinberg, 1992, p. 82)

If the probabilities arise because of the epistemological constitution of the physicist-observer, our most scientifically fundamental description and explanation of nature is not fully mind-independent. Weinberg is clearly committed to a fully mind-independent account. He says:

> What one needs is a quantum-mechanical model with a wave function that describes not only various systems under study but also something representing a conscious observer. With such a model, one would try to show that, as a result of repeated interactions of the observer with individual systems, the wave function of the combined system evolves with certainty to a final wave function in which the observer has become convinced that the probabilities of the individual measurements are what are prescribed in the Copenhagen interpretation. (p. 84)

This is of course to take the position that consciousness, at least insofar as it is involved in quantum mechanical measurement, is completely explainable in mind-independent terms.

9 Understanding naturalism to be the view that science can in principle supply a mind-independent description and explanation of everything.

References

Kalin, N. (1993) "The neurobiology of fear," *Scientific American* 268(5) (May), pp. 54–60.

Lewis, D. (1971) "An argument for the identity theory," in D. M. Rosenthal (ed.) *Materialism and the Mind–Body Problem*, Englewood Cliffs, NJ: Prentice-Hall, pp. 162–71; first published 1966 in *Journal of Philosophy* 63, pp. 17–25.

Nagel, T. (1979) "Subjective and objective," in *Mortal Questions*, Cambridge: Cambridge University Press, pp. 196–213.

Scheffler, I. (1967) *Science and Subjectivity*, Indianapolis, Ind.: Bobbs-Merrill.

Taylor, C. (1985) Introduction, *Philosophical Papers*, vol. 1, *Human Agency and Language*, Cambridge: Cambridge University Press.

Weinberg, S. (1992) *Dreams of a Final Theory*, New York: Pantheon Press.

Part I
Physicalist Perspectives

1
Mind and Brain

J. J. C. Smart

Ever since Gilbert Ryle at Oxford persuaded me to reject the last vestiges of Cartesian dualism, I have been a materialist about the mind. Admittedly the philosophy of mind to which Ryle attracted me was a sort of behaviorism, which I later came to reject (mainly owing to the influence of a younger colleague of mine at the University of Adelaide in South Australia, U. T. Place (see Place, 1956)). Ryle, roughly speaking, held that when we talk about the mind we are concerned with hypothetical propositions about behavior, not, as Descartes thought, with categorical propositions about a nonphysical entity (see Ryle, 1949, esp. p. 46). Where I possibly differed from Ryle (who at least used a lot of antimaterialist rhetoric) was that I was convinced that these hypotheticals should be at least in principle explicable by a categorical basis provided by neurophysiology and the emerging science of cybernetics. Indeed I now think that Ryle was wrong in thinking that hypothetical propositions could, so to speak, float in free air. They need a categorical, or relatively more categorical, basis. Nevertheless the place where I came to feel dissatisfied first with a behavioristic approach was in the case of *experiences*, such as that of having a toothache or an afterimage or of seeing a banana. In such cases we seem to be aware of a very concrete process going on in us.

When we attend to such experiences, we are tempted to think that we are aware of them as nonphysical. I think that is due to confusion of thought. We can so easily jump from "we are not aware of X being Y" to "we are aware of X as being not Y." The transition is natural but logically illegitimate. As D. M. Armstrong (1968) has pointed out, it has been made use of by illusionists, as when a woman has her head covered by a black cloth against a black background, while her body is brightly illuminated.

Because the audience do not see her head they think wrongly that they see that she has no head. Similarly, because we are not aware in consciousness of our experiences as physical (neurological) processes we think that we are aware of them as nonphysical. A neurological process may extend over all or part of our brain. It is true that in introspection we are not aware of our experiences as located or extended in space. But not to be aware of them as such is by no means to be aware that they are *not* so located or extended.

How are we aware of them? I hold that we are aware of their *neutral* properties – neutral, that is, between a physicalist and a nonphysicalist metaphysics of mind. Here one can draw support from Wittgenstein's criticisms of the notion of private experience, his stress on the fact that we individuate our experiences in terms of their typical external stimuli and their typical behavioral effects. One may consider also the elusiveness of the idea of a "raw feel" put forward by certain psychologists (see Farrell, 1950). Thus when I say that I have a yellow afterimage I am indicating such a thing as that what is going on in me is like what goes on in me when a lemon is before my eyes, my eyes are open, I'm awake, and so on. Materialist me and immaterialist Descartes could agree on this. My assertion that my experience is in fact a neurophysiological process is then put forward as the most plausible in the light of total science. For example, it is hard to see how nonphysical entities could have arisen through the process of evolution by natural selection and genetic mutation and recombination. The same goes for metaphysically emergent *properties*. In science we do need to talk of emergence, but only in the harmless sense in which a jumble of inductances, capacitances, resistors, etc. will not oscillate at a certain frequency, whereas properly connected together they may. Our awareness of "raw feels" is just awareness of bare likenesses and unlikenesses between them, and also of certain neutral properties such as of being intermittent, becoming more or less intense and so on.

When I have a yellow afterimage, say, this having an afterimage is the going on in me of a process like that which goes on in me when I see a banana, say. It is the banana that is yellow, not my experience. My experience is the having of a yellow afterimage, and the having of a yellow image is not itself yellow. (Note: I do not believe that images exist but only the havings of them. Much as there are no dances but only dancings.) It is the banana that is yellow. Now as a physicalist I want to say that the yellowness of the banana or rather the particular shade of yellow is a *reflectance*. The reflectance of a surface is got by plotting a curve showing the proportions of light of all the wavelengths over the visible spectrum that are reflected from the surface. It is a more abstract physical property than the particular constitutions of the minute parts of the surface, but is a physical property nonetheless (see Hilbert, 1987, esp. ch. 4).

Common sense (in my view rightly) holds that beliefs and desires are causes of actions. Just as I asserted that experiences are physical processes in the brain, so I assert that beliefs and desires are physical states of the brain. The states can be thought of as often mutually interacting entities of commonsense psychology, postulated in order to explain actions and other behavior, though common sense is neutral as to whether the states are physical or nonphysical. The neutral state can be thought of as a *functional* state. Let us pretend (contrary to fact, I believe) that telepathy exists. Suppose that Mary has a telephone line to her brother John and a telepathy channel to her sister Elizabeth. In either case there is a communication channel. "Communication channel" is an abstract "functional" expression, neutral between the material and the ghostly.

Though functionalism has come to be widely thought of as superseding the identity theory, I think that functionalists exaggerate the difference between the two types of theory. Functionalists mostly believe, like the identity theorist, that a particular functional state is embodied in a particular neural state. The functionalist's talk of functional processes and states is still of concrete processes and states, even though abstractly described. A particular functional process or state is identical to a particular process or state, which a scientific-minded functionalist must think of as neurophysiological. A functional process is not as abstract a thing as a function. Certainly having a pain does not feel like something abstract. The main bone of contention between functionalists and identity theorists seems to be that the functionalist tends to accuse the identity theorist of thinking that your pain or belief must be a neural process or state that is in detail like mine, or even that some extra-terrestrial silicon-based experience of pain must be very similar to my carbon-based one. As an identity theorist I would take a conciliatory position on this. I think that within one person experiences of a particular sort must be importantly similar since, as I have suggested, in inner experience we are reacting to likenesses and unlikenesses in our inner goings on. It is also plausible that identical twins' experiences are very similar neurophysiologically, and one can surely conjecture that the experiences of genetically different humans, and even of extra-terrestrials, may have neurophysiological similarities even if in extreme cases only of a wave pattern or something like that. With beliefs and desires such conjectures are on shakier ground, as the ways in which the propositional contents of our beliefs and desires are encoded will depend on all sorts of accidents of biography and perhaps of brain structure. Perhaps the identity theorist should conjecture similarities, but these will be very much a matter of degree. The neurophysiological structures need not be anatomically distinct. They may even overlap in "hardware," much as in a "transceiver radio" part of the transmitter circuit uses part of the hardware of the receiver circuit.

An identity theorist who believes that beliefs and desires are brain states must take note of a challenging and fashionable argument that they cannot be "in the head." It will be sufficient for present purposes to consider one such argument. Consider Jim's belief that the parrot on the eucalyptus tree is white. Jim individuates the parrot-cum-tree as a certain patchwork of colored objects at a certain distance and angle from him. It could also be said that Jim believes that there is a tree and a parrot at a certain distance and angle from him. Here there is no indexical word such as "that." This belief could exist in Jim whether or not the parrot and tree existed. Jim might be under some sort of illusion. Perhaps he is looking at a huge cleverly constructed painting stuck among the bushes and other trees. Jim's belief that the parrot on *that* tree is white could not exist unless the tree existed. So it may be said that the tree is partly what constitutes Jim's belief. In the fashionable jargon, Jim's belief that there is a white parrot on *that* tree has "wide content," whereas his belief that there is a white parrot in *a* tree has "narrow content." In principal a brain in a vat, manipulated by a mad scientist of the far future with electric impulses to sense receptors in the brain, could have the same narrow belief. (The mad scientist gives the brain in the vat all the sensory inputs that normally come from the outside world and receives on an instrument the neural impulses that normally would go from the brain to cause behavior. So the brain in the vat might believe that he or she was kicking a football, even though there was no leg and no football.) Clearly we should say that it is only the narrow belief that is in the head or identifiable with a brain state. We can also allow that a mention of the wide belief will indirectly identify the narrow belief and the brain state. It is the narrow belief that is causally efficacious in behavior. If the reference to "that tree" fails because Jim is under an illusion that there is such a tree, nevertheless this means only that the belief is not correctly described as "about a parrot on that tree," and the narrow belief will be the same as it would be if the wide description were correct. Commonsense language does not clearly make the distinction between wide and narrow belief. One can sense an ambiguity here. Even though it is not the case that wide belief is causally efficacious in behavior, it can be explanatory. It can indirectly point to the appropriate narrow belief. To use an example of Frank Jackson and Philip Pettit (1988),[1] the explanation of acceleration of particle A being the same as that of particle B may be that they have the same forces on them. Nevertheless particle A's force is not causally efficacious on particle B. There is no great mystery about wide belief that should worry a mind–brain identity theorist or a functionalist. What I have said about the distinction between wide and narrow beliefs also applies of course to a similar distinction between wide and narrow desires.

Because of their intentionality beliefs and desires can seem mysterious and hence ghostly. We have a tendency to think that by making something spiritual it can do anything, even the impossible! For example I can believe in or desire unicorns even though there are no unicorns. "I desire a unicorn" is clearly different from "I kick a football." You can't kick a football unless there is a football to be kicked. "Believes" and "desires" do not signify relations. However let us construe "I believe that unicorns exist" as "I believe-true the proposition 'unicorns exist' " and "I desire a unicorn" as "I desire-true of me the property "possesses a unicorn." Believings-true and desirings-true are relations between a brain and a proposition or property, and the proposition or property individuates a brain state. It does so fuzzily, because propositions and properties are fuzzy classes of intertranslatable linguistic expressions. So commonsense psychology is fuzzy, but useful for all that, and we have no reason to believe that our ordinary language of belief and desire will be superseded by scientific advance, any more than our talk of "rain," "cloud," or "thunderstorm" will be. Fuzzy though it is, our commonsense psychological talk implicitly, even though not necessarily explicitly, has a theoretical structure of its own, and is remarkably successful in a way that suggests it is true (see Jackson and Pettit, 1990). The fuzziness comes from the notion of "translatable" in "class of intertranslatable expressions." I have mentioned classes. Reference to classes, numbers and other abstract entities, as well as not typically "material" things such as space-time points, seems to be needed in physics. That is why I prefer to call myself a physicalist rather than a materialist.

Note

1   This important paper dispels much of the mystery that has been generated by proponents of "broad content."

References

Armstrong, D. M. (1968) "The headless woman illusion and the defence of materialism," *Analysis* 29, pp. 48–9.
Farrell, B. A. (1950) "Experience," *Mind* 59, pp. 170–98.
Hilbert, D. R. (1987) *Color and Color Perception*, Stanford, Calif.: CSLI.
Jackson, F. and Pettit, P. (1988) "Functionalism and broad content," *Mind* 97, pp. 381–400.
Jackson, F. and Pettit, P. (1990) "In defence of folk psychology," *Philosophical Studies* 59, pp. 31–54.
Place, U. T. (1956) "Is consciousness a brain process?", *British Journal of Psychology* 47, pp. 44–50.
Ryle, G. (1949) *The Concept of Mind*, London: Hutchinson.

2
The Mind–Body Problem

Jerry A. Fodor

Modern philosophy of science has been devoted largely to the formal and systematic description of the successful practices of working scientists. The philosopher does not try to dictate how scientific inquiry and argument ought to be conducted. Instead he tries to enumerate the principles and practices that have contributed to good science. The philosopher has devoted the most attention to analyzing the methodological peculiarities of the physical sciences. The analysis has helped to clarify the nature of confirmation, the logical structure of scientific theories, the formal properties of statements that express laws and the question of whether theoretical entities actually exist.

It is only rather recently that philosophers have become seriously interested in the methodological tenets of psychology. Psychological explanations of behavior refer liberally to the mind and to states, operations, and processes of the mind. The philosophical difficulty comes in stating in unambiguous language what such references imply.

Traditional philosophies of mind can be divided into two broad categories: dualist theories and materialist theories. In the dualist approach the mind is a nonphysical substance. In materialist theories the mental is not distinct from the physical; indeed, all mental states, properties, processes, and operations are in principle identical with physical states, properties, processes, and operations. Some materialists, known as behaviorists, maintain that all talk of mental causes can be eliminated from the language of psychology in favor of talk of environmental stimuli and behavioral responses. Other materialists, the identity theorists, contend that there are mental causes and that they are identical with neurophysiological events in the brain.

In the past fifteen years a philosophy of mind called functionalism that is neither dualist nor materialist has emerged from philosophical reflection on developments in artificial intelligence, computational theory, linguistics, cybernetics and psychology. All these fields, which are collectively known as the cognitive sciences, have in common a certain level of abstraction and a concern with systems that process information. Functionalism, which seeks to provide a philosophical account of this level of abstraction, recognizes the possibility that systems as diverse as human beings, calculating machines, and disembodied spirits could all have mental states. In the functionalist view the psychology of a system depends not on the stuff it is made of (living cells, metal or spiritual energy) but on how the stuff is put together. Functionalism is a difficult concept, and one way of coming to grips with it is to review the deficiencies of the dualist and materialist philosophies of mind it aims to displace.

The chief drawback of dualism is its failure to account adequately for mental causation. If the mind is nonphysical, it has no position in physical space. How, then, can a mental cause give rise to a behavioral effect that has a position in space? To put it another way, how can the nonphysical give rise to the physical without violating the laws of the conservation of mass, of energy and of momentum?

The dualist might respond that the problem of how an immaterial substance can cause physical events is not much obscurer than the problem of how one physical event can cause another. Yet there is an important difference: there are many clear cases of physical causation but not one clear case of nonphysical causation. Physical interaction is something philosophers, like all other people, have to live with. Nonphysical interaction, however, may be no more than an artifact of the immaterialist construal of the mental. Most philosophers now agree that no argument has successfully demonstrated why mind – body causation should not be regarded as a species of physical causation.

Dualism is also incompatible with the practices of working psychologists. The psychologist frequently applies the experimental methods of the physical sciences to the study of the mind. If mental processes were different in kind from physical processes there would be no reason to expect these methods to work in the realm of the mental. In order to justify their experimental methods many psychologists urgently sought an alternative to dualism.

In the 1920s John B. Watson of Johns Hopkins University made the radical suggestion that behavior does not have mental causes. He regarded the behavior of an organism as its observable responses to stimuli, which he took to be the causes of its behavior. Over the next thirty years psychologists such as B. F. Skinner of Harvard University developed Watson's ideas into an elaborate worldview in which the role of psychology was to catalogue the laws that determine causal relations between stimuli and responses. In this "radical behaviorist" view the problem of explaining the nature of the mind–body interaction vanishes; there is no such interaction.

Radical behaviorism has always worn an air of paradox. For better or worse the idea of mental causation is deeply ingrained in our everyday language and in our ways of understanding our fellow men and ourselves. For example, people commonly attribute behavior to beliefs, to knowledge, and to expectations. Brown puts gas in his tank because he believes the car will not run without it. Jones writes not "acheive" but "achieve" because he knows the rule about putting *i* before *e*. Even when a behavioral response is closely tied to an environmental stimulus, mental processes often intervene. Smith carries an umbrella because the sky is cloudy, but the weather is only part of the story. There are apparently also mental links in the causal chain: observation and expectation. The clouds affect Smith's behavior only because he observes them and because they induce in him an expectation of rain.

The radical behaviorist is unmoved by appeals to such cases. He is prepared to dismiss references to mental causes, however plausible they may seem, as the residue of outworn creeds. The radical behaviorist predicts that as phychologists come to understand more about the relations between stimuli and responses they will find it increasingly possible to explain behavior without postulating mental causes.

The strongest argument against behaviorism is that psychology has not turned out this way; the opposite has happened. As psychology has matured, the framework of mental states and processes that is apparently needed to account for experimental observations has grown all the more elaborate. Particularly in the case of human behavior psychological theories satisfying the methodological tenets of radical behaviorism have proved largely sterile, as would be expected if the postulated mental processes are real and causally effective.

Nevertheless, many philosophers were initially drawn to radical behaviorism because, paradoxes and all, it seemed better than dualism. Since a psychology committed to immaterial substances was unacceptable, philosophers turned to radical behaviorism because it seemed to be the only alternative materialist philosophy of mind. The choice, as they saw it, was between radical behaviorism and ghosts.

By the early 1960s philosophers began to have doubts that dualism and radical behaviorism exhausted the possible approaches to the philosophy of mind. Since the two theories seemed unattractive, the right strategy might be to develop a materialist philosophy of mind that nonetheless allowed for mental causes. Two such philosophies emerged, one called logical behaviorism and the other called the central-state identity theory.

Logical behaviorism is a semantic theory about what mental terms mean. The basic idea is that attributing a mental state (say thirst) to an organism is the same as saying that the organism is disposed to behave in a particular way (for example to drink if there is water available). On this view every mental ascription is equivalent in meaning to an if – then statement (called a behavioral hypothetical) that expresses a behavioral disposition. For example, "Smith is thirsty" might be taken to be equivalent to the dispositional statement "If there were water available, then Smith would drink some." By definition a behavioral hypothetical includes no mental terms. The if-clause of the hypothetical speaks only of stimuli and the then-clause speaks only of behavioral responses. Since stimuli and responses are physical events, logical behaviorism is a species of materialism.

The strength of logical behaviorism is that by translating mental language into the language of stimuli and responses it provides an interpretation of psychological explanations in which behavioral effects are attributed to mental causes. Mental causation is simply the manifestation of a behavioral disposition. More precisely, mental causation is what happens when an organism has a behavioral disposition and the if-clause of the behavioral hypothetical expressing the disposition happens to be true. For example, the causal statement "Smith drank some water because he was thirsty" might be taken to mean "If there were water available, then Smith would drink some, and there was water available."

I have somewhat oversimplified logical behaviorism by assuming that each mental ascription can be translated by a unique behavioral hypothetical. Actually the logical behaviorist often maintains that it takes an open-ended set (perhaps an infinite set) of behavioral hypotheticals to spell out the behavioral disposition expressed by a mental term. The mental ascription "Smith is thirsty" might also be satisfied by the hypothetical "If there were orange juice available, then Smith would drink some" and by a host of other hypotheticals. In any event the logical behaviorist does not usually maintain he can actually enumerate all the hypotheticals that correspond to a behavioral disposition expressing a given mental term. He only insists that in principle the meaning of any mental term can be conveyed by behavioral hypotheticals.

The way the logical behaviorist has interpreted a mental term such as thirsty is modeled after the way many philosophers have interpreted a physical disposition such as fragility. The physical disposition "The glass is fragile" is often taken to mean something like "If the glass were struck, then it would break." By the same token the logical behaviorist's analysis of mental causation is similar to the received analysis of one kind of physical causation. The causal statement "The glass broke because it was fragile" is taken to mean something like "If the glass were struck, then it would break, and the glass was struck."

By equating mental terms with behavioral dispositions the logical behaviorist has put mental terms on a par with the nonbehavioral dispositions of the physical sciences. That is a promising move because the analysis of nonbehavioral dispositions is on relatively solid philosophical ground. An explanation attributing the breaking of a glass to its fragility is surely something even the staunchest materialist can accept. By arguing that mental terms are synonymous with dispositional terms, the logical behaviorist has provided something the radical behaviorist could not: a materialist account of mental causation.

Nevertheless, the analogy between mental causation as construed by the logical behaviorist and physical causation goes only so far. The logical behaviorist treats the manifestation of a disposition as the sole form of mental causation, whereas the physical sciences recognize additional kinds of causation. There is the kind of causation where one physical event causes another, as when the breaking of a glass is attributed to its having been struck. In fact, explanations that involve event–event causation are presumably more basic than dispositional explanations, because the manifestation of a disposition (the breaking of a fragile glass) always involves event–event causation and not vice versa. In the realm of the mental many examples of event–event causation involve one mental state's causing another, and for this kind of causation logical behaviorism provides no analysis. As a result the logical behaviorist is committed to the tacit and implausible assumption that psychology requires a less robust notion of causation than the physical sciences require.

Event–event causation actually seems to be quite common in the realm of the mental. Mental causes typically give rise to behavioral effects by virtue of their interaction with other mental causes. For example, having a headache causes a disposition to take aspirin only if one also has the desire to get rid of the headache, the belief that aspirin exists, the belief that taking aspirin reduces headaches, and so on. Since mental states interact in generating behavior, it will be necessary to find a construal of psychological explanations that posits mental processes: causal sequences of mental events. It is this construal that logical behaviorism fails to provide.

Such considerations bring out a fundamental way in which logical behaviorism is quite similar to radical behaviorism. It is true that the logical behaviorist, unlike the radical behaviorist, acknowledges the existence of mental states. Yet since the underlying tenet of logical behaviorism is that references to mental states can be translated out of psychological explanations by employing behavioral hypotheticals, all talk of mental states and processes is in a sense heuristic. The only facts to which the behaviorist is actually committed are facts about relations between stimuli and responses. In this respect logical behaviorism is just radical behaviorism in a semantic form. Although the former theory offers a construal of mental causation, the construal is Pickwickian. What does not really exist cannot cause anything, and the logical behaviorist, like the radical behaviorist, believes deep down that mental causes do not exist.

An alternative materialist theory of the mind to logical behaviorism is the central-state identity theory. According to this theory, mental events, states and processes are identical with neurophysiological events in the brain, and the property of being in a certain mental state (such as having a headache or believing it will rain) is identical with the property of being in a certain neurophysiological state. On this basis it is easy to make sense of the idea that a behavioral effect might sometimes have a chain of mental causes; that will be the case whenever a behavioral effect is contingent on the appropriate sequence of neurophysiological events.

The central-state identity theory acknowledges that it is possible for mental causes to interact causally without ever giving rise to any behavioral effect, as when a person thinks for a while about what he ought to do and then decides to do nothing. If mental processes are neurophysiological, they must have the causal properties of neurophysiological processes. Since neurophysiological processes are presumably physical processes, the central-state identity theory ensures that the concept of mental causation is as rich as the concept of physical causation.

The central-state identity theory provides a satisfactory account of what the mental terms in psychological explanations refer to, and so it is favored by psychologists who are dissatisfied with behaviorism. The behaviorist maintains that mental terms refer to nothing or that they refer to the parameters of stimulus–response relations. Either way the existence of mental entities is only illusory. The identity theorist, on the other hand, argues that mental terms refer to neurophysiological states. Thus he can take seriously the project of explaining behavior by appealing to its mental causes.

The chief advantage of the identity theory is that it takes the explanatory constructs of psychology at face value, which is surely something a philosophy of mind ought to do if it can. The identity theory shows how the mentalistic explanations of psychology could be not mere heuristics but literal accounts of the causal history of behavior. Moreover, since the identity theory is not a semantic thesis, it is immune to many arguments that cast in doubt logical behaviorism. A drawback of logical behaviorism is that the observation "John has a headache" does not seem to mean the same thing as a statement of the form "John is disposed to behave in such and such a way." The identity theorist, however, can live with the fact that "John has a headache" and "John is in such and such a brain state" are not synonymous. The assertion of the identity theorist is not that these sentences mean the same thing but only that they are rendered true (or false) by the same neurophysiological phenomena.

The identity theory can be held either as a doctrine about mental particulars (John's current pain or Bill's fear of animals) or as a doctrine about mental universals, or properties (having a pain or being afraid of animals). The two doctrines, called respectively token physicalism and type physicalism, differ in strength and plausibility. Token physicalism maintains only that all the mental particulars that happen to exist are neurophysiological, whereas type physicalism makes the more sweeping assertion that all the mental particulars there could possibly be are neurophysiological. Token physicalism does not rule out the logical possibility of machines and disembodied spirits having mental properties. Type physicalism dismisses this possibility because neither machines nor disembodied spirits have neurons.

Type physicalism is not a plausible doctrine about mental properties even if token physicalism is right about mental particulars. The problem with type physicalism is that the psychological constitution of a system seems to depend not on its hardware, or physical composition, but on its software, or program. Why should the philosopher dismiss the possibility that silicon-based Martians have pains, assuming that the silicon is properly organized? And why should the philosopher rule out the possibility of machines having beliefs, assuming that the machines are correctly programmed? If it is logically possible that Martians and machines could have mental properties, then mental properties and neurophysiological processes cannot be identical, however much they may prove to be coextensive.

What it all comes down to is that there seems to be a level of abstraction at which the generalizations of psychology are most naturally pitched. This level of abstraction cuts across differences in the physical composition of the systems to which psychological generalizations apply. In the cognitive sciences, at least, the natural domain for psychological theorizing seems to be all systems that process information. The problem with type physicalism is that there are possible information-processing systems with the same psychological constitution as human beings but not the same physical organization. In principle all kinds of physically different things could have human software.

This situation calls for a relational account of mental properties that abstracts them from the physical structure of their bearers. In spite of the objections to logical behaviorism that I presented above, logical behaviorism was at least on the right track in offering a relational interpretation of mental properties: to have a headache is to be disposed to exhibit a certain pattern of relations between the stimuli one encounters and the responses one exhibits. If that is what having a headache is, however, there is no reason in principle why only heads that are physically similar to ours can ache. Indeed, according to logical behaviorism, it is a necessary truth that any system that has our stimulus-response contingencies also has our headaches.

All of this emerged ten or fifteen years ago as a nasty dilemma for the materialist program in the philosophy of mind. On the one hand the identity theorist (and not the logical behaviorist) had got right the causal character of the interactions of mind and body. On the other the logical behaviorist (and not the identity theorist) had got right the relational character of mental properties. Functionalism has apparently been able to resolve the dilemma. By stressing the distinction computer science draws between hardware and software the functionalist can make sense of both the causal and the relational character of the mental.

The intuition underlying functionalism is that what determines the psychological type to which a mental particular belongs is the causal role of the particular in the mental life of the organism. Functional individuation is differentiation with respect to causal role. A headache, for example, is identified with the type of mental state that among other things causes a disposition for taking aspirin in people who believe aspirin relieves a headache, causes a desire to rid oneself of the pain one is feeling, often causes someone who speaks English to say such things as "I have a headache" and is brought on by overwork, eye-strain and tension. This list is presumably not complete. More will be known about the nature of a headache as psychological and physiological research discovers more about its causal role.

Functionalism construes the concept of causal role in such a way that a mental state can be defined by its causal relations to other mental states. In this respect functionalism is completely different from logical behaviorism. Another major difference is that functionalism is not a reductionist thesis. It does not foresee, even in principle, the elimination of mentalistic concepts from the explanatory apparatus of psychological theories.

The difference between functionalism and logical behaviorism is brought out by the fact that functionalism is fully compatible with token physicalism. The functionalist would not be disturbed if brain events turn out to be the only things with the functional properties that define mental states. Indeed, most functionalists fully expect it will turn out that way.

Since functionalism recognizes that mental particulars may be physical, it is compatible with the idea that mental causation is a species of physical causation. In other words, functionalism tolerates the materialist solution to the mind–body problem provided by the central-state identity theory. It is possible for the functionalist to assert both that mental properties are typically defined in terms of their relations and that interactions of mind and body are typically causal in however robust a notion of causality is required by psychological explanations. The logical behaviorist can endorse only the first assertion and the type physicalist only the second. As

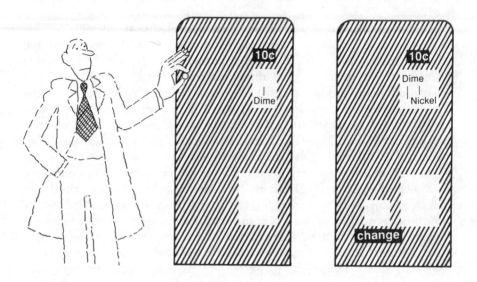

Two Coke Machines bring out the difference between behaviorism (the doctrine that there are no mental causes) and mentalism (the doctrine that there are mental causes). Both machines dispense a Coke for 10 cents and have states that are defined by reference to their causal role. The machine at the left is a behavioristic one: its single gate (*S0*) is defined solely in terms of the input and the output. The machine at the right is a mentalistic one: its two states (*S1*, *S2*) must be defined not only in terms of the input and the output of the Coke machine depends on the state the machine is in as well as on the input. The functionalist philosopher maintains that mental states are interdefined, like the internal states of the mentalistic Coke machine.

a result functionalism seems to capture the best features of the materialist alternatives to dualism. It is no wonder that functionalism has become increasingly popular.

Machines provide good examples of two concepts that are central to functionalism: the concept that mental states are interdefined and the concept that they can be realized by many systems. The illustration contrasts a behavioristic Coke machine with a mentalistic one. Both machines dispense a Coke for 10 cents. (The price has not been affected by inflation.) The states of the machines are defined by reference to their causal roles, but only the machine on the left would satisfy the behaviorist. Its single state (*S0*) is completely specified in terms of stimuli and responses. *S0* is the state a machine is in if, and only if, given and a dime as the input, it dispenses a Coke as the output.

The machine on the right in the illustration has interdefined states (*S1* and *S2*), which are characteristic of functionalism. *S1* is the state a machine is in if, and only if, (1) given a nickel, it dispenses nothing and proceeds to *S2*, and (2) given a dime, it dispenses a Coke and stays in *S1*. *S2* is the state a machine is in if, and only if, (1) given a nickel, it dispenses a Coke and proceeds to *S1*, and (2) given a dime, it dispenses a Coke and a nickel and proceeds to *S1*. What *S1* and *S2* jointly amount to is the machine's dispensing a Coke if it is given a dime, dispensing a Coke and a nickel if it is given a dime and a nickel and waiting to be given a second nickel if it has been given a first one.

Since *S1* and *S2* are each defined by hypothetical statements, they can be viewed as dispositions. Nevertheless, they are not behavioral dispositions because the consequences an input has for a machine in *S1* or *S2* are not specified solely in terms of the output of the machine. Rather, the consequences also involve the machine's internal states.

Nothing about the way I have described the behavioristic and mentalistic Coke machines puts constraints on what they could be made of. Any system whose states bore the proper relations to inputs, outputs, and other states could be one of these machines. No doubt it is reasonable to expect such a system to be constructed out of such things as wheels, levers, and diodes (token physicalism for Coke machines). Similarly, it is reasonable to expect that our minds may prove to be neurophysiological (token physicalism for human beings).

Nevertheless, the software description of a Coke machine does not logically require wheels, levers, and diodes for its concrete realization. By the same token, the software description of the mind does not logically require neurons. As far as functionalism is concerned a Coke machine with states *S1* and *S2* could be made of ectoplasm, if there is such stuff and if its states have the right causal properties. Functionalism allows for the possibility of disembodied Coke machines in exactly the same way and to the same extent that it allows for the possibility of disembodied minds.

To say that *S1* and *S2* are interdefined and realizable by different kinds of hardware is not, of course, to say that a Coke machine has a mind. Although interdefinition and functional specification are typical features of mental states, they are clearly not sufficient for mentality. What more is required is a question to which I shall return below.

Some philosophers are suspicious of functionalism because it seems too easy. Since functionalism licenses the individuation of states by reference to their causal role, it appears to allow a trivial explanation of any observed event *E*, that is, it appears to postulate an *E*-causer. For example, what makes the valves in a machine open? Why, the operation of a valve opener. And what is a valve opener? Why, anything that has the functionally defined property of causing valves to open.

In psychology this kind of question-begging often takes the form of theories that in effect postulate homunculi with the selfsame intellectual capacities the theorist set out to explain. Such is the case when visual perception is explained by simply postulating psychological mechanisms that process visual information. The behaviorist has often charged the mentalist, sometimes justifiably, of mongering this kind of question-begging pseudo-explanation. The charge will have to be met if functionally defined mental states are to have a serious role in psychological theories.

The burden of the accusation is not untruth but triviality. There can be no doubt that it is a valve opener that opens valves, and it is likely that visual perception is mediated by the processing of visual information. The charge is that such putative functional explanations are mere platitudes. The functionalist can meet this objection by allowing functionally defined theoretical constructs only where mechanisms exist that can carry out the function and only where he has some notion of what such mechanisms might be like. One way of imposing this requirement is to identify the mental processes that psychology postulates with the operations of the restricted class of possible computers called Turing machines.

A Turing machine can be informally characterized as a mechanism with a finite number of program states. The inputs and outputs of the machine are written on a tape that is divided into squares each of which includes a symbol from a finite alphabet. The machine scans the tape one square at a time. It can erase the symbol on a scanned square and print a new one in its place. The machine can execute only the elementary mechanical operations of scanning, erasing, printing, moving the tape and changing state.

The program states of the Turing machine are defined solely in terms of the input symbols on the tape, the output symbols on the tape, the elementary operations and the other states of the program. Each program state is therefore functionally defined by the part it plays in the overall operation of the machine. Since the functional role of a state depends on the relation of the state to other states as well as to inputs and outputs, the relational character of the mental is captured by the Turing-machine version of functionalism. Since the definition of a program state never refers to the physical structure of the system running the program, the Turing-machine version of functionalism also captures the idea that the character of a mental state is independent of its physical realization. A human being, a roomful of people, a computer, and a disembodied spirit would all be a Turing machine if they operated according to a Turing-machine program.

The proposal is to restrict the functional definition of psychological states to those that can be expressed in terms of the program states of

Turing machines. If this restriction can be enforced, it provides a guarante that psychological theories will be compatible with the demands of mechanisms. Since Turing machines are very simple devices they are in principle quite easy to build. Consequently by formulating a psychological explanation as a Turing machine program the psychologist ensures that the explanation is mechanistic, even though the hardware realizing the mechanism is left open.

There are many kinds of computational mechanisms other than Turing machines, and so the formulation of a functionalist psychological theory in Turing-machine notation provides only a sufficient condition for the theory's being mechanically realizable. What makes the condition interesting, however, is that the simple Turing machine can perform many complex tasks. Although the elementary operations of the Turing machine are restricted, iterations of the operations enable the machine to carry out any well-defined computation on discrete symbols.

An important tendency in the cognitive sciences is to treat the mind chiefly as a device that manipulates symbols. If a mental process can be functionally defined as an operation on symbols, there is a Turing machine capable of carrying out the computation and a variety of mechanisms for realizing the Turing machine. Where the manipulation of symbols is important the Turing machine provides a connection between functional explanation and mechanistic explanation.

The reduction of a psychological theory to a program for a Turing machine is a way of exorcising the homunculi. The reduction ensures that no operations have been postulated except those that could be performed by a familiar mechanism. Of course, the working psychologist usually cannot specify the reduction for each functionally individuated process in every theory he is prepared to take seriously. In practice the argument usually goes in the opposite direction; if the postulation of a mental operation is essential to some cherished psychological explanation, the theorist tends to assume that there must be a program for a Turing machine that will carry out that operation.

The "black boxes" that are common in flow charts drawn by psychologists often serve to indicate postulated mental processes for which Turing reductions are wanting. Even so, the possibility in principle of such reductions serves as a methodological constraint on psychological theorizing by determining what functional definitions are to be allowed and what it would be like to know that everything has been explained that could possibly need explanation.

Such is the origin, the provenance, and the promise of contemporary functionalism. How much has it actually paid off? This question is not easy to answer because much of what is now happening in the philosophy of mind and the cognitive sciences is directed at exploring the scope and limits of the functionalist explanations of behavior. I shall, however, give a brief overview.

An obvious objection to functionalism as a theory of the mind is that the functionalist definition is not limited to mental states and processes. Catalysts, Coke machines, valve openers, pencil sharpeners, mousetraps and ministers of finance are all in one way or another concepts that are functionally defined, but none is a mental concept such as pain, belief, and desire. What, then, characterizes the mental? And can it be captured in a functionalist framework?

The traditional view in the philosophy of mind has it that mental states are distinguished by their having what are called either qualitative content or intentional content. I shall discuss qualitative content first.

It is not easy to say what qualitative content is; indeed, according to some theories, it is not even possible to say what it is because it can be known not by description but only by direct experience. I shall nonetheless attempt to describe it. Try to imagine looking at a blank wall through a red filter. Now change the filter to a green one and leave everything else exactly the way it was. Something about the character of your experience changes when the filter does, and it is this kind of thing that philosophers call qualitative content. I am not entirely comfortable about introducing qualitative content in this way, but it is a subject with which many philosophers are not comfortable.

The reason qualitative content is a problem for functionalism is straight forward. Functionalism is committed to defining mental states in terms of their causes and effects. It seems, however, as if two mental states could have all the same causal relations and yet could differ in their qualitative content. Let me illustrate this with the classic puzzle of the inverted spectrum.

It seems possible to imagine two observers who are alike in all relevant psychological respects except that experiences having the qualitative content of red for one observer would have the qualitative content of green for the other. Nothing about their behavior need reveal the difference because both of them see ripe tomatoes and flaming sunsets as being similar in color and both of them call that color "red." Moreover, the causal connection between their (qualitatively distinct) experiences and their other mental states could also be identical. Perhaps they both think of Little Red Riding Hood when they see ripe tomatoes, feel depressed when they see the color green, and so on. It seems as if anything that could be packed into the notion of the causal role of their experiences could be shared by them, and yet the qualitative content of the experiences could be as different as you like. If this is possible, then the functionalist account does not work for mental states that have qualitative content. If one person is having a green experience while another person is having a red one, then surely they must be in different mental states.

The example of the inverted spectrum is more than a verbal puzzle. Having qualitative content is supposed to be a chief factor in what makes a mental state conscious. Many psychologists who are inclined to accept the functionalist framework are nonetheless worried about the failure of functionalism to reveal much about the nature of consciousness. Functionalists have made a few ingenious attempts to talk themselves and their colleagues out of this worry, but they have not, in my view, done so with much success. (For example, perhaps one is wrong in thinking one can imagine what an inverted spectrum would be like.) As matters stand, the problem of qualitative content poses a serious threat to the assertion that functionalism can provide a general theory of the mental.

Functionalism has fared much better with the intentional content of mental states. Indeed, it is here that the major achievements of recent cognitive science are found. To say that a mental state has intentional content is to say that it has certain semantic properties. For example, for Enrico to believe Galileo was Italian apparently involves a three-way relation between Enrico, a belief, and a proposition that is the content of the belief (namely the proposition that Galileo was Italian). In particular it is an essential property of Enrico's belief that it is about Galileo (and not about, say, Newton) and that it is true if, and only if, Galileo was indeed Italian. Philosophers are divided on how these considerations fit together, but it is widely agreed that beliefs involve semantic properties such as expressing a proposition, being true or false and being about one thing rather than another.

It is important to understand the semantic properties of beliefs because theories in the cognitive sciences are largely about the beliefs organisms have. Theories of learning and perception, for example, are chiefly accounts of how the host of beliefs an organism has are determined by the character of its experiences and its genetic endowment. The functionalist account of mental states does not by itself provide the required insights. Mousetraps are functionally defined, yet mousetraps do not express propositions and they are not true or false.

There is at least one kind of thing other than a mental state that has intentional content: a symbol. Like thoughts, symbols seem to be about things. If someone says "Galileo was Italian" his utterance, like Enrico's belief, expresses a proposition about Galileo that is true or false depending on Galileo's homeland. This parallel between the symbolic and the mental underlies the traditional quest for a unified treatment of language and mind. Cognitive science is now trying to provide such a treatment.

The basic concept is simple but striking. Assume that there are such things as mental symbols (mental representations) and that mental symbols have semantic properties. On this view having a belief involves being related to a mental symbol, and the belief inherits its semantic properties from the mental symbol that figures in the relation. Mental processes (thinking, perceiving, learning, and so on) involve causal interactions among relational states such as having a belief. The semantic properties of the words and sentences we utter are in turn inherited from the semantic properties of the mental states that language expresses.

Associating the semantic properties of mental states with those of mental symbols is fully compatible with the computer metaphor, because it is natural to think of the computer as a mechanism that manipulates symbols. A computation is a causal chain of computer states and the links in the chain are operations on semantically interpreted formulas in a machine code. To think of a system (such as the nervous system) as a computer is to raise questions about the nature of the code in which it computes and the semantic properties of the symbols in the code. In fact, the analogy between minds and computers actually implies the postulation of mental symbols. There is no computation without representation.

The representational account of the mind, however, predates considerably the invention of the computing machine. It is a throwback to classical epistemology, which is a tradition that includes philosophers as diverse as John Locke, David Hume, George Berkeley, René Descartes, Immanuel Kant, John Stuart Mill, and William James.

Hume, for one, developed a representational theory of the mind that included five points. First, there exist "Ideas," which are a species of mental symbol. Second, having a belief involves entertaining an Idea. Third, mental processes are causal associations of Ideas. Fourth, Ideas are like pictures. And fifth, Ideas have their semantic properties by virtue of what they resemble: the Idea of John is about John because it looks like him.

Contemporary cognitive psychologists do not accept the details of Hume's theory, although they endorse much of its spirit. Theories of computation provide a far richer account of mental processes than the mere association of Ideas. And only a few psychologists still think that imagery is the chief vehicle of mental representation. Nevertheless, the most significant break with Hume's theory lies in the abandoning of resemblance as an explanation of the semantic properties of mental representations.

Many philosophers, starting with Berkeley, have argued that there is something seriously wrong with the suggestion that the semantic relation between a thought and what the thought is about could be one of resemblance. Consider the thought that John is tall. Clearly the thought is true only of the state of affairs consisting of John's being tall. A theory of the semantic properties of a thought should therefore explain how this particular thought is related to this particular state of affairs. According to the resemblance theory, entertaining the thought involves having a mental image that shows John to be tall. To put it another way, the relation between the thought that John is tall and his being tall is like the relation between a tall man and his portrait.

The difficulty with the resemblance theory is that any portrait showing John to be tall must also show him to be many other things: clothed or naked, lying, standing or sitting, having a head or not having one, and so on. A portrait of a tall man who is sitting down resembles a man's being seated as much as it resembles a man's being tall. On the resemblance theory it is not clear what distinguishes thoughts about John's height from thoughts about his posture.

The resemblance theory turns out to encounter paradoxes at every turn. The possibility of construing beliefs as involving relations to semantically interpreted mental representations clearly depends on having an acceptable account of where the semantic properties of the mental representations come from. If resemblance will not provide this account, what will?

The current idea is that the semantic properties of a mental representation are determined by aspects of its functional role. In other words, a sufficient condition for having semantic properties can be specified in causal terms. This is the connection between functionalism and the representational theory of the mind. Modern cognitive psychology rests largely on the hope that these two doctrines can be made to support each other.

No philosopher is now prepared to say exactly how the functional role of a mental representation determines its semantic properties. Nevertheless, the functionalist recognizes three types of causal relation among psychological states involving mental representations, and they might serve to fix the semantic properties of mental representations. The three types are causal relations among mental states and stimuli, mental states and responses, and some mental states and other ones.

Consider the belief that John is tall. Presumably the following facts, which correspond respectively to the three types of causal relation, are relevant to determining the semantic properties of the mental representation involved in the belief. First, the belief is a normal effect of certain stimulations, such as seeing John in circumstances that reveal his height. Second, the belief is the normal cause of certain behavioral effects, such as uttering "John is tall." Third, the belief is a normal cause of certain other beliefs and a normal effect of certain other beliefs. For example, anyone who believes John is tall is very likely also to believe someone is tall. Having the first belief is normally causally sufficient for having the second belief. And anyone who believes everyone in the room is tall and also believes John is in the room will very likely believe John is tall. The third belief is a normal effect of the first two. In short, the functionalist maintains that the proposition expressed by a given mental representation depends on the causal properties of the mental states in which that mental representation figures.

The concept that the semantic properties of mental representations are determined by aspects of their functional role is at the center of current work in the cognitive sciences. Nevertheless, the concept may not be true. Many philosophers who are unsympathetic to the cognitive turn in modern psychology doubt its truth, and many psychologists would probably reject it in the bald and unelaborated way that I have sketched it. Yet even in its skeletal form, there is this much to be said in its favor: it legitimizes the notion of mental representation, which has become increasingly important to theorizing in every branch of the cognitive sciences. Recent advances in formulating and testing hypotheses about the character of mental representations in fields ranging from phonetics to computer vision suggest that the concept of mental representation is fundamental to empirical theories of the mind.

The behaviorist has rejected the appeal to mental representation because it runs counter to his view of the explanatory mechanisms that can figure in psychological theories. Nevertheless, the science of mental representation is now flourishing. The history of science reveals that when a successful theory comes into conflict with a methodological scruple, it is generally the scruple that gives way. Accordingly the functionalist has relaxed the behaviorist constraints on psychological explanations. There is probably no better way to decide what is methodologically permissible in science than by investigating what successful science requires.

3
Intertheoretic Reduction: a Neuroscientist's Field Guide

Paul M. Churchland and Patricia S. Churchland

"Reductionism" is a term of contention in academic circles. For some, it connotes a rightheaded approach to any genuinely scientific field, an approach that seeks intertheoretic unity and real systematicity in the phenomena. It is an approach to be vigorously pursued and defended.

For others, it connotes a wrongheaded approach that is narrow-minded and blind to the richness of the phenomena. It is a bullish instance of "nothing-butery," insensitive to emergent complexity and higher-level organization. It is an approach to be resisted.

This latter reaction is most often found within the various social sciences, such as anthropology, sociology, and psychology. The former attitude is most often found within the physical sciences, such as physics, chemistry, and molecular biology. Predictably then, the issue of reductionism is especially turbulent at the point where these two intellectual rivers meet: in the discipline of modern neuroscience.

The question at issue is whether it is reasonable to expect, and to work toward, a reduction of all psychological phenomena to neurobiological and neurocomputational phenomena. A large and still respectable contingent within the academic community remains inclined to say no. Their resistance is principled. Some point to the existence of what philosophers call "qualia" – the various subjective qualitative characters displayed in our sensations: think of pain, the smell of a rose, the sensation of redness, and so forth. These qualia, it is held, are beyond the possibility of any materialist explanation or reduction (Jackson, 1982; Nagel, 1974). Others point to the semantic content or *intentionality* of our thoughts, and make a similar claim about its irreducibility (Popper, 1978; Searle, 1980, 1990). Others claim that the most important aspects of human behavior are explicable only in terms of high-level *emergent properties* and their correlative regularities, properties that irreducibly encompass the social level, properties such as loyalty to a moral ideal, perception of a political fact, or the recognition of a personal betrayal (Taylor, 1970, 1987). Yet others see a conflict with the important and deeply entrenched idea of *human freedom* (Popper and Eccles, 1978). Finally, some materialists raise what is called the problem of *multiple instantiation*. They point to the presumed fact that conscious intelligence could be sustained by physical systems other than the biochemistry peculiar to humans – by a system of transistors, for example – just as a nation's financial economy can be sustained by tokens other than silver coins and paper bills. But no one thinks that macroeconomics can be reduced to the chemistry of metals and paper. So why think that psychology should be reducible to the neurobiology of terrestrial humans? (Fodor, 1975).

Our aim here is threefold. First, we will try to provide a useful overview of the general nature of intertheoretic reduction, as it appears in the many examples to be found in the history of science. Expanding our horizons here is important, since little is to be learned from simply staring long and hard at the problematic case at issue, namely, the potential reduction of psychological phenomena to neural phenomena. Instead, we need to look at cases where the dust has already settled and where the issues are already clear. Second, we will identify the very real virtues that such cases display, and the correlative vices to be avoided. And finally, we will attempt to apply these historical lessons to the case here at issue – cognitive neuroscience – and we will try to meet the salient objections listed above.

Intertheoretic Reduction: Some Prototypical Cases

Since nothing instructs like examples, let us briefly examine some. One of the earliest cases of intertheoretic reduction on a grand scale was the reduction of Kepler's three laws of astronomical motion by the newly-minted mechanics of Isaac Newton. Kepler's theory was specific to the motions of the solar planets, but Newton's theory at least purported to be the correct account of bodily motions in general. It was therefore a great triumph when Newton showed that one could deduce all three of Kepler's laws from his own theory, given only the background assumption that the mass of any planet is tiny compared to the great mass of the sun.

Kepler's three planetary laws are:
(1) All planets move on ellipses with the sun at one focus; (2) A given planet always sweeps out equal areas in equal times; (3) The square of planet's period is proportional to the cube of its mean orbital radius.

Newton's three laws of motion are:
(1) Inertial motion is constant and rectilinear; (2) Acceleration = force/mass; (3) For any change in momentum something suffers an equal and opposite change in momentum. To these laws we must add his gravitation law:

$$F = Gm_1 m_2 / R^2.$$

Kepler's account thus turned out to be just a special case or a special application of Newton's more encompassing account. And astronomical motions turned out to be just a special instance of the inertial and force-governed motions of massive bodies in general. The divine or supernatural character of the heavens was thereby lost forever. The sublunary and the superlunary realms were thereby united as a single domain in which the same kinds of objects were governed by one and the same set of laws.

Newton's mechanics also provides a second great example of intertheoretic reduction, one that did not emerge until the nineteenth century. If his mechanics successfully comprehends motion at both the astronomical and the human-sized scales, then what, it was asked, about motions at the microscopic scale? Might these be accounted for in the same way?

The attempts to construct such an account produced another unification, one with an unexpected bonus concerning the theory of heat. If we assume that any confined body of gas consists in a swarm of submicroscopic corpuscles bouncing around inside the container according to Newton's three laws, then we can deduce a law describing the pressure they will collectively exert on the container's walls by repeatedly bouncing off them. This "Kinetic" law has the form

$$PV = 2n/3 \cdot mv^2/2$$

This law had the same form as the then already familiar "ideal gas law,"

$$PV = \mu R \cdot T$$

(Here P is pressure and V is volume.) Although they are notationally different, the expressions "$2n/3$" and "μR" both denote the amount of gas present in the container (n denotes the number of molecules in the container; μ denotes the fraction of a mole). The only remaining difference, then, is that the former law has an expression for the *kinetic energy of an average corpuscle* ($mv^2/2$) in the place where the latter has an expression for *temperature* ($Tsoze4$). Might the phenomenon we call "temperature" thus *be* mean kinetic energy at the molecular level? This striking convergence of principle, and many others like it, invited Bernoulli, Joule, Kelvin, and Boltzmann to say yes. As matters were further pursued, mean molecular kinetic energy turned out to have *all* of the causal properties that the classical theory had been ascribing to temperature. In short, temperature turned out to *be* mean molecular kinetic energy. Newtonian mechanics had another reductive triumph in hand. Motion at all three scales was subsumed under the same theory, and a familiar phenomenal property, *temperature*, was reconceived in a new and unexpected way.

It is worth emphasizing that this reduction involved identifying a familiar *phenomenal* property of common objects with a highly unfamiliar microphysical property. (By "phenomenal," we mean a property one can reliably discriminate in experience, but where one is unable to articulate, by reference to yet simpler discriminable elements, just how one discriminates that property.) Evidently, reduction is not limited to conceptual frameworks hidden away in the theoretical stratosphere. Sometimes the conceptual framework that gets subsumed by a deeper vision turns out to be a familiar piece of our commonsense framework, a piece whose concepts are regularly applied in casual observation on the basis of our native sensory systems. Other examples are close at hand: before Newton, *sound* had already been identified with compression waves in the atmosphere, and *pitch* with wavelength, as part of the larger reduction of commonsense sound and musical theory to mechanical acoustics. A century and a half after Newton, *light* and its various *colors* were identified with electromagnetic waves and their various wavelengths, within the larger reduction of geometrical optics by electromagnetic theory, as outlined by Maxwell in 1864. *Radiant heat*, another commonsense observable, was similarly reconceived as long-wavelength electromagnetic waves in a later articulation of the same theory. Evidently, the fact that a property or state is at the prime focus of one of our native discriminatory faculties does not mean that it is exempt from possible reconception within the conceptual framework of some deeper explanatory theory.

This fact will loom larger later in the paper. For now, let us explore some further examples of intertheoretic reduction. The twentieth-century reduction of classical (valence) chemistry by atomic and sub-atomic (quantum) physics is another impressive case of conceptual unification. Here the structure of an atom's successive electron shells, and the character of stable regimes of electron-sharing between atoms, allowed us to reconstruct, in a systematic and thus illuminating way, the electronic structure of the many atomic elements, the classical laws of valence-bonding, and the gross structure of the periodic table. As often happens in intertheoretic reductions, the newer theory also allowed us to explain much that the old theory had been unable to explain, such as the specific heat capacities of various substances and the interactions of chemical compounds with light.

This reduction of chemistry to physics is notable for the further reason that it is not yet complete, and probably never will be. For one thing, given the combinatorial possibilities here, the variety of chemical compounds is effectively endless, as are their idiosyncratic chemical, mechanical, optical, and thermal properties. And for another, the calculation of these diverse properties from basic quantum principles is computationally daunting, even when we restrict ourselves to merely approximate results, which for purely mathematical reasons we generally must. Accordingly, it is not true that all chemical knowledge has been successfully reconstructed in quantum-mechanical terms. Only the basics have, and then only in approximation. But our experience here firmly suggests that quantum physics has indeed managed to grasp the underlying elements of chemical reality. We thus expect that any particular part of chemistry can be approximately reconstructed in quantum-mechanical terms, when and if the specific need arises.

The preceding examples make it evident that intertheoretic reduction is at bottom a relation between two distinct conceptual frameworks for describing the phenomena, rather than a relation between two distinct domains of phenomena. The whole point of a reduction, after all, is to show that what we thought to be two domains is actually one domain, though it may have been described in two (or more) different vocabularies.

Perhaps the most famous reduction of all is Einstein's twentieth-century reduction of Newton's three laws of motion by the quite different mechanics of the Special Theory of Relativity (STR). STR subsumed Newton's laws in the following sense. If we make the (false) assumption that all bodies move with velocities much less than the velocity of light, then STR entails a set of laws for the motion of such bodies, a set that is experimentally indistinguishable from Newton's old set. It is thus no mystery that those old Newtonian laws seemed to be true, given the relatively parochial human experience they were asked to account for.

But while those special-case STR laws may be experimentally indistinguishable from Newton's laws, they are logically and semantically quite different from Newton's laws: they ascribe an importantly different family of features to the world. Specifically, in every situation where Newton ascribed an intrinsic property to a body (e.g. mass, or length, or momentum, and so forth), STR ascribes a *relation*, a *two*-place property (e.g. x has a mass-relative-to-an-inertial-frame-F, and so on), because its portrait of the universe and what it contains (an unitary 4-D space-time continuum with 4-D world-lines) is profoundly different from Newton's.

Here we have an example where the special-case resources and deductive consequences of the new and more general theory are not identical, but merely similar, to the old and more narrow theory it purports to reduce. That is to say, the special-case reconstruction achieved within the new theory parallels the old theory with sufficient systematicity to explain why the old theory worked as well as it did in a certain domain, and to demonstrate that the old theory could be displaced by the new without predictive or explanatory loss within the old theory's domain; and yet the new reconstruction is not perfectly isomorphic to the old theory. The old theory turns out not just to be narrow, but to be false in certain important respects. Space and time are not distinct, as Newton assumed, and there simply are no intrinsic properties such as mass and length that are invariant over all inertial frames.

The trend of this example leads us toward cases where the new and more general theory does not sustain the portrait of reality painted by the old theory at all, even as a limiting special case or even in its roughest outlines. An example would be the outright displacement, without reduction, of the old phlogiston theory of combustion by Lavoisier's oxygen theory of combustion. The older theory held that the combustion of any body involved the *loss* of a spirit-like substance, phlogiston, whose precombustion function it was to provide a noble wood-like or metal-like character to the baser ash or calx that is left behind after the process of combustion is complete. It was the "ghost" that gave metal its form. With the acceptance of Lavoisier's contrary claim that a purely material substance, oxygen, was being somehow *absorbed* during combustion, phlogiston was simply eliminated from our overall account of the world.

Other examples of theoretical entities that have been eliminated from serious science include carloric fluid, the rotating crystal spheres of Ptolemaic astronomy, the four humours of medieval medicine, the vital spirit of pre-modern biology, and the luminiferous ether of pre-Einsteinian mechanics. In all of these cases, the newer theory did not have the resources adequate to reconstruct the furniture of the older theory or the laws that supposedly governed their behavior; but the newer theory was so clearly superior to the old as to displace it regardless.

At one end of the spectrum then, we have pairs of theories where the old is smoothly reduced by the new, and the ontology of the old theory (that is, the set of things and properties that it postulates) survives, although redescribed, perhaps, in a new and more penetrating vocabulary. Here we typically find claims of cross-theoretic identity, such as "Heat is identical with mean molecular kinetic energy" and "Light is identical with electromagnetic waves." In the middle of the spectrum, we find pairs of theories where the old ontology is only poorly mirrored within the vision of the new, and it "survives" only in a significantly modified form. Finally, at the other end of the spectrum we find pairs where the older theory, and its old ontology with it, is eliminated entirely in favor of the more useful ontology and the more successful laws of the new.

Before closing this quick survey, it is instructive to note some cases where the older theory is neither subsumed under nor eliminated by the aspirant and allegedly more general theory. Rather, it successfully resists the takeover attempt, and proves not to be just a special case of the general theory at issue. A clear example is Maxwell's electromagnetic theory (hereafter, EM theory). From 1864 to 1905 it was widely expected that EM theory would surely find a definitive reduction in terms of the mechanical properties of an all-pervading ether, the elastic medium in which EM waves were supposedly propagated. Though never satisfactorily completed, some significant attempts at reconstructing EM phenomena in mechanical terms had already been launched. Unexpectedly, the existence of such an absolute medium of luminous propagation turned out to be flatly inconsistent with the character of space and time as described in Einstein's 1905 Special Theory of Relativity. EM theory thus emerged as a fundamental theory in its own right, and not just as a special case of mechanics. The attempt at subsumption was a failure.

A second example concerns the theory of stellar behavior accumulated by classical astronomy in the late nineteenth century. It was widely believed that the pattern of radiative behavior displayed by a star would be adequately explained in mechanical or in chemical terms. It became increasingly plain, however, that the possible sources of chemical and mechanical energy available to any star would sustain their enormous outpourings of thermal and luminous energy for only a few tens of millions of years. This limited time-scale was at odds with the emerging geological evidence of a history numbered in the *billions* of years. Geology notwithstanding, Lord Kelvin himself was prepared to bite the bullet and declare the stars to be no more than a few tens of millions of years old. The conflict was finally resolved when the enormous energies in the atomic nucleus were discovered. Stellar astronomy was eventually reduced all right, and very beautifully, but by quantum physics rather than by mere chemistry or mechanics. Another reductive attempt had failed, though it was followed by one that succeeded.

The Lessons for Neuroscience

Having seen these examples and the spectrum of cases they define, what lessons should a neuroscientist draw? One lesson is that intertheoretic reduction is a normal and fairly commonplace event in the history of science. Another lesson is that genuine reduction, when you can get it, is clearly a good thing. It is a good thing for many reasons, reasons made more powerful by their conjunction.

First, by being displayed as a special case of the (presumably true) new theory, the old theory is thereby *vindicated*, at least in its general outlines, or at least in some suitably restricted domain. Second, the old theory is typically *corrected* in some of its important details, since the reconstructed image is seldom a perfect mirror image of the old theory, and the differences reflect improvements in our knowledge. Third, the reduction provides us with a much *deeper insight* into, and thus a *more effective control* over, the phenomena within the old theory's domain. Fourth, the reduction provides us with a *simpler* overall account of nature, since apparently diverse phenomena are brought under a single explanatory umbrella. And fifth, the new and more general theory immediately *inherits all the evidence* that had accumulated in favor of the older theory it reduces, because it explains all of the same data.

It is of course a bad thing to try to force a well-functioning old theory into a procrustean bed, to try to effect a reduction where the aspirant reducing theory lacks the resources to do reconstructive justice to the target old theory. But whether or not the resources are adequate is seldom clear beforehand, despite people's intuitive convictions. And even if a reduction is impossible, this may reflect the old theory's radical falsity instead of its fundamental accuracy. The new theory may simply eliminate the old, rather than smoothly reduce it. Perhaps folk notions such as "beliefs" and "the will," for example, will be eliminated in favor of some quite different story of information storage and behavior initiation.

The fact is, in the neuroscience and psychology case there are conflicting indications. On the one side, we should note that the presumption in favor of an eventual reduction (or elimination) is far stronger than it was in the historical cases just examined. For unlike the earlier cases of light, or heat, or heavenly motions, in general terms we already know how psychological phenomena arise: they arise from the evolutionary and ontogenetic articulation of matter, more specifically, from the articulation of biological organization. We therefore *expect* to understand the former in terms of the latter. The former is produced by the relevant articulation of the latter.

But there are counter indications as well, and this returns us at last to the five objections with which we opened this paper. From the historical perspective outlined above, can we say anything useful about those objections to reduction? Let us take them in sequence.

The first concerns the possibility of explaining the character of our subjective sensory qualia. The negative arguments here all exploit the very same theme, namely our inability to imagine how any possible story about the objective nuts and bolts of neurons could ever explain the inarticulable subjective phenomena at issue. Plainly this objection places a great deal of weight on what we can and cannot imagine, as a measure of what is and isn't possible. It places more, clearly, than the test should bear. For who would have imagined, before James Clark Maxwell, that the theory of charged pith balls and wobbling compass needles could prove adequate to explain all the phenomena of light? Who would have thought, before Descartes, Bernoulli, and Joule, that the mechanics of billiard balls would prove adequate to explain the prima facie very different phenomenon of heat? Who would have found it remotely plausible that the pitch of a sound is a frequency, in advance of a general appreciation that sound itself consists in a train of compression waves in the atmosphere?

We must remember that a successful intertheoretic reduction is typically a complex affair, as it involves the systematic reconstruction of all or most of the old conception within the resources of the new conception. And not only is it complex, often the reconstruction is highly surprising. It is not something that we can reasonably expect anyone's imagination to think up or comprehend on rhetorical demand, as in the question, "How could *As possibly* be nothing but *Bs*?"

Besides, this rhetorical question need not stump us if our imagination is informed by recent theories of sensory coding. The idea that taste sensations are coded as a four-dimensional vector of spiking frequencies (corresponding to the four types of receptor on the tongue) yields a representation of the space of humanly possible tastes which unites the familiar tastes according to their various similarities, differences, and other relations such as betweenness (Bartoshuk, 1978). Land's retinex theory of color vision (Land, 1977) suggests a similar arrangement for our color sensations, with similar virtues. Such a theory also predicts the principal forms of color blindness, as when one's three-dimensional color space is reduced to two dimensions by the loss of one of the three classes of retinal cones.

Here we are already reconstructing some of the features of the target phenomena in terms of the new theory. We need only to carry such a reconstruction through, as in the historical precedents of the objective phenomenal properties noted earlier (heat, light, pitch). Some things may indeed be inarticulably phenomenal in character, because they are the target of one of our basic discriminatory modalities. But that in no way makes them immune to an illuminating intertheoretic reduction. History already teaches us the contrary.

The second objection concerned the meaning, or semantic content, or intentionality of our thoughts and other mental states. The antireductionist arguments in this area are very similar to those found in the case of qualia. They appeal to our inability to imagine how meaning could be just a matter of how signals interact or how inert symbols are processed (Searle

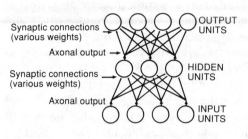

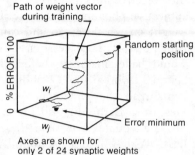

A simple feedforward artificial "neural network." Inputs are coded as a pattern or vector of activation levels across the input units. This pattern is conveyed toward the hidden units, but is transformed as it passes through the bank of intervening synaptic connections of various weights. Each hidden unit then sums the weighted inputs it receives and assumes an activation level appropriate to that sum. Thus results a second pattern or vector of activation levels across the hidden units. The story is repeated for the final layer of output units, which assumes a third pattern of activations. The network is thus a vector-to-vector transformer. Precisely what transformation it em-bodies is dictated by the specific configuration of its synaptic weights. With sigmoid output functions at the first two layers, networks of this kind can approximate any computable transformation whatever.

A schematic portrayal of an abstract "weight space" for the simple network. Learning in such a network consists in the successive modification of its weight configuration in order to incrementally reduce its performance error. This process continues until the network finally performs the input–output transformation implicit in the many examples on which it was trained. (From Churchland, P. M., 1989)

1980, 1990; for a rebuttal, see Churchlands 1990. Searle, strictly speaking, objects only to a purely computational reduction, but that is an important option for neuroscience so we shall include him with the other antireductionists.) Such appeals, as before, are really arguments from ignorance. They have the form, "I can't *imagine* how a neurocomputational account of meaningful representations could possibly work; therefore, it can't possibly work." To counter such appeals in the short term, we need only point out this failing.

To counter them in the long term requires more. It requires that we actually produce an account of how the brain represents the external world and the regularities it displays. But that is precisely what current theories of neural network function address. According to them, real-time information about the world is coded in high-dimensional activation vectors, and general information about the world is coded in the background configuration of the network's synaptic weights. Activation vectors are processed by the weight configurations through which they pass, and learning consists in the adjustment of one's global weight configuration (see the figure). These accounts already provide the resources to explain a variety of things, such as the recognition of complex objects despite partial or degraded sensory inputs, the swift retrieval of relevant information from a vast content-addressable memory, the appreciation of diffuse and inarticulable similarities, and the administration of complex sensorimotor coordination (P. M. Churchland, 1989). We are still too ignorant to insist that hypotheses of this sort will prove adequate to explain all of the representational capacities of mind. But neither can we insist that they are doomed to prove inadequate. It is an empirical question, and the jury is still out.

The third objection complains that what constitutes a human consciousness is not just the intrinsic character of the creature itself, but also the rich matrix of relations it bears to the other humans, practices, and institutions of its embedding culture. A reductionistic account of human consciousness and behavior, insofar as it is limited to the microscopic activities in an individual's brain, cannot hope to capture more than a small part of what is explanatorily important.

The proper response to this objection is to embrace it. Human behavior is indeed a function of the factors cited. And the character of any individual human consciousness will be profoundly shaped by the culture in which it develops. What this means is that any adequate neuro-computational account of human consciousness must take into account the manner in which a brain comes to represent, not just the gross features of the physical world, but also the character of the other cognitive creatures with which it interacts, and the details of the social, moral, and political world in which they all live. The brains of social animals, after all, learn to be interactive elements in a community of brains, much to their cognitive advantage. We need to know how they do it.

This is a major challenge, one that neuroscientists have not yet addressed with any seriousness, nor even much acknowledged. This is not surprising. Accounting for a creature's knowledge of the spatial location of a fly is difficult enough. Accounting for its knowledge of a loved one's embarrassment, a politician's character, or a bargaining opponent's hidden agenda, represents a much higher level of difficulty. And yet we already know that artificial neural networks, trained by examples, can come to recognize and respond to the most astonishingly subtle patterns and similarities in nature. If physical patterns, why not social patterns? We confront no problem in principle here. Only a major challenge.

It may indeed be unrealistic to expect an exhaustive global account of the neural and behavioral trajectory of a specific person over any period of time. The complexity of the neural systems we are dealing with may forever preclude anything more than useful approximations to the desired ideal account. The case of chemistry and its relation to quantum physics comes to mind. There also, the mathematics of complex dynamical systems imposes limits on how easily and accurately we can reconstruct the chemical facts from the physical principles. This means that our reduction will never be truly complete, but we rightly remain confident that chemical phenomena are nothing but the macro-level reflection of the underlying quantum physical phenomena even so. As with chemical phenomena, so with psychological phenomena.

This brings us to the fourth objection, concerning the threat that a reduction would pose to human freedom. Here we shall be brief. Whether and in what sense there is any human freedom, beyond the relative autonomy that attaches to any complex dynamical system that is partially isolated from the world, is an entirely empirical question. Accordingly, rather than struggle to show that a completed neuroscience will be consistent with this, that, or the other preconceived notion of human freedom, we recommend that we let scientific investigation *teach us* in what ways and to what degrees human creatures are "free." No doubt this will entail modifications for some people's current conceptions of human freedom, and the complete elimination of some others. But that is preferable to making our current confusions into a standard that future theories must struggle to be consistent with.

The fifth and final objection claims an irreducibly abstract status for psychology, on grounds that a variety of quite different physical systems could realize equally well the abstract organization that constitutes a cognitive economy. How can we reduce psychological phenomena to neurobiology, if other physical substrates might serve just as well?

The premise of this objection will likely be conceded by all of us. But the conclusion against reduction does not follow. We can see this clearly by examining a case from our own scientific history. Temperature, we claimed earlier, is identical with mean molecular kinetic energy. But strictly speaking, this is true only for a gas, where the molecules are free to move in a ballistic fashion. In a solid, where the particles oscillate back and forth, their energy is constantly switching between a kinetic and a potential mode. In a high-temperature plasma, there are no molecules at all to consider, since everything has been ripped into sub-atomic parts. Here temperature is a complex mix of various energies. And in a vacuum, where there is no mass at all, temperature consists in the wave-length distribution – the 'black-body curve' – of the EM waves passing through it.

What these examples show us is that reductions can be domain specific: in a gas, temperature is one thing; in a solid, temperature is another thing; in a plasma, it is a third; in a vacuum, a fourth; and so on. (They all count as "temperature," since they interact, and they all obey the same laws of equilibrium and disequilibrium.) None of this moves us to say that classical thermodynamics is an autonomous, irreducible science, forever safe from the ambitions of the underlying microphysical story. On the contrary, it just teaches us that there is more than one way in which energy can be manifested at the microphysical level.

Similarly, visual experience may be one thing in a mammal, and a slightly different thing in an octopus, and a substantially different thing in some possible metal-and-semiconductor android. But they will all count as visual experiences because they share some set of abstract features at a higher level of description. That neurobiology should prove capable of explaining all psychological phenomena in humans is not threatened by the possibility that some *other* theory, say semiconductor electronics, should serve to explain psychological phenomena in *robots*. The two reductions would not conflict. They would complement each other.

We have elsewhere provided more comprehensive accounts of how recent work in neuroscience illuminates issues in psychology and cognitive theory (P. S. Churchland, 1986; P. M. Churchland, 1989). We conclude here with two cautionary remarks. First, while we have here been very upbeat about the possibility of reducing psychology to neuroscience, producing such a reduction will surely be a long and difficult business. We have here been concerned only to rebut the counsel of impossibility, and to locate the reductive aspirations of neuroscience in a proper historical context.

Second, it should not be assumed that the science of psychology will somehow disappear in the process, nor that its role will be limited to that of a passive target of neural explanation. On the contrary, chemistry has not disappeared through the quantum-mechanical explication of its basics; nor has the science of biology disappeared, despite the chemical explication of its basics. Moreover, each of these higher-level sciences has helped to shape profoundly the development and articulation of its underlying science. It will surely be the same with psychology and neuroscience. At this level of complexity, intertheoretic reduction does not appear as the sudden takeover of one discipline by another; it more closely resembles a long and slowly maturing marriage.

References

Bartoshuk, L. M. (1978) "Gustatory system," in R. B. Masterton (ed.) *Handbook of Behavioral Neurobiology*, vol. 1, *Sensory Integration*, New York: Plenum Press, pp. 503–67.
Churchland, P. M. (1989) *A Neurocomputational Perspective: the Nature of Mind and the Structure of Science*, Cambridge, Mass.: MIT Press.

Churchland, P. M. and Churchland, P. S. (1990) "Could a machine think?" *Scientific American* 262, pp. 32–7.

Churchland, P. S. (1986) *Neurophilosophy: Toward a Unified Understanding of the Mind / Brain*, Cambridge, Mass.: MIT Press.

Fodor, J. A. (1975) *The Language of Thought*, New York: Crowell.

Jackson, F. (1982) "Epiphenomenal qualia," *Philosophical Quarterly* 32, pp. 127–36.

Land, E. (1977) "The retinex theory of color vision," *Scientific American* 237, pp. 108–28.

Nagel, T. (1974) "What is it like to be a bat?" *Philosophical Review* 83, pp. 435–50.

Popper, K. and Eccles, J. (1978) *The Self and its Brain*, New York: Springer.

Searle, J. (1980) "Minds, brains, and programs," *Behavioral and Brain Sciences* 3, pp. 417–57.

Searle, J. (1990) "Is the brain's mind a computer program?" *Scientific American* 262, pp. 26–31.

Taylor, C. (1970) "Mind–body identity: a side issue?", in C. V. Borst (ed.) *The Mind / Brain Identity Theory*, Toronto: Macmillan, pp. 231–41.

Taylor, C. (1987) "Overcoming epistemology," in K. Baynes, J. Bohman, T. McCarthy (eds) *After Philosophy: End or Transformation?*, Cambridge, Mass.: MIT Press, pp. 464–88.

4
The Mind–Body Problem

Sydney Shoemaker

In common with many other contemporary philosophers, I see the mind–body problem, not as the problem of how a nonphysical mind can interact with a physical body, but rather as the problem of how minds can be part of a fundamentally physical reality. In part this is the problem of how certain widespread "Cartesian" intuitions about mind can be either explained away, i.e. shown to be illusions, or else shorn of their apparent dualist implications. More generally, it is the problem of how distinctive features of the mental – intentionality, consciousness, subjectivity, etc. – can have a place in a naturalistic worldview which sees minds as a product of biological evolution and as having a physico-chemical substrate in just the way other biological phenomena do.

I see these issues as most fruitfully approached within the framework of the view that has come to be known as "functionalism": the view that mental states are defined, or individuated, in terms of their causal relations to "inputs" (sensory stimuli and the like), outputs (behavior), and one another. Thus, for example, what makes a state the belief that it is raining is that it has certain characteristic causes (including rain and, more proximally, experiences of rain), that in combination with certain other states (e.g. the desire to keep dry) it gives rise to certain behavior (e.g. taking an umbrella), that in combination with certain mental states (e.g. the belief that rain makes the streets wet) it gives rise to yet other mental states (e.g. the belief that the streets are wet), and so on. Such a view is clearly compatible with materialism, for such a functionally defined state can be realized in, or implemented in, the states of a physical (normally biological) mechanism in much the sense in which a computer program can be realized or implemented in the hardware of a computer. But this view is compatible with the Cartesian intuition that such a mental state cannot be identical with any specific physical state; there will be no such identity if, as seems plausible, such functional states are "multiply realizable," i.e. can be physically realized or implemented in any of a variety of different ways.

If a materialist can (by accepting functionalism) agree with the Cartesian intuition that mental states and properties are not identical with physical states and properties, he can also agree with the Cartesian intuition that a person, or the mind of a person *qua* subject of that person's mental states, is not identical to his body or any part of it. The latter will be true if the identity conditions for persons (minds) are different from those for human bodies and their parts. That this is so is a consequence of a view of personal identity which is in the spirit of the view advanced by John Locke in chapter 27 of book II of his *Essay Concerning Human Understanding*; this is, in its modern form, the view that the identity of persons over time consists in a certain sort of psychological continuity. Such a view allows for the possibility of a person having different bodies, and perhaps even different brains, at different times, and so precludes any identification of persons (minds) and bodies (brains). Yet it is entirely compatible with the materialist view that mental phenomena are always realized in, or con- stituted out of, physical phenomena.

The view I favor is, then, a radically "nonreductive" version of materialism. Neither in the case of properties and states nor in the case of particulars will it hold that there is any neat mapping of our commonsense mentalistic taxonomy on to the taxonomies of the physical sciences. In this it agrees with Cartesian intuitions. But the sense in which psychology (whether it be commonsense psychology or scientific psychology) does not reduce to chemistry and physics is the same as the sense in which biology and geology do not reduce to chemistry and physics, and in which chemistry does not reduce to physics. No one doubts that the entities and phenomena that are the subject matter of geology, biology, and chemistry are ultimately composed of entities and phenomena that are the subject matter of physics. There is good reason to think that the same is true of mental phenomena. The philosophical task here is not to carry out a reduction but to make it intelligible that there is this compositional relationship.

There is still a great deal to be explained. One of the most active areas of research in contempoary philosophy of mind is that which concerns "intentionality" or (what I here equate with this) mental representation. Given that mental states are realized in neurophysiological states of the brain, how can they have intentional representational content; how can they be thoughts about Iraq, beliefs that the Cold War is over, hopes that global warming can be arrested? If functional characterizations of mental states are construed "narrowly," i.e. as referring only to causal relations between what goes on "inside the head" (and at its periphery), it seems clear that they will be insufficient to bestow representational content; this is clear from the work of Hilary Putnam and others. It seems pretty clear that in some way or other relations to things outside our heads, to things in our environments, enter into bestowing on our mental states the contents they have. The aim of those who want to "naturalize" intentionality is to show that these relations consist ultimately in relations, e.g. causal ones, for which there is room in a materialist ontology. Various proposals have been put forward about how mental representation can be naturalized, and each of these has met with a variety of objections. All that can be said with confidence is that the problem is far from being solved.

Another main area of research in contemporary philosophy of mind concerns the nature of consciousness and subjectivity. This has been the primary focus of my own recent work. This is an area rife with Cartesian intuitions. To begin with, people seem to have a "privileged access" to their own mental states which, on the face of it, it is difficult to reconcile with materialist views about the nature of such states. One knows what one is thinking and feeling, and, normally, what one believes, desires, etc., without having to ground this knowledge on evidence about one's behavior and bodily circumstances. And in being aware of one's own mental states one certainly is not aware of them *as* physical states of any sort. Nor, and this is a prima-facie objection to functionalist views, does one seem to be aware of them *as* functional states, i.e. as states defined by functional or causal roles. And sometimes we seem to know the nature of our mental states in a way that seems incompatible with that nature being what materialist and functionalist accounts say it is.

This last seems true in the case of what have come to be known as "qualia," and are also referred to as the "phenomenal features" of feelings, sensations, and perceptual states: the felt features of pains and itches that make them (so one wants to say) the kinds of sensations they are, the distinctive feature of a visual experience of redness that determines "what it is like" to see red and distinguishes this from what it is like to see green, blue, yellow, and so on. It is natural to say that in being aware of these features of an experience one is aware of its "intrinsic nature," and aware of something whose nature cannot consist in its aptness for playing a certain causal role. Moreover, there are arguments that purport to show that qualia cannot be physical properties and cannot be functionally defined. Frank Jackson's "knowledge argument" points out that someone could know all of the relevant physical facts about the seeing of red without knowing what it is like to see red, and concludes that there is something the physical facts leave out, and that physicalism is false (see Jackson, 1982). Similar ideas are expressed by Thomas Nagel in his well-known paper "What is it like to be a bat?" (1974). And the conceivability of "spectrum inversion" (red things looking to one person the way green things look to another, and vice versa), and more generally "qualia inversion," has been used to argue that qualia are not functionally definable. For, allowing the conceivability of this, it seems possible that there should be creatures who are functionally exactly alike (at the psychological level of description) but who differ in the qualitative character of their experiences.

Some writers friendly to functionalism and materialism have responded to the qualia-based arguments by arguing that the very existence of qualia is an illusion. For example, Gilbert Harman (1990) has argued that the only features of experiences that are accessible to consciousness are their intentional (i.e. representational) features, and that there are no qualia as usually conceived. And Daniel Dennett has argued that "conscious experience has *no* properties that are special in *any* of the ways qualia have been supposed to be special," and that qualia should be "quined" (1988). While I think there is truth in what Harman and Dennett claim, I think both go too far. I think we can give an account of qualia which answers to most, if not all, of the intuitions that motivate the use of the term, and which allows materialists and functionalists to acknowledge their existence.

Briefly, I allow that the inverted qualia argument shows that individual qualia (e.g. the one that characterizes my experiences of red) cannot be functionally defined, but I hold that the notion of a quale is nonetheless a functional concept. The key notion here is that of qualitative similarity. This can be functionally defined in terms of its role in perceptual discrimination and recognition, and in the fixation of perceptual beliefs. In terms of this we can define a notion of qualitative identity, and in terms of that we can explain what it is for a property to be a quale. Having this much of a functional account allows us to speak of qualia as being physically realized or implemented (in the sense in which any functional property can be physically realized or implemented), and makes their existence compatible with materialism (Shoemaker, 1975, 1982). I think that the Jackson–Nagel "knowledge argument" can likewise be answered, but shall not attempt to give my answer here.

Returning to the more general question of consciousness and self-knowledge, I think that a promising way of taming Cartesian intuitions about our special access to our own mental states is to show that some of them, at least, are consequences of a plausible functionalist account of the nature of such states (and are compatible with materialism because functionalism is). A common view about "introspective" self-knowledge, due largely to D. M. Armstrong, is that awareness of one's mental states is basically a matter of having higher-order beliefs about one's own mental states that are produced, via a reliable mechanism in the mind – brain, by the very states they are about (see Armstrong, 1968). What I would add to this is that in many cases it belongs to the very essence of a mental state (its functional nature) that, normally, its existence results, under certain circumstances, in there being such awareness of it. It should be noted that much of the explanatory role of some mental states *vis-à-vis* behavior is a role they can play only via their subject's higher-order beliefs about them (the beliefs which if true count as awarenesses of them). This is true of the role of pain in explaining such behavior as seeking medical treatment. And it is arguably true of the role of beliefs in explaining such speech acts as assertions; what one sincerely asserts is what one believes that one believes. Moreover, it is arguable that being the subject of certain kinds of states, in particular beliefs and desires, requires at least a minimal degree of rationality, and that it is of the essence of rationality that one be aware (or can become aware on demand) of one's own beliefs and desires, since only so can one detect and eradicate inconsistencies and incoherencies in one's belief–desire system, or make the rationality required revisions of it in the light of new experience (see Shoemaker, 1988).

What these considerations suggest is that a functionalist account of mind can accept a version of the Cartesian intuition that (some) mental states are "self-intimating." A companion Cartesian intuition to this is that awareness of one's own mental states is infallible. I doubt if this can be defended for most kinds of mental states, although I think that a functionalist case can be made for the slightly weaker claim that, as a matter of necessity, introspective beliefs about one's sensations and current thoughts are nearly always correct (see Shoemaker, 1990). But in the special case of beliefs about what one believes, I think that an infallibility claim may be defensible. One can certainly be wrong in thinking that one does not believe something; this happens in some cases of self-deception. But it is arguable that if someone believes that he does believe something, then he does believe that thing (although he may also believe something incompatible with it). For someone who believes that he believes that *P* will be disposed to use the proposition that *P* as a premise in his reasonings, including his practical reasonings, and so will be disposed to act on the assumption that *P*. As we might put it, being disposed to act on the assumption that one believes that *P* brings with it being disposed to act on the assumption that *P* – and, arguably, having the latter disposition is sufficient for believing that *P*.

Much of what I have just said is controversial, and would be disputed by many philosophers who share my general outlook. What I have tried to do is to suggest ways in which Cartesian intuitions can be accommodated within a functionalist–materialist framework. As I said at the outset, for a materialist a large part of solving the mind–body problem will consist in either "explaining away" Cartesian intuitions away or, what is my preference, showing how they can be accommodated within a materialist account.

References

Armstrong, D. M. (1968) *A Materialist Theory of the Mind*, London: Routledge & Kegan Paul.
Dennett, D. (1988) "Quining qualia," in A. J. Marcel and E. Bisiach (eds) *Consciousness in Contemporary Science*, Oxford: Clarendar Press, pp. 42–77.
Harman, G. (1990) "The intrinsic quality of experience," *Philosophical Perspectives* 4, pp. 31–52.
Jackson, F. (1982) "Epiphenomenal qualia," *Philosophical Quarterly* 32, pp. 127–3.
Nagel, T. (1974) "What is it like to be a bat?" *Philosophical Review* 83, pp. 435–50.
Shoemaker, S. (1975) "Functionalism and qualia," *Philosophical Studies* 27, pp. 291–315, reprinted 1984 in *Identity, Cause and Mind: Philosophical Essays* Cambridge: Cambridge University Press.
Shoemaker, S. (1982) "The inverted spectrum," *Journal of Philosophy* 79, pp. 357–81; reprinted 1984 in *Identity, Cause and Mind, Philosophical Essays*, Cambridge: Cambridge University Press.
Shoemaker, S. (1988) "On knowing one's own mind," *Philosophical Perspectives* 2, pp. 183–209.
Shoemaker, S. (1990) "First-person access," *Philosophical Perspectives* 4, pp. 187–214.

Part II
Is the Mind–Body Problem Well Posed?

5
Consciousness and Objective Reality

Thomas Nagel

We do not at present have even the outline of an adequate theory of the place of mind in the natural order. We know that conscious mental processes occur as part of animal life, and that they are intimately connected with behavior and with the physical activity of our nervous systems and those of other animals. But at the more general, one might say cosmological, level, we know essentially nothing, for we do not understand why those particular connections exist. Our knowledge is entirely empirical and *ad hoc*, not theoretical.

Much discussion in the philosophy of mind is concerned with the problem of intentionality: what it means to attribute content to mental states like belief, desire, thought, perception, and so forth. This topic also links discussion of the relation between the mind and the brain with discussion of the relation between natural and artificial intelligence, and of the possibility of ascribing mental states to computers, in some distant future stage of their development. However I believe that the most fundamental problem in the area is that of consciousness. While consciousness in the form of pure sensation does not in itself guarantee intentionality, I believe true intentionality cannot occur in a being incapable of consciousness. The nature of this relation is very unclear to me, but its truth seems evident. We may assign meaning to the operations and output of an unconscious computer, as we can assign meaning to words in a book, but the computer can't mean or intend anything itself by what it says or does.

For this reason I believe it is at present not possible to speculate fruitfully about the question whether artificially created physical systems could have minds. We can say nothing interesting about this when we know so little about why *we* have minds, or why the other natural organisms to which we find it natural to attribute mental states have them. What is it about a system constructed as we are that explains why it can feel, perceive, want, believe, and think? Until we can begin to answer that question at some level of generality, we are unlikely to say anything useful about whether systems of a radically different physical type could do those things.

Ultimately, a person's opinion concerning this question will depend not merely on his scientific beliefs but on his philosophical beliefs about the mind–body problem. That is because it is a philosophical question, what a general theory of mind would have to account for to be adequate.

There are those who believe, for example, that mental states can be defined in terms of their causal role in the control of the organism. When this definition refers to a system of interacting states, definable entirely in terms of their relations to physical inputs, behavioral outputs, and to one another, the view is called functionalism. If functionalism were correct as an account of what it is for a being to have a mind, or to be the subject of mental states, then nothing more would be required for a general theory of the physical conditions of mind than an account of how physical materials can be put together to construct systems whose functional organization was of the right type. To explain this would be a stupendous task; and it is not at all obvious that the same functional organization that characterizes a mouse, let alone a human, could be embodied in a completely different type of physical system, in the way that much simpler functions like addition can be carried out by different physical machines. But at least we can understand the general character of the question. The possibility of an alternative physical realization of visual perception, for example, would depend both on the functional analysis of that mental faculty and on the possibility of replicating that type of functional operation in a structure physically quite different from the standard biological model. Such a theory would enable us to consider the possibility of the eventual construction of artificial minds, through the creation of systems which mimic the behavior and functional organization of human and other animal organisms.

I believe, however, that functionalism, though part of the truth, is not an adequate theory of mind, and that the complete truth is much more complicated and more resistant to understanding. In addition to their functional role in the explanation of behavior and their concrete physiological basis, conscious mental states have characteristics of a third type, familiar to us all, namely their subjective experiential quality: how they are or how they appear or feel from the point of view of their subjects. However true it may be that mental states and processes play a functional

role in the behavioral life of the organism, these experiential or phenomenological qualities of conscious experience are not simply *equivalent* to
those functional roles. And however closely tied these phenomenological
qualities may be to specific neurophysiological conditions, they are quite
clearly not analyzable in terms of the physical description of those
conditions.

If this is correct, then an adequate general theory of the place of mind
in the natural order must systematically relate three seemingly disparate
things: functional organization, physical constitution, and subjective appearance. We know a certain amount about how these three are related in
human sensory perception, and perhaps more generally in mammalian
perception. We know parts of the story about other aspects of mind, in
ourselves and other animals. But we have not even the glimmerings of a
general theory which explains *why* the particular physical operation of the
human central nervous system gives rise to the sort of conscious life that
it does – though we understand a bit more in certain respects about how
it makes possible the organism's behavior in dealing with its environment.
But unless our theory of mind includes a theory of consciousness, it cannot
give us any basis for speculating either positively or negatively about the
possibility of alternative physical bases of mind, different from the familiar
biological examples. And at present we have simply no idea what *in general*
the occurrence of conscious processes depends on.

We have increasing knowledge of a fascinating character about the
physical conditions of particular types of conscious states, but these
correlations, even if substantially multiplied, do not amount to a general
explanatory theory. In order to achieve a real understanding of these
matters, we would have to make progress of a fundamental kind with the
mind–body problem: progress which constituted a conceptual advance,
rather than merely more empirically ascertainable information, however
interesting. A theory which succeeded in explaining the relation between
behavior, consciousness, and the brain would have to be of a fundamentally different kind from theories about other things: it cannot be generated
by the application of already existing methods of explanation.

The reason for this is simple. The mind–body problem is a natural
outgrowth or by-product of the overwhelmingly successful methods of
physical science which have driven the permanent scientific revolution of
our era since the seventeenth century. That is why the problem received
its essential modern formulation from Descartes, who participated in the
beginnings of that revolution.

What has made modern physical science possible is the method of
investigating the observable physical world not with respect to the way it
appears to our senses – to the species-specific view of human perceivers –
but rather as an objective realm existing independently of our minds.

(I realize that this description may be thought not to fit certain developments of contemporary physics, but that is a complication I leave aside, as it is not relevant to the present issue.) In order to do this, it was necessary to find ways of detecting and measuring and describing features of the physical world which were not inextricably tied to the ways things looked, sounded, and felt to us; and this resulted in the discovery of objective, essentially spatiotemporal properties of the physical world which could be mathematically described and related by general laws of extraordinary power and universality, thus enabling us to transcend the rough and particular associations available at the level of merely human appearances. The result is an understanding of objective physical reality almost unrecognizably different from the familar world of our theoretically unaided experience.

But it was a condition of this remarkable advance that the subjective appearances of things be excluded from what had to be explained and described by our physical theories. And what was done with those appearances instead was that they were detached from the physical world and relocated in our minds. The whole idea of objective physical reality depends on excluding the subjective appearances from the external world and consigning them to the mind instead.

But it follows inexorably from this strategy that the same methods of objective physical understanding cannot be successfully applied to the subjective contents of the mind themselves. The method can be used on the body, including its central nervous system, and on the relation of neural activity to observable behavioral functioning, because these are all aspects of objective physical reality. But for the subjective qualities of experience themselves, we need a different form of understanding. We cannot hope to understand them completely as an aspect of objective physical reality, because the concept of objective physical reality depends on excluding them from what has to be understood. They are excluded, because they are tied to a species-specific point of view that the objectivity of physical science requires us to leave behind.

So when science turns to the effort to explain the subjective quality of experience, there is no further place for these features to escape to. And since the traditional, enormously successful method of modern physical understanding cannot be extended to this aspect of the world, that form of understanding has built into it a guarantee of its own essential incompleteness – its intrinsic incapacity to account for everything.

One consequence is that the traditional form of scientific explanation, reduction of familiar substances and processes to their more basic and in general imperceptibly small component parts, is not available as a solution to the analysis of mind. Reductionism within the objective domain is essentially simple to understand, for it uses the uncomplicated geometrical idea of the part–whole relation. Geometry is the basic imaginative tool which made possible the formulation of atomic theory, and in more and more sophisticated versions it has allowed physical understanding to expand. But it depends on first stripping familiar objects of all but their spatiotemporal, or primary, qualities and relations. That makes possible their reduction to more basic and law-governed objective phenomena from which the familiar properties can be seen to arise by necessity, as the mass and hardness of a diamond can be seen to result from the combined mass and structural arrangement of its carbon atoms, or the liquidity of water can be seen to result from the relations of its molecules to one another.

No correspondingly straightforward psychophysical reduction is imaginable, because it would not have the simple character of a relation between one objective level of description and another. We at present lack the conception of a complete analysis of subjective, phenomenological features of mental reality in terms of an objective, physical basis, and there is no reason to believe that such a thing is possible.

Surprisingly, there are some who believe this is a reason to deny the reality of the third, subjective aspect of the mental; they call themselves eliminative materialists. But this is an irrational and, I might add, unscientific attitude. The first rule of science is not to ignore the data, and the existence of phenomenological features of mental life is one of the most obvious and unavoidable categories of data with which we are presented. To regard it as unreal because it cannot be accounted for by the methods of current physical science is to get things backwards. The data are not determined by our methods; rather the adequacy of our methods is determined by whether they can account for the data. To admit to reality only what can be understood by current methods is a sure recipe for stagnation.

The limits of the classical methods of objective physical science are not surprising, since those methods were developed to deal with a definite, though universal, type of subject matter. If we are to take the next great step, to a truly theoretical understanding of the mental, we must proceed by regarding this limitation as a challenge to develop a new form of understanding appropriate to a subject whose exclusion from physical science was essential to its progress. This is in my view the most interesting and difficult scientific challenge we now face, and I have no idea how it might be met. My own instincts are in the direction of a Spinozistic monism, which will reveal both the mental and the physical as incomplete descriptions of a more fundamental reality that explains them both, as well as their necessary connection – but of which we have at present no conception. The possibility of the development of conscious organisms must have been built into the world from the beginning: it cannot be an accident. (Nor can it be explained through the theory of evolution, in terms of the survival value of consciousness. Evolution can explain only why a trait has survived and not been extinguished, not how it is possible in the first place.) But such speculation is at this point idle.

Machines won't have minds unless they have points of view, and at present we know practically nothing about the general conditions under which subjective points of view arise out of the activities of the physical world. In some respects we understand quite well how that world works, and we are making significant progress in extending this physical form of understanding to biology, including neurophysiology. But until we discover a way to stand theoretically astride the boundary between objective spatiotemporal physical reality and the subjective contents of experience, we cannot claim to be in possession of the basic intellectual tools needed for a comprehensive understanding of conscious life. This may be unattainable, but without it we cannot have a general cosmology.

6
The Experiential and the Non-experiential

Galen Strawson

1 Introduction

Consider a human being persisting through time. Consider this portion of reality and ask what it contains. It certainly contains experiential phenomena, by which I mean all the phenomena of consciousness or conscious experience, whose reality I take for granted and in no need of laborious definition for present purposes.[1] And it also contains non-experiential phenomena. I assume this, since I am by faith a materialist, although the existence of non-experiential phenomena is epistemologically more dubious than that of experiential phenomena. (It is arguable that one can be a materialist and hold that all experiential phenomena are physical phenomena without committing oneself to belief in non-experiential phenomena. But I will take it that to be a materialist is to believe that there are non-experiential phenomena.)

The question is then this: What is the relation between the experiential and the non-experiential, in this portion of reality? I think this is the only hard part of the mind–body problem. That is, I think that it is only the experiential mental phenomena that cause problems, on the "mind" side of the mind–body problem. One may hold that there are also *non-experiential* mental phenomena, e.g. dispositional, propositional-attitude phenomena, or sub-experiential phenomena like the processes postulated in the Marr–Nishihara theory of vision. But these are not a serious problem when it comes to the mind–body problem.[2]

2 "Experience" and "Experiential"

What is the relation between the experiential and the non-experiential? Having put the question this way, let me make a terminological ruling. Most contemporary analytic philosophers are materialists who suppose that experiences not only have experiential (or conscious-experience-involving) aspects, but also have non-experiential aspects, aspects whose description does not require reference to any conscious experience. They may well be right, and I will reserve the plural-accepting, count-noun use of "experience" for talking of experiences as things – events – that may have nonconscious or non-experiential properties as well as conscious and experiential properties. Concurrently, I will reserve the word "experiential," and the word "experience" considered as a "mass" term with no plural, for talking about the character that experiences have precisely and only insofar as they involve conscious experience. I will take these words to refer only to the (experiential) "what-it's-like-ness" of experience considered in all its extraordinary variety and complication, as one swims the Hellespont, eats apricots, or lies awake at night thinking about the mind–body problem.

3 Agnostic Materialism

What, then, is the relation between the experiential and the non-experiential? I suppose this is ultimately a question for scientists, but philosophers also have something to say, and there are some reasons for thinking that scientists may never be able to produce a satisfactory answer (McGinn, 1989). I approach the question as an *agnostic materialist*, one who believes that we must be radically ignorant of the nature of the physical if materialism is true. The main ground for this agnostic materialism is the belief that the apparent difficulty of the mind–body problem cannot plausibly be thought to stem from any hopeless inadequacy or error in our concepts of the mental, and in particular of the experiential (as Dennett, for example, supposes); and that the failure of these concepts to connect satisfactorily with our concepts of the non-experiential – as deployed in current physics, for example, and in those sciences generally held to be reducible to physics – must therefore stem from some other sort of radical (and possibly irremediable) inadequacy in our concepts of the nature of the physical. In Section 7 I will consider one rather high-level attack on this view. But I will begin by discussing a problem that arises for nonreductive identity theorists or nonreductive monists: those who hold, briefly, that although mental goings on are identical with physical goings on, statements attributing mental properties cannot be reduced to – cannot in any sense be equivalent to – statements containing only the nonmental terms of physics.

4 Real Materialism

According to materialism, every natural thing is wholly physical. It follows that experience – recall the restriction of the term in Section 2 – is wholly physical. For experience is indubitably a real and natural phenomenon. It is as real as rock, as real as everything physical whose existence is not a matter of experience. Serious materialists must hold experiences to be physical phenomena in *every* respect, and hence even in respect of their having the experiential character they have; and thus not just in respect of their having the character they appear to have to physics and neurophysiology as they inspect the brain.

It follows that they cannot talk of the physical *as opposed to* the mental or experiential at all. If they do talk like this – and they do all the time – they can only really mean to talk of the non-experiential physical as opposed to the experiential physical (or the mental physical as opposed to the nonmental physical). The distinction that concerns them when it comes to the mind–body problem cannot be a distinction between the mental and the physical, because it is a distinction that must be drawn entirely *within* the realm of the physical. If one is a materialist, to say that there is a fundamental distinction between mental or experiential phenomena, on the one hand, and physical phenomena, on the other hand, is like saying that there is a fundamental distinction between cows and animals: that on the one hand there are cows, and on the other hand there are animals.

The mental-physical distinction seems very natural. Materialist books and articles about the mind–body problem speed along in the standard idiom. But the question always arises: what exactly are they saying, given their materialist premise? What they tend to mean, of course, is that there is a problem about the relation between the experiential or mental and the physical *as conceived of by current physics*. And of course there is. This is the whole problem and it is the old problem.[3] But to be a materialist is to believe that the experiential is as much of a physical phenomenon as electric charge. It is to hold that there is no more difficulty (no more difficulty, ontologically speaking) in the idea that physical things can have the wholly physical property of having experience, as well as the physical properties currently discerned by physics, than there is in the idea that physical things can have mass as well as extension.

Let me try to block a misunderstanding, by recalling again the ruling about the words "experience" and "experiential" in section 2. When I say that the experiential "just is" physical, or that experiential properties "just are" physical properties, I don't mean to be saying *anything like* what I think some materialists have meant by saying such things as that "experience is really just neurons firing." I don't mean to be saying that all that is really going on is what can be discerned and accounted for by current physics, or what could be discerned and accounted for by any nonrevolutionary or conceptually conservative extension of current physics. Such a view is obviously false (it amounts to some kind of radical eliminativism). To say that the experiential just is physical is not to say anything like this. For "the experiential" here refers *only* to that part of reality which consists of the (indisputably real) phenomenon of experiences' having the (conscious) experiential character they do for those who have them as they have them. It is this – the experiential as such – the portion of reality we have to do with when we consider experiences specifically and solely in respect of their experiential character for those who have them as they have them – that "just is" physical. It is your experience considered solely in respect of the experiential character it has for you as you read this or eat apricots that just is physical, and that must, specifically in respect of its complex experiential character, be as comprehensively accounted for by any hypothetical complete physics as the motions of billiard balls – if materialism is true.

5 Real Materialism and Reduction

This point has consequences for the question of reduction, and I will now comment on this.

Reductionism has many varieties – one may for example distinguish between semantic and ontological reductionism – but I wish to say as little about this as possible, because I do not think it matters much for present purposes.[4] I will treat reduction as a relation between properties rather than sentences or statements (the talk of properties can always be converted into talk of sentences or statements). I will suppose the fundamental entailment of "X is reducible to Y" to be "X is (fully) theoretically explicable by reference to Y," and take the notion of explanation for granted until section 7.[5] In order to keep things simple I will restrict attention to basic, sensory experiential properties like the property of having color-experience or sound-experience.

One reason for doing this is that some materialists feel that experiential phenomena like the phenomenon of someone's consciously wondering whether Goldbach's Conjecture is true are patently irreducible to the terms of physics (although they are wholly physical phenomena), because their explication necessarily involves reference to linguistic conventions, and so on. It is not at all clear that they can maintain this position, if, as is likely, they accept the "asymmetry thesis" discussed in the next section, but I will leave the difficult questions raised by such phenomena to one side because the point I wish to make can be made by reference to more basic, patently nonconventional, sensory-experiential properties such as the having of color-experience.

If one is a serious materialist, and (therefore) a real realist about experiential properties, one holds that experiential properties like the property of having color-experience just are physical properties, as already remarked. They are real, natural properties of natural living things, and all such properties are physical. As a materialist, then, it seems that one faces a choice. Either experiential properties, being natural physical properties, are reducible to other natural physical properties, in something like the way we take physical properties such as liquidity or acidity to be, or they are not. But if they are not so reducible, then at least some of them must themselves be fundamental physical properties like (e.g.) extension or electric charge, not reducible to (or theoretically explicable in terms of) any other physical properties. There is no other plausible option, so long as one is a materialist and a (real) realist about experiential properties. It seems, then, that nonreductive materialist monists must hold at least some experiential properties to be fundamental physical properties like extension or electric charge – even if some experiential properties are reducible to others. They must hold this if they are real materialists.

Some will think this sounds very alarming. And it is perhaps not surprising that many philosophers who think of themselves as materialists are not really realists about many mental properties, such as dispositional propositional-attitude properties. But here the primary concern is with occurrent experiential properties. These are the difficult properties, when it comes to the mind–body problem, and they cannot possibly be thought to admit of any antirealist or irrealist treatment of the sort sometimes applied to dispositional propositional-attitude properties. So serious materialists do face the choice described in the last paragraph. By definition, they hold that the experiential (or phenomenal, or what-it's-like-ness) properties of experiences are entirely physical properties (they are natural, nonconventional properties, and all such natural properties are entirely physical properties). So either these experiential physical properties are reducible to other, non-experiential physical properties, and do not feature as fundamental in an optimal physics; or they are not reducible to non-experiential physical properties, and at least some of them feature as fundamental in an optimal physics. There is no other possibility. Materialists who cannot accept the idea that experiential properties might be fundamental physical properties – that *experientiality*, like extension, might be a fundamental physical property with many "modes" – must suppose that their appearance of constitutive irreducibility to the terms of physics is an illusion, an artifact of the limits on human understanding and human physics.

To be a nonreductive materialist monist, then, is either to hold that reduction of experiential to non-experiential properties is in principle possible, and that the appearance of irreducibility merely shows that human physics is fundamentally incomplete; or it is to hold that such reduction is in principle impossible. But to hold this second thing, as a materialist who is also a real realist about experiential properties, is simply to hold that experiential properties are – that experientiality is – among the fundamental properties that must be adverted to in a completed or optimal physics. Some have been lulled into thinking that there is a comfortable and strictly materialist middle position that combines rejection of the idea that any experiential properties are fundamental physical properties with endorsement of the idea that they are in principle irreducible to non-experiential properties. To see that this won't do, one has to register fully the point that to be a materialist is to grant that these experiential properties, these natural (nonconventional) properties of physical beings like ourselves, are wholly physical properties.

6 Materialism and Asymmetry

Standard materialism is committed to the *asymmetry thesis*. It is committed to the idea that there is a crucial asymmetry in the status of mental and physical phenomena, and in particular in the status of experiential and non-experiential phenomena, given which it is correct to say (1) that the experiential is based in, or "realized by," or otherwise dependent on, the non-experiential, and incorrect to say either (2) that the non-experiential is based in, or realized by, or otherwise dependent on, the experiential or (3) that they coexist in such a way that neither can be said to be based in, or realized by, or in any way asymmetrically dependent on, the other.

One reason why the asymmetry thesis seems so attractive is this: we find it natural to suppose that wherever and whenever there is experiential reality there is non-experiential reality, but that the converse of this is not true: there can, we think, be non-experiential reality without experience. And this immediately makes it seem that experiential reality must *depend* on non-experiential reality in some way; or, more cautiously, that there is an asymmetrical relation of existential dependence of experiential features of physical reality on features of physical reality that are taken account of in a physics that, like our current physics, takes itself to contain predicates only for non-experiential features of physical reality.

According to this view, then, (1) some things have experiential physical properties, (2) all those that do also have non-experiential physical properties, and (3) they have the particular experiential physical properties they have in virtue of having certain of the non-experiential physical properties they have – whatever exactly "in virtue of" means.[6]

The asymmetry thesis can sound very plausible. But it is important to be clear about what it amounts to, if one is both a materialist, and a realist (as one must be) about experiential properties. I suggest, to return to the theme of section 5, that it must in the end amount to the claim that experiential physical properties like the property of having color-experience resemble non-experiential physical properties like liquidity in one crucial respect, *however much they may also differ from them*: they resemble such properties in being physical properties that are possessed by things in virtue of their possession of other physical properties which we naturally think of as more fundamental physical properties. The reason why it seems that this is all the asymmetry thesis can really amount to is that it seems that this is really the only relevant sort of asymmetrical dependency that one natural physical property can be said to have on another, within the materialist scheme of things.

This conclusion about what the asymmetry thesis amounts to appears to have a very striking consequence. It appears to have the consequence – which some will think clearly false – that if one accepts the asymmetry thesis one must reject the *irreducibility thesis*, and vice versa. Given the asymmetry thesis, and materialism, experiential physical properties must be reducible to non-experiential physical properties in a way which is, ultimately, similar to the way in which the property of liquidity is held to be reducible to van de Waals molecular interaction properties, and so on – however great the difference between the two cases may also be. (The case of liquidity is not chosen because it is comfortable or tractable as an analogy. It isn't. There is no comfortable analogy, and that is part of the point.)

This reduction is of course very hard – impossible – to imagine. If one thinks of reduction in a standard way as semantic or ontological reduction, then it looks as if it amounts to the claim that when you have said all there is to say about a segment of the world (say a person) in non-experiential terms, there is a fundamental sense in which you have described everything there is to describe; so that although there may perhaps be other natural, perspicuous, and theoretically interesting ways of putting things, they will not advert to facts, or aspects of facts, other than those already detailed in non-experiential terms. But this claim cannot possibly be true, for you will not, in deploying only non-experiential terms, have described the person's experience considered just as such. The problem is not diminished if one thinks of reduction in the way proposed in section 5, and takes the fundamental entailment of "X is reducible to Y" to be "X is (fully) theoretically explicable by reference to Y." For how can the nature and existence of an experiential property be thought to be fully explained by reference to essentially non-experiential properties?

It is accordingly easy to sympathize with nonreductive monists who think the irreducibility thesis is just obviously true. But it is arguable that they will have to abandon the standard asymmetry thesis. They will either have to abandon the asymmetry thesis, or treat the irreducibility thesis as a rather banal thesis about the limitations on human understanding. That is, they will have to grant that there is no irreducible irreducibility, that experiential properties are reducible to non-experiential properties in some possible optimal physics, and that the appearance of irreducibility is just an illusion generated by human ignorance. This seems profoundly implausible, given the nature of the case.

Some may talk of levels of description, and of how facts registered at one level of description (e.g. the sociological level) may be dependent on facts registered at another (e.g. the level of physics) while being clearly irreducible to them. But even if this case of irreducibility were to be granted it would not provide a good analogy for the present case, because all sorts of convention-involving properties – properties which depend for their existence on human conventions – are ascribed at the sociological level, and there is no parallel for this alleged source of in-principle irreducibility in the case of basic, non-convention-involving, sensory experiential properties like color-experience or sound-experience.

Once again, then, if experiential phenomena (like color-experience) really are somehow (wholly) dependent on non-experiential phenomena, then naturalistic materialist realism about them necessarily involves the idea that there is a correct way of describing things given which one can relate color-experience, considered just as such, to the non-experiential phenomena on which it is supposed to depend, in such a way that the dependence is at least as intelligible as the dependence of the liquidity of water on the interaction properties of individual molecules. The alternative, after all, is that there should be total dependence that is not intelligible or explicable in any possible physics, dependence that is unintelligible and inexplicable even to God, as it were. It may be objected that I am simply assuming that if there is a single, unified, non-miraculous physical reality, there must be some possible valid unified theoretical account of it. I admit it and return to the question in the next section.

In sum. The question that must be faced by nonreductive monists who are unconvinced by the present discussion, but who are genuine realists about the experiential, is "How is it possible for there to be asymmetrical dependence without reducibility in some possible or optimal physics?" I feel I will have got somewhere if I have managed to revive anyone's sense that a positive answer to this question is very hard, if not impossible. There can't be (1) wholly physical properties that are (2) wholly dependent on other physical properties and (3) wholly irreducible to them, or wholly inexplicable by reference to them in any possible valid physics. As far as I can see many nonreductive monists want to accept (2) and (3), in the case of experiential properties, although they are committed to the view that experiential properties satisfy (1) if they are genuine materialists.

It may finally be protested that I have failed to consider an "emergentist" suggestion about how to combine asymmetry and irreducibility within the materialist framework. Some may hold that asymmetry thesis is compatible with the view that there is an essentially *indirect* dependency relation between the experiential and the non-experiential. Experiential physical properties simply cannot be instantiated, at a given time and place, unless non-experiential physical properties are also instantiated, while the converse is not true. But this is not because the experiential physical properties are dependent on the non-experiential physical properties in a way that implies the reducibility in principle of (statements about) the former to (statements about) the latter in some possible, optimal physics. It is because although the former are not directly dependent on the latter, they somehow just need the presence or company of the latter. Some who want to talk of experiential properties as "emergent" relative to non-experiential properties may feel that this represents their position accurately, although it seems to turn the relation between the experiential and the non-experiential into a guaranteed mystery, where before it was merely a mystery.

7 Experience, Explanation, and Theoretical Integration

Serious materialists have to be outright realists about the experiential. So they are obliged to hold that experiential phenomena just are physical phenomena, although current physics cannot account for them. As an acting materialist, I accept this, and assume that experiential phenomena are "based in" or "realized in" the brain (to stick to the human case). But this assumption doesn't solve any problems for materialists. Instead it obliges them to admit ignorance of the nature of the physical, to admit that they don't have a fully adequate idea of what the physical is, and hence of what the brain is.

In talking of ignorance I have one well-known thing in mind: when we consider the brain as current physics and neurophysiology presents it to us, we have to admit that we do not know how experience as such – experiential "what-it's-like-ness" as such – is or even could be based in the brain. That is why any serious statement of materialism should *explicitly incorporate* the thought that our current physical-science conception of the physical is incomplete in certain basic respects. The physics (and neurophysiological) story of my brain is rich and detailed, but it fails to provide any theoretically satisfying account of how something undeniably real is even so much as possible: it just leaves out the phenomenal or experiential character of my experience. If I am watching a tree in the wind, there is a remarkable electrochemical, computational, photons-and-retina-and-rods-and-cones-involving story of what is happening to me. But this story leaves out the experiential properties of my experience. It fails to say anything about these properties. It fails to explain even how they are possible.

This is a familiar claim. I repeat it in order to consider an objection which directly challenges this use of the notion of explanation. In one form, it goes like this: science is not really (or ultimately) concerned with explanation at all. It is true that we cannot really explain (or understand) the relation between experiential phenomena and non-experiential phenomena. But there is no special failure here, because we cannot really explain (or understand) the relations between non-experiential phenomena either.

The objection concedes that we use the idiom of explanation. We use the word "because." We say that *A* happened *because B* happened. We say that the reason why billiard ball *B* moved off in direction *D* at velocity *V* is that it was struck by billiard ball *A* in the particular way that it was. And if we are questioned, we may talk of impact and energy transfer, momentum, force, and mass. But we may be pressed further, and if we are we will eventually come to the end of our explanatory resources. And when we are asked why the facts appealed to in our final explanation are as they are, we will not be able to say anything but "This is (just) how things are."

The claim is then this: since explanation must come to an end, nothing in science is ever really truly or ultimately explained. There are scientific explanations that seem completely satisfying given what they take for granted. But the question "Why?" can always be raised about what they take for granted, and in the end one will be unable to give any further answer. It follows from this (according to the objection) that all science really delivers, in the end, are statements of correlation, causal or otherwise, e.g. statements of the form "When events of type *A* occur, events of type *B* occur," statements to the effect that this is just how things are. What is more (the objection continues), we may eventually be just as successful in the attempt to formulate well-confirmed statements of correlation that link experiential predicates to non-experiential predicates as we have been in the attempt to formulate well-confirmed statements of correlation that link non-experiential physics predicates to each other. If so, there will be no special failure of physics, or of explanation, when it comes to giving an account of the experiential and its place in nature. There will be no need to suppose any special inadequacy in this area (for a powerful statement of this view see Hume, 1978, pp. 246–8).

Now there are various problems with the idea that we could produce well-confirmed exceptionless statements of correlation linking experiential predicates and non-experiential predicates. (Cf. Strawson, forthcoming, 3.6) But they are not important at present. For even when it is allowed that we can produce them the essential point remains: mere correlations cannot be seen as providing any sort of explanation or understanding of the existence of experience or "what-it's-like-ness" or qualia in physical-science terms.

But what exactly does this point come to? It has been granted that explanation comes to an end, and that when we are pressed in science, we end up with statements about how things just are (and just are correlated) which offer no (ultimate) explanation of why they are that way. And it has been granted that for us to feel that we have been given an *explanation*, in science, when someone says "*A* happened because of *B*," as opposed to a statement of essentially unexplained correlation which happens to use the idiom "because," is really just a matter of what we find theoretically satisfying, given other things we already accept. So what does this point about explanation amount to?

One point is this. The weak-looking notion of what we find theoretically satisfying is not unimportant. Even if explanations come to an end, there are many explanations which we do find theoretically satisfying in science, and this satisfaction is one of the things we aim at in scientific inquiry. It is, as Quine remarks, the goal of *understanding*; of what we take to be understanding, of what satisfies us as constituting understanding (Quine, 1990, p. 2). It is something we feel we manage to achieve in many areas of physics, and something which we find we have utterly failed to achieve in the case of the relations between experiential phenomena and non-experiential phenomena, and will still have failed to achieve even if we manage to come up with promising statements of correlation.

This is why it seems reasonable to say that we should – as materialists who think that experiential phenomena, like non-experiential phenomena, are entirely physical phenomena – suppose ourselves to be ignorant of the nature of the physical in a specific way that will remain undiminished until we have achieved something like the sort of theoretical satisfaction, in our account of the relation between experiential and non-experiential phenomena, that we are familiar with in other areas of science; the sort of theoretical satisfaction that regularly leads us to say that we can explain or understand why things behave in the way they do, or are related in the way that they are. Obviously the experience of theoretical satisfaction is not self-validating, and can be unwarranted; and it always presupposes a background of things taken for granted. But this is compatible with the view that it is sometimes justified, and with the fact that it appears attainable in some areas of science and utterly unattainable (at present) when it comes to the question of the relation between experiential and non-experiential phenomena.

Next objection. One cannot infer ignorance of the nature of the physical from the unavailability of any sort of theoretically satisfying account of why or how some feature of it is as it is relative to the rest of physics. For we can give no such account of certain fundamental physical constants, for example, but we are not therefore necessarily ignorant of what they are, or of the nature of the physical. We may, for example, be untroubled by the "this is just how things are" status of Planck's Constant relative to the rest of physics. Planck's Constant fits smoothly into our theory of the physical in spite of having this status. But the same cannot be said of experiential phenomena, when considered relative to the non-experiential features of the brain as described by physics. Serious materialists – and physicists committed to the advance of their subject – cannot so easily pass over our dramatic lack of theoretical understanding of how experiential phenomena relate to non-experiential phenomena in the brain, by saying nothing more than "Well, that's just how things are." They might decide to say this, but it would not change the fact that experiential phenomena simply do not fit into our existing theory of the physical. That is why they raise a problem which does not exist in the case of things like Planck's Constant, or in the case of features of the universe that are the products of "symmetry-breaking." And that is why it seems reasonable to talk of ignorance and incompleteness when confronted with them.

It may next be objected that quantum mechanics, often called the most successful theory in the history of science, notoriously fails to provide us with the feeling that we can really explain or understand why things happen as they do at the quantum level (e.g. why light behaves as it does in the two-slit experiment). Why then should one criticize a theory that successfully correlated types of experiential phenomena with types of non-experiential phenomena for failing to deliver any real understanding of the relation of the phenomena in question? It seems that it is not in general true that a satisfactory scientific theory must supply one with some sense of understanding the phenomena it deals with. A theory may be found theoretically satisfactory – beautiful and powerful – without sup-plying a sense of understanding. Perhaps it is not even generally true that lack of understanding indicates a certain sort of ignorance of the nature of the phenomena in question.

In response, let me try to put the present difficulty differently. There is felt to be a certain sort of strong *theoretical integratedness* or *homogeneity* (or at least nonheterogeneity) among many of the existing predicates of physics (and among those predicates and the predicates of other sciences which are held, with good reason, to be reducible to physics). These predicates recognizably form part of the same family, the same overall system of description. The problem is that experiential predicates do not fit into this family or system of description. And we have, at present, no idea of how they might be integrated. We assume, as materialists, that all experiential phenomena are physical phenomena, but we cannot fit them into the account of the physical delivered by physics. We know that they are actual, but we do not understand how they are possible, or why they occur in the way they do, given all that we know about the physical as described by physics. We do not understand why they occur as they do in the way that we feel we understand why many other physical phenomena occur as they do, given the account of the physical delivered by physics.

We can hope to be able to relate the *range* features or "abstract morphology" of the experiential phenomena of a given sense modality to aspects of brain structure: we can see how the structure of the brain can provide for extremely fine discriminatory abilities, and we can correlate variations in *intensity* of experiential phenomena with variations in intensity of non-experiential phenomena (cf. e.g. Churchland, 1986; Edelman, 1992, ch. 3; Lockwood, 1989, ch. 7). It is the basic qualitative modalities of sense experience considered just as such that seem completely resistant to genuine theoretical integration with physics, and continue to seem so even after we have made such unverifiable (and implausible) simplifying assumptions as the assumption that all those who have normal verbal color-discrimination abilities have it on the basis of exactly the same qualitative experience; so that the predicate "experience of pillar-box red," say, has a unique determinate reference. Such theoretical integration would require more than the formulation of statements of correlation linking experiential predicates (e.g. "the experience of pillar-box red," "the experience of middle C played on a flute") and non-experiential predicates, exceptionless or not. It would require a kind of the theoretical homogenization which seems at present unimaginable.

It is on these grounds, I suggest, that we must admit fundamental if partial ignorance of the nature of the physical. We have an atomic physics, and all parts of physics integrate with each other, but we don't have a qualitative-character-of-experience physics at all. We don't have a physics of phenomenology, let alone one that integrates with the rest of physics. The view that this must indicate ignorance, and that it must be possible in principle to achieve some deep theoretical homogenization of such experiential terms and non-experiential terms is, on the present view, a necessary concomitant of the idea that materialism is true, and that there is indeed a single, unified physical reality.

This returns to a question raised earlier. The move is from the claim that there is a single unified physical (system of) reality to the claim that there must be a single, unified or homogeneous system of theoretical description of that reality, whether or not is is attainable by us. (Note that dualists can endorse the last sentence, after removing the word "physical.") If anyone says "That's just an assumption," so be it. It is an assumption that I make. If a thing X is a natural phenomenon, there must be a perspective from which it does not appear mysterious, relative to the rest of what is known about the natural; for it is not mysterious in fact, relative to the rest of the natural. There must be a perspective which integrates its account of X into its account of the rest of the natural. This is what we lack, in the case of the experiential. And perhaps we experience and conceptualize the non-experiential physical in such a way that the existence of the experiential physical will always appear mysterious or inexplicable, relative to our conception of the rest of the physical (cf. McGinn, 1989). If so, our understanding of the nature of the physical will always seem incomplete in a certain respect: with respect to the relation between the experiential and the non-experiential.

Objection. Our physics is necessarily a human physics. It is an account of reality which is necessarily conditioned by the particular perspective on reality that we have as members of a species with a particular kind of sensory-intellectual equipment; so that we cannot suppose that we could ever reach The Truth of the matter, or think of our physics as giving the complete story. This is true, but it does not mean that we cannot identify specific areas in which our current physics appears dramatically lacking or incomplete even on its own terms, for example, on account of its failure to provide any satisfactory theoretical integration of two sorts of phenomenon that appear to us as indubitably real. True, our physics is a human physics; but there are aspects of the physical of which we nevertheless feel we have a genuine understanding. And it is relative to that standard of understanding, not some impossible godlike standard, that it is true to say that if materialism is true, then there is something fundamental that we have not grasped about the physical, and will not have grasped until we have achieved some sort of (valid) theoretical integration of experiential terms and non-experiential terms.

It may again be objected that the mysteries of quantum mechanics lie at the bottom of all physics and that there are terminological heterogeneity problems within quantum mechanics which are as acute as the terminological heterogeneity problems raised by experiential and non-experiential terms. This can be doubted, for things can seem inexplicable, in the way that they do in quantum mechanics, without there being any perceived problem of radical heterogeneity of terms. But it can also be granted. For if it were true it would merely show something that few would deny: that we are in certain ways ignorant of the nature of quantum reality. It would not undermine the suggestion that our inability to achieve a deep theoretical integration of experiential and non-experiential terms shows (given that materialism is true) that our current conception of the nature of the physical is dramatically incomplete on its own terms. Explanation and understanding must stop somewhere. But it does not follow from this that the satisfaction of the homogeneity principle is impossible. For a science could very well reach a stage at which there were things which prompted us to say that we could not understand or explain why they were as they were (we would say of them, "That's just how things are"), but at which we nevertheless felt that all the terms of the science were fundamentally theoretically homogeneous with each other, recognizably part of the same overall system of theoretical description.

It may be pointed out that facts about what satisfies us as explanations are sociological facts, and that human beings may at some future time find statements correlating non-experiential descriptions of brain events with descriptions of experiential events as theoretically satisfying as statements correlating billiard ball impacts with billiard ball movements. In reply: the present position on explanation and understanding allows this as a possibility. The fact remains that there is a difference between being very familiar with a fact and finding it theoretically unproblematic. Familiarity does not necessarily lead to a sense that something is theoretically unproblematic. Even if we become very familiar with the fact that non-experiential brain events of type X were reliably correlated with experiential events of type Y, this could not lead us to think of the relation between them as theoretically unproblematic in the billiard ball way, so long as we continued to operate with our current physics, or some nonrevolutionary extension of it. It may be denied that what billiard balls do is theoretically unproblematic; and it is true – once again – that what they do seems theoretically unproblematic only relative to things we take for granted. But at this point I am content for my claim to be classified as sociological in character.

It may finally be said that the claim about the intractability of the problem of experience or consciousness is exactly like the claim that used to be made about the "mystery" of life; just as life ceased to seem problematic within the frame of physics, so too will experience. Reply: one should never underestimate the "silent permeative genius of science" (Pattison, 1988, p. 154), but one shouldn't overestimate it either. A revolution is still needed, that's my prediction. Dennett (1991) has suggested that those who insist on our failure of understanding *want* there to be an irreducible mystery. But most, I suspect, are materialists who would give a lot for a convincing naturalistic theory of experience, one that would explain how experience is possible given the rest of what we know about the physical. Most of those who insist on the acuity of the problem are merely concerned to keep it clearly in view, in the face of all those who are trying to sideline it or deny its existence.

8 Conclusion

Our existing notions of the physical and the mental or experiential cannot be reconciled or theoretically integrated as they stand. So one or both of the two sets of notions will have to be radically modified if we are going to be able to understand how monism is true. Some eliminativists think that the source of the problem lies in our notions of the mental or experiential, and that these notions will ultimately be discarded in a perfected philosophy or science of mind. With their more moderate allies, these eliminativists still appear to represent the majority view in contemporary philosophy of mind: they hold that the principal cause of the intractability of the problem lies in the defective nature of our existing concepts of the mental or experiential. Concentrating on the experiential-mental, I have suggested that it is the other way round, and that it is the descriptive scheme of physics that will have to change dramatically if there is to be an acceptable theoretical unification with the mental scheme. If eliminativists or instrumentalists claim that the best *predictive science of behavior* will not have any use for our common mental and (in particular) experiential notions, then we may doubt it, but we may also concede it cheerfully for the sake of argument, because what then becomes clear is that this predictive science of behavior is going to say nothing about the hard part of the mind–body problem, the problem posed by the existence of experience given the current terms of physics. This predictive science of behavior will perhaps be useful, powerful, and stylish, but it will sail straight past the hard part of the mind–body problem.

Having built a heavy (Lockean) element of agnosticism into the term "materialist," I continue to call myself a materialist. Some may wonder why, but I stand beside Quine (1961) in Humean natural belief: as a "lay physicist," I "believe in physical objects" although they are posits "comparable, epistemologically, to the gods of Homer." According to agnostic materialism, the idea that the mind–body problem is particularly perplexing flows from our unjustified and relatively modern faith that we have an adequate grasp of the fundamental nature of matter at some crucial *general* level of understanding, even if we are still uncertain about many details. Agnosticism seems called for because it seems so clear that this cannot be right – if materialism is true. As things stand, the best we can do is to take James Clerk Maxwell's advice and try to maintain ourselves in that state of "thoroughly conscious ignorance which is a prelude to every real advance in knowledge" (Maxwell, 1877, pp. 245–6).[7]

Notes

1 Personalized ostensive definition will do: one says to each reader, "You know what it is like from your own case, as you burn your finger, listen to Beethoven, give birth, and so on."

2 I defend this claim in chapters 4.4, 6.6, and 7 of *Mental Reality* (Strawson, forthcoming). Those who doubt it can take what follows as a discussion of just one hard part of the mind–body problem while denying that it is the only hard part.

3 Perhaps it only came to seem acute in the sixteenth and seventeenth centuries, with the evolution of a scientific conception of the physical as nothing more than particles in motion, which made it unclear how experiential phenomena could be physical.

4 Generally, the issue of reduction arises when it is suspected that what seems to be talk about two sorts of thing is really talk in two different vocabularies about only one sort of thing. Semantic reductionism is explicitly stated as a thesis about language, and says that the content of sentences in a certain (e.g. mentalistic vocabulary) can be expressed without loss in another (e.g. physical-science) vocabulary. Such semantic reductionism may be distinguished from ontological reductionism, and it seems one can endorse the latter without endorsing the former, but I think there is a key sense in which they ultimately come down to the same thing: roughly, faced with the two vocabularies, both versions of reductionism claim that the aspects of reality apparently talked about by means of the first vocabulary do not really exist as aspects of reality which are fundamentally or genuinely ontologically distinct from the aspects of reality talked about by means of the second vocabulary.

5 Here it may help to note that a strong and well-confirmed correlation statement of the form "X occurs when and only when Y occurs" is no sort of explanation.

6 Note that some may argue (unhelpfully, I think) that (1)–(3) present a relatively strong version of the general dependency thesis, in employing the "in virtue of" idiom, one that is not forced on one merely by acceptance of the view that wherever there is experiential reality there is non-experiential reality but not conversely. See the last paragraph of this section.

Note also that there is no need to say, as here, that a being B's experiential properties depend only on its own non-experiential properties, and do not also depend on certain of the wider world's non-experiential properties. Nor is there any need to restrict attention to B's nonrelational non-experiential properties. I do so here in order to bypass interesting but currently unimportant complications that have to do with "broad" content. I am at present concerned with the asymmetry thesis only as applied to phenomena discernible at the "purely experiential" or "narrow" level of description of content (the level at which I and my twin-earth twin and vat-twin have identical experiences). One reason why these phenomena are all that need concern us at present is that the mind–body problem arises already in all its glory for a being whose experiences have no content relating to an external world. It arises in all its fullness for a being that

suddenly comes into existence by chance and lies in a sealed room with its sense organs inoperative having experiences just like yours or mine on account of the internal activity of its brain.
7 I am grateful to Ron Chrisley, Sebastian Gardner, Mark Greenberg, Derek Parfit and Paul Snowdon for their comments on earlier versions of this paper.

References

Churchland, P. M. (1986) "Some reductive strategies in cognitive neurobiology," *Mind* 95, pp. 279–309.

Dennett, D. C., (1991). *Consciousness Explained*, Boston, Mass.: Little, Brown.

Edelman, G. (1992) *Bright Air, Brilliant Fire: on the Matter of the Mind*, Harmondsworth: Penguin.

Hume, D. (1978) *A Treatise of Human Nature*, ed. L. A. Selby-Bigge and P. H. Nidditch, 2nd edn., Oxford: Clarendon Press.

Lockwood, M. (1989) *Mind, Brain, and the Quantum: the Compound "I"*, Oxford: Blackwell.

Maxwell, J. C. (1877) "The kinetic theory of gases," *Nature* 16, pp. 245–6.

McGinn, C., (1989) "Can we solve the mind–body problem?" *Mind* 98, pp. 349–66.

Pattison, M. (1988) *Memoirs of an Oxford Don*, London: Cassell.

Quine, W. V. (1961) "Two Dogmas of Empiricism," in *From a Logical Point of View: Nine Logico-Philosophical Essays*, New York: Harper & Row, pp. 20–46.

Quine, W. V. (1990) *Pursuit of Truth*, Cambridge, Mass.: Harvard University Press.

Strawson, G. (forthcoming) *Mental Reality*, Cambridge, Mass.: Bradford Books MIT Press.

7
Supervenience, Recognition, and Consciousness

Steven J. Wagner

What was once called the mind–body problem is no longer a serious issue. But a closely related problem, always implicit and sometimes explicit in writings from the seventeenth century on, is more vexing than ever. It is, moreover, a characteristically philosophical question, not one science may be expected to answer in due course.

We usually trace the mind–body problem to the discussions of dualism and mechanism in Descartes, Hobbes, and their contemporaries. But the principal seventeenth-century debate is over. It concerned the capacities of matter: can a purely physical system achieve thought through its purely mechanical (or, say, electromagnetic) operations? The answer is yes. Very few philosophers would doubt that putting physical parts together in the right way makes a thinking thing. Human brains, or embodied human brains, are such things, as are the brains of at least some animals. So, *in principle*, are suitably configured robots, perhaps with hybrid architectures (analog-digital or parallel-serial). Each of these actual or possible systems performs physical operations that amount to thought. We now know that matter can think.

Two related seventeenth-century questions have equally definite answers. One motive for investigations of materialism was the hope of surviving bodily death. Locating our mental operations in something other than our bodies would have offered some prospect although no guarantee. But no such prospect obtains. The early modern philosophers also wondered whether there are any thinkers besides the embodied systems we encounter in everyday life – perhaps angels or gods. Again, this hypothesis lacks the least support. As far as we can guess, every thinker is a physical system that thinks by performing physical operations.

The agreement that the philosophical community has reached on these questions is a remarkable development in the history of thought. If there is still a mind–body problem, what is it? Here are some possibilities:

(1)   Given that as far as we can guess, only material things *do* think, one might ask whether only these *can* think. Are there possible immaterial thinkers, or must every mind be physical?

This is really two questions. The first asks whether we can usefully conceive thinking that does not consist in physical operations. Such a quest for alternative models is often important in science and philosophy. One may ask, for example, whether life would be possible without carbon or whether a noncapitalist economy could generate a given level of wealth. The present issue is whether we have reason to grant the possibility of nonphysical thinking things. And the answer is a clear no. No one has ever offered a minimally plausible description of a nonphysical thinking system.

But to deny that this possibility has been made out is not to assert the impossibility of a nonphysical thinker. (Compare: although there is no good evidence for cold fusion, we can also not support an impossibility claim.) Since such an assertion would require more knowledge than we have, nonphysical thinkers have not been ruled out. This point, however, is of limited significance for the philosophy of mind. It derives from the abstract possibility – not one we can now *usefully* imagine – of a nonphysical theory of nature.

Current science does not strictly bound our concept of physical theory. It offers a paradigm of physics, but possible theories with different structures or vocabularies would likewise count as physics if they exhibit sufficient similarity to the physics we know. (Thus, "physics" is a concept implicitly involving certain similarity judgments. Other examples are "game," "socialism," and "automobile," indeed perhaps most of the concepts we express by general terms.) We have no grasp of just how far this concept extends or whether we could ever have good reason to leave physical theory behind. Admittedly, any successor theory would be mathematical and would in large measure preserve the results and explanatory structures of our physics. Hence it would incorporate physics. But it might also contain more general elements that we would no longer count as physics. In this sense, nonphysical reality is an epistemically open possibility. Hence also, we have no clear reason to claim that every mental process must be physical. The limits of what we would be willing to recognize as mental might lie farther out.

This is a negative result, due purely to the indefinite boundaries of our concept of the physical. This indefiniteness shows that the question of nonphysical mentality is not, at present, well posed. We can assert that all thinking systems now known or describable are physical, because they are all clear cases. But speculation about nonphysical mentality would require a tolerably clear notion of nonphysical nature. It would require a grasp not just of the center but of the periphery of our concept. Without that, the question is best shelved.

These remarks answer a well-known position of Chomsky's, who has long claimed that materialism (physicalism) has been a nonissue since the demise of seventeenth-century conceptions of matter. Without a clear notion of the physical, on what grounds or to what end, he asks, would one assert that the mental is physical? But this challenges only the absolute form of materialism just dismissed. Our science permits the description of numerous clearly physical systems. To hold that some of these think and that we can make no useful sense of thinking systems of any other kind is highly significant, as the historical perspective shows.

We may note, in leaving (1), that the notion of the mental has a certain autonomy. It is not tied to our physical science as are the notions of particle or force. It may apply where our notion of the physical does not, and its explication or illumination may not be a task for physical science. This will be important below.

(2)   The answer to the central seventeenth-century question is that physical systems can think. Some materialist philosophers have found this insufficient. True physicalism, they maintain, requires not only that the thinking subjects be physical things but that mental *properties* (or states) be classified as physical properties. Thus, the seventeenth-century question invites a generalization, one that our recognition of thinking organisms or (possibly) machines does not settle. This further question, however, is ill-conceived.

To begin, we are presumed to *want* a sweeping physicalism, a thesis to the effect that everything, including every property, is physical. Serious acceptance of science is taken to commit one to such a claim; this is one form of the position known as naturalism. I believe that naturalism is unmotivated in all forms. Specifically, no appreciation of science and no project of scientific inquiry requires or even encourages an exclusionary ontological claim, a thesis that everything is physical.

Any claim to the effect that all properties are physical is, moreover, particularly treacherous. It is not that we lack a notion of physical property. Numerous properties can be identified as belonging to the ontology of physics, hence are physical properties in a good sense. But physics places no obvious limit on its abstract ontology. It does not say just what the physical properties are, nor does it clarify the notion of a nonphysical property. (This is similar to our earlier point about the boundaries of the physical.) In fact, the entire notion of "all properties" seems obscure, and at least as bad as the notorious totality of sets. To assume this notion in order to advance a thesis that all properties are physical is to enter into an exceedingly dubious transaction.

The naturalist arguments concerning the ontology of properties bear out this skepticism. They characteristically involve the invention – or better – the positing, of a standard of property identity: one that allows the classification, as physical, of various undoubtedly real properties not evidently mentioned in the language of physics. Otherwise a "physical" status for, say, "chair," "exchange rate," or "parasite" is ruled out. But scientific practice grounds no such standard of identity. And philosophers importing one for their own purposes invariably use devices, such as a notion of coextensiveness across all metaphysically possible worlds, that lead to a conceptual morass and lack motivation once the urge to assert some sweeping ontological naturalism – if one could only find a way to say it – is abandoned.

Contemporary materialists have increasingly resorted to supervenience theories. The supervenience of the mental on the physical means, roughly, that there is no difference without a physical difference; that any two physically alike things would share all mental properties. Such theories are notoriously uninformative about the nature of the mental. To be told that two psychologically distinct systems must differ in at least one among the countless properties that physics recognizes is to learn nothing about the specific connections of mental to physical states. This holds even if we assume some restricted base of physical properties, by claiming, say, that any two psychologically distinct systems must differ in the nature or arrangement of their atoms. But for the supervenience theorist, this is the point. Specifying the connections of mental to physical states falls under the heading of psychophysical reduction. The aim of supervenience theory is to formulate a materialism that does not depend on the unclear prospect of reduction. If we are unable to find reductions, indeed even to agree on what this notion (a twin to "property identification") would mean in the psychophysical case, yet still want to assert a significant materialism, then a supervenience thesis is the likely result.

Yet this attempt to formulate a general materialism shares the flaws of its predecessors. Since the boundaries of the physical remain obscure, the claim that mental differences require physical differences lacks useful content. And if mentalistic concepts might apply to things outside our concept of the physical, then supervenience claims could even be false. We are not, as remarked, in any position seriously to evaluate this possibility, since there is no good existing concept of nonphysical reality. The supervenience theorist, however, absolutely rules the possibility out – on no visible grounds.

(3) The claim that physical operations constitute thought admits an interesting variant interpretation. There is no doubt that brains consist of physical particles whose particular structures and motions are our thinking. But calling mental operations physical may be held to imply something stronger: that natural science can explain their mental properties. The question becomes whether thought can be brought into an explanatory fold that includes physics, chemistry, and biology. That is obviously open, since we can rarely know what future science will explain and where it will fail. Often, though, certain outcomes are foreseeable. At some point we will most likely have effective cancer treatments and settle the issue of proton decay. It is less clear whether any features of thought pose fundamental obstacles to scientific understanding. Philosophers have tended to assume that if physical things can think, then physical science will tell us how. Yet the further question is separate. Lacking an answer, we do not have a full solution to the mind–body problem.

I wish to approach this new question indirectly, via a return to supervenience. (1) and (2) failed by stressing our concept of the physical more than it can bear. We can improve by abandoning the obsession with drawing an ontological line, a boundary of the physical that necessarily includes the mental. Let us drop the concern with materialism. If we do not regard supervenience theory as strengthening our answer to Descartes and Hobbes, we can extract an important truth. A natural line of thought will then return us, in the end, to the question of the scope of natural science.

It is at best misleading to say that mental states supervene on the physical, but the fact is that they must supervene. Any thinking consists in a set of operations that are not themselves, taken separately, acts of thinking but that amount to thought when they occur together in the right order. (Let us call such operations or processes submental.) More strongly, the specific nature and content of any thought – its being, say, a wish for a relaxing afternoon or an image of a cube – is determined by the specific submental processes that make it up. Change the thought, and you must somehow change these. Although the claim that the mental must supervene on the physical lacks useful content, it is correct that the mental can supervene on the physical and must supervene on something.

Computational accounts of thought provide the obvious illustration. To desire this or remember that is, on such an account, to perform a host of information-processing operations, none itself a thought, that constitute thought when properly coordinated. Of course the idea is more general. The language of digital computation may not suffice to describe the subprocesses on which thought depends. What is certain is that thinking does not simply happen; that it is determined by what one might call a substrate of operations.

This idea is a legacy of the seventeenth-century mechanistic philosophers. It generates a descendant of the earlier mind–body problem that is now called the problem of content. Given that thought depends on submental operations, which operations must be present for thinking to occur? Specifically, which operations would constitute a memory of fire, a desire for snow, or the belief that Theaetetus flies? We are asking for a detailed, quasi-mechanistic analysis of thought.

The problem of content is not the original mind–body problem because it is freed from the category of body crucial to materialism. We are not positing a definite or absolute category of the physical in order to ask how the mental is related to it. Inquiries into the analysis of content are perfectly compatible with dualism or neutral monism. One good illustration is Hume, who recognizably posed the problem of content although the status of body in his system remains problematic. Yet there is a close link to materialist concerns. Suppose we understand how the mental and the submental are linked. We should then be able to specify well-understood physical processes that would allow a physical system to think. This would show how mind and body were related for that system. Once we give up grander materialist ambitions, this is what solving the mind–body problem would mean.

The problem of content is frequently represented as a problem of matching two vocabularies. There is, on the one hand, the everyday language of attitudes, sensations, and emotions; the way of talking about our selves that seems to be part of the common human inheritance. This language (or conceptual framework) has become known as folk psychology. (I use this term without the disparagement it sometimes involves.) On the other hand, there is some yet unspecified language of information-processing, perhaps a language of inputs, algorithms, and data structures. The second language is supposed to describe the submental processes that amount to thought; to identify those features of my neural processing, for example, owing to which I am now thinking that it is cold outside. We may call this the language of cognitive models or structures. (Thinking that it is cold outside may require certain submental processes *situated in a certain environment*; the internal structures alone may not suffice. I touch on this point below but will omit the qualification whenever possible.) Posing the problem in terms of these two languages is useful because it encourages us to ask how features of one discourse or the other might impede a solution.

I should remark that certain naturalist writers claim already to have offered or at least adumbrated solutions to the problem of content: definitions, in scientific vocabulary, of what it is to believe that p or to think about object A. These analyses, however, are so radically deficient as to be paradigms of the triumph of hope over sense. The rest of this essay will review some of the immediate obstacles to progress. Beyond these, no doubt, lie others.

Much of the literature on content deals with what Putnam has called the contribution of the environment: can an individual on earth be thinking about water while her neuro-computational double on twin-earth is thinking about the local substance XYZ? At stake is the balance of internal and environmental factors in determining mental contents. I will not enter into this issue beyond remarking that the extant argumentation is generally slipshod and unconvincing even by philosophical standards. Of greater interest to us is the underlying difficulty that makes this controversy possible. The problem of intentionality is usually regarded as one of finding analyses for known contents. We assume a working, commonsense grasp of when someone believes that crows are black or wants a glass of water; our task is to express the conditions in submental terms. Arguments about the contribution of the environment, however, show a striking weakness in our ordinary understanding of intentionality. In the twin-earth (and related) cases, the kind of evidence available for assignments of content does not easily settle fairly simple questions. Since the problem is not a lack of evidence – these are our imagined cases, in which we can imagine all the evidence we want – our intentional concepts themselves must be more poorly defined than we might expect.

Other studies point in the same direction. The literature on translation and indirect speech underscores the limits of our propositional attitude idioms. Continuing debates over the logical form of belief sentences, for example, show that we cannot even agree on what follows immediately by logic from "Jane believes that Frege was a logician." Our language of belief is, however familiar, evidently quite obscure to us in certain ways. Discussions of *akrasia*, self-deception, experimentally induced reasoning error, neurosis, and other vagaries of deliberation and choice reveal further difficulties. The subtleties of human thinking, including our forms of confusion and error, often obstruct the application of such concepts as belief, intention, decision, desire, or reason. Do I or do I not believe that the chocolate truffle I am reaching for will likely harm me? In what sense do I prefer *A* to *B* if this is part of an intransitive set of preferences? And so on. Such questions (which may be far more complex than indicated here) often seem to be defeat our psychological vocabulary.

The problem of content would be hard enough if our folk language were precise and well defined. We would face a difficult process of inventing and refining cognitive models with an eye to their capacity to realize intentional states. Yet the problem might for all that be a hard technical problem, like weather prediction or the machine translation of Japanese news articles into English. The questions would be well understood, and answers would admit ready evaluation. But quite apart from the technical complexities, which are daunting enough, we lack a clear idea of what we are talking about on the folk-psychological side of the matter.

One possible response is that the ills of the folk vocabulary need not impede the project of analysis, since an analysis may, among other things, capture various kinds of ambiguity or indeterminacy. This is correct as far as it goes. A difficulty, however, arises if we cannot even accurately identify or describe the semantic ills of the folk language, as seems to be the case. Also, folk psychology might be pathological enough to cast doubt on its status as a candidate for translation into any scientific language.

One might now call for the further development in extending, clarifying, and making more precise our folk vocabulary as part of the attack on the problem of content. Cleaning up that vocabulary would, this idea runs, turn the problem into a technical one. But the projected clean-up is quite problematic. Among the unanswered questions are: how much cleaning up is possible? Are some ways of doing it more reasonable than others? At what point would "cleaning up" our folk notions amount to abandoning them? Perhaps most important, no one knows how the clean-up should proceed or whether any plausible evolution of folk psychology would meet the demands of a theory of content. Philosophers, psychologists, novelists, and others have long contributed to the development of folk concepts. This process will undoubtedly continue. But there is no clear reason to think that it will remove the difficulties that obstruct cognitive modeling. If the proposal is that we should not rely on "normal" conceptual evolution but instead undertake a sanitation project specifically geared to the needs of a theory of content, then no one has any good idea of how to start or how far we could get.

I have tried to indicate how certain features of the folk language prevent us from viewing the problem of content as merely a (difficult) technical problem. It cannot be assimilated to standard cases of scientific reduction because the intended object of reduction too little resembles a science. Hence it is very unclear how much help is to be expected from progress in cognitive neuroscience, artificial intelligence, and related areas. Philosophical programs that pin their hopes on such progress need reconsideration.

Yet these reflections also lead to a conundrum. A philosopher's question about the nature of thought has a characteristic generality that prima facie rules out a scientific answer. Neuroscience can, we think, answer certain questions of cognitive engineering: a full account of human brain function would tell us how one biological system achieves thought. The philosopher's question is more general: what is the difference between thought and non-thought? Which possible systems think (with what contents), and which don't? An answer would appear if science were to provide, along with the design of the brain, a specification of just what features of this design were *essential* to thinking. But that may not (as Kant in effect noted) be in the neuroscientist's line of work.

This mismatch between the philosopher's desires and what science apparently provides may then suggest that the philosopher wants the wrong thing. An interest in the necessary and sufficient conditions for thinking (with given contents) seems to lead to a suspect project of conceptual analysis, an armchair project of classifying all possible systems as to their mentality. Even if one believes, as I do, that conceptual analysis has an important place in philosophy, this particular quest does not look promising. So one is tempted to settle for neuroscience: let us describe the engineering of one thinking system (or class of these), banishing other questions about thought to the realm of idle speculation.

Yet I would not dismiss the philosophical question with which we started. The inquiry into content was motivated not just by an interest in the workings of the brain but by curiosity over what it is about us that makes us thinkers. If the question of brain engineering alone admits a useful answer, that would be a defeat. Because the notion of thought is so interesting and so important to our definition of ourselves, we seek a more general understanding. I suspect that the dichotomy between scientific investigation of the brain (of robots, etc.) and pure conceptual analysis is too simple. Reflection on the models in a sufficiently advanced cognitive science should improve our ability to ask conceptual questions and evaluate their answers. After enough experience with various possibilities for cognitive engineering, we may be in a position to say which sets of subprocesses we would count as implementing (genuine) thought. So the attempt to confront our intuitions with the empirical models should continue. It may even lead to a satisfactory resolution. Even so, I would emphasize how poorly we understand the problem of content and the methods it requires.

I have emphasized the importance, for the problem of content, of the vagaries of folk language, the puzzles connected to ordinary attributions of mental states. This now requires some correction. Let us set these puzzles aside and suppose that folk psychology is perfectly clear and precise in its everyday applications, that we have no trouble identifying a speaker's beliefs, wants, feelings, and so on. Theorists of content are then expected to make progress by examining various cognitive models, perhaps computer programs or descriptions of brain architecture, in order to determine which ones realize which mental states (if any). This procedure faces two obstacles.

The first is in a sense purely technical, yet formidable nonetheless and widely overlooked. Assume that the kind of thought we are trying to analyze requires a physical system even roughly as complex as the human brain (a chimpanzee, if you like). Our rudimentary neuroscience shows that the brain is *staggeringly* complex. Relative to the entertaining of propositional attitudes, such phenomena as color vision or the control of auditory attention must be elementary, yet their investigation already opens up labyrinths. Quite possibly, any model of full-blown thinking rich enough to be taken seriously would simply be too complex for us to understand, too complex even for teams of investigators, let alone individuals. To get a sense of the difficulties, remember how easily surprising features ("bugs") arise in what are, cognitively, very stupid pieces of software. I see no guarantee that we would be able to understand what is going on in potential models of the human mind. If solving the problem of content means being able to say what a given cognitive structure is thinking, then we may simply not be smart enough to make much progress.

The hope, of course, is that the essential features of any such system will admit a perspicuous description. By way of comparison, we have (up to a point) a reasonable model of color vision, even though many neural intricacies remain unknown. Philosophers expecting progress on the mind–body problem, however, should offer foundations for their hopes.

Second, our everyday criteria for attributing mental states might be perfectly in order without suiting the needs of cognitive theory. We might reliably discern when fellow humans believe that Theaetetus flies without being to read possession of this belief off from a computer program (embodied or otherwise). It is a little as though someone who had never seen musical instruments, but could infallibly recognize them by sound, were suddenly asked to pick out the trumpets in a shop display. Her command of the musical vocabulary might be impeccable in its own way without providing useful criteria in the new situation. Similarly, the skills we use to identify each other's mental states might not apply in our encounters with cognitive models.

One could duck this issue along various behaviorist or Wittgensteinian lines. If the grounds for ascribing content are simply behavioral, then we should determine what a cognitive system thinks by seeing what it does and attributing mental states on that basis. (Thus the question of mentality arises only given suitable embodiment.) The obvious problem with this reaction is that such behavioral views of mentality seem wrong. We take thought to be a matter of what is going on inside; of cognitive structure in some sense. Such intuitions aside, philosophical behaviorism runs into fatal difficulties over questions of holism and indeterminacy. And the problem of content would not be solved in any case. No one knows how good our behavioral criteria for ascribing beliefs are, let alone whether we would be able to state these, as a solution to the problem of content requires. Similar remarks hold for Wittgenstein's idea that mental states are properly ascribed only to our fellow humans or quite similar beings. It is far from clear how much this restriction would help with the problem of content, and in any case it seems false. (Note that Wittgenstein, unlike at least some philosophical behaviorists, was not trying to solve and would indeed totally have rejected, the problem of content.)

We have encountered an old difficulty. Leibniz famously argued that an observer walking through a suitably enlarged brain would see nothing reconizable as the operations of consciousness. He plausibly took this as an antimaterialist argument, one showing that the operations aren't there. This was wrong, since brains are perfectly material objects that achieve consciousness. But Leibniz had a powerful idea. Suppose our question is not whether matter can think but how submental processes determine content. If we cannot read contents off from information-processing descriptions of systems, how are we to proceed? Let us call this the recognition problem. Recall that it is additional to, although exacerbated by, problems arising from the semantic or epistemic ills of the folk language. Also exacerbating it, of course, is the sheer complexity of the structures whose possession of mentality would be at issue.

With this we have returned to version (3) of the mind–body problem. The difficulties about folk language, complexity, and recognition all obstruct a unified science of mind and body. A more direct pursuit of (3) would most naturally have introduced considerations on the current state of psychological theory, but I believe the problems would in the end have been the same.

I have no solutions. Yet I have already stated that philosophers of mind should continue to press the joint strategies of exploring the folk scheme and reflecting on the models that cognitive science provides. This should produce light, although we cannot guess the amount or just where it will fall. The prospects for ultimately solving the problem of content are obscure. I do, however, want to conclude by dissociating myself from an excessive pessimism.

Some philosophers discern an absolute barrier to cognitive theorizing. Certain features of thought or consciousness are held to preclude an analysis into submental processes. One candidate feature is our alleged incorrigibility about some mental states. Another lies in the qualitative (phenomenal, subjective) aspects of experience. Of these arguments, the former now enjoys less currency, since any brand of incorrigibility can apparently be modeled in information-processing terms. Whatever reliable conscious access you think we have can be built into a cognitive model. Subjective experience, however, is more challenging. The problem is not that it obstructs supervenience theses. Our subjective experiences (qualia) undoubtedly arise from the operations of our brains. At issue, rather, are the limits of human understanding. If we cannot explain how a given cognitive structure would yield a given subjective appearance, then we would appear unable to justify any rules associating one kind of item with the other. We could not say how experiences supervene on submental processing, in spite of our assurance that they do.

One reaction, Thomas Nagel's, is to put conscious events under a distinct ontological heading of subjective facts. The old mind–body dualism is replaced by a division between objective things, which are the province of natural science, and subjective things, which some other form of inquiry may or may not illuminate. This improves on Locke, for whom qualia were a miracle, a proof of the existence of God. Yet Nagel's leap to a profoundly obscure diagnosis is premature.

Subjective experience seems rather to yield an acute instance of the recognition problem. Our language for describing qualia is even less adequate than our language of propositional attitudes, and identifying another's qualia is much harder than attitude ascription. One's understanding of phenomenal concepts – the way lilacs smell, for example – seems strongly tied to one's first-person position. I know how lilacs smell to me and conjecture, relying on little more than our general similarities, that they smell about the same to you. In contrast, I can have decisive grounds for crediting you with the belief that lilacs bloom in the doorway and are enchantingly fragrant this year. The difference lies in the looser association of qualia with behavior (including speech behavior). A state we know best from our own case will be particularly hard to ascribe to a cognitive model.

It is not surprising that the recognition problem should be more acute in some cases than in others. The harder cases do not call for a distinct ontological category or, as far as we can now tell, for some radically different methodology. In this way, I make less of subjective experience than some other writers on the mind–body problem. But I find the recognition problem very serious in general. And I affirm its status as a genuine problem. Human beings want to know what thought is, not just how various information-processing systems are engineered and what they can do. Hence our quest for an analysis. It remains to be seen whether we are making progress or just pressing our noses harder against the candy-store window.

8
Can We Solve the Mind–Body Problem?

Colin McGinn

How it is that anything so remarkable as a state of consciousness comes about as a result of initiating nerve tissue, is just as unaccountable as the appearance of the Djin, where Aladdin rubbed his lamp in the story...
                                                                    T. H. Huxley

We have been trying for a long time to solve the mind–body problem. It has stubbornly resisted our best efforts. The mystery persists. I think the time has come to admit candidly that we cannot resolve the mystery. But I also think that this very insolubility – or the reason for it – removes the philosophical problem. In this paper I explain why I say these outrageous things.

The specific problem I want to discuss concerns consciousness, the hard nut of the mind–body problem. How is it possible for conscious states to depend upon brain states? How can technicolor phenomenology arise from soggy grey matter? What makes the bodily organ we call the brain so radically different from other bodily organs, say the kidneys – the body parts without a trace of consciousness? How could the aggregation of millions of individually insentient neurons generate subjective awareness? We know that brains are the *de facto* causal basis of consciousness, but we have, it seems, no understanding whatever of how this can be so. It strikes us as miraculous, eerie, even faintly comic. Somehow, we feel, the water of the physical brain is turned into the wine of consciousness, but we draw a total blank on the nature of this conversion. Neural transmissions just seem like the wrong kind of materials with which to bring consciousness into the world, but it appears that in some way they perform this mysterious feat. The mind–body problem is the problem of understanding how the miracle is wrought, thus removing the sense of deep mystery. We want to take the magic out of the link between consciousness and the brain.[1]

Purported solutions to the problem have tended to assume one of two forms. One form, which we may call constructive, attempts to specify some natural property of the brain (or body) which explains how consciousness can be elicited from it. Thus functionalism, for example, suggests a property – namely, causal role – which is held to be satisfied by both brain states and mental states; this property is supposed to explain how conscious states can come from brain states.[2] The other form, which has been historically dominant, frankly admits that nothing merely natural could do the job, and suggests instead that we invoke supernatural entities or divine interventions. Thus we have Cartesian dualism and Leibnizian pre-established harmony. These "solutions" at least recognize that something pretty remarkable is needed if the mind–body relation is to be made sense of; they are as extreme as the problem. The approach I favor is naturalistic but not constructive: I do not believe we can ever specify what it is about the brain that is responsible for consciousness, but I am sure that whatever it is it is not inherently miraculous. The problem arises, I want to suggest, because we are cut off by our very cognitive constitution from achieving a conception of that natural property of the brain (or of consciousness) that accounts for the psychophysical link. This is a kind of causal nexus that we are precluded from ever understanding, given the way we have to form our concepts and develop our theories. No wonder we find the problem so difficult!

Before I can hope to make this view plausible, I need to sketch the general conception of cognitive competence that underlies my position. Let me introduce the idea of *cognitive closure*. A type of mind M is cognitively closed with respect to a property P (or theory T) if and only if the concept-forming procedures at M's disposal cannot extend to a grasp of P (or an understanding of T). Conceiving minds come in different kinds, equipped with varying powers and limitations, biases and blind-spots, so that properties (or theories) may be accessible to some minds but not to others. What is closed to the mind of a rat may be open to the mind of a monkey, and what is open to us may be closed to the monkey. Representational power is not all or nothing. Minds are biological products like bodies, and like bodies they come in different shapes and sizes, more or less capacious, more or less suited to certain cognitive tasks.[3] This is particularly clear for perceptual faculties, of course: perceptual closure is hardly to be denied. Different species are capable of perceiving different properties of the world, and no species can perceive every property things may instantiate (without artificial instrumentation anyway). But such closure does not reflect adversely on the reality of the properties that lie outside the representational capacities in question; a property is no less real for not being reachable from a certain kind of perceiving and conceiving mind. The invisible parts of the electromagnetic spectrum are just as real as the visible parts, and whether a specific kind of creature can form conceptual representations of these imperceptible parts does not determine whether they exist. Thus cognitive closure with respect to P does not imply irrealism about P. That P is (as we might say) *noumenal* for M does not show that P does not occur in some naturalistic scientific theory T. It shows only that T is not cognitively accessible to M. Presumably monkey minds and the property of being an electron illustrate this possibility. And the question must arise as to whether human minds are closed with respect to certain true explanatory theories. Nothing, at least, in the concept of reality shows that everything real is open to the human concept-forming faculty – if, that is, we are realists about reality.[4]

Consider a mind constructed according to the principles of classical empiricism, a Humean mind. Hume mistakenly thought that human minds were Humean, but we can at least conceive of such a mind (perhaps dogs and monkeys have Humean minds). A Humean mind is such that perceptual closure determines cognitive closure, since "ideas" must always be copies of "impressions"; therefore the concept-forming system cannot transcend what can be perceptually presented to the subject. Such a mind will be closed with respect to unobservables; the properties of atoms, say, will not be representable by a mind constructed in this way. This implies that explanatory theories in which these properties are essentially mentioned will not be accessible to a Humean mind.[5] And hence the observable phenomena that are explained by allusion to unobservables will be inexplicable by a mind thus limited. But notice: the incapacity to explain certain phenomena does not carry with it a lack of recognition of the theoretical problems the phenomena pose. You might be able to appreciate a problem without being able to formulate (even in principle) the solution to that problem (I suppose human children are often in this position, at least for a while). A Humean mind cannot solve the problems that our physics solves, yet it might be able to have an inkling of what needs to be explained. We would expect, then, that a moderately intelligent inquiring Humean mind will feel permanently perplexed and mystified by the physical world, since the correct science is forever beyond its cognitive reach. Indeed, something like this was precisely the view of Locke. He thought that our ideas of matter are quite sharply constrained by our perceptions and so concluded that the true science of matter is eternally beyond us, that we could never remove our perplexities about (say) what solidity ultimately is.[6] But it does not follow for Locke that nature is itself inherently mysterious; the felt mystery comes from our own cognitive limitations, not from any objective eeriness in the world. It looks today as if Locke was wrong about our capacity to fathom the nature of the physical world, but we can still learn from his fundamental thought: the insistence that our cognitive faculties may not be up to solving every problem that confronts us. To put the point more generally: the human mind may not conform to empiricist principles, but it must conform to *some* principles, and it is a substantive claim that these principles permit the solution of every problem we can formulate or sense. Total cognitive openness is not guaranteed for human beings and it should not be expected. Yet what is noumenal for us may not be miraculous in itself. We should therefore be alert to the possibility that a problem that strikes us as deeply intractable, as utterly baffling, may arise from an area of cognitive closure in our ways of representing the world.[7] That is what I now want to argue is the case with our sense of the mysterious nature of the connection between consciousness and the brain. We are biased away from arriving at the correct explanatory theory of the psychophysical nexus. And this makes us prone to an illusion of objective mystery. Appreciating this should remove the philosophical problem: consciousness does not, in reality, arise from the brain in the miraculous way in which the djin arises from the lamp.

I now need to establish three things: (1) there exists some property of the brain that accounts naturalistically for consciousness; (2) we are cognitively closed with respect to that property; but (3) there is no philosophical (as opposed to scientific) mind–body problem. Most of the work will go into establishing (2).

Resolutely shunning the supernatural, I think it is undeniable that it must be in virtue of *some* natural property of the brain that organisms are conscious. There just *has* to be some explanation for how brains subserve minds. If we are not to be eliminativists about consciousness, then some theory must exist which accounts for the psychophysical correlations we observe. It is implausible to take these correlations as ultimate and inexplicable facts, as simply brute. And we do not want to acknowledge radical emergence of the conscious with respect to the cerebral: that is too much like accepting miracles *de re*. Brain states cause conscious states, we know, and this causal nexus must proceed through necessary connections of some kind, the kind that would make the nexus intelligible *if* they were understood.[8] Consciousness is like life in this respect. We know that life evolved from inorganic matter, so we expect there to be some explanation of this process. We cannot plausibly take the arrival of life as a primitive brute fact, nor can we accept that life arose by some form of miraculous emergence. Rather, there must be some natural account of how life comes from matter, whether or not we can know it. Eschewing vitalism and the magic touch of God's finger, we rightly insist that it must be in virtue of some natural property of (organized) matter that parcels of it get to be alive. But consciousness itself is just a further biological development, and so it too must be susceptible of some natural explanation – whether or not human beings are capable of arriving at this explanation. Presumably there exist objective natural laws that somehow account for the upsurge of consciousness. Consciousness, in short, must be a natural phenomenon, naturally arising from certain organizations of matter. Let us then say that there exists some property P, instantiated by the brain, in virtue of which the brain is the basis of consciousness. Equivalently, there exists some theory T, referring to P, which fully explains the dependence of conscious states on brain states. If we knew T, then we would have a constructive solution to the mind–body problem. The question then is whether we can ever come to know T and grasp the nature of P.

Let me first observe that it is surely *possible* that we could never arrive at a grasp of P; there is, as I said, no guarantee that our cognitive powers permit the solution of every problem we can recognize. Only a misplaced idealism about the natural world could warrant the dogmatic claim that everything is knowable by the human species at this stage of its evolutionary development (consider the same claim made on behalf of the intellect of Cro-Magnon man). It *may* be that every property for which we can form a concept is such that *it* could never solve the mind–body problem. We *could* be like 5-year-old children trying to understand Relativity Theory. Still, so far this is just a possibility claim: what reason do we have for asserting, positively, that our minds are closed with respect to P?

Longstanding historical failure is suggestive, but scarcely conclusive. Maybe, it will be said, the solution is just around the corner, or it has to wait upon the completion of the physical sciences? Perhaps we simply have yet to produce the Einstein-like genius who will restructure the problem in some clever way and then present an astonished world with the solution?[9] However, I think that our deep bafflement about the problem, amounting to a vertiginous sense of ultimate mystery, which resists even articulate formulation, should at least encourage us to explore the idea that there is something terminal about our perplexity. Rather as traditional theologians found themselves conceding cognitive closure with respect to certain of the properties of God, so we should look seriously at the idea that the mind–body problem brings us bang up against the limits of our capacity to understand the world. That is what I shall do now.

There seem to be two possible avenues open to us in our aspiration to identify P: we could try to get to P by investigating consciousness directly, or we could look to the study of the brain for P. Let us consider these in turn, starting with consciousness. Our acquaintance with consciousness could hardly be more direct; phenomenological description thus comes (relatively) easily. "Introspection" is the name of the faculty through which we catch consciousness in all its vivid nakedness. By virtue of possessing this cognitive faculty we ascribe concepts of consciousness to ourselves; we thus have "immediate access" to the properties of consciousness. But does the introspective faculty reveal property P? Can we tell just by introspecting what the solution to the mind–body problem is? Clearly not. We have direct cognitive access to one term of the mind–brain relation, but we do not have such access to the nature of the link. Introspection does not present conscious states *as* depending upon the brain in some intelligible way. We cannot therefore introspect P. Moreover, it seems impossible that we should ever augment our stock of introspectively ascribed concepts with the concept P, that is, we could not acquire this concept simply on the basis of sustained and careful introspection. Pure phenomenology will never provide the solution to the mind–body problem. Neither does it seem feasible to try to extract P from the concepts of consciousness we now have by some procedure of conceptual analysis – any more than we could solve the life – matter problem simply by reflecting on the concept *life*.[10] P has to lie outside the field of the introspectable, and it is not implicitly contained in the concepts we bring to bear in our first-person ascriptions. Thus the faculty of introspection, as a concept-forming capacity, is cognitively closed with respect to P; which is not surprising in view of its highly limited domain of operation (*most* properties of the world are closed to introspection).

But there is a further point to be made about P and consciousness, which concerns our restricted access to the concepts of consciousness themselves. It is a familiar point that the range of concepts of consciousness attainable by a mind M is constrained by the specific forms of consciousness possessed by M. Crudely, you cannot form concepts of conscious properties unless you yourself instantiate those properties. The man born blind cannot grasp the concept of a visual experience of red, and human beings cannot conceive of the echolocatory experiences of bats.[11] These are cases of cognitive closure within the class of conscious properties. But now this kind of closure will, it seems, affect our hopes of access to P. For suppose that we were cognitively open with respect to P; suppose, that is, that we had the solution to the problem of how specific forms of consciousness depend upon different kinds of physiological structure. Then, of course, we would understand how the brain of a bat subserves the subjective experiences of bats. Call this type of experience B, and call the explanatory property that links B to the bat's brain PI. By grasping PI it would be perfectly intelligible to us how the bat's brain generates B-experiences; we would have an explanatory theory of the causal nexus in question. We would be in possession of the same kind of understanding we would have of our own experiences if we had the correct psychophysical theory of them. But then it seems to follow that grasp of the theory that explains B-experiences would *confer* a grasp of the nature of those experiences: for how could we understand that theory without understanding the concept *B* that occurs in it? How could we grasp the *nature* of *B*-experiences without grasping the *character* of those experiences? The true psychophysical theory would seem to provide a route to a grasp of the subjective form of the bat's experiences. But now we face a dilemma, a dilemma which threatens to become a reductio: either we *can* grasp this theory, in which case the property *B* becomes open to us; or we *cannot* grasp the theory, simply because property *B* is *not* open to us. It seems to me that the looming reductio here is compelling: our concepts of consciousness just *are* inherently constrained by our own form of consciousness, so that any theory the understanding of which required us to transcend these constraints would *ipso facto* be inaccessible to us. Similarly, I think, any theory that required us to transcend the finiteness of our cognitive capacities would *ipso facto* be a theory we could not grasp, and this despite the fact that it might be needed to explain something we can see needs explaining. We cannot simply stipulate that our concept-forming abilities are indefinitely plastic and unlimited just because they would have to be to enable us to grasp the truth about the world. We constitutionally lack the concept-forming capacity to encompass all possible types of conscious state, and this obstructs our path to a general solution to the mind–body problem. Even if we could solve it for our own case, we could not solve it for bats and Martians. *P* is, as it were, too close to the different forms of subjectivity for it to be accessible to all such forms, given that one's form of subjectivity restricts one's concepts of subjectivity.[12]

I suspect that most optimists about constructively solving the mind–body problem will prefer to place their bets on the brain side of the relation. Neuroscience is the place to look for property *P*, they will say. My question then is whether there is any conceivable way in which we might come to introduce *P* in the course of our empirical investigations of the brain. New concepts have been introduced in the effort to understand the workings of the brain, certainly; could not *P* then occur in conceivable extensions of this manner of introduction? So far, indeed, the theoretical concepts we ascribe to the brain seem as remote from consciousness as any ordinary physical properties are, but perhaps we might reach *P* by diligent application of essentially the same procedures: so it is tempting to think. I want to suggest, to the contrary, that such procedures are inherently closed with respect to *P*. The fundamental reason for this, I think, is the role of *perception* in shaping our understanding of the brain – the way that our perception of the brain constrains the concepts we can apply to it. A point whose significance it would be hard to overstress here is this: the property of consciousness itself (or specific conscious states) is not an observable or perceptible property of the brain. You can stare into a living conscious brain, your own or someone else's, and see there a wide variety of inslantiated properties – its shape, colour, texture, etc. – but you will not thereby *see* what the subject is experiencing, the conscious state itself. Conscious states are simply not potential objects of perception: they depend upon the brain but they cannot be observed by directing the senses on to the brain. In other words, consciousness is noumenal with respect to perception of the brain.[13] I take it this is obvious. So we know there *are* properties of the brain that are necessarily closed to perception of the brain; the question now is whether *P* is likewise closed to perception.

My argument will proceed as follows. I shall first argue that *P* is indeed perceptually closed; then I shall complete the argument to full cognitive closure by insisting that no form of *inference* from what is perceived can lead us to *P*. The argument for perceptual closure starts from the thought that nothing we can imagine perceiving in the brain would ever convince us that we have located the intelligible nexus we seek. No matter what recondite property we could see to be instantiated in the brain we would always be baffled about how it could give rise to consciousness. I hereby invite you to try to conceive of a perceptible property of the brain that might allay the feeling of mystery that attends our contemplation of the brain–mind link: I do not think you will be able to do it. It is like trying to conceive of a perceptible property of a rock that would render it perspicuous that the rock was conscious. In fact, I think it is the very impossibility of this that lies at the root of the felt mind–body problem. But why is this? Basically, I think, it is because the senses are geared to representing a spatial world; they essentially present things in space with spatially defined properties. But it is precisely *such* properties that seem inherently incapable of resolving the mind–body problem: we cannot link consciousness to the brain in virtue of spatial properties of the brain. There the brain is, an object of perception, laid out in space, containing spatially distributed processes; but consciousness defies explanation in such terms. Consciousness does not seem made up out of smaller spatial processes; yet perception of the brain seems limited to revealing such processes.[14] The senses are responsive to certain *kinds* of properties – those that are essentially bound up with space – but these properties are of the wrong sort (the wrong *category*) to constitute *P*. Kant was right, the form of outer sensibility is spatial; but if so, then *P* will be noumenal with respect to the senses, since no spatial property will ever deliver a satisfying answer to the mind–body problem. We simply do not understand the idea that conscious states might intelligibly arise from spatial configurations of the kind disclosed by perception of the world.

I take it this claim will not seem terribly controversial. After all, we do not generally expect that every property referred to in our theories should be a potential object of human perception: consider quantum theory and cosmology. Unrestricted perceptual openness is a dogma of empiricism if ever there was one. And there is no compelling reason to suppose that the property needed to explain the mind–brain relation should be in principle perceptible; it might be essentially "theoretical," an object of thought, not sensory experience. Looking harder at nature is not the only (or the best) way of discovering its theoretically significant properties. Perceptual closure does not entail cognitive closure, since we have available the procedure of hypothesis formation, in which *un*observables come to be conceptualized.

I readily agree with these sentiments, but I think there are reasons for believing that no coherent method of concept introduction will ever lead us to *P*. This is because a certain principle of *homogeneity* operates in our introduction of theoretical concepts on the basis of observation. Let me first note that consciousness itself could not be introduced simply on the basis of what we observe about the brain and its physical effects. If our data, arrived at by perception of the brain, do not include anything that brings in conscious states, then the theoretical properties we need to explain these data will not include conscious states either. Inference to the best explanation of purely physical data will never take us outside the realm of the physical, forcing us to introduce concepts of consciousness.[15] Everything physical has a purely physical explanation. So the property of consciousness is cognitively closed with respect to the introduction of concepts by means of inference to the best explanation of perceptual data about the brain.

Now the question is whether *P* could ever be arrived at by this kind of inference. Here we must be careful to guard against a form of magical emergentism with respect to concept formation. Suppose we try out a relatively clear theory of how theoretical concepts are formed: we get them by a sort of analogical extension of what we observe. Thus, for example, we arrive at the concept of a molecule by taking our perceptual representations of macroscopic objects and conceiving of smaller scale objects of the same general kind. This method seems to work well enough for unobservable material objects, but it will not help in arriving at *P*, since analogical extensions of the entities we observe in the brain are precisely as hopeless as the original entities were as solutions to the mind–body problem. We would need a method that left the base of observational properties behind in a much more radical way. But it seems to me that even a more unconstrained conception of inference to the best explanation would still not do what is required: it would no more serve to introduce *P* than it serves to introduce the property of consciousness itself. To explain the observed physical data we need only such theoretical properties as bear upon those data, not the property that explains consciousness, which does not occur in the data. Since we do not need consciousness to explain those data, we do not need the property that explains consciousness.

We will never get as far away from the perceptual data in our explanations of those data as we need to get in order to connect up explanatorily with consciousness. This is, indeed, why it seems that consciousness is theoretically epiphenomenal in the task of accounting for physical events. No concept needed to explain the workings of the physical world will suffice to explain how the physical world produces consciousness. So if P is perceptually noumenal, then it will be noumenal with respect to perception-based explanatory inferences. Accordingly, I do not think that P could be arrived at by empirical studies of the brain alone. Nevertheless, the brain *has* this property, as it has the property of consciousness. Only a magical idea of how we come by concepts could lead one to think that we can reach P by first perceiving the brain and then asking what is needed to explain what we perceive.[16] (The mind–body problem tempts us to magic in more ways than one.)

It will help elucidate the position I am driving towards if I contrast it with another view of the source of the perplexity we feel about the mind–brain nexus. I have argued that we cannot know which property of the brain accounts for consciousness, and so we find the mind–brain link unintelligible. But, it may be said, there is another account of our sense of irremediable mystery, which does not require positing properties our minds cannot represent. This alternative view claims that, even if we *now* had a grasp of P, we would *still* feel that there is something mysterious about the link, because of a special epistemological feature of the situation. Namely this: our acquaintance with the brain and our acquaintance with consciousness are necessarily mediated by distinct cognitive faculties, namely perception and introspection. Thus the faculty through which we apprehend one term of the relation is necessarily distinct from the faculty through which we apprehend the other. In consequence, it is not possible for us to use one of these faculties to apprehend the nature of the psychophysical nexus. No single faculty will enable us ever to apprehend the fact that consciousness depends upon the brain in virtue of property P. Neither perception alone nor introspection alone will ever enable us to witness the dependence. And this, my objector insists, is the real reason we find the link baffling: we cannot make sense of it in terms of the deliverances of a single cognitive faculty. So, even if we now had concepts for the properties of the brain that explain consciousness, we would still feel a residual sense of unintelligibility; we would still take there to be something mysterious going on. The necessity to shift from one faculty to the other produces in us an illusion of inexplicability. We might in fact have the explanation right now but be under the illusion that we do not. The right diagnosis, then, is that we should recognize the peculiarity of the epistemological situation and stop trying to make sense of the psychophysical nexus in the way we make sense of other sorts of nexus. It only *seems* to us that we can never discover a property that will render the nexus intelligible.

I think this line of thought deserves to be taken seriously, but I doubt that it correctly diagnoses our predicament. It is true enough that the problematic nexus is essentially apprehended by distinct faculties, so that it will never reveal its secrets to a single faculty; but I doubt that our intuitive sense of intelligibility is so rigidly governed by the "single-faculty condition." Why *should* facts only seem intelligible to us if we can conceive of apprehending them by one (sort of) cognitive faculty? Why not allow that we can recognize intelligible connections between concepts (or properties) even when those concepts (or properties) are necessarily ascribed using different faculties? Is it not suspiciously empiricist to insist that a causal nexus can only be made sense of by us if we can conceive of its being an object of a single faculty of apprehension? Would we think this of a nexus that called for touch and sight to apprehend each term of the relation? Suppose (*per impossible*) that we were offered *P* on a plate, as a gift from God: would we still shake our heads and wonder how that could resolve the mystery, being still the victims of the illusion of mystery generated by the epistemological duality in question? No, I think this suggestion is not enough to account for the miraculous appearance of the link: it is better to suppose that we are permanently blocked from forming a concept of what accounts for that link.

How strong is the thesis I am urging? Let me distinguish *absolute* from *relative* claims of cognitive closure. A problem is absolutely cognitively closed if no possible mind could resolve it; a problem is relatively closed if minds of some sorts can in principle solve it while minds of other sorts cannot. Most problems, we may safely suppose, are only relatively closed: armadillo minds cannot solve problems of elementary arithmetic but human minds can. Should we say that the mind–body problem is only relatively closed or is the closure absolute? This depends on what we allow as a possible concept-forming mind, which is not an easy question. If we allow for minds that form their concepts of the brain and consciousness in ways that are quite independent of perception and introspection, then there may be room for the idea that there are possible minds for which the mind–body problem is soluble, and easily so. But if we suppose that *all* concept formation is tied to perception and introspection, however loosely, then *no* mind will be capable of understanding how it relates to its own body; the insolubility will be absolute. I think we can just about make sense of the former kind of mind, by exploiting our own faculty of a priori reasoning. Our mathematical concepts (say) do not seem tied either to perception or to introspection, so there does seem to be a mode of concept formation that operates without the constraints I identified earlier. The suggestion might then be that a mind that formed all of its concepts in this way – including its concepts of the brain and consciousness – would be free of the biases that prevent *us* from coming up with the right theory of how the two connect. Such a mind would have to be able to think of the brain and consciousness in ways that utterly prescind from the perceptual and the introspective, in somewhat the way we now (it seems) think about numbers. This mind would conceive of the psychophysical link in totally a priori terms. Perhaps this is how we should think of God's mind, and God's understanding of the mind–body relation. At any rate, something pretty radical is going to be needed if we are to devise a mind that can escape the kinds of closure that make the problem insoluble for us – if I am right in my diagnosis of our difficulty. *If* the problem is only relatively insoluble, then the type of mind that can solve it is going to be very different from ours and the kinds of mind we can readily make sense of (there may, of course, be cognitive closure here too). It certainly seems to me to be at least an open question whether the problem is absolutely insoluble; I would not be surprised if it were.[17]

My position is both pessimistic and optimistic at the same time. It is pessimistic about the prospects for arriving at a constructive solution to the mind–body problem, but it is optimistic about our hopes of removing the philosophical perplexity. The central point here is that I do not think we need to do the former in order to achieve the latter. This depends on a rather special understanding of what the philosophical problem consists in. What I want to suggest is that the nature of the psychophysical, connection has a full and non-mysterious explanation in a certain science, but that this science is inaccessible to us as a matter of principle. Call this explanatory scientific theory T: T is as natural and prosaic and devoid of miracle as any theory of nature; it describes the link between consciousness and the brain in a way that is no more remarkable (or alarming) than the way we now describe the link between the liver and bile.[18] According to T, there is nothing eerie going on in the world when an event in my visual cortex causes me to have an experience of yellow, however much it seems to *us* that there is. In other words, there is no intrinsic conceptual or metaphysical difficulty about how consciousness depends on the brain. It is not that the correct science is compelled to postulate miracles *de re*; it is rather that the correct science lies in the dark part of the world for us. We confuse our own cognitive limitations with objective eeriness. We are like a Humean mind trying to understand the physical world, or a creature without spatial concepts trying to understand the possibility of motion. This removes the philosophical problem because it assures us that the entities *themselves* pose no inherent philosophical difficulty. The case is unlike, for example, the problem of how the abstract world of numbers might be intelligibly related to the world of concrete knowing subjects: here the mystery seems intrinsic to the entities, not a mere artifact of our cognitive limitations or biases in trying to understand the relation.[19] It would not be plausible to suggest that there exists a science, whose theoretical concepts we cannot grasp, which completely resolves any sense of mystery that surrounds the question how the abstract becomes an object of knowledge for us. In this case, then, eliminativism seems a live option. The *philosophical* problem about consciousness and the brain arises from a sense that we are compelled to accept that nature contains miracles, as if the merely metallic lamp of the brain could really spirit into existence the Djin of consciousness. But we do not need to accept this: we can rest secure in the knowledge that some (unknowable) property of the brain makes everything fall into place. What creates the philosophical puzzlement is the assumption that the problem must somehow be scientific but that any science *we* can come up with will represent things as utterly miraculous. And the solution is to recognize that the sense of miracle comes from us and not from the world. There is, in reality, nothing mysterious about how the brain generates consciousness. There is no *metaphysical* problem.[20]

So far that deflationary claim has been justified by a general naturalism and certain considerations about cognitive closure and the illusions it can give rise to. Now I want to marshall some reasons for thinking that consciousness is actually a rather simple natural fact; objectively, consciousness is nothing very special. We should now be comfortable with the idea that our own sense of difficulty is a fallible guide to objective complexity: what is hard for us to grasp may not be very fancy in itself. The grain of our thinking is not a mirror held up to the facts of nature.[21] In particular, it may be that the extent of our understanding of facts about the mind is not commensurate with some objective estimate of their intrinsic complexity: we may be good at understanding the mind in some of its aspects but hopeless with respect to others, in a way that cuts across objective differences in what the aspects involve. Thus we are adept at understanding action in terms of the folk psychology of belief and desire, and we seem not entirely out of our depth when it comes to devising theories of language. But our understanding of how consciousness develops from the organization of matter is nonexistent. But now, think of these various aspects of mind from the point of view of evolutionary biology. Surely language and the propositional attitudes are more complex and advanced evolutionary achievements than the mere possession of consciousness by a physical organism. Thus it seems that we are better at understanding some of the more complex aspects of mind than the simpler ones. Consciousness arises early in evolutionary history and is found right across the animal kingdom. In some respects it seems that the biological engineering required for consciousness is less fancy than that needed for certain kinds of complex motor behavior. Yet we can come to understand the latter while drawing a total blank with respect to the former. Conscious states seem biologically quite primitive, comparatively speaking. So the theory *T* that explains the occurrence of consciousness in a physical world is very probably less objectively complex (by some standard) than a range of other theories that do not defy our intellects. If only we could know the psychophysical mechanism it might surprise us with its simplicity, its utter naturalness. In the manual that God consulted when he made the earth and all the beasts that dwell thereon the chapter about how to engineer consciousness from matter occurs fairly early on, well before the really difficult later chapters on mammalian reproduction and speech. It is not the *size* of the problem but its *type* that makes the mind–body problem so hard for us. This reflection should make us receptive to the idea that it is something about the tracks of our thought that prevents us from achieving a science that relates consciousness to its physical basis: the enemy lies within the gates.[22]

The position I have reached has implications for a tangle of intuitions it is natural to have regarding the mind–body relation. On the one hand, there are intuitions, pressed from Descartes to Kripke, to the effect that the relation between conscious states and bodily states is fundamentally contingent.[23] It can easily seem to us that there is no necessitation involved in the dependence of the mind on the brain. But, on the other hand, it looks absurd to try to dissociate the two entirely, to let the mind float completely free of the body. Disembodiment is a dubious possibility at best, and some kind of necessary supervenience of the mental on the physical has seemed undeniable to many. It is not my aim here to adjudicate this longstanding dispute; I want simply to offer a diagnosis of what is going on when one finds oneself assailed with this flurry of conflicting intuitions. The reason we feel the tug of contingency, pulling consciousness loose from its physical moorings, may be that we do not and cannot grasp the nature of the property that intelligibly links them. The brain has physical properties we can grasp, and variations in these correlate with changes in consciousness, but we cannot draw the veil that conceals the manner of their connection. Not grasping the nature of the connection, it strike us as deeply contingent; we cannot make the assertion of a necessary connection intelligible to ourselves. There *may* then be a real necessary connection; it is just that it will always strike us as curiously brute and unperspicuous. We may thus, as upholders of intrinsic contingency, be the dupes of our own cognitive blindness. On the other hand, we are scarcely in a position to assert that there *is* a necessary connection between the properties of the brain we can grasp and states of consciousness, since we are so ignorant (and irremediably so) about the character of the connection. For all we know, the connection may be contingent, as access to *P* would reveal if we could have such access. The link between consciousness and property P is not, to be sure, contingent – virtually by definition – but we are not in a position to say exactly how P is related to the "ordinary" properties of the brain. It may be necessary or it may be contingent. Thus it is that we tend to vacillate between contingency and necessity; for we lack the conceptual resources to decide the question, or to understand the answer we are inclined to give. The indicated conclusion appears to be that we can never really know whether disembodiment is metaphysically possible, or whether necessary supervenience is the case, or whether spectrum inversion could occur. For these all involve claims about the modal connections between properties of consciousness and the ordinary properties of the body and brain that we can conceptualize; and the real nature of these connections is not accessible to us. Perhaps P makes the relation between C-fiber firing and pain necessary or perhaps it does not: we are simply not equipped to know. We are like a Humean mind wondering whether the observed link between the temperature of a gas and its pressure (at a constant volume) is necessary or contingent. To know the answer to that you need to grasp atomic (or molecular) theory, and a Humean mind just is not up to attaining the requisite theoretical understanding. Similarly, we are constitutionally ignorant at precisely the spot where the answer exists.

I predict that many readers of this paper will find its main thesis utterly incredible, even ludicrous. Let me remark that I sympathize with such readers: the thesis is not easily digestible. But I would say this: if the thesis *is* actually true, it will still strike us as hard to believe. For the idea of an explanatory property (or set of properties) that is noumenal for us, yet is essential for the (constructive) solution of a problem we face, offends a kind of natural idealism that tends to dominate our thinking. We find it taxing to conceive of the existence of a real property, under our noses as it were, which we are built not to grasp – a property that is responsible for phenomena that we observe in the most direct way possible. This kind of realism, which brings cognitive closure so close to home, is apt to seem both an affront to our intellects and impossible to get our minds around. We try to think of this unthinkable property and understandably fail in the effort; so we rush to infer that the very supposition of such a property is nonsensical. Realism of the kind I am presupposing thus seems difficult to hold in focus, and any philosophical theory that depends upon it will also seem to rest on something systematically elusive.[24] My response to such misgivings, however, is unconcessive: the limits of our minds are just not the limits of reality. It is deplorably anthropocentric to insist that reality be constrained by what the human mind can conceive. We need to cultivate a vision of reality (a metaphysics) that makes it truly independent of our given cognitive powers, a conception that includes these powers as a proper part. It is just that, in the case of the mind–body problem, the bit of reality that systematically eludes our cognitive grasp is an aspect of our own nature. Indeed, it is an aspect that makes it possible for us to have minds at all and to think about how they are related to our bodies. This particular transcendent tract of reality happens to lie within our own heads. A deep fact about our own nature as a form of embodied consciousness is thus necessarily hidden from us. Yet there is nothing inherently eerie or bizarre about this embodiment. We are much more straightforward than we seem. Our weirdness lies in the eye of the beholder.

The answer to the question that forms my title is therefore "No and Yes."[25]

Afterword

The perspective developed in this paper can be seen as the convergence of two ideas. On the one hand, there is a general conception of mind and cognitive capacity that can be traced through Descartes, Locke, Hume, Kant, and most recently Chomsky, which stresses the constitutive internal structure of the knowing faculties, especially as this structure determines the limits of human knowledge. Under this conception, in its modern version, human cognitive capacity is a biologically based modular system, with certain specific strengths and weaknesses, and there is every reason to expect that its powers do not spread uniformly across the natural world. Thus some natural phenomena are likely to elude our capacities for understanding, as is patently the case with respect to the intelligence of other evolved species. On the other hand, the mind–body problem, construed as a problem about the emergence of consciousness from matter, presents deep and intractable problems of understanding, manifested in the miraculous-seeming character of the psychophysical link. We do not possess the theoretical tools with which to make any headway with the problem. The basic thesis of "Can we solve the mind–body problem?" is then this: the problem of consciousness is a plausible example of the kind of cognitive closure we would predict on general grounds. That there should exist problems that systematically escape our best theoretical efforts is antecedently highly probable, and the problem of consciousness looks like an instance of just such a problem. In this sense, philosophy confirms biology.

There are three main additions I would now make to the original paper. First, I was inclined then to think that consciousness is unique among philosophical problems in being susceptible to this kind of treatment, and I cited free will and knowledge of abstract entities as areas in which such an approach does not seem plausible. Subsequent reflection, however, has caused me to conclude that the cognitive closure diagnosis is more generally applicable than I thought, and indeed that it provides a plausible general metaphilosophical position. In *Problems in Philosophy* (McGinn, 1993) I develop this broader thesis, taking in the self, meaning, free will, a priori knowledge, and skepticism; I also offer a general account of philosophical perplexity and the scope of reason. For details, I refer interested readers to that work.

Second, I spoke in the original paper as if property *P* was going to be a property of the brain alone, assuming that consciousness itself is essentially fully open to cognitive penetration. I quickly came to see, however, that this could not be right: consciousness too must possess a hidden nature, in which *P* plays a mediating role. The resulting realism about consciousness is explained and defended in "The hidden structure of consciousness," in my book *The Problem of Consciousness* (McGinn, 1991). We need to view introspection as far less omniscient with respect to its objects than has typically been assumed.

Third, I failed in my early thinking to reckon with the following possibility: though conscious reason is inherently incapable of solving the mind–body problem (among others), some other type of epistemic system might be free of the limitations that generate such closure. Certainly it does not follow from the admission that conscious reason has these limits that *every* type of representational system is thus confined. And I now think that there are good grounds for supposing that there do exist epistemic systems that contain the kind of philosophical information denied to conscious reason: specifically, subconscious brain representations and the genetic code. The latter provides the simplest illustration of this point: encoded in the genes is a body of information that is necessary and sufficient to engineer organisms with certain bodily and mental characteristics, among them consciousness. So the genes must somehow encode principles that enable them to manufacture conscious state from physical materials. They must then have already solved the problem of emergence. The genes of any conscious organism possess the kind of philosophical aptitude denied to conscious human reason. I explore this idea in chapter 8 of *Problems in Philosophy*. I take it to reinforce the naturalism claimed for my overall position.

Let me finally urge an open mind on the question of whether we can solve every problem we can formulate: it can scarcely be a necessary truth that the problems of philosophy have solutions that lie along the path of human cognitive endeavor.

Notes

1 One of the peculiarities of the mind–body problem is the difficulty of formulating it in a rigorous way. We have a sense of the problem that outruns

our capacity to articulate it clearly. Thus we quickly find ourselves resorting to invitations to look inward, instead of specifying precisely *what* it is about consciousness that makes it inexplicable in terms of ordinary physical properties. And this can make it seem that the problem is spurious. A creature without consciousness would not properly appreciate the problem (assuming such a creature could appreciate other problems). I think an adequate treatment of the mind–body problem should explain why it is so hard to state the problem explicitly. My treatment locates our difficulty in our inadequate conceptions of the nature of the brain and consciousness. In fact, if we knew their natures fully we would already have solved the problem. This should become clear later.

2 I would also classify panpsychism as a constructive solution, since it attempts to explain consciousness in terms of properties of the brain that are as natural as consciousness itself. Attributing specks of proto-consciousness to the constituents of matter is not supernatural in the way postulating immaterial substances or divine interventions is; it is merely extravagant. I shall here be assuming that panpsychism, like all other extant constructive solutions, is inadequate as an answer to the mind–body problem, as (of course) are the supernatural "solutions." I am speaking to those who still feel perplexed (almost everyone, I would think, at least in his heart).

3 This kind of view of cognitive capacity is forcefully advocated by Noam Chomsky (1975) in *Reflections on Language* and by Jerry Fodor (1983) in *The Modularity of Mind*. Chomsky distinguishes between "problems," which human minds are in principle equipped to solve, and "mysteries," which systematically elude our understanding; and he envisages a study of our cognitive systems that would chart these powers and limitations. I am here engaged in such a study, citing the mind–body problem as falling on the side of the mysteries.

4 See Thomas Nagel's discussion of realism in *The View From Nowhere*, (1986, ch. 6). He argues there for the possibility of properties we can never grasp. Combining Nagel's realism with Chomsky–Fodor cognitive closure gives a position looking very much like Locke's in the *Essay Concerning Human Understanding*: the idea that our God-given faculties do not equip us to fathom the deep truth about reality. In fact, Locke held precisely this about the relation between mind and brain: only divine revelation could enable us to understand how "perceptions" are produced in our minds by material objects.

5 Hume, of course, argued, in effect, that no theory essentially employing a notion of objective causal necessitation could be grasped by our minds – and likewise for the notion of objective persistence. We might compare the frustrations of the Humean mind to the conceptual travails of the pure sound beings discussed in ch. 2 of P. F. Strawson's *Individuals* (1959); both are types of mind whose constitution puts various concepts beyond them. We can do a lot better than these truncated minds, but we also have our constitutional limitations.

6 See the *Essay*, Book II, ch. IV. Locke compares the project of saying what solidity ultimately is to trying to clear up a blind man's vision by talking to him.

7 Some of the more arcane aspects of cosmology and quantum theory might be thought to lie just within the bounds of human intelligibility. Chomsky suggests that the causation of behavior might be necessarily mysterious to human investigators (see Chomsky, 1975, p. 156). I myself believe that the mind–body problem exhibits a qualitatively different level of mystery from this case (unless it is taken as an aspect of that problem).

8 Cf. Nagel's discussion of emergence in "Panpsychism," in *Mortal Questions* (1979). I agree with him that the apparent radical emergence of mind from matter has to be epistemic only, on pain of accepting inexplicable miracles in the world.

9 Despite his reputation for pessimism over the mind–body problem, a careful reading of Nagel reveals an optimistic strain in his thought (by the standards of the present paper): see, in particular, the closing remarks of "What is it like to be a bat?" (Nagel, 1979). Nagel speculates that we might be able to devise an "objective phenomenology" that made conscious states more amenable to physical analysis. Unlike me, he does not regard the problem as inherently beyond us.

10 This is perhaps the most remarkably optimistic view of all – the expectation that reflecting on the ordinary concept of pain (say) will reveal the manner of pain's dependence on the brain. If I am not mistaken, this is in effect the view of commonsense functionalists: they think that P consists in causal role, and that this can be inferred analytically from the concepts of conscious states. This would make it truly amazing that we should ever have felt there to be a mind–body problem at all, since the solution is already contained in our mental concepts. What optimism!

11 See "What is it like to be a bat?" (Nagel, 1979). Notice that the fugitive character of such properties with respect to our concepts has nothing to do with their "complexity"; like fugitive color properties, such experiential properties are "simple." Note too that such properties provide counterexamples to the claim that (somehow) rationality is a faculty that, once possessed, can be extended to encompass all concepts, so that if *any* concept can be possessed then *every* concept can.

12 It might be suggested that we borrow Nagel's idea of "objective phenomenology" in order to get around this problem. Instead of representing experiences under subjective descriptions, we should describe them in entirely objective terms, thus bringing them within our conceptual ken. My problem with this is that, even allowing that there could be such a form of description, it would not permit us to understand how the subjective aspects of experience depend upon the brain, which is really the problem we are trying to solve. In fact, I doubt that the notion of objective phenomenology is any more coherent than the notion of subjective physiology. Both involve trying to bridge the psychophysical gap by a sort of stipulation. The lesson here is that the gap cannot be bridged just by applying concepts drawn from one side to items that belong on the other side; and this is because neither sort of concept could ever do what is needed.

13 We should distinguish two claims about the imperceptibility of consciousness: (1) consciousness is not perceivable by directing the senses on to the brain;

(2) consciousness is not perceivable by directing the senses anywhere, even towards the behavior that "expresses" conscious states. I believe both theses, but my present point requires only (1). I am assuming, of course, that perception cannot be unrestrictedly theory-laden; or that if it can, the infusions of theory cannot have been originally derived simply by looking at things or tasting them or touching them or . . .

14 Nagel discusses the difficulty of thinking of conscious processes in the spatial terms that apply to the brain in *The View From Nowhere* (1986, pp. 50–1), but he does not draw my despairing conclusion. The case is exactly *un*like (say) the dependence of liquidity on the properties of molecules, since here we do think of both terms of the relation as spatial in character; so we can simply employ the idea of spatial composition.

15 Cf. Nagel: 'it will never be legitimate to infer, as a theoretical explanation of physical phenomena alone, a property that includes or implies the consciousness of its subject,' 'Panpsychism,' in *Mortal Questions*, (Nagel, 1979, p. 183).

16 It is surely a striking fact that the microprocesses that have been discovered in the brain by the usual methods seem no nearer to consciousness than the gross properties of the brain open to casual inspection. Neither do more abstract "holistic" features of brain function seem to be on the right lines to tell us the nature of consciousness. The deeper science probes into the brain the more remote it seems to get from consciousness. Greater knowledge of the brain thus destroys our illusions about the kinds of properties that might be discovered by traveling along this path. Advanced neurophysiological theory seems only to deepen the miracle.

17 The kind of limitation I have identified is therefore not the kind that could be remedied simply by a large increase in general intelligence. No matter how large the frontal lobes of our biological descendants may become, they will still be stumped by the mind–body problem, so long as they form their (empirical) concepts on the basis of perception and introspection.

18 Or again, no more miraculous than the theory of evolution. Creationism is an understandable response to the theoretical problem posed by the existence of complex organisms; fortunately, we now have a theory that renders this response unnecessary, and so undermines the theism required by the creationist thesis. In the case of consciousness, the appearance of miracle might also tempt us in a "creationist" direction, with God required to perform the alchemy necessary to transform matter into experience. Thus the mind–body problem might similarly be used to prove the existence of God (no miracle without a miracle-maker). We cannot, I think, refute this argument in the way we can the original creationist argument, namely by actually producing a non-miraculous explanatory theory, but we can refute it by arguing that such a naturalistic theory must *exist*. (It is a condition of adequacy upon any account of the mind–body relation that it avoid assuming theism.)

19 See Paul Benacerraf (1973) for a statement of this problem about abstract entities. Another problem that seems to me to differ from the mind–body problem is the problem of free will. I do not believe that there is some

unknowable property Q which reconciles free will with determinism (or indeterminism); rather, the concept of free will contains internal incoherencies, as the concept of consciousness does not. This is why it is much more reasonable to be an eliminativist about free will than about consciousness.

20 A test of whether a proposed solution to the mind–body problem is adequate is whether it relieves the pressure towards eliminativism. If the data can only be explained by postulating a miracle (i.e. not explained), then we must repudiate the data; this is the principle behind the impulse to deny that conscious states exist. My proposal passes this test because it allows us to resist the postulation of miracles; it interprets the eeriness as merely epistemic, though deeply so. Constructive solutions are not the only way to relieve the pressure.

21 Chomsky suggests that the very faculties of mind that make us good at some cognitive tasks may make us poor at others (see Chomsky, 1975, pp. 155–6). It seems to me possible that what makes us good at the science of the purely physical world is what skews us away from developing a science of consciousness. Our faculties bias us towards understanding matter in motion, but it is precisely this kind of understanding that is inapplicable to the mind–body problem. Perhaps, then, the price of being good at understanding matter is that we cannot understand mind. Certainly our notorious tendency to think of everything in spatial terms does not help us in understanding the mind.

22 I get this phrase from Fodor (1983, p. 121). The intended contrast is with kinds of cognitive closure that stem from exogenous factors – as, say, in astronomy. Our problem with P is not that it is too distant or too small or too large or too complex; rather, the very structure of our concept-forming apparatus points us away from P.

23 Saul Kripke, (1980). Of course, Descartes explicitly argued from (what he took to be) the essential natures of the body and mind to the contingency of their connection. If we abandon the assumption that we know these natures, then agnosticism about the modality of the connection seems the indicated conclusion.

24 This is the kind of realism defended by Nagel (1986) in ch. 6 of *The View From Nowhere*: to be is not to be conceivable by us. I would say that the mind–body problem provides a demonstration that there *are* such concept-transcending properties, not merely that there *could* be. I would also say that realism of this kind should be accepted precisely because it helps solve the mind–body problem; it is a metaphysical thesis that pulls its weight in coping with a problem that looks hopeless otherwise. There is thus nothing "epiphenomenal" about such radical realism: the existence of a reality we cannot know can yet have intellectual significance for us.

25 Discussions with the following people have helped me work out the ideas of this paper: Anita Avramides, Jerry Katz, Ernie LePore, Michael Levin, Thomas Nagel, Galen Strawson, Peter Unger. My large debt to Nagel's work should be obvious throughout the paper: I would not have tried to face the mind–body problem down had he not first faced up to it.

References

Benacerraf, P. (1973) "Mathematical truth," *Journal of Philosophy* 70, pp. 661–79.
Chomsky, N. (1975) *Reflections on Language*, New York: Pantheon Press.
Fodor, J. (1983) *The Modularity of Mind: an Essay on Faculty Psychology*, Cambridge, Mass.: Bradford Books/MIT Press.
Kripke, S. (1980) *Naming and Necessity*, Oxford: Blackwell.
McGinn, C. (1991) *The Problem of Consciousness: Essays Towards Resolution*, Oxford: Blackwell.
McGinn, C. (1993) *Problems in Philosophy*, Oxford: Blackwell.
Nagel, T. (1979) *Mortal Questions*, Cambridge: Cambridge University Press.
Nagel, T. (1986) *The View from Nowhere*, Oxford and New York: Oxford University Press.
Strawson, P. F. (1959) *Individuals: an Essay in Descriptive Metaphysics*, London: Methuen.

9
Consciousness, Intentionality, and the Philosophy of Mind

Richard Rorty

The term "philosophy of mind" came into currency in the English-speaking world in the 1950s, largely as a description of the debates initiated by Gilbert Ryle's pioneering book *The Concept of Mind*, published in 1949. Ryle's book was a polemic against the Cartesian idea that mental states are states of an immaterial substance. This polemic, and the ensuing discussion, turned on the question of the reducibility of mental events to behavioral dispositions. Ryle's central argument was that we had misconceived the "logic" of such words as "belief," "sensation," "conscious," etc. He thought that the traditional, Cartesian, theory of mind, had "misconstrued the type-distinction between disposition and exercise into its mythical bifurcation of unwitnessable mental causes and their witnessable physical effects" (Ryle, 1949, p. 32). Ryle's attempt to do philosophy of mind as "conceptual analysis" was founded on the pre-Quinean idea that philosophical puzzles arose out of "misunderstandings of the logic of our language."

Almost as soon as Ryle's book was published, this conception of philosophy began to fall into disrepute. Quinean and Wittgensteinian doubts that there was any such thing as "the logic of our language" began to make themselves felt. Furthermore, there were doubts that Ryle had done enough to explain the plausibility of Cartesianism. He had given us too little help in understanding why anyone had ever misunderstood our language as badly as the Cartesians purportedly had – why anyone had made what Ryle called "absurd category mistakes." Ryle thought it enough to say that Descartes's admiration for Galilean mechanics committed him to viewing the mind as a quasi-mechanical process (Ryle, 1949, p. 19). But this was hardly enough to explain how Descartes had gotten everybody to swallow the idea of nonspatial causal mechanisms, how he had gotten them to confuse a behavioral disposition with an inner event. Something had to be said about the markedly counterintuitive character of Ryle's claim that the notion of "the mind" was simply the product of a misleading way of describing the organism's behavior.

The next stage beyond Ryle is dominated by the writings, during the 1950s and 1960s, of J. J. C. Smart and David Armstrong, the most prominent of the so-called "central-state materialists." These philosophers said we should just give up Ryle's counterintuitive claim that when we thought we were talking about inner events we were "really" talking about dispositions to behave. No "conceptual analysis" could show that the "real meaning" of mentalistic discourse consisted in reference to dispositions. But that merely showed, smart and Armstrong thought, that philosophers should not think of themselves as concerned with doing linguistic analysis. They should give up the positivistic idea that one can validate philosophical claims by an appeal to "meanings," or do philosophical work by "analyzing" meanings.

Instead, Smart and Armstrong proposed, philosophers should think of themselves as reconciling natural science and common sense by showing how various words of ordinary language can be interpreted as referring to the sorts of processes, e.g. brain states, which natural science knows how to investigate. Such interpretations were proposals, rather than discoveries, proposals dictated not by "the logic of our language" but by the state of our empirical science. In the materialists' view, the reason why Descartes went so badly wrong was that in his day brain physiology was too primitive to make a physicalistic, microstructural account of cognition sound like a plausible research program. So it was reasonable for Descartes to call up a "ghost in the machine." We moderns, however, are now within hailing distance of such an account. So now philosophy's task is to clear away the Cartesian debris which makes us think that psychology is more than a place-holder for biology. More specifically, its task is to persuade us that, as Armstrong put it,

> The concept of a mental state is the concept of that, whatever it may turn out to be, which is brought about in a man by certain stimuli and which in turn brings about certain responses. (Amstrong, 1968, p. 79)

As Armstrong noted, however, his own view and Ryle's were counterintuitive in the same way. As he put it:

> The view that our notion of mind is nothing but that of an inner principle apt for bringing about certain sorts of behavior may be thought to share a

certain weakness with [Ryle's] Behaviorism. Modern philosophers have put the point about Behaviorism by saying that although Behaviorism may be a satisfactory account of the mind from an *other-person point of view*, it will not do as a *first-person* account . . . We are conscious, we have experiences. Now can we say that to be conscious, to have experiences, is simply for something to go on within us apt for the causing of certain sorts of behavior? (Armstrong, 1980, p. 197)

Armstrong's reply to these questions was to say that we should interpret the notion of experience, of consciousness, as that of acquisition of beliefs about our inner states. To be conscious of being in pain, for example, is a matter of acquiring a belief about the state of our nerves. Armstrong summed up by saying

Consciouness of our own mental state . . . may then be conceived of as an inner state or event giving a capacity for selective behavior, in this case selective behavior toward our own mental state . . . Consciousness is a self-scanning mechanism in the central nervous system. (p. 199)

The next stage in the development of philosophy of mind was, however, a move back from Armstrong's emphasis on physiology in the direction of claiming a certain autonomy for the psychological. The principal motive for this antimaterialist move was Hilary Putnam's argument that many different states of a brain could cause the same behavioral disposition. Brains might be as diverse as computer hardware, but, just as the same program could run on lots of different machines (made of lots of different materials and constructed according to quite different principles), so the same mental states could occur independently of any particular physiological event.

This analogy between the study of computer hardware and physiology on the one hand, and between the study of computer software and psychology on the other, was the beginning of a transition from philosophy of mind to philosophy of psychology. Instead of the question of the 1950s and 1960s – "How can we refute Descartes?" – the question of the 1970s became "How can we make sense of the various research programs upon which cognitive psychologists are embarked?" The answer was: by thinking of mental states as *functional* states, states which mediate between input and output in the way in which program states of computers do and which can, like program states, be viewed as symbolic representations of states of affairs – as sentential attitudes. For the next twenty years or so "functionalism" became the dominant school of thought among Anglo-Saxon philosophers interested in the mind–body problem.

It is important to emphasize that the functionalists adopted the same attitude toward consciousness as had Ryle and the central-state materialists.

As Searle has rightly said, the entire history of philosophy of mind since Ryle is marked by a refusal to take consciousness seriously, or, more exactly, by an insistence on taking "conscious experience" to be a matter of *having beliefs*. This insistence enabled the functionalists to shrug off the question "Are computers conscious?" by saying that computers can be programmed to report on their own program states, (see Putnam, 1961, p. 148), to represent symbolically their own symbolic representations. Such an ability is, they said, all the notion of "conscious experience" amounts to.

The refusal to take Cartesianism seriously which was common to Ryle, Armstrong, and Putnam was thus not so much a result of their inability to take the idea of a state of an immaterial entity seriously as of their inability to take the notion of "conscious experience distinct from the having of a belief" seriously. So when Thomas Nagel complained that all these philosophers had neglected the *phenomenology* of conscious experience – *what it is like* to be conscious – Daniel Dennett thought it enough to reply that "thinkings that *p* . . . exhaust our immediate awareness" (1978, p. 165).

Dennett's identification of experience and belief should be seen as part of the same line of thought which led philosophers away from the Lockean notion of words as names of ideas – of words as able to have meaning by naming experiences – and toward the holistic view (shared by Quine and Wittgenstein) that words have meaning by virtue of their place in a language-game. Following this line led them to become steadily more naturalistic: to accept the principle "If natural science cannot tell us more about how it works, then it does not exist." The link between a holistic philosophy of language and this naturalistic (or, if you like, "objectivistic") attitude is the view that *to understand something is to discover its lawlike relations to other things*. The view that understanding *x* is a matter of finding lawlike regularities which tie its behavior in with the behavior of *y*, *z*, and so on (rather than a matter of contemplating it in isolation, penetrating into its inner nature, finding its *intrinsic* properties, and the like) is the familiar legacy of Galileo's substitution of a law–event framework of scientific explanation for Aristotle's thing–nature framework. Galileo's example taught us to be wary of the notion of an *intrinsic* property of an entity, one which could *not* be viewed as a set of relationships between that entity and other entities.

If one shares this Galilean outlook one will distrust appeals to immediate experience, and especially the idea that certain experiences cannot be put into words and made the subject of argument. For that outlook predisposes one to think, with Wittgenstein, that if the phrase "what it is like to be conscious" has a meaning, then there must be criteria for deciding when and whether this property applies: when it merely seems to someone that she recognizes the presence of this property and when she actually does. Thus Dennett says,

A defender of the subjective realm such as Nagel must grant that in general, whether or not it was like something to be *x*, whether or not the subject *experienced* being *x* – questions that *define* the subjective realm – are questions about which the subject's subsequent subjective opinion is not authoritative. But if the subject's own convictions do not settle the matter, and if, as Nagel holds, no objective considerations are conclusive either, the subjective realm floats out of ken altogether, except perhaps for the subject's convictions about the specious present. (1978, p. 143)

What links Ryle, Armstrong, Putnam, and Dennett together, and seperates them from Nagel, Kripke, and Searle, is that the former philosophers are content to *let* the subjective realm float out of ken, and out of philosophy, altogether. They think that if philosophy is ever going to join hands with natural science, it must eliminate the unverifiable, not to mention the ineffable. So the claim that to talk of "conscious experience" is merely a misleading way of talking about beliefs gets its plausibility not from any particular discovery about experiences, but rather from a very general metaphilosophical outlook.

By contrast, philosophers such as Nagel and Searle insist that attention to the subjective realm is just what is needed if philosophy is not to relapse into dogmatism.[2] Nagel began his seminal paper "What is it like to be a bat?" by saying, "Consciousness is what makes the mind–body problem really intractable." His principal point is made in the following sentence from that article:

> Certainly it *appears* unlikely that we will get closer to the real nature of human experience by leaving behind the particularity of our human point of view and striving for a description in terms accessible to beings that could not imagine what it was like to be us. (1980, p. 164)

Searle echoes this point when he says that the view that "mental states can be entirely defined in terms of their causal realtions" has never been reached

> by a close scrutiny of the phenomena in question. No one ever considered his own terrible pain or his deepest worry and concluded that they were just Turing machine states or that they could be entirely defined in terms of their causes and effects or that attributing such states to themselves was just a matter of taking a certain stance toward themselves. (1983, pp. 262–3)

For Nagel's and Searle's opponents, however, all this talk of "what it is like", "real nature," and "close scrutiny" is pre-Galilean obscurantism. For them, mind is whatever psychology studies, and psychology is a discipline which finds lawlike relationships between public events. No correlations of this sort are going to involve close scrutiny of what it is like to have a pain, much less of what it is like to have a belief.

I have not worked in the philosophy of mind in recent years, partially because my interests have changed, but partially also because Dennett and Davidson seem to me to be saying almost everything that I should want to say – and saying it more clearly than I could. Reading Davidson has convinced me that I was still too much of a physicalist when I wrote *Philosophy and the Mirror of Nature*. A pragmatist should not say, as I was still half-inclined to say in 1979, that physics tells us all we need to know about the way the world is, but rather should follow Goodman and Putnam in saying that there is no "Way the World Is." As I said in an exposition of Davidson called "Non reductive physicalism," the moral of Davidson's "anomalous monism" is that mentalistic language is no more a way of describing a portion of physical reality than physicalistic language is a way of describing (among other things) mental reality.

As I see it, Dennett's philosophy of mind nicely complements the Wittgensteinian–Davidsonian philosophy of language. Reading Dennett has made me more aware of the importance of the holistic character of belief-ascription than I was when I wrote *Philosophy and the Mirror of Nature*. This holism ties in with the thoroughgoing holism which leads Davidson to say that "there is no such thing as a language, not if a language is anything like what many philosophers and linguists have supposed" (1986, p. 446). This latter Davidsonian doctrine seems to me to harmonize nicely with the connectionist approach to artificial intelligence and with Dennett's "multiple drafts" model of how the mind works.

However, Dennett is not as ready as I am to abandon the notion of representation, and to say with Davidson that "beliefs represent nothing" (Davidson, 1989, pp. 165–6).[3] The residual disagreement between Dennett and myself is not so much about philosophy of mind as about metaphilosophy: about whether philosophy of mind should be thought of as a study of mental representations, or rather as the therapeutic dissolution of representationalist notions.[4]

Notes

1 In this seminal paper – the first to develop the program–mind analogy in detail – Putnam uses an Armstrong-like notion of self-scanning as an analogy to introspection.
2 See Nagel (1986, p. 11): "In the name of liberation, these movements have offered us intellectual repression." See Dennett's discussion of this passage at p. 5 of *The Intentional Stance*, as well as Nagel's explanation (at p. 106) of why his position is incompatible with a Wittgensteinian conception of language.

3 For a sort of anti-representationalist manifesto, see the Introduction ("Antire-presentationalism, ethnocentrism, and liberalism") to my *Objectivity, Relativism and Truth* (Rorty, 1991). That book also contains the essay "Non-reductive physicalism" to which I refer above.
4 I have offered some criticisms of Dennett's residual representationalism in my "Holism, intrinsicality and the ambition of transcendence" (Rorty, 1993). Dennett's reply is included in the same volume.

References

Armstrong, D. M. (1968) *A Materialist Theory of the Mind*, London: Routledge & Kegan Paul.
Armstrong, D. M. (1980) "The nature of mind," in N. Block (ed.) *Readings in the Philosophy of Psychology*, vol. 1, Cambridge, Mass.: Harvard University Press, pp. 191–9.
Davidson, D. (1986) "A nice derangement of epitaphs," in E. LePore (ed.) *Truth and Interpretation: Perspectives on the Philosophy of Donald Davidson*, Oxford: Blackwell, 433–46.
Davidson, D. (1989) "The myth of the subjective," in M. Krausz (ed.) *Relativism: Interpretation and Confrontation*, Notre Dame, Ind.: Notre Dame University Press, pp. 159–72.
Dennett, D. C. (1978) "Toward a cognitive theory of consciousness," in *Brainstorms: Philosophical Essays on Mind and Psychology*, Montgomery, Vt.: Bradford Books/MIT Press, pp. 149–73.
Dennett, D. C. (1987) *The Intentional Stance*, Cambridge, Mass.: Bradford Books/MIT Press.
Nagel, T. (1980) "What is it like to be a bat?" in N. Block (ed.) *Readings in the Philosophy of Psychology*, vol. 1, Cambridge, Mass.: Harvard University Press, pp. 159–68.
Nagel, T. (1986) *The View from Nowhere*, Oxford and New York: Oxford University Press.
Putnam, H. (1961) "Minds and machines," in S. Hook (ed.) *Dimensions of Mind: a Symposium*, New York: Collier, pp. 138–64.
Rorty, R. (1991) *Philosophical Papers*, vol. 1, *Objectivity, Relativism and Truth*, Cambridge: Cambridge University Press.
Rorty, R. (1993) "Holism, intrinsicality and the ambition of transcendence," in B. Dahlbom (ed.) *Dennett and His Critics: Demystifying Mind*, Oxford: Blackwell, pp. 184–202.
Ryle, G. (1949) *The Concept of Mind*, London: Hutchinson.
Searle, J. (1983) *Intentionality: an Essay in the Philosophy of Mind*, Cambridge: Cambridge University Press.

Part III
Intentionality, Cognitive Science, and the Mind–Body Problem

10
Mind and Brain

Fred Dretske

I am a materialist. Mental states are simply physical states of the organism. The physical states (or facts) with which mental states (or facts) are to be identified may be very complex, of course; they may be, or include, facts about the *relations* that exist (or existed) between an organism and its environment. The physical relationships underlying the mental life of an organism may be causal, informational, functional, or historical. I happen to believe that the important relations are informational and historical: facts having to do with the way an organism developed (during learning) to more efficiently service its own needs. But, from the point of view of materialism, the crucial point is that whatever set of facts we select to analyze the mental are facts which, taken individually, are recognizably physical – the sort that exist, or can exist, in a world devoid of minds.

My materialism does not mean that I'm not a realist about the mind. On the contrary. I think we really do have thoughts and desires. Our thoughts are *about* things and our desires are *for* things. Furthermore, these thoughts and desires are causally efficacious, and they influence behavior in virtue of what they are thoughts about and desires for. We really do see, know, and remember, and that is why it is predictively useful to describe ourselves as seeing, knowing, and remembering. It is not, as some have argued, acceptable (or true?) to talk this way merely because it is predictively useful or convenient.

Aside from this general orientation, an orientation that I presumably share with most people in cognitive science, I have a basic principle that guides my thinking about the mind. To put it crudely, this principle says that the mind must be good for something over and above what the brain is good for. It must *do* something that the brain doesn't (or can't) do. If this isn't true, I don't see what point there is in having a mind (or, if we've got one nonetheless, why there would be any interest in studying it). This is not to say that the mind has to be some sort of object working alongside the brain. No, it is merely to say that whatever set of facts it is – and, given my materialism, this set of facts must be physical facts – that makes it true to say that a person thinks and knows, sees and remembers, is a set of facts that has a role to play in the explanation of why that person behaves the way he does. If, for example, belief is a form of internal representation (and representation, in turn, is understood in some appropriate physical way), then this fact, the fact that the brain represents external affairs in a certain way, had better contribute to the explanation of why the animal in which that brain resides behaves the way it does. If the mind has a genuine place in nature, as realists like myself suppose, then it must, I am convinced, be an explanatory place.

Given this assumption, it seems entirely reasonable to suppose (as I do) that whatever may be the case with other parts of the mind (those having to do with conation, feeling, emotion, and so on), the primary function of such cognitive structures as knowledge, perception, belief, memory, reasoning, and inference is the coordination of behavior with conditions, typically external conditions, on which survival and well-being depend. If seeing and knowing, thinking and planning, reasoning and remembering do not improve performance in need- and desire-related taks, in getting one what one has to have, or wants to have, why bother?

If this is, indeed, the primary function (or at least one of the important functions) of cognition (broadly construed), then it is easy to see why cognitive systems *must* be representational systems of a rather powerful sort (just how powerful will depend, of course, on the scope and variety of the organism's needs and desires). If a physical system has no way of representing the external conditions on which its survival and well-being depend, nothing inside to indicate what is going on outside, then (aside from possible coincidences) it cannot act when, where, and how it must act in order to flourish and survive. This is why animals come equipped with internal representational mechanisms of great power. If they didn't, they wouldn't be here.

According to this way of thinking, then, what we describe ourselves as knowing, seeing, remembering, inferring, judging, believing, and concluding are the various ways we (internally) represent the world as being. Thought and belief are the basic representational modes, basic ways of "saying" how things stand elsewhere in the world. Perception is a process for acquiring, memory a process for preserving, and reasoning and inference a process for articulating and enlarging the kind of information needed to construct accurate and timely representations. When the representational processes are working right, we call the results knowledge.

Hence, the central role of representation in the cognitive dimension of our mental life. Cognition requires representation because its mission – that of coordinating behavior with external conditions – cannot be achieved without it. This being so, the mind – at least that much of it devoted to cognitive affairs – can be understood as simply the brain in its representational mode. Neuroscience studies the brain as an organ of the body, as a lump of matter having a variety of intrinsic (electrical and chemical) properties (and, of course, various relations to other internal organs). Psychology, on the other hand, studies the brain as a consumer of information about its surroundings, as a lump of matter having extrinsic relations to an environment in which action must take place. We have one physical object – the brain – with two sets of properties. The intrinsic properties (the ones studied by neurobiologists) define it as a physical organ of a certain sort. The extrinsic properties, those which (I would argue) we describe when we talk of what the organism believes and knows, what it sees and remembers, are the *relations* (primarily informational relations) this physical organ bears to the rest of the universe, the way this internal object represents the rest of the world. Just as a photograph is an ordinary physical object (possessing the usual array of intrinsic properties: mass, color, size, etc.) whose extrinsic properties make it a representation of something else, so is a thought an ordinary state of the brain (possessing the usual array of neurobiological properties) whose extrinsic properties make it a representation of, a thought about, something else in the world.

As I see it, then, the philosophical task is twofold. We must first try to say, more precisely, what representation is and how it is realized in living systems, those systems that actually perceive, think and remember (i.e. those which, in this respect, *have* a mind). This will tell us, in physical terms, what belief actually is; it will tell us how this kind of representation – cognitive representation – differs from other familiar sorts of representation (e.g. that found in gauges and instruments). I believe that an information-theoretic approach is most promising here. But the words aren't really important. One needn't use the *word* "information." One might (as I often do) speak of one condition or state of affairs "indicating" another in the same way in which tracks on the ground indicate something about the kind of animals nearby. Or one can use the more familiar idiom of causality. Whatever words are used, though, it is essential to stress the fundamental role of correlation in the business of representation. For if representation is to play its fundamental role, then representation must be understood in terms of the relations – and, specifically, the *co*rrelations – between the internal events that perform the representing and the external conditions they represent. Without this correlation (at some level and to some degree), internal structures, whatever their intrinsic character, are cognitively worthless. They cannot perform their function: the function of synchronizing output with the conditions on which the success of that output depends. A resemblance theory of representation, for instance, is totally worthless in this regard. Of what help is it to have internal pictures of predators, internal objects that *resemble* a predator, if the occurrence of these pictures is not correlated with the actual presence of a predator? For cognitive purposes what the rabbit needs in its head (directing output) is not something that resembles the fox, but something that, no matter what it looks like, *co-occurs* with the approach of a fox.

So we need an information-theoretic (or, if you will, a correlational) account of representation if we are to think of cognitive activities in representational terms. But what we need is not only an account which exhibits the informational basis of representation, but also an account that exhibits the respects and degree to which representation is something *more than* mere correlation. For if, as now being suggested, we are to think of belief as a form of internal representation, then, since (as we all know) we can have false beliefs, we need to understand how *mis*representation can occur. Beliefs, when true, when they are knowledge, are useful in directing behavior. But beliefs are not always true. We sometimes misrepresent our surroundings. So a theory of representation must allow for the fact that internal representations may not correspond with the facts, and it is not at all clear how a causal or informational account can provide for this possibility. I think the right approach to this problem is to think of representation in terms of what information an event is *supposed* to carry, what it has the function of carrying, where ontogeny (and, in some cases, phylogeny) provides the basis for the teleological element in this analysis. Some things in the brain are supposed to carry information in the same sense that something in the chest cavity, the heart, is supposed to pump blood. This, though, is a technical matter and I haven't the space for details. My own theory can be found in *Knowledge and the Flow of Information* (1981) and (in more developed form) in *Explaining Behavior* (1988).

But I said there were, basically, two philosophical tasks that confronted this approach to the relation between mind and body. Giving a satisfactory theory of representation is only one of them. That tells us what beliefs is, but not what beliefs do. The other job, equally important, at least for a realist (about the mind) like myself, is showing that the facts that underlie the representational aspect of the brain, the facts that thereby comprise the mental (at least the cognitive) life of an organism, are facts that help explain something about its behavior. If, as I earlier urged, the mind is supposed to do something the brain doesn't (or can't) do, if (in other words) it is to be of any use having a mind (in addition to a brain), then those facts (about the brain) that make it a cognitive (i.e. mental) system

– in this case facts about what the brain *represents* – must be shown to be facts that are explanatorily relevant to why the organism behaves the way it does. There is no use having a theory of representation, and showing that the brain is a representational device, if the fact that the brain represents conditions in the animal's environment doesn't help explain something about the way the animal operates in that environment.

This problem is not properly solved by merely pointing to the causal efficacy of representations. For it is clear (given my orientation) that a representation, being a physical state, has, like all physical states, physical effects. The fact that A (some representation in the head) represents B doesn't prevent A from causing C (e.g. some bodily movement). There is no reason, then, why an internal representations (a belief) shouldn't be among the causes of useful (need-satisfying) bodily movements.

But this doesn't tell us what we need to know to understand why thought makes a difference, why representations, *in virtue of being representations*, are capable of having effects on (and, therefore, figuring in the explanation of) animal behavior. One could as well try to show the causal efficacy of, say, linguistic meaning by showing that speech (sounds having linguistic meaning) have physical effects on ear drums. If one wants to show the physical influence of meaning, its explanatory relevance, what must be shown is not just that objects with meaning have effects like this, but that, in addition, the *fact* that the sounds have this meaning is relevant to their producing this effect. In the case of speech, the fact that the sounds have the meaning they have is (presumably) irrelevant to why these sounds vibrate eardrums. So the fact that the sounds have meaning is causally irrelevant to the vibration of eardrums even if the sounds that have this meaning are the cause of vibration. The situation is no different with those internal representations that we mean to identify with beliefs. To show that internal representations, *qua* representations, *qua* cognitive states, *qua* mental, are relevant to behavior, what must be shown is not just that these representations cause behavior, but that they cause the behavior they do *in virtue* of their representational (mental) properties.

That, I say, is the second major task that a materialist (who, like myself, is a realist about the mind) faces. This is the task of saying what explanatory difference mind-facts (in this case, facts about what the brain represents) make in the life of an organism. This is a task that I have undertaken in *Explaining Behavior*; there I argue that it is only in the learning situation, only in the *ontogeny* of cognitive systems, that the representational aspect of brain events, the fact that the brain represents things as thus and so, acquires a genuine relevance in the causal explanation of an animal's behavior. But that, once again, is a matter of details available elsewhere.

References

Dretske, F. (1981) *Knowledge and the Flow of Information*, Cambridge, Mass.: Bradford Books/MIT Press.
Dretske, F. (1988) *Explaining Behavior: Reasons in a World of Causes*, Cambridge, Mass.: Bradford Books/MIT Press.

11
Psychological Externalism

Joseph Owens

Psychological externalism, the thesis that psychological content is not logically independent of external factors, is a natural outgrowth of semantic externalism. On classical theories of reference, e.g. those of Frege and Russell, the reference of a word is determined by internal mental states of the speaker, by internalized concepts or descriptions. This familiar picture of reference, which was the target of Kripke's famous lectures on naming and necessity, has now been widely abandoned and replaced by a picture of reference as determined by external contextual factors (see Kripke, 1980).[1] On this new model the reference of names and natural kind terms (e.g. "tiger") is determined at least in part, by external causal and historical factors. In using a name a, for example, a speaker S refers to x in virtue of the fact that a traces back, through one speaker after another, to the individual x. It was quickly recognized that these externalist intuitions could not be confined to reference, that meaning (or sense) is also a function of contextual factors. Hilary Putnam used the following kind of thought experiment to illustrate this latter point (Putnam, 1975). Suppose an English speaker, Alf, ignorant of chemical theory, has acquired the term "aluminum" and uses it in a very ordinary way; he says, for example, such things as, "Pots are made of aluminum," "Aluminum is light," etc. Think now of another world, one very like ours, indeed just like ours except for the fact that in it a metal other than aluminum is used where we would have used aluminum. Suppose that this other metal has all the surface properties of aluminum, and, indeed, that the inhabitants of this world use the term "aluminum" when speaking of it. This, however, is just an accidental feature of their language; this other metal is not aluminum and their word "aluminum" means something other than ours. Let us, then, introduce a word, "twalum", to translate their term "aluminum." One further supposition: Alf has a physical replica on this twin-earth; call him "Alf*." Like Alf, Alf* says such things as "Pots are made of aluminum," "Aluminum is light," etc. Putnam rightly concluded that the meaning of their respective utterances are different, despite the lack of any physical difference in the twins. Meaning, like reference, is not determined by the physical states of the speaker; you can alter the meaning while leaving the physical makeup unchanged. In advancing this argument Putnam assumed that the physical identity between the twins guaranteed sameness in explanatory psychological states (at least sameness in belief).[2] This latter assumption is what I want to focus on in this essay. It is at the subject of heated debate; there are good reasons for thinking it false, and once we abandon this assumption we have, I argue, little or no choice but to give up much of the traditional Cartesian picture of the mental.[3]

Arguments to the effect that physical twins such as Alf and Alf* can differ in belief (and other intentional states) were independently made by a number of theorists at roughly the same time, most explicitly, however, by Tyler Burge, (see Burge, 1979, 1982; McGinn, 1982; Stich, 1978). There are numerous variations on these arguments but the central idea is a simple one. Though these two speakers are physically identical (they are particle for particle replicas) and utter the same words (e.g. "Aluminum is light"), *what they say (under interpretation) is different*: their respective utterances have different truth conditions. Each one is sincere, believing what he says, and so we have every reason to say that they *believe* different things. Alf believes that aluminum is light, while Alf* believes that twalum is light. Psychological content, like reference and meaning, is a function of external factors.[4] In what follows I will discuss the following: first, a few remarks on the externalist thesis and a brief look at some attempts to undermine it. Second, I will examine some of the epistemological implications of externalism. Finally, I will look at the relevance of externalism for our understanding of commonsense psychological explanation and cognitive theory.

(1)   The externalist advances a metaphysical thesis; he rejects the view that individuals who agree in internal physical states must also agree in their psychological explanatory states (states such as belief). That is, he rejects what is now known as "psychophysical supervenience."[5] This externalist rejection of psychophysical supervenience tells against many popular theories and programs; it tells against all reductionistic accounts of the mental and indeed against token-identity theories. Advocates of these threatened programs were quick to respond. Initially, many theorists tried to directly fault the argument by citing, for example, Alf's limited knowledge of aluminum. None

of these initial responses has proven very attractive. When we use a term *a* in reporting what a speaker says or thinks we don't require or presuppose that the speaker fully understands the nature of the things denoted by *a*. For example, we certainly want to allow that one may wonder whether whales are fish. Clearly, one who wonders about this lacks information that is central to the determination of the reference of the term "whale" (lacks vital information about whales), but this does *not* impede our using this term literally in characterizing what it is the subject is wondering about, in characterizing the contents of his thoughts. Alternative accounts which would bar our saying of Alf that he believes that aluminum is light because he lacks some information about aluminum would also eliminate the very possibility of wondering whether whales are fish, etc. And this is simply absurd.[6]

There is today a growing recognition that such twins do indeed merit different belief characterizations even in the absence of any corresponding internal physical difference; psychological *characterizations* apparently do not supervene on the physical. In particular, the sentence "He believes that aluminum is light" appears to be true of Alf but not his twin. Some objectors grant this much but then try to minimize its impact by denying the further claim that such twins differ in psychological *state*. There are a number of ways in which one might try to block this inference from difference in characterization to difference in state. One possibility is to simply reject the intuitive conception of the attitudes as content-individuated states. Lewis, for example, has argued that psychological expressions are best construed as abbreviating functional descriptions and as *contingently* designating the neurophysiological states that happens to satisfy the abbreviated descriptions (See Lewis, 1966, 1972).[7] On this understanding of the psychological vocabulary, the expression "Alf's belief that aluminum is light" is construed as designating a neurophysiological state, the one that happens to play the characteristic role of this belief (the causal inferential role we commonsensically suppose this belief to play). By hypothesis, Alf* also instantiates this (physiological) state, but in him it plays a slightly different role: it is casually linked to a different environmental entity. Our characterizations are sensitive to such differences in role, and hence we don't say of Alf* that he believes that aluminum is light. Lewis is ready to allow that twin-earth examples are revealing in that they expose ways in which belief ascriptions are context sensitive, but he denies the metaphysical claim that they tell against psychophysical supervenience.

This strategy, however, has not proven popular. First, the analysis itself is faced with a number of serious problems; there are good reasons for rejecting the claim that our psychological expressions abbreviate functional descriptions (see Owens, 1986). Second, and more important, the remedy being offered is more costly than the original problem: in effect this response avoids the conclusion that the twins differ in psychological states by denying that there are psychological states – states with identity conditions that are recognizably psychological in character. According to this objection, the externalist is mistaken in supposing that Alf and Alf* differ in psychological states, not because they agree in such states, but because there are no such states. This is tough medicine and few want to swallow it. A far more popular strategy has been to try to block the inference from difference in content ascription to difference in psychological state by distinguishing between different kinds of content, and in particular by distinguishing between "propositional or wide content" and "narrow or psychological content." Theorists who opt for this route allow that propositional content – ordinary content – is a function of contextual factors. This, they claim, explains why it is we get to say different things about the twins. But this content, they argue, should be sharply distinguished from "narrow content," which is internal to the subject and logically independent of all contextual factors. It is this narrow content that is relevant to the individuation of psychological states, and since the twins don't differ in narrow content, they don't difer in phychological states. So, even though the twins satisfy different psychological characterizations, they don't differ in psychological state. Psychophysical supervenience is saved, externalism rejected, and all of this without the radical medicine prescribed by Lewis-style theorists, without abandoning the link between the attitudes and content.[8] This kind of response was popular for a number of years, but is now in decline (see Owens, 1987, 1990). The plausibility of the response clearly turns on the question as to whether or not there are independent reasons for thinking that there is such a thing as narrow content, genuine content that supervenes on the physical. Various efforts have been made to articulate such a notion of content, and all have proven unsatisfactory. Motivated by the fact that things must "seem" the same to each of the twins, some have appealed to "phenomenological content." Fodor, for example, has suggested that the apparent psychological differences between Alf and Alf* can be put aside once we recognize that in characterizing the real content of Alf's belief (and likewise for Alf*) we should talk about him not as believing that "aluminum is light" but as believing something like "the stuff around here that we use in the manufacture of pots, pans, etc. is light" (see Fodor, 1982). Viewed from this perspective, there are simply no differences in content between the corresponding states of Alf and Alf*. The problem with this proposal is that it amounts to a simple, undefended rejection of the externalists' intuitive claim that one can really believe that aluminum is such and such in the absence of complete information about the nature of aluminum. Of course, one who has this "aluminum" belief has other "phenomenological" beliefs, but these are different beliefs. The externalists' argument is that this specific "aluminum" belief does not supervene and one cannot avoid this challenge by talking about other beliefs unless one offers independent reason for thinking that one cannot have the problematic "aluminum" beliefs.

Others have suggested that the problem posed by the twins is analogous to that posed by indexicals; the twins' utterances of "aluminum is light" differ and agree in content in much the same way as different utterances of "I am ill" differ and agree in content. Given appropriate contextual differences, these indexical utterances clearly serve to express different propositions, but there is also a sense in which they can be said to agree in meaning. (In the familiar terminology of Kaplan, they agree in "character.") Likewise with the twins; the different mental and verbal tokenings of "aluminum is light" agree in meaning, but given the contextual differences they also serve to express different propositions (see, e.g., Perry, 1979). Once again, there is simply no argument here. The fact that it is useful to distinguish between two notions of "content" in developing a semantics for sentences containing indexical elements provides no support for the thought that this distinction may be applied across the board, to sentences which apparently lack indexical elements. This distinction, after all, was meant to capture one of the distinctive features of sentences containing indexicals, and *the intuitive semantic considerations that motivated distinguishing between propositional and nonpropositional content in indexical sentences provide no support for introducing a notion of nonpropositional content that is constant across twin worlds* (for details see Owens, 1989, 1990).

These and other efforts to provide for a notion of psychological content that is invariant across these different contexts have failed. The mere fact that there are striking similarities between the twins give us no reason to think that they agree in *content* of any kind. So far as I can tell the attraction of narrow content is due solely to the fact that such content would save internalism. Externalism, it seems, is here to stay.

(2) Though externalism is primarily a metaphysical thesis it has some striking, if controversial, epistemological implications. Some have argued that extenalism provides us with a decisive response to

traditional skeptical concerns, while others have argued to the contrary, that externalism serves to extend the scope of skepticism.[9] Now
it is true that skeptical concerns about our claims to know the external
world are traditionally advanced in ways that presuppose internalism.
Descartes, for example, presupposed that we could have the beliefs
we have in the absence of an external world, or in the presence of one
which is very different than we commonly suppose. The Cartesian
assumes that one could, for example, have the belief that aluminum
is light even in a world devoid of aluminum or anything of that sort.
If externalists are correct, this presupposition is mistaken; one can
have this kind of belief only if one inhabits a world in which one has
some kind of link (perhaps tenuous) to aluminum. The question
arises then as to whether externalism provides a direct and simple
answer to skepticism. The quick answer is that it does not; it simply
requires one to be more cautious in formulating the skeptical position.
The externalist grants that a subject's stream of consciousness, his
experiential life, might be just as it is even if the external world were
very different than it is, and this is all it takes to generate skeptical
worries. This, however, is but the short answer; it does not address
the fact that *externalism seems to provide one with a new and powerful
argument against the skeptic.* If it is true, as the externalist claims, that
our thoughts have the content they have only if the external world is
of a certain kind, then it may seem that our introspective knowledge
of our thoughts *should* afford knowledge of this same external world.
If I know that I believe that aluminum is light and I know that
externalism is true, then surely I am in a position to infer that my
world is of a certain kind? This seems to be all I need to know that
I am not a denizen of twin-earth, that I am not a brain in a vat,
that my experience is not merely the product of Descartes's demons.[10]
This contemporary transcendental argument is problematic for the
externalist in that it suggests that he must either a reject the premise,
denying that we are in a position to know the contents of our
own occurrent thoughts, or he must accept the conclusion and
dismiss traditional skeptical concerns as the product of a mistaken
view of mental content. Neither option is attractive. We appear to
have direct and authoritative knowledge of our own occurrent beliefs,
and traditional concerns about the reliability of claims to know
the external world seem to be independent of specific theories of
mental content. In section (a) I examine the linkage between externalism and self-knowledge, and then in (b) I return to the issues of
skepticism.

(a)   A number or authors have argued that externalism tells against
first-person knowledge of occurrent beliefs. The essential intuition is

a simple one: since the content of one's beliefs is a function of the way the world is, and since a subject does not have any special access to this external world, it follows that a subject has no special access to the contents of his occurrent beliefs. There is undoubtedly a certain attractiveness to this intuition, but it is mistaken. Externalism is perfectly compatible with self-knowledge, with the kind of knowledge we intuitively suppose ourselves to have of our own mental states. Externalism would threaten genuine self-knowledge if the dependency of mental content on external factors made for a new source of error by somehow undermining the ability of a subject to recognize the contents of her own mental states. It would undermine self-knowledge *if it somehow provided us new grounds for doubting the accuracy of sincere, first-person attitude reports.* Externalism, however, provides no such grounds. The original intuition that seemed to undermine first-person authority can be fleshed out in the following way. Suppose I think "aluminum is light" and I then make the second-order judgment that I am now entertaining the thought that aluminum is light. If, unbeknownst to me, my world is of the twin-earth kind, then this judgment is mistaken. Since more than mere rational introspection is necessary to rule out the possibility that I am in a twin-earth context, more than introspection is needed to eliminate this kind of error. Hence, I cannot be said to introspectively *know* the contents of my own mind. This argument rests on a crucial misreading of the externalists' picture. True, the contents of one's beliefs are in part a function of external factors, but this does not provide for a new source of error; these same factors ensure a match between our beliefs and our introspective awareness of what we believe. In fashioning and reporting our second-order beliefs, beliefs about our own beliefs, we employ the concepts or vocabulary used in the first-order beliefs and this ensures a matching. Those features of the external world that play a role in determining the content of a first-order belief (e.g. the belief that aluminum is light) play a parallel role in determining the contents of the corresponding second-order belief (e.g. the belief that I believe that aluminum is light). Alf believes that aluminum is light and he believes that he believes that aluminum is light. His twin, Alf*, believes something else, and he believes that he believes something else. All of this despite the fact that these differences don't show up in any experiential fashion. Externalism is fully compatible with the intuitive conception of ourselves as having authoritative knowledge of of our own attitudes.[11] But if this is so, where does it leave the skeptic? Why not dismiss skepticism as simply the product of a mistaken, internalist conception of mind and mental content?

(b) To see that externalism does not provide for this easy dismissal of skepticism, we need to distinguish between two different kinds of introspective capacities: first, the capacity of a subject to recognize the contents of her explicit thoughts, and second, the capacity of a subject to introspectively determine sameness and difference in her beliefs. It is intuitive to suppose that a rational subject has the first kind of capacity, and we have just argued that externalism does not tell against this conception of rational introspection. So far as the second capacity goes, we find in the literature little or no explicit discussion of how subjects are supposed to determine sameness and difference in mental content, but it is quite clear that rational introspection was implicitly assigned the task. This, for example, is what lies behind the long-standing intuition that a fully rational subject would never subscribe to explicit contradiction, would never believe both *P* and not-*P*.[12] There seems to be no doubt but that externalism *does* tell against this element in the traditional picture. Alf would have a different belief were he on twin-earth but this difference is not one that reveals itself to introspective awareness. Rational introspection alone won't enable him determine whether the belief that aluminum is light is the same or different from the belief that twalum is light. To make *this* determination he needs crucial empirical information; he needs to know whether the stuff he calls "aluminum" is the same as the stuff we have been calling "twalum." He needs to know whether he is an inhabitant of earth or twin-earth. *Externalism is incompatible with the intuition that one can always determine sameness and difference in one's own thoughts by mere rational introspection.*

But this does not tell against externalism. There is simply no reason to think that we have this kind of introspective access. Consider the following simple example. Rudolf, we assume, is proficient in the use of the terms "coriander" and "cilantro." He is familiar with cilantro as the parsley-like herb characteristic of Mexican cuisine. His acquaintance with coriander, however, is limited to dried and ground coriander. He is partial to both and indeed recalls himself as entertaining the thought(s), "I relish the flavor of cilantro" and "I relish the flavor of coriander." Informed that "cilantro" and "coriander" are synonyms, Rudolf asks himself: "Did I or did I not entertain the same belief on these two occasions?" How is Rudolf to answer this question?

Externalism aside, there is every reason to think that in answering this question, Rudolf should give some weight to the issue of whether or not the terms employed actually are synonyms; this, after all, is what prompted the questions in the first place. Likewise, we want Rudolf to take some account of the fact that his knowledge of the relevant terms, and their linkage in the language, is less than perfect. But to suppose this much is to suppose that when a subject employs linguistic items (e.g. "coriander") in fashioning his thoughts, then the character of these items, the objective relations they bear to each other, and his knowledge of all of this, *is* relevant when it comes to determining whether or not the thought he entertains now is the same or different from the one he entertained then. But this kind of information is not derived from introspection. More generally, in determining whether the token thoughts are the same or different, it seems entirely reasonable to suppose that Rudolf should take into consideration whatever relevant theory there is, be it linguistic, psychological, or philosophical. Once again, this kind of information, however, is not acquired by introspective examination; it is acquired from dictionaries, native speakers, linguists, philosophers, and psychologists.

Complex beliefs provide a different and even more dramatic illustration of the limitations of introspection. Consider the following variation on a well-known puzzle.[13]

1 Nobody doubts that whoever believes that Mary is a physician believes that Mary is a physician.

2 Nobody doubts that whoever believes that Mary is a doctor believes that Mary is a physician.

Each of us is proficient in English, we are familiar with the terms employed in (1) and (2); accordingly, there is no reason to suppose that either one of us fails to understand what is meant by these sentences, and there is no good reason to suppose that we don't know the thoughts we express using these same sentences. But now ask yourself the following question: Do I or do I not entertain the same thought when I entertain thought (1) and when I entertain (2)? I know what I think when I entertain (1) and I know what I think when I entertain (2), and so do you. But if you are at all like me, you do not know the answer to this last question. You do not know whether you expressed the same thought by (1) and (2). This kind of example raises all kinds of interesting issues, but one thing does seem to be clear: introspection is of little or no use in answering this question. One has no choice but to turn to theory, to linguistics, psychology, and philosophy.[14]

If these simple but intuitive considerations are at all reliable, then our capacity to determine sameness and difference in belief *is* contingent on external information. Externalism does have *some* bearing on self-knowledge: it does not undermine genuine self-knowledge but it does highlight its nature and scope. Rational introspection may enable one to determine *what* one believes, but it does not enable one to determine sameness and difference in one's own thoughts; empirical information about one's context may be needed for this. This result is extremely important: it casts doubt on the traditional conception of the rational subject as one who would never subscribe to explicit contradiction, and it thereby serves to resolve a number of important semantic puzzles, e.g. Kripke's puzzle about belief (see Kripke, 1979; Owens, 1989). More important, it exposes the fallacy in the problematic argument that self-knowledge combined with externalism provides one with an easy refutation of skepticism. The details are complex and delicate, but the central idea is fairly clear.[15] The central issue is this: Can I use externalist intuitions and the knowledge I have of my occurrent beliefs to infer that the external world must be of a certain kind, to infer that I am not on twin-earth, to infer that I am not a brain in a vat, and so on? As an externalist, I know that the contents of my thoughts are in part determined by external factors, and that they would be different if I were in a different environment. Furthermore, I know that I am now thinking the thought that aluminum is light. Why can't I use this information to infer that I am an inhabitant of earth rather than twin-earth or to infer that I am not a brain in a vat? I can't draw this inference for the simple reason that even though I introspectively know that I am entertaining the thought that aluminum is light, I do not introspectively know that I am not entertaining the thought that twalum is light. This follows only if these are different beliefs; and I cannot determine whether or not they are different without appealing to the contexts in which the beliefs are tokened. The belief I entertain when I internally token "aluminum is light" is the belief that twalum is light, if my context is that of twin-earth; it is a different belief if my context is the more familiar earth. As a skeptic, I cannot avail myself of this kind of information, and hence I can't rule out the possibility that my "aluminum" thought is really a twalum thought; hence I can't rule out the possibility that I am a denizen of twin-earth or a brain in a vat. In conclusion, the externalist can admit that we know that we believe that aluminum is such and such, and that we could not have the beliefs we have unless the world is a certain way. But we can not use this against the skeptic, for the simple reason that even though we introspectively know that we believe that aluminum is such and such, we don't in like fashion – i.e. independent of investigation of our world – know that this belief is different from the twalum belief. We do not have to examine our worlds to know the contents of our thoughts, but this same introspective knowledge is "thin"; it does not enable us to say whether or not our "aluminum" thoughts are the same as "twalum" thoughts. To conclude this discussion of the epistemological consequences: externalism can't be used to extend the scope of skepticism to the contents of our minds, nor can it be used to summarily dismiss traditional skeptical concerns about claims to know the external world.

(3) The nature of psychological explanation has been a subject of controversy for most of this century, but today the received view is that ordinary psychological explanation, explanation in terms of beliefs and other mental states, is causal in character.[16] This causal construal of psychological explanation is cast into doubt by externalist models of the mental. The reason is simple: Alf and Alf* are physical doppelgangers. From the physical perspective they are as alike as two identical metal spheres, and there is no more reason to distinguish between their causal powers than there is to distinguish between the causal powers of the metal spheres. Though Alf and Alf* don't differ in causal powers, they do differ in psychological states and these different states are such as to *explain* different kinds of behaviors. Alf's token belief that aluminum is light is explanatorily linked to his saying that aluminum is light, while Alf*'s belief that twalum is light is explanatorily linked to a different action (intentionally characterized). This difference in explanatory linkage cannot be cashed out in terms of the two tokens being such as to *cause* different actions (in terms of some difference in causal powers). It is this that tells against the causal interpretation of psychological explanation.[17]

Though there is no reason to think that such twins differ in causal powers, the examples could have been constructed in such a way as to clearly illustrate differences in causal powers, i.e. they could have been constructed in a way that linked differences in psychological state to differences in causal powers. And it is informative to see exactly why they were not constructed in this way; it gives us another perspective on the difficulty of retaining the causal thesis once one has abandoned internalism and it helps reinforce the intuition that the twins don't differ in causal powers. In the familiar examples, twins such as Alf and Alf* *never* differ physically; indeed the whole point of such examples is that they come to differ psychologically in the absence of any physical difference. But consider now a "strengthened" twin example: Bart and Bart* are twins from their inception at t_1 to some later time t_n. They are physically identical throughout this period, though by t_n they have come to differ psychologically, and they have come to have different beliefs. Since we want this example to illustrate how such differences in belief make for differences in *causal* powers, let us now suppose that they start to exhibit different behaviors at t_{n+1}. At t_{n+1} the individuals diverge, not only under intentional characterization, but physically: they produce different sounds, different bodily motions, and so on. These physical differences are not the result of any earlier physical differences in composition or input, since, by hypothesis, they are physically identical over the period $t_1 - t_n$. At t_n they have come to differ in belief, and this difference, since it entails a difference in causal powers, is wholly responsible for their different physical behaviors at t_{n+1}. This example differs from the original twin-earth examples in taking the causal thesis seriously; here there is no need to speak of the subjects as coming to exhibit different behaviors only under this or that special characterization; they simply come to diverge, and they continue to diverge. (This, of course, is not to deny that there won't be descriptions under which they don't differ; there will always be such.)

Now the original examples don't take this form, and with good reason. It is a familiar thought that, quantum indeterminacies aside, the ongoing physical states and behavior of an organism are fully determined by earlier physical states (inputs, etc.), and since Bart and Bart* have the same physical history from t_1 through t_n it is implausible to suppose that they can physically diverge at t_{n+1} (in the absence of any difference in physical input, etc.). This kind of physical determinism is, of course, not without ambiguity and is not subscribed to by everyone.[18] Nevertheless, determin-istic intuitions are widely held, and they are certainly not challenged by twin-earth examples. These are explicitly designed to satisfy deterministic constraints, and I shall assume here that determinism is not at issue.

But what then of phychological causation? What kind of genuine causality is left for the psychological if the ongoing physical life and activities of an organism are fully determined by its earlier physical states? There has always been an element of tension between the causal thesis and this intuitive brand of physical determinism. Malcolm, for example, argues that one can't have both the causal thesis and a complete physical (e.g. neurophysiological) explanation of each bodily movement.

> Let us remember that the postulated neurophysiological theory is compre-hensive. It is assumed to provide complete causal explanations for all bodily movements that are not produced by external physical forces ... If the neurophysiological theory were true, then in no cases would desires, intentions, purposes be necessary conditions of any human movements ... Purposive explanations of human bodily movements would *never* be true. Desires and intentions would not be even potential causes of human movements in the actual world. (Malcolm, 1968, p. 56)

When pressed to respond, to explain why the physical determination of a subject's ongoing life and activities doesn't negate the causal efficacy of the psychological, the defender of the causal thesis had one convenient fallback: it is true that Bart and Bart* cannot diverge physically at t_{n+1}, given that they are physically identical from t_1 through t_n, but this does not undermine the causal thesis for the simple reason that the physical identity of Bart and Bart* from t_1 to t_n also ensures their psychological identity over this time. Since they can't differ in psychological states, there is no reason to suppose that the causal activity of the psychological should make for the possibility of different physical behaviors at t_{n+1}. I think it fair to say that traditional defenders of the causal thesis understood the thesis as entailing that different psychological states could cause different physical behaviors, and they reconciled this with physical determinism by assuming in one way or another (e.g. by opting for some kind of identity theory) that the physical determines the psychological; this effectively blocks the problem cases (cases in which there is psychological but no physical difference). So Kim, for example, writes,

> If a mental event M has a simultaneous physiological equivalent, it becomes a dangling cause, dangling from its physical correlate, and its causal role is threatened . . . there is an irresistible push towards accepting the physical correlate as the *real substantive* cause of whatever the mental event is initially thought to cause. The causal potency of the mental is in need of vindication . . . It is now clear that the identity solution is extremely appealing – in fact all but compelling – as a response to these problems. If we say that pain is identical with its neural correlate, there would be no problem of accounting for the causal role of pain independently of the correlated neural processes. (Kim, 1979, pp. 36–40)

Like others, such as Davidson, Kim sees the identity theory as *one* way of safeguarding the causal efficacy of the psychological in the face of physical determinism. It is worth noting that he himself does not opt for this response; he attempts to reconcile the causal thesis with physical determinism by appealing directly to psychophysical supervenience.

All of this is very familiar, but the point of interest here is that this strategy is simply not available to us once we have abandoned internalism. Indeed, it is entirely unclear as to how one is supposed to reconcile physical determinism and the causal thesis *once one has abandoned supervenience*. If physically identical individuals can differ psychologically, then such psychological differences should, on the causal model, provide for the possibility of differences in physical output (contrary to the thesis of physical determinism), and attempts to emasculate this causal efficacy, construing the behavioral differences as appearing only under intentional description, seem to reduce it to a shadowy nothing. Certainly this kind of causal efficacy is not going to satisfy those who want the psychological to make for a real difference in this world; they are not likely to be happy with the suggestion that this anemic difference between Alf and Alf* is indicative of the causal contribution of the psychological.

Externalism seriously threatens the causal interpretation of commonsense psychology and this in turn threatens the foundations of cognitive science, the theoretical analogue of commonsense psychology. The commonsense theory provides cognitive theory with its distinctive taxonomy and agenda. It gives us that fundamental distinction between actions, which stand in need of psychological explanation, and mere happenings which don't, and it provides us with the initial inventory of those intellectual capacities which likewise call out for psychological explanation. In addition, this folk or commonsense theory provides cognitive theory with its *explanatory paradigm*: intentional explanation or explanation by appeal to representational states.[19] The cognitive theorist attempts to analyze and explain our complex intellectual capacities as resulting from the interplay of information-bearing states; she attempts to extend the analysis, however, to deeper levels, providing explanations for many of the capacities that folk theory takes to be primitive. (e.g. the capacity to compute the "meanings" of complex expressions from the "meanings" of the constituent expressions), postulating, when necessary, new theoretical representational structures and sub-capacities (e.g. representations of underlying "deep structures"). And, in proposing intentional explanations of this sort, the cognitive theorist thinks of herself as proposing causal explanations.[20] The behaviors are supposed to causally result from the interaction of the various representational states. The attraction of this model – the very idea that it is possible to causally explain behavior by citing content-individuated states – is largely due to the presumption that this is a familiar and acceptable form of explanation, familiar from commonsense psychology. If commonsense psychology is noncausal in character, then we lose the only model we have for contemporary cognitive theory.

To summarize: externalism is probably here to stay, and this metaphysical thesis not only undermines various reductionistic programs, it also casts into doubt some central elements in the contemporary model of the mental; it casts into doubt entrenched intuitions about the individuation of mental states, our access to them, and the role they play in psychological explanation.

Notes

1 Kripke has often been criticized for downplaying important differences between Russell and Frege, for imposing too much of the Russellian descriptional view on Frege (who has so little to say about proper names beyond the one unfortunate footnote). However, even though Kripke does tend to underestimate the differences between Russell and Frege, he is justified in treating them

uniformly insofar as they both conceive of singular reference as being deter-mined by something in the speaker's head; on classical models it is this speaker's contribution that dictates the reference of the name, rather than its public use or history (the issue as to whether this mental thing is strictly descriptional or not is secondary). This is the picture Kripke rejects, urging, in its place, a conception of naming in which reference is determined by external factors. While I think it correct to interpret both Frege and Russell in this internalist fashion (an internalism, however, which is at odds with Frege's general theoretic apparatus), it is not correct to include Wittgenstein. True, in discussing what is meant by the name "Moses" he writes as though he were indorsing a "cluster theory" of names (*Philosophical Investigations*, § 79). But this should be balanced by the fact that his goal in this passage is largely negative, rejecting the idea that there must be something in common (e.g. one specific description) behind each use of the name. More important, he repeatedly attacks those who think of reference as being determined by some-thing in the speaker's head, something lying behind and giving life and meaning to otherwise meaningless sounds. The following passage from the *Blue Book* is just one of many in which he strikes this theme:

Someone says "Mr. N. will come to see me this afternoon"; I ask "Do you mean him?" pointing to someone present, and he answers "Yes." In this conversation a connection was established between the word "Mr. N." and Mr. N. But we are tempted to think that while my friend said, "Mr. N. will come to see me", and meant what he said, his mind must have made the connection. (Wittgenstein, 1958, p. 39)

This is a clear rejection of internalist intuitions, those very intuitions that played a large role in motivating descriptional theories of names. The reference is established by the earlier contextual act of pointing, not by something in the speaker's head at the time of speaking.

2 Strictly speaking such twins are not physically identical, since they occupy different environments and hence satisfy different relational characterizations. They are, however, particle for particle replicas, and the differences between their worlds can be quite remote and need not impinge on them in any interesting physical fashion; these differences need not, for example, provide for any compositional differences in the twins or in their proximate environ-ments. Following established practice, I will speak of such twins as not differing in their "internal physical states."

3 In a number of cases, I merely sketch the outlines of an argument. Details are available in the various works cited.

4 Burge offered two different arguments for the externalist thesis. One argument, like the one sketched in the main text, looks to twins ensconced in physically different environments and sees the difference in content as reflecting this dif-ference in context (Burge, 1982). The other argument, however, is one to the effect that a difference in content can arise even when there is no comparable difference in *physical* environment; all we need suppose is that they are members of linguistic communities that differ in appropriate ways (Burge, 1979).

5 See Kim (1978, 1979, 1982, 1984) for some general discussions of supervenience and of psychophysical supervenience in particular.

6 For amplification see Burge, 1979. The central intuition is this: an individual may use a concept *C* with an incomplete or erroneous view of the extension of the concept, and in such cases we don't routinely reinterpret this individual's usage so as to understand him as employing a different concept, *B*, one that accords with the extension he mistakenly assigns to the original concept.

7 In characterizing this response as a "Lewis-style response," I simply mean that it is line with the analysis Lewis defends in these early papers. I do not mean to suggest that Lewis has endorsed this line of response to externalist examples. He has not.

8 For variations on this approach see Block (1986); Fodor (1987); Loar (1988); McGinn (1982).

9 In a series of influential articles and books Putnam argues that externalism provides us with a new and powerful "transcendental argument" against skepticism. See especially Putnam (1981). The negative thesis, that externalism undermines self-knowledge, has been argued by Brueckner (1986); Woodfield (1982); and others.

10 The thought that I might be a brain in a vat, electronically stimulated to have the experiences I have, is Putnam's contemporary version of the familiar Cartesian thought that our experiences might be the product of demonic manipulation.

11 For a discussion of these issues, see Burge (1988); Davidson, (1963); Owens (1992); Falvey and Owens (forthcoming).

12 The supposition that we have introspective access to sameness and difference in content also plays an important role in many Fregean arguments against interchanging codesignative proper names in intentional contexts. However, one should not suppose that abandoning this kind of introspective access legitimizes such interchange. For discussion, see Owens (1990).

13 This, of course, is a version of Mates's puzzle. See Mates (1950).

14 For detailed arguments against the traditional picture of introspective access, see Owens (1989, 1990).

15 For some of the details and the complexities, see Falvey and Owens (forthcoming).

16 This causal construal of psychological explanation is a powerful testimony to the influence of Davidson's (1963) "Actions, reasons, and causes." 1943.

17 Some theorists, e.g. Burge (1989) and Van Gulick (1988), have argued that such physically identical twins differ in causal powers. See Owens (1993) for a discussion of these arguments.

18 See Earman (1986) for a critical discussion.

19 My concern is with "classical" cognitive science, with those theoretical approaches which seek to explain by postulating symbolic, representational structures. One may construe alternative theoretical approaches, e.g. connectionist approaches, as abandoning any such appeal to representational states. Such accounts are not touched by the arguments of this paper, though they face difficult problems of their own.

20 The commitment to intentional/representational explanation is central in the work of theorists such as Marr and Chomsky. Here, for example, is how Marr characterizes the task of the vision theorist:

> Our overall goal is to understand vision completely, that is, to understand how descriptions of the world may efficiently and reliably be obtained from images of it. The human system is a working example of a machine that can make such descriptions, and as we have seen one of our aims is to understand it thoroughly at all levels. What kind of information does the human system represent, what kinds of computations does it perform to obtain this information, and why? How does it represent this information, and how are the computations performed and with what algorithms? (Marr, 1982, p. 99)

In addition these parallels between folk psychology and cognitive psychology have been explicitly emphasized by many, most persuasively by Jerry Fodor and Zenon Pylyshyn. Pylyshyn, for example writes,

> Although the need to use a special class of terms (especially terms that refer to semantic content) may surprise some, the situation here [in cognitive theory] is no different from the one we have already encountered [in folk psychological explanation]. The principle that leads us to postulate representational states (individuated by their content) that are distinct from functional states is exactly the same as the principle that leads us to functional states that are distinct from physical states. In both cases we want to capture certain generalizations. (Pylyshyn, 1985, p. 32)

Fodor is perhaps the most impassioned and articulate defender of representationalism in both folk and theoretical psychology. This is a constant theme in his writings, but see especially Fodor (1981a, 1981b, 1987).
In most contemporary discussions, the causal interpretation of both folk and theoretical psychology is just assumed. But for some defense, see Fodor (1981a, 1987).

References

Block, N. (1986) "Advertisement for a semantics for psychology," in *Midwest Studies in Philosophy*, vol. 10, pp. 615–78.

Brueckner, A. (1986) "Brains in a vat," *Journal of Philosophy* 83, pp. 148–67.

Burge, T. (1979) "Individualism and the mental," in *Midwest Studies in Philosophy*, vol. 4, pp. 73–121.

Burge, T. (1982) "Other bodies," in A. Woodfield (ed.) *Thought and Object: Essays on Intentionality*, Oxford: Clarendon Press, pp. 97–120.

Burge, T. (1988) "Individualism and self- knowledge," *Journal of Philosophy* 85, pp. 649–63.

Burge, T. (1989) "Individuation and causation in philosophy," *Pacific Philosophical Quarterly* 70, pp. 303–22.

Davidson, D. (1963) "Actions, reason, and causes," *Journal of Philosophy* 60, pp. 685–700.

Davidson, D. (1987) "Knowing one's own mind," *Proceedings and Addresses of the American Philosophical Association* 60, pp. 441–58.

Earman, J. (1986) *A Primer on Determinism*, Dordrecht: Reidel.

Falvey, K. and Owens, J. (forthcoming) "Psychological externalism, self-knowledge, and skepticism."

Fodor, J. (1981a) "Propositional attitudes," in *Representations: Philosophical Essays on the Foundations of Cognitive Science*, Cambridge, Mass.: MIT Press, pp. 177–203.

Fodor, J. (1981b) "Three cheers for propositional attitudes," in *Representations: Philosophical Essays on the Foundations of Cognitive Science*, Cambridge, Mass.: MIT Press, pp. 100–23.

Fodor, J. (1982) "Cognitive science and the Twin-Earth problem," *Notre Dame Journal of Formal Logic* 23, pp. 98–118.

Fodor, J. (1987) *Psychosemantics: the Problem of Meaning in the Philosophy of Mind*, Cambridge, Mass.: MIT Press.

Kim, J. (1978) "Supervenience and nomological incommensurables," *American Philosophical Quarterly* 15, pp. 149–56.

Kim, J. (1979) "Causality, identity and supervenience in the mind – body problem," in *Midwest Studies in Philosophy*, vol. 4, pp. 31–49.

Kim, J. (1982) "Psychophysical supervenience," *Philosophical Studies* 41, pp. 51–70.

Kim, J. (1984) "Concepts of supervenience," *Philosophy and Phenomenological Research* 45, pp. 153–76.

Kripke, S. (1979) "A puzzle about belief," in A. Margalit (ed.) *Meaning and Use*, Dordrecht: Reidel, pp. 239–83.

Kripke, S. (1980) *Naming and Necessity*, Oxford: Blackwell.

Lewis, D. (1966) "An argument for the identity theory," *Journal of Philosophy* 63, pp. 17–25.

Lewis, D. (1972) "Psychophysical and theoretical identifications," *Australiasian Journal of Philosophy* 50, pp. 249–58.

Loar, B. (1988) "Social content and psychological content," in R. H. Grimm and D. D. Merrill (eds) *Contents of Thought*, Tucson, Ariz.: University of Arizona Press, pp. 99–139.

Malcolm, N. (1968) "The conceivability of mechanism," *Philosophical Review* 77, pp. 45–72.

Marr, D. (1982) *Vision: a Computational Investigation into the Human Representation and Processing of Visual Information*, San Francisco: W. H. Freeman.

Mates, B. (1950) "Synonymity," *University of California Publications in Philosophy* 25.

McGinn, C. (1977) "Charity interpretation and belief," *Journal of Philosophy* 74, pp. 521–35.

McGinn, C. (1982) "The structure of content," in A. Woodfield (ed.) *Thought and Object: Essays on Intentionality*, Oxford: Clarendon Press, pp. 207–58.

Owens, J. (1986) "The failure of Lewis's functionalism," *Philosophical Quarterly* 36, pp. 159–73.

Owens, J. (1987) "In defense of a different doppelganger," *Philosophical Review* 96, pp. 521–54.

Owens, J. (1989) "Contradictory belief and cognitive access," in *Midwest Studies in Philosophy*, vol. 14, pp. 289–316.

Owens, J. (1990) "Cognitive access and semantic puzzles," in C. A. Anderson and J. Owens (eds) *Propositional Attitudes: the Role of Content in Logic, Language, and Mind*, Stanford, Calif.: CSLI Press, pp. 147–73.

Owens, J. (1992) "Psychophysical supervenience: its epistemological foundation," *Synthese* 90, pp. 89–117.

Owens, J. (forthcoming) "Content, causation, and psychophysical supervenience," *Philosophy of Science*.

Perry, J. (1979) "The problem of the essential indexicals," *Noûs* 13, pp. 3–21.

Putnam, H. (1975) "The meaning of 'meaning,' " in K. Gunderson (ed.) *Language, Mind, and Knowledge*, Minneapolis, Minn.: University of Minnesota Press, pp. 131–93.

Putnam, H. (1981) *Reason, Truth and History*, Cambridge: Cambridge University Press.

Pylyshyn, Z. (1985) *Computation and Cognition: Toward a Foundation for Cognitive Science*, Cambridge, Mass.: Bradford Books/MIT Press.

Stich, S. (1978) "Autonomous psychology and the belief-desire thesis," *The Monist* 61, pp. 573–91.

Van Gulick, R. (1988) "Metaphysical arguments for internalism and why they don't work," in S. Silvers (ed.) *Re-representations: Readings in the Philosophy of Mental Representation*, Dordrecht: Reidel.

Wittgenstein, L. (1958) *The Blue and Brown Books*, Oxford: Blackwell.

Woodfield, A. (1982) *Thought and Object: Essays on Intentionality*, Oxford: Clarendon Press.

12
Minds and Bodies

John Heil

1 Mental Causation

Among English-speaking philosophers, it is widely supposed that the
mind–body problem is no longer a problem. Dualism has lost its appeal,
and traditional objections to materialist construals of mind no longer carry
conviction. This is not to say that the philosophical community has
embraced some single, definitive account of mind. Even so, most philosophers today seem to assume at least that mental predicates apply to
conscious beings in virtue of the physical constitution of those beings. The
relationship may be indirect: an agent may be in a particular mental state
because his brain is in a particular *functional* state, for instance. But then
the functional state is thought itself to be *realized* by the brain state.

If this is so, then the mind–body problem appears to vanish. How
mental items might interact with physical items ceases to puzzle once one
accepts the view that mental items are realized by physical systems.
Compare being a painful sensation with being liquid. A substance is liquid
in virtue of its molecular structure, perhaps; that structure *realizes*
liquidity. Similarly, I might experience a painful sensation *in virtue of*
being in a certain neural condition; the condition realizes my sensation. In
neither case is there an embarrassing gap between a thing's possessing one
sort of property (being liquid, being a painful sensation) and its possessing
another sort of property (having a particular kind of molecular structure,
being a particular sort of neural condition). Now, if we suppose that neural
conditions unproblematically enter into causal relations, there seems no

reason to doubt that mental items – at least in their physical guises – figure in perfectly ordinary causal relations.

Difficulties remain, however. Consider, again, a substance's being liquid. We are imagining that its being liquid depends on its possessing a certain sort of molecular structure. Suppose now that we observe that the substance behaves in a certain way, it pours, for instance, and takes the shape of its container. Informally we might explain these characteristics by reference to the substance's liquidity: it pours and conforms to its container *because it is liquid*. But is this quite right? The substance's behavior under these circumstances is, as we know, explicable by reference to its molecular structure. Its being liquid adds nothing to the picture. Certainly its being liquid does not endow the substance with causal powers over and above those it possesses owing to its possession of a particular molecular structure. An exactly parallel point could be made about my painful sensation. If there is a causal story to be told in that case, it must, it would seem, refer exclusively to my neural condition. That this neural condition realizes my painful sensation seems not to matter to its causal character.

It should be noted that, if this were *not* so, if "higher-level" characteristics like being liquid and being a painful sensation *added* causal powers to objects over and above the powers those objects possessed in virtue of their "lower-level" character, we should have an apparent violation of the closedness of the physical domain. Something like this, perhaps, is what "emergentists" (Lloyd Morgan and C. D. Broad, for instance) regarded as an inevitable if inexplicable feature of a complex world (see, e.g. Broad, 1951 ch. 21 and Morgan, 1923). Nowadays emergentism strikes many philosophers as far-fetched.[1] It seems to require an abandonment of physicalism, the doctrine that basic physics provides an exhaustive account of the causal structure of the world. In any case, it would be risky to hang a defense of mental causation on the acceptance of emergence. To do so, rather than addressing a puzzle, simply replaces one puzzle with another.

Perhaps, then, the difficulty could be resolved by supposing that the relation between liquidity and certain sorts of molecular structure, or painful sensations and certain sorts of neural condition, is one of identity: being liquid just *is* to possess a particular molecular structure; being in pain *is* to be in a particular neural condition. This approach, property- or type-identity, apparently runs afoul of two much-discussed difficulties. First, the higher-level properties in question seem capable of *multiple realization*. Liquidity can be realized by a variety of distinct sorts of molecular structure; and there is ample neurobiological evidence to suggest that the same may be so for painful sensations. By itself, this point establishes little. One could preserve type-identity by allowing that the lower-level property is a complex one, a property constructed, so to speak, from a disjunction of simple lower-level properties. The disjunction might prove infinite, but that, in itself, need not threaten its legitimacy.[2]

A much more serious difficulty facing type-identity theorists, a difficulty that threatens to undermine the prospects for a robust notion of mental causation altogether, arises from a consideration of a distinct category of mental state. I have focused thus far on sensations of pain. Such things seem dependent on local features of a creature's nervous system. But when we consider intentional states, this is by no means obvious. My believing that there is water in the pitcher in front of me seems to depend, not solely on my physical state at the time, but also on my environment, my history, and perhaps on my linguistic community as well. This, at least, is standardly taken to follow from various thought experiments promoted by Tyler Burge, Donald Davidson, and, originally, by Hilary Putnam (see, e.g. Burge, 1979; Davidson, 1987; Putnam; 1975).[3]

Imagine that a molecule-for-molecule duplicate of me, twin-me, inhabits a molecule-for-molecule duplicate of earth, twin-earth, that exists in some remote galaxy. Twin-earth differs from earth in one important respect: on twin-earth, there is no H_2O. The stuff that runs in rivers on twin-earth, that fills bathtubs, and that falls from the sky looks, tastes, and feels exactly like H_2O, but is in fact some different chemical compound, XYZ. Of course (twin-)English-speaking inhabitants of twin-earth *call* XYZ, "water," but twin-water is not water: *water* is H_2O. Thus, when my twin and I simultaneously form beliefs we should express by saying, "There is water in that pitcher," my twin's belief differs from mine: my belief is about water, his concerns XYZ, twin-water.

It seems possible to generate endless examples of this sort, all of which push in the direction of an *externalist* perspective on the contents of intentional states. This has led many philosophers to suppose that the contents of such states must be fixed, not just by the intrinsic properties of agents possessing them, but by the circumstances of those agents as well. On such a view, the intentional character of states of mind are taken to depend, in part, on *relational* features of those states. If this is so, however, the prospects for mental causation begin to fade.

It is widely held that the causal powers of an object depend exclusively on that object's nonrelational, here-and-now characteristics. This is the intuition driving Stephen Stich's principle of autonomy ("the states and processes that ought to be of interest to the psychologist are those that supervene on the current, internal, physical state of the organism") and Jerry Fodor's "methodological solipsism" (see Fodor, 1980; Stich, 1983). Thus, while mental states could turn out to be bodily states, we might nevertheless doubt that these states' distinctively *mental* features had any bearing on their causal powers. These doubts stem from a very natural conviction: although an object's total contribution to causal transactions of which it is a constituent may reflect all of the object's properties, not every property is equally implicated in every effect. The brick in my hand has countless properties: it is red, rectangular, it has a certain mass, it was manufactured in 1923. When I toss the brick toward my neighbour's cat, it may shatter a window pane. The shattering is caused by the brick solely in virtue of characteristics "supervenient" on the brick's current physical condition, however: its mass, shape, and velocity. Its being red and its being manufactured in 1923 seem patently irrelevant to its producing that effect.[4]

Two points bear mention here. First, one who reasons in this way need not endorse the idea that only intrinsic properties could be causally relevant. At the very least, the brick's spatial and temporal location *vis-à-vis* the window are germane to its effect. Second, whatever "intrinsic" means, we must suppose that it means something other than "essential." An object's intrinsic properties are its nonrelational properties. If objects have essential properties, however, these could well include relational properties. It might be held, for instance, that my having a particular causal origin is an essential property of me. My aim here is simply to expose a conviction that, though rarely articulated, seems often to be taken for granted.

Now, it is possible that a state's being mental is like a brick's having mass. Were that so, there might be no special difficulty in understanding how its mental features might exhibit bodily effects. Were a state's mental character like its being manufactured in 1923, in contrast, then a neural state might possess mental characteristics *and* be a cause of behavior without thereby being a cause of behavior *in virtue of* those mental characteristics.

The second possibility, as we have noted, is more than just fanciful. If we suppose, as many theorists now do, that mental states owe their nature in part to the historical circumstances of agents – in something like the way a chess piece owes its significance to its role in a range of human activities – then it may seem to follow that mentality, like the redness or the historical origin of the brick, is, with respect to behavior, *causally otiose*. The venerable Cartesian problem is reintroduced in a materialist guise. A chess piece may have a host of causal powers, but these need have nothing at all to do with its being a chess piece. Suppose, for instance, I deploy a rook as a paperweight. The rook causes a piece of paper to stay put when it otherwise might blow away. But its being a rook seems irrelevant to its possessing *this* causal power. Any object with a similar weight and shape, a stone I found on the beach that resembled a rook, might have exactly the same effects.

If our states of mind – or at any rate, the intentional characteristics, the *meanings* of those states of mind – depend on our historical circumstances in something like the way a thing's being a rook (and thereby having a certain chess significance) depends on its having a certain kind of history, it is difficult to see how mental characteristics *could* be causally implicated in the production of behavior. A state's causal powers, no less than a rook's, are determined exclusively by its here-and-now makeup. A molecular duplicate of the rook with a different history, a rook-shaped piece of rock carved by the action of waves and never used for chess, would possess all the causal powers possessed by my rook. Similarly, were my history and circumstances such that the states responsible for my deeds exhibited very different intentional contents, or even no contents at all, they would nevertheless produce identical bodily movements. Or at least, it is hard to imagine why they would not.

Before saying a word about my own approach to the problem of mental causation, I shall mention two maneuvers that might seem altogether to avoid the problem. Each, however, brings with it difficulties of its own.

First, one might appeal, as does Fodor, to an attenuated conception of mental content, so-called "narrow" content. Narrow content is content shared by molecular duplicates. My thoughts about water and my twin's thoughts about twin-water differ in respect to their "broad" content, but share a particular, and perhaps ineffable, narrow content. Whereas broad content is fixed partly by an agent's relational characteristics, narrow content, in Stich's words, "supervenes on the current, internal, physical state of the organism." Appeals to narrow content, while rendering the problem of mental causation more tractable, appear to do so at the cost of sacrificing our ordinary notion of mental content. Narrow content, whatever it is, is not *intentional* content. And it is difficult to see how such a shadowy conception of mentality could be thought to preserve what is distinctive in psychological – reason-giving – explanation.

Appeals to a notion of narrow content "solve" the problem of mental causation by deflating the mental. A second maneuver aims at a deflationary conception of the role of causation in psychological explanation. The once popular view that reasons and actions were not causally related is enjoying a minor revival. My own view on this matter is that Donald Davidson, thirty years ago, provided excellent reasons for resisting any such suggestion (see Davidson, 1963; cf. Ginet, 1990; Wilson, 1989). Davidson, echoing Aristotle, argued that reasons *explain* (or "rationalize") actions only to the extent that they figure causally in the production of those actions. Hamlet may *have* many reasons to kill the king. A reason *for which* he acts, however, is a reason that causes his action. Indeed, it is arguably a conceptual truth about action that actions – or, at any rate, intentional actions – are events caused by reasons.

Attempts to sidestep the problem of mental causation by appealing to narrow content or by denying that mental items have a role in the causing of behavior look unpromising. If that is so, we must either find some workable solution to the problem or face the prospect of eliminativism, the view that there are no intentional states, that explanations of intelligent behavior featuring appeals to intentional items are to be eliminated or replaced by neurobiological explanations.

2 Counterfactuals and Causality

It is tempting, under the circumstances, to appeal to certain counterfactual and subjunctive conditional truths holding of agents in virtue of their possession of particular states of mind, and to argue that these truths support a suitable conception of mental causation (e.g., recently, Horgan, 1989; LePore and Loewer, 1989). I shall say a few words about how this might work, then mention some residual difficulties. To focus the discussion, I shall pretend that intentional content is fixed in part by agents' causal histories. The problem is to see how anything of this sort could have a role in the production of behavior.

First, and very roughly, we can see that a thing's causal history uncontroversially contributes to its being as it is at any given moment. If we imagine that agents possess intentional states partly in virtue of their historical circumstances, then, were those circumstances different, agents would, at least in many cases, lack the here-and-now features causally responsible for their bodily movements. Imagining away agents' causal histories, in such cases, results in imagining away as well their current states, replacing them by different states with different causal powers. If my yen to toss a brick at my neighbour's cat is a matter of my being in a certain internal state *and* my having a certain history, it may well be true of me that, were I to lack *that* history, I would lack, as well, the state responsible for my brick-tossing. (Suppose, for instance, that I deliberated prior to tossing the brick, and narrowed my options to two: tossing the brick or playing the piano, and that I elected to toss the brick. It is, at the time, true of me that had I not decided earlier to toss the brick, I would have decided to play the piano, and I would now be behaving very differently.)

Might this be enough to establish the causal efficacy of the mental? Probably not. Notice that, if epiphenomenalism were true, if mental items invariably accompanied physical events but were themselves inert, the very same counterfactuals would hold. Something more would seem to be required, then, some grounding for the relevant counterfactuals and subjunctive conditionals. In many cases – though not in every case – where causation is at issue, we expect to discover appropriate causal *mechanisms*. So far, it is not clear that we have any reason to hope that such mechanisms will be uncovered in cases of mental causation. This may be due in some large measure to a prior conviction that the intentional content of mental states is fixed by relational features of the systems to which they belong. And it is far from clear how characteristics thus fixed *could* have a place in the operation of a causal mechanism.

Here is one possibility. Mental states are states, not of brains *per se*, but states of agents, complex systems that are themselves embedded in larger social and biological systems. Psychological explanation focuses on agents and agents' states of mind as components of such systems. A tacit recognition that this is so, perhaps, accounts for our ambivalence toward the sorts of twin-earth thought experiments discussed above. Twin-earth cases are decidedly far-fetched; still, they make salient the idea that physically indistinguishable items embedded in distinguishable systems may require very different explanations. Were that so, we should be faced with a choice. We could abandon the notion that mental characteristics have any interesting causal relevance to behavior; we could opt for a Fodor-style conception of "narrow content," mental content that supervenes on an agent's local neural condition; we could revise our conception of psychological explanation to include – essentially – agents' circumstances.

A second possibility is worth mentioning. I have supposed that the most serious challenge to a sensible account of mental causation is posed by externalism. Perhaps externalism is overrated, however. Perhaps, as C. B. Martin contends,[5] we can make sense of the ofness and aboutness of states of mind without adverting to agents' circumstances (see Martin and Pfcifer, 1986). Martin points out that dispositional states have a projective character, that need not depend on their causal history. A given substance, for instance, might be soluble in XYZ, but not H_2O, even if it never encounters XYZ. Similarly, my thoughts might concern XYZ (but not H_2O), even though I have never been in causal contact with XYZ, provided those thoughts were the expression of a particular sort of disposition. Looked at this way, the brains of intelligent agents realize complex systems of dispositions, and it is in virtue of these that agents exemplify intentional characteristics.

A view of this sort upholds the traditional distinction between meaning, intentional content, and reference. Dispositional characteristics are of or for types or kinds, not particulars, though of course some types or kinds may have single, unique instantiations. Arguably, this is a virtue of the approach. It preserves the intuition that molecular duplicates must be psychologically indistinguishable. My twin and I think alike, although our thoughts may refer to very different things. That difference, however, is psychologically irrelevant.

Whether an internalist view of this sort can be worked out in detail remains to be seen. Even if it can, we are still some distance from a solution to the mind–body problem. I have focused on intentional mental characteristics. This leaves untouched the sensational, experiential characteristics. How these might be reconciled with a broadly physicalist outlook is perhaps less easy to anticipate.[6]

Notes

This paper develops ideas advanced in John Heil and Alfred Mele, "Mental causes," (1991), and chs 2 and 4 of *The Nature of True Minds* 1992. See also Alfred Mele, *Springs of Action* (1992, ch. 2).

1 An apparent exception is Nancy Cartwright; see her *How the Laws of Physics Lie* (1983), essay 6. Another possibility is that our current picture of the physical domain is incomplete. Properties that now strike us as physically anomalous may find a place in a more comprehensive physics. On this, see Galen Strawson, *Mental Reality* (forthcoming).

2 It is more accurate, perhaps, to speak of disjunctive or complex *predicates*. And it might certainly turn out that a complex predicate picks out a single property. Is such a property complex? To be sure, its *name* is complex; but that might easily be fixed by substituting a single term for the complex original.

3 The example used in the next paragraph is, of course, due to Putnam.

4 This is not to say that these properties are in some absolute sense causally inert, only that this occurrence of the property of being a shattering owes nothing to them.

5 In "A new view of the mind," (unpublished) See also Martin (forthcoming) and Martin and Pfeifer (1986).

6 This topic is the focus of William Seager's *Metaphysics of Consciousness* (1991).

References

Broad, C. D. (1951) *The Mind and its Place in Nature*, London: Routledge & Kegan Paul, ch. 2.

Burge, T. (1979) "Individualism and the mental," *Midwest Studies in Philosophy* 4, pp. 73–121.

Cartwright, N. (1983) *How the Laws of Physics Lie*, Oxford: Clarendon Press.

Davidson, D. (1963) "Actions, reasons, and causes," *Journal of Philosophy* 60, pp. 685–700; reprinted 1980 in *Essays on Actions and Events*, Oxford: Clarendon Press, pp. 229–44.

Davidson, D. (1987) "Knowing one's own mind," *Proceedings and Addresses of the American Philosophical Association* 60, pp. 441–58.

Fodor, J. (1980) "Methodological solipsism considered as a research strategy in cognitive psychology," *Behavioral and Brain Sciences* 3, pp. 63–73.

Ginet, C. (1990) *On Action*, Cambridge: Cambridge University Press.

Heil, J. and Mele, A. R. (1992) "Mental causes," *American Philosophical Quarterly* 28, pp. 61–71.

Heil, J. and Mele, A. R. (1992) *The Nature of True Minds*, Cambridge: Cambridge University Press.

Horgan, T. (1989) "Mental Quausation," *Philosophical Perspectives* 3, pp. 47–76.

LePore, E. and Loewer, B. (1989) "More on making mind matter," *Philosophical Topics* 17, pp. 175–91.

Martin, C. B. (forthcoming) "The need for ontology: some alternatives," *Philosophy*.

Martin, C. B. "A new view of the mind," unpublished manuscript.

Martin, C. B. and Pfeifer, K. (1986) "Intentionality and the non-psychological," *Philosophy and Phenomenological Research* 46, pp. 531–54.

Mele, A. R. (1992) *Springs of Action*, New York: Oxford University Press.

Morgan, C. L. (1923) *Emergent Evolution*, London: Williams & Norgate.

Putnam, H. (1975) "The meaning of 'meaning' " in K. Gunderson (ed.) *Language, Mind, and Knowledge* (*Minnesota Studies in the Philosophy of Science*, vol. 7), Minneapolis, Minn.: University of Minnesota Press, pp. 131–93; reprinted 1975 in *Mind, Language, and Reality*, Cambridge: Cambridge University Press, pp. 215–71.

Seager, W. (1991) *Metaphysics of Consciousness*, London: Routledge.

Stich, S. (1983) *From Folk Psychology to Cognitive Science: the Case against Belief*, Cambridge, Mass.: Bradford Books/MIT Press.

Strawson, G. (forthcoming) *Mental Reality*, Cambridge, Mass.: Bradford Books/MIT Press.

Wilson, G. M. (1989) *The Intentionality of Human Action*, Stanford, Calif.: Stanford University Press.

13
The Mind–Body Problem and Contemporary Psychology

John Macnamara

If contemporary psychology neglects the mind–body problem, it is not because it has successfully defused that problem, much less solved it, but because contemporary psychology systematically ignores the core of cognition, which is referring. Reference is the main relation between symbols and what they symbolize; as such it is a strictly logical relation. It has a psychological counterpart, referring, which is the intentional contact a symbol user makes by means of symbols with what the symbols symbolize. No one has a good idea how a system under physical description (e.g. a computer) or physiological description (e.g. a brain) can make such intentional contact with objects outside the system. This is frequently called the "aboutness" problem. To characterize the problem thus, however, is to miss its core. The crux is that all referring involves intentional contact with abstract objects: precisely the type of object that eludes purely physical/physiological explanation. The difficulty extends to actions, for actions are individuated by beliefs and belief-informed desires. For this reason actions, too, elude physical/physiological explanation. But these declarations merit comment.

It may come as a surprise that cognitive psychology ignores the issue of referring. It is little wonder that physiological psychology, with its talk of neural networks and neural transmitters should. But cognitive psychology, with its emphasis on language, word meaning, and concept formation? The great effort of cognitive psychologists, however, is to discover the form and function of mental representations, not the relation between such representations and what they represent. Indeed there is little attention to what they represent, the common supposition being that what a word like "dog" represents is either a concept of dog in the mind or the physical creatures that are dogs, such as Freddie, Spot, and Towser. These suppositions do not survive a moment's serious reflection. When I say "Freddie is a dog" I am certainly not saying that Freddie is a mental concept. Neither am I saying that Freddie is one in the list: Freddie, Spot, Towser . . . For one thing, not all dogs have had names and could not, then, be listed; yet, they are nonetheless dogs. Instead I am saying that Freddie is a member of the kind Dog. "Dog," then, names a universal. Contemporary psychology pays no heed whatsoever to what universals are. It thus cannot but fail to take adequate account of referring.

The role of universals is more extensive than people realize. Take the proper name "Freddie"; to what does it refer? And what, so to speak, keeps it on the right referential track? To individuate the bearer of the name a universal is needed. The bearer is a *dog*. This excludes the collar he may be wearing and the mud on his paws; it includes the whole invisible interior as well as the visible exterior. There is also need to trace identity correctly so that we can talk about the same Freddie in past, present, and counterfactual circumstances as well as in present ones. To see what must be handled consider that although Freddie has an intimate relation with the set of molecules that compose his body, he is not identical with those molecules. For, while Freddie was born, the set in question was not born, being far too large. What traces Freddie's identity is the kind dog. It follows that the correct interpretation of "Freddie" requires intentional appeal to the kind Dog. The universal is essential.

The problem of referring is that universals are abstract objects. They do not reside in space and time or take part in spatiotemporal events. There is, then, no giving an account of intentional contact with them in the language of physics or physiology. If we realize that all reference, even to physical objects, involves abstract objects we begin to grasp the force of Brentano's celebrated question: How do we give an account of reference to an object in purely physical or physiological terms?

What does this mean for the mind–body problem? Does it mean that man's mind is not purely physical? I am not clear that it does; but it certainly means that the theory of cognition cannot be translated without remainder into the language of physiological psychology. In particular it means that accounts of intentional states, which essentially involve reference to abstract objects, cannot be wholly translated into statements expressed exclusively in the primitives of physiological psychology: "neural network," "cell firing," "neural transmitter," and so forth.

There are several standard responses to this position. One drastic one is to deny the reality of such intentional states as beliefs, a line explicitly taken by Paul Churchland (1984) and Patricia Churchland (1986) and gestured towards by Dennett (1978, 1987), and Stich (1983). These are all philosophers, I might add. Psychologists seem less sensitive to the issue. The line is drastic because it does away with reference and in consequence, as Putnam (1988) observes, with logic.

A less drastic response is to canvass the logical opacity of belief and desire states and to claim that reference is of no consequence to the theory of cognition. To illustrate: if Joe believes there is a tiger in the garden he will avoid the garden. It makes no difference to behavior whether there really is a tiger there or not. The theory of cognition, this line argues, is concerned with the nature of mental representations and with their transformations as an explanation of action. This position, called methodological solipsism, was proposed by Fodor (1980) and is accommodated by the psychologist Pylyshyn (1985). But this position also seems disastrous for cognitive psychology. It obliterates the theoretical distinction between the states of seeing a tiger and hallucinating one. It also obliterates the theoretical distinction between healthy thought processes and deranged ones that happen to obey the mental transformation rules. Moreover, since it denies the importance of reference for cognition, methodological solipsism delivers a dangerous impulse towards idealism in a field already inclined to tilt in that direction.

One of the reasons for the penchant for idealism is cognitive psychology's long-standing affair with the computer and its predilection for theories of cognition in the form of computer programs. Now the computer is a mathematical engine designed by Turing to solve a mathematical problem: the decidability of arithmetical sentences. It was a condition on the success of Turing's project that the engine he invented not interpret its symbols, because insight into models of arithmetical sentences might have led the engine to make steps that were not justified by purely formal considerations. What had to be avoided were steps justified by something other than the formal descriptions of machine states and rules for transforming such states. The computer was born blind to reference and remains so to this day. One result of cognition's affair with the computer is that it is content with cognitive theories that are blind to reference. Grasp this and you understand contemporary psychology's neglect of the mind–body problem.

The only way ahead for cognitive psychology is to admit such primitives as reference and referring and acknowledge that they cannot be reduced to the language of neural science. This is to concede a certain "dualism" among the sciences that deal with the nature of man. Whether this entails metaphysical dualism I see as an open question.

It is commonplace in contemporary psychology to treat cognition as an extension of perception, that is, to treat the two as a single complex system. There is obviously some sense in which this is correct, because we gain knowledge by perceiving. At the same time there is a well-grounded theoretical distinction, recognized by Aristotle in the *de Anima*, between the two. Failure to grasp the distinction invites confusion in discussions of the mind–body problem.

The reason is that perception depends on causal interaction with the environment. The environment sends us informatively structured light, sound, tactile signals . . . that we are equipped to process and thus learn about the environment. It follows that a causal account of perception is possible, while I have been saying that no causal account of cognition is possible. It follows further that the position I have been urging presupposes a distinction between perception and cognition deep enough to explain the difference just pointed to. Ultimately what is at stake is that the theory of perception does not make the same sort of appeal to universals as the theory of cognition.

It is easy to demonstrate a deep division between perception and cognition. A single perceptual presentation can be conceptualized as a male poodle, a poodle, a dog, a quadruped, a mammal, an animal. Correspondingly a single conceptualization, say animal, is appropriate for such perceptually diverse presentations as a dog, a bird, a worm, a fish, a flea. This means that perception and cognition can vary independently. Their theories are thus distinct.

A little more dramatically, the visual illusions do not go away once their illusory nature is known. *Knowledge* that the two lines in the Müller–Lyer illusion are the same length does not make them *look* the same length. Knowledge that a movie is a sequence of stills does not make it look like a sequence of stills. Knowledge that a shadow is not a physical object does not deprive a shadow of its looking like an object. These can be taken as so many indications that perception is controlled by the environment impinging on the perceptual systems in such a way that a causal explanation seems possible. This is not to deny all top-down effects of cognition on perception. But such effects seem like short cuts. The perceptual systems seem designed in the first instance to respond to bottom-up stimulation. To put the matter in Chomsky's language: the competence theory of perception is bottom-up; that of cognition is not, or at least it does not build on the same bottom.

This is all by way of indicating that the theory of perception need not implicate universals in the direct manner that the theory of cognition does. The two are distinct. Not to understand this is not to understand the original motivation in Plato for a metaphysical distinction between mind and body. For Aristotle, certainly as interpreted by St Thomas Aquinas, that metaphysical distinction is not between entities but between properties. Both Plato and Aristotle were sensitive to the distinction I drew between perception and cognition. Not to recognize that distinction results in blindness to the roots of the mind–body distinction.

I stated earlier that human actions, being individuated by beliefs and belief-informed desires, cannot be reduced to neural science. Could human actions, nevertheless, be subject to laws that preclude freedom of action in the sense that is incompatible with determinism? For if they were, one dimension of mind that was of concern to dualists (and indeed humanists), namely freedom of the will, would have proved to be illusory. I mean, of course, freedom of the will in the sense that excludes determinism. Once again, my position is more guarded than I find satisfactory. It is simply that if human actions are subject to causal laws of an intentional sort, we can never discover them. With two collaborators I published a long article on the matter (Macnamara, Govitrikar, and Doan, 1988), which I cannot adequately distill here. Perhaps the gist of the argument can be suggested by observing that while actions are individuated by beliefs and desires, the true importance or centrality of a person's beliefs and desires, as distinct from his profession of their importance for him, is evidenced best by his actions. The circularity in this does not preclude enough insight into motives and actions to ground our everyday understanding of one another. What it precludes is the sharpening of this insight into precisely stated causal laws to cover actions. Our paper goes on to argue that this conclusion does not rule out a useful science of human action. The upshot is that the issue of freedom of the will is neutral with respect to the scientific aspirations of cognitive psychology. One can go further and say that the issue of dualism (mind–body distinction) is neutral with respect to such scientific aspirations.

I fear I have not resolved the mind–body issue to my own satisfaction. Nevertheless, I hope to have thrown some light on its neglect in contemporary psychology and also to have placed my finger on its core. I have also shown (in Macnamara, Govitrikar, and Doan, 1988) that, since a dualist solution to the problem would not threaten the scientific aspirations of psychology, there is no reason for contemporary psychologists to fear a serious reappraisal of the issue.

Notes

Many of the ideas in this paper emerged in discussions with my friends Gonzalo Reyes and Marie Reyes.

References

Churchland, P. M. (1984) *Matter and Consciousness: a Contemporary Introduction to the Philosophy of Mind*, Cambridge, Mass.: Bradford Books/MIT Press.

Churchland, P. S. (1986) *Neurophilosophy: Toward a Unified Understanding of the Mind–Brain*, Cambridge, Mass.: Bradford Books/MIT Press.

Dennett, D. (1978) *Brainstorms: Philosophical Essays on Mind and Psychology*, Montogomery, Vt.: Bradford Books.

Dennett, D. (1987) *The Intentional Stance*, Cambridge, Mass.: Bradford Books/MIT Press.

Fodor, J. A. (1980) "Methodological solipsism considered as a research strategy in cognitive psychology," *Behavioral and Brain Sciences* 3, pp. 63–73.

Macnamara, J., Govitrikar, V., and Doan, B. (1988) "Actions, laws and scientific psychology," *Cognition* 29, pp. 1–27.

Putnam, H. (1988). *Representation and Reality*, Cambridge, Mass.: Bradford Books/MIT Press.

Pylyshyn, Z. W. (1985). *Computation and Cognition: Toward a Foundation for Cognitive Science*, Cambridge Mass.: Bradford Books/MIT Press.

Stich, S. (1983) *From Folk Psychology to Cognitive Science: the Case against Belief*, Cambridge, Mass.: Bradford Books/MIT Press.

14
What is a Theory of Mental Representation?

Stephen P. Stich

1 Introduction

Theories of mental content or mental representation are very fashionable these days. And as with many fashionable products, the market offers a dizzying range of options. There are causal co-variation theories, teleological theories, functional role theories, and theories inspired by the causal theory of reference. There are single factor theories, multiple factor theories, narrow theories, wide theories, and a profusion of variations on all of these themes.[1] Indeed, it often seems that it is hard to find a current volume of a major journal in the area that does not have at least one article offering an argument for, or (more typically) against, someone's theory of mental representation. Moreover much of this literature has an unmistakable tone of urgency to it. The quest for an adequate theory of mental representation is not just a popular pursuit, many writers insist, it is a vitally important one. Jerry Fodor, who is rarely accused of understanding the case, tells us that producing a naturalistic theory of mental content is an essential step in vindicating commonsense intentional psychology. And "if commonsense intentional psychology really were to collapse, that would be, beyond comparison, the greatest intellectual catastrophe in the history of our species" (Fodor, 1987, p. xii). Fred Dretske uses similarly apocalyptic terms. Without a suitably naturalistic theory of mental content, he suggests darkly, we might ultimately have to "relinquish a conception of ourselves as human agents" (1988, p. x).

While there is no shortage of debate about the merits and demerits of various accounts of mental content, there has been remarkably little discussion about what a theory of mental representation is supposed to do. What question (or questions) is a theory of mental representation supposed to answer? And what would count as getting the answer right? These are the questions that will be center stage in the current paper. In trying to answer them, it will prove useful to start by asking another question: Why do so many people *want* a theory of mental representation; what makes the project of producing such a theory seem so urgent? This is the question I'll try to answer in section 2.

Though it is unfortunate that questions about what a theory of mental representation is supposed to do have been so often neglected, it is hardly surprising. The sort of methodological self-consciousness that these questions engender has rarely been fashionable in philosophy. As a result, it is all too often the case that philosophers provide elaborate solutions for which there is no clear problem; or, as Fodor has put it, they offer cures for which there is no adequate disease. Thus I would urge, as a basic principle of philosophical method, that we spend a fair amount of time getting clear about the question, before we start worrying about the answer. When we apply this strategy to theorizing about mental representation, some very surprising conclusions begin to emerge.

Here is a preview of the conclusions that I will be defending in the pages to follow.

1 Once we start thinking about what a theory of mental representation is supposed to do, it becomes clear that there are actually several very different answers that might be offered. There is not one project here but several. These projects divide into two different families, though even within a single family, there are important differences to be noted.

2 With a single (and controversial) exception, the projects that I will sketch cannot readily be pursued by philosophers using the familiar techniques of philosophical analysis that predominate in the literature. Rather, they are intrinsically interdisciplinary projects in which the construction and testing of empirical theories plays a central role. However (again with a few exceptions) the sort of interdisciplinary work that would be necessary to make serious progress on these projects is notably absent in the literature.

3 This last fact might be taken as an indication that the projects people are actually pursuing are different from the ones that I will describe – that I have simply failed to figure out what those who are searching for a theory of mental representation are up to. But without some details on what those alternative projects might be, I am inclined to draw a darker conclusion. It is my contention that most of the players in this very crowded field have *no* coherent project that could possibly be pursued successfully with the methods they are using.

4 Even if we put these worries to one side, it is unlikely that any of the projects I will sketch will be of much help in responding to the concerns that have led many to feel it is a matter of some urgency to produce a theory of mental representation.
5 But I will also argue that those concerns themselves are deeply misguided.

So much for threats and promises. It is time to get to work.

2 Why would We Want a Theory of Mental Representation?

No doubt there are lots of reasons why people might want a theory of mental representation. But among these many motives, one stands out. Concern about *eliminativism* has been a central theme in the philosophy of mind during the last decade, and producing a theory of mental representation is seen to be a central step in the debate. Though eliminativists have rarely been clear or careful in setting out their thesis, I think the doctrine is best viewed as making a pair of ontological claims, one of which is much stronger, and more unsettling, than the other. The weaker claim is that the representational states of commonsense psychology – states like beliefs and desires – will play no role in a mature theory about the causes of human behavior. If we use the label "cognitive science" as a catch-all for the various scientific disciplines that will play a role in the explanation of human behavior, then what the eliminativist is claiming is that the intentional states posited by commonsense psychology are not part of the ontology of cognitive science. The stronger claim is that these common-sense mental states do not even exist. *There are no such things*, just as there are no such things as phlogiston, caloric fluid, or witches. Those who endorse both of these claims typically suppose that the first can be marshalled in support of the second, though it is far from clear how the argument is supposed to run.[2] There can be little doubt that many people think a theory of mental representation has a major role to play in the debate over eliminativism. But exactly what this role is supposed to be is less clear. In section 3 and section 4 we will be looking at a pair of views on what a theory of mental representation is. When we've made some progress on that topic, we will return, in section 6, to the question of how a theory of mental representation might be exploited in arguing for or against eliminativism.

There are various arguments for the weaker of the two eliminativist theses, the claim that beliefs and desires won't play a role in a mature cognitive science. One family of arguments focuses on the *structure* of the cognitive processes and mechanisms portrayed by folk psychology. These structures, it is maintained, are incompatible with the structures posited in one or another putatively promising scientific paradigm (see, for example, Ramsey, Stich, and Garon, 1990). A second family of arguments focuses on the *semantic* or *intentional* properties of mental states, as these are construed in commonsense psychology. Some of the arguments in this second family are fairly fussy and technical. They exploit sophisticated notions such as supervenience, individualism, and meaning holism. But, as Fodor has noted, for many people the most worrisome fact about semantic properties is their intuitive ontological oddness.

> [T]he deepest motivation for intentional irrealism derives not from . . . relatively technical worries about individualism and holism . . . but rather from a certain ontological intuition: that there is no place for intentional categories in a physicalistic view of the world; that the intentional can't be *naturalized*. (1987, p. 97)

This worry goes a long way toward explaining a widely accepted constraint on any acceptable theory of mental representation. The theory must be *naturalistic*. It must show how representational properties of mental states can be explained in terms that are compatible with the broader, physicalistic view of nature provided by the natural sciences. Despite its widespread acceptance, I am inclined to think that the naturalism constraint is deeply misguided. I will say a bit about the reasons for my misgivings in section 7.

Even if one accepts the naturalism constraint, however, it is obvious that this constraint can only be part of the story about what it is to get a theory of mental representation right. For on any plausible unpacking of the naturalism constraint, it will be possible to tell lots of naturalistic stories about mental representation, and these stories will differ from one another in lots of ways. We surely don't want to say that all of these accounts are correct. So let us now ask what distinguishes the good ones from the bad ones. What counts as getting a theory right?

3 Describing a Commonsense Concept: a First Family of Projects

A prominent feature of our everyday discourse about ourselves and about other people is our practice of identifying mental states by adverting to their content. Examples are everywhere:

> Bush believes that Gorbachev is in Moscow.
> I think it is going to rain this afternoon.
> My wife hopes that I won't be late for dinner.

In these, and in a vast range of other cases, the attribution of content is effortless, unproblematic, and unquestionably useful. Moreover, in the typical case, there is widespread inter subjective agreement about these attributions. Plainly, there must be a mental mechanism of some complexity underlying this ubiquitous practice, and it seems plausible to suppose that the mechanism in question includes a store of largely tacit knowledge about the conditions under which it is (and is not) appropriate to characterize a mental state as the belief or the desire *that p*. If we adopt the relatively loose use of the term "concept" that prevails in psychology, this amounts to the assumption that the mechanism underlying our practice embodies a concept of mental representation. And one perfectly plausible goal for a theory of mental content would be to describe that concept. To get the theory right is to give an accurate description of the concept, or the body of tacit knowledge, that underlies our quotidian practice.[3]

The project of describing the conceptual structure underlying judgments about content is at least roughly analogous to a variety of other projects that have been pursued in philosophy and cognitive science. In generative linguistics it is common to assume that a speaker's linguistic judgments and practice are subserved by a substantial body of tacit grammatical knowledge, and that the task of the linguist is to give an explicit account of what the speaker tacitly knows. In cognitive psychology there has been a fair amount of work aimed at making explicit the concepts and knowledge structures underlying various social and practical skills. One of the most fascinating projects along these lines has been the effort to uncover the concepts and principles of "folk physics," the system of information about the physical world that we exploit as we wander around in it. What makes this research particularly intriguing is the finding that many people exploit a folk physics that is mistaken about the physical world, and not just in detail. The tacit theory that apparently guides these people's physical judgments and their actions is closer to medieval impetus theory than it is to Newtonian physics (see McCloskey, Caramazra, and Green, 1980 and McCloskey, 1983). Findings like this may make the eliminativist's thesis a bit more plausible. If people can rely on a seriously mistaken physical theory to assist them in moving around in the world, surely it is at least possible that they rely on an equally mistaken psychological theory when they describe, explain, and predict people's behavior.

A third endeavor that bears a significant resemblance to the project of describing our commonsense concept of mental representation is the sort of conceptual analysis that has provided intermittent employment for philosophers since the time of Socrates. The rules of the game have changed very little over the last 2,500 years. It goes something like this:

S (Socrates, as it might be): Tell me please, what is X? (where "X" may be replaced by "justice" or "piety" or "knowledge" or "causation" or "freedom" . . .)

C (Cephalus, perhaps, or Chisholm): I will tell you gladly. To be an instance of X, something must be y and z.

S But that can't be right. For surely you will grant that a is X, but it is neither y nor z.

C You are quite right. Let me try again. To be an instance of X something must be either y and z or it must be w.

S I'm afraid that won't work either, since b is w, but clearly it is not X.

The game comes to an end when S runs out of counter-examples, or C runs out of definitions. And, though no one has kept careful records in this sport, the smart money usually bets on S.

This philosophical game of definition and counter examples makes little sense unless we make a pair of assumptions about the concepts it aims to analyze. The first of these is that the target concept can be characterized, or defined, by specifying necessary and sufficient conditions. To win a round, S can either produce an example which is an instance of the concept but is not captured by the definition, or he can produce an example which fits the definition but is not an instance of the concept. Moreover, it is generally assumed that the definition will be a Boolean concatenation of properties, or some relatively straightforward variation on that theme. The second assumption is that the players come equipped with enough information about the target concept to enable them to judge whether or not it applies in a wide range of cases, real and hypothetical, that they have never before imagined. To see this second point, consider a pair of well-known examples:

1 If someone asks you to keep his weapons, and then asks for them back after he has gone insane, does justice demand, that you return them?
2 Suppose that Smith has just signed the papers to buy the Ford in the dealership showroom. Though Smith doesn't know it, the dealership does not have clear title to the car. However, moments before and far away, Granny Smith died, and title to her old Ford passes to Smith. So Smith believes he owns a Ford, and his belief is both justified and true. Does Smith *know* he owns a Ford?

It is hard to see how we could expect people to answer questions like these, or why we should take their answers seriously, unless we suppose that they already tacitly know something very much like the set of necessary and sufficient conditions that we are trying to make explicit.

There are two reasons why I have gone on at some length about the traditional philosophical approach to conceptual analysis. The first is that much of the philosophical literature on mental representation seems to fit squarely within the definition and counter example paradigm. Philosophical theories about the nature of mental representation typically offer what purport to be necessary and sufficient conditions for claims of the form:

Mental state M has the content p.

And objections to these theories typically turn on intuitive counterexamples, cases in which the definition says that M has the content p, but intuition denies it, or vice versa (see, for example: Block, 1986, p. 660; Field, 1986, p. 444; Jones, Mulaire, and Stich, 1991, §4.2; Loewer, 1987, p. 296).[4] The second reason is that there is now a fair amount of evidence suggesting that the assumptions underlying this traditional philosophical project may be simply mistaken. And if they are, then the project which dominates the philosophical literature on mental representation will be seriously undermined.

In the psychological literature, perhaps the most widely known challenge to the assumptions underlying traditional philosophical analysis derives from the work of Eleanor Rosch and her co-workers.[5] On the Roschian view, the mental structures that underlie people's judgments when they classify items into categories do not exploit tacitly known necessary and sufficient conditions for category membership, or anything roughly equivalent. Exactly what they do use is an issue that has motivated a great deal of empirical research since the late 1970s, and continues to be actively explored. Early on Rosch proposed that categorization relies on *prototypes*, which may be thought of as idealized descriptions of the most typical or characteristic members of the category. The prototype for "bird", for example, might include such features as flying, having feathers, singing, and a variety of others. In determining whether a particular instance falls within the category, subjects assess the similarity between the prototype and the instance being categorized. However, the features specified in the prototype are not even close to being necessary or sufficient conditions for membership. So, for example, an animal can lack one or many of the features of the prototypical bird, and still be classified as a bird. Emus are classified as birds though they neither fly nor sing. An alternative to the prototype theory is the hypothesis that categorization is subserved by *exemplars*, which can be thought of as detailed mental descriptions of specific members of the category that are familiar to the person doing the categorizing. On this account, too, people determine whether an item is a member of a category by making a tacit similarity judgment. However, on the exemplar theory, the item being classified is compared to exemplary members of the category.[6]

More recent research has made it clear that for many concepts neither the prototype nor the exemplar account will explain all the data comfortably. For some concepts it has been proposed that subjects' judgments rely on something very much like a tacitly known scientific theory. In other cases it has been suggested that there is no enduring concept underlying categorization judgments. Rather, it is argued, subjects construct concepts of various different sorts "on the fly," in response to the situation in which the need to categorize arises (Barsalou, 1987; Murphy and Medin 1985; Rips, 1989).

Although there has been an enormous amount of work on concepts and categorization in recent years, there has been no systematic empirical study of *intentional* categories, categories like *believing that p*, or *desiring that q*. Thus at present we can only speculate about what such an investigation would reveal. Perhaps the safest bet is that whatever the mental mechanism underlying intentional categorization may be, it will not utilize "classical" concepts, the sort that can be defined with a set of necessary and sufficient conditions. The argument here is straightforwardly inductive: *no* commonsense concept that has been studied has turned out to be analyzable into a set of necessary and sufficient conditions. Indeed, given currently available evidence, it looks as if there are no classical concepts. A second plausible speculation is that the concepts or "knowledge structures" underlying intentional categorization are much more complex than those traditionally offered in philosophical analyses. It's my guess that our "concept" of mental content is going to look more like a theory than like a Platonic definition.

Suppose these speculations are right, what follows? The most obvious consequence is that in seeking to build a theory of mental representation, the traditional philosophical method of proposing definitions and hunting for intuitive counterexamples will have to be abandoned. That method tries to specify a set of conditions that all and only the cases which intuitively fall under the target concept will satisfy. But if our intuitions about whether a state has the content *that p* are guided by prototypes, or exemplars, or tacit theories, or if the mental structures that determine our intuitve judgments are constructed partly in response to the circumstances in which the judgment is called for, then there will be no such conditions. So if using the method of definition and counterexample is the hallmark of a philosophical theory in this area, and if the commonsense concept of mental representation is like every other concept that has been studied empirically, there is a sense in which *there can be no philosophical theory of content*.

It is important not to read too much into this conclusion, however. For, although the traditional method of philosophical analysis may have to be abandoned, there is no reason why we cannot use other methods in constructing a descriptive theory about the ordinary concept of mental representation. Linguists, cognitive psychologists, and cognitive anthropologists have developed a variety of methods for exploring the structure of commonsense concepts, none of which presuppose that these concepts have a classical structure that can be captured by a set of necessary and sufficient conditions. With a bit of ingenuity, one or more of these methods might well be used to probe the mechanisms underlying our intuitive judgments about mental representation.

We began this section by asking what a theory of mental representation was supposed to do. And we now have at least the outlines of one plausible answer. A theory of mental representation is supposed to describe the concept or knowledge structure underlying people's ordinary judgments about the content of beliefs, desires and other intentional states. However, if *this* is the sort of theory that philosophers want when they set out to build a theory of mental representation, then it is a good bet that they will have to give up "doing philosophy" (as traditionally conceived) and start doing cognitive science instead.

4 Mental Representation as a Natural Phenomenon: a Second Family of Projects

The description of commonsense concepts, when not encumbered by a priori philosophical requirements on what such a description must look like, is a perfectly reasonable activity. But it is not the only project that those who seek a theory of mental representation might have in mind. To see what the alternative might be, consider the concept of disease. There is a substantial anthropological literature aimed at describing the concept of disease as it is used in various cultures see, for example, Murdock, 1980. And if you are interested in how people conceive of disease, this is the place to look. But if you are interested in what disease is then it is biology or medicine you should be studying, not cognitive anthropology. An entirely analogous point could be made about gold, or space, or mass, or heredity. If you want to know how people conceive of them, then the description of commonsense concepts or knowledge structures is the project to pursue. But if you want to know what gold, or space, or mass, or heredity is really like, then you should be studying chemistry or physics or genetics.

Sometimes the relevant science will be pretty explicit about how it conceives of the item of interest. *The Handbook of Physics and Chemistry* will tell you all you want to know about gold, and then some. But in lots of other cases a science will use a concept quite successfully without providing a fully explicit or philosophically satisfying account of that concept. In those cases, philosophers of science often step in and try to make the notion in question more explicit. In recent years, there have been illuminating studies of fitness, grammaticality, space-time and a wide variety of other notions for fitness, see Sober, 1984; for grammaticality, see Fodor, 1981; for space-time see Sklar, 1974. Part of this work can be viewed as straightforward conceptual description – trying to do for scientific concepts and theories what linguists, cognitive psychologists, and cognitive anthropologists have tried to do for commonsense concepts and theories. Indeed, in recent years a number of philosophers of science have begun using the techniques of cognitive science in the analysis of science, often with intriguing results see, for example, Giere 1988; Glymour et al., 1987; Langley et al., 1987; Nersessian, 1992; Thagard, 1988. Sometimes, however, the concepts philosophers find, and the theories in which they play a role, are uncomfortably vague or poorly developed. And in these cases it is not at all uncommon for philosophers of science to propose improvements in the concepts and theories they are describing. It is often no easy matter to say where description stops and construction begins, and for most purposes it hardly matters.

It looks as if we now have the beginnings of a second, rather different, answer to the question of what a theory of mental representation is supposed to do. On this second account, a theory of mental representation doesn't much care about the commonsense conception of mental representation. The intuitions and tacit knowledge of the man or woman in the street are quite irrelevant. The theory seeks to say what mental representation really is, not what folk psychology takes it to be. And to do this it must describe, and perhaps patch up, the notion of mental representation as it is used by the best cognitive science we have available. So on this account, a theory of mental representation begins as part of the cognitive psychology of cognitive science, though it may end up contributing to the conceptual foundations of the science it sets out to describe.

In the large literature on mental representation, I know of only one author who explicitly undertakes the project I have been sketching. The author is Robert Cummins, and in his recent book, *Meaning and Mental Representation* (1989), he offers a detailed account of a notion of mental representation. But he goes out of his way to stress that the notion he is concerned with is not the folk psychological concept that underlies our ordinary language of intentional characterization (Cummins, p. 26). Rather, Cummins's goal is to give an account of the notion of mental representation that is used in one venerable and still vigorous research tradition in cognitive science, the tradition that seeks to build what he calls "orthodox" computational theories of cognition. This tradition "assumes that cognitive systems are automatic interpreted formal systems" (p. 13), and much of the work on problem-solving, planning, language processing, and higher-level visual processing that has been done during the last two decades falls squarely within the orthodox computational paradigm.

An essential part of Cummins's project is an explication of the explanatory strategy of computational theories of cognition. He offers an account of what these theories are trying to explain, and of what successful explanations in this paradigm must do. This explanatory structure imposes strong constraints on an account of mental representation since the notion of representation used in computational theories must make sense of the explanations being offered. Here's how Cummins characterizes his approach:

> First determine what explanatory role representation plays in some particular representation-invoking scientific theory or theoretical framework; then ask what representation has to be – how it is to be explicated – if it is to play that role. (p. 145).

Though Cummins's target is the notion of representation exploited in computational theories of cognition, he recognizes that this is not the only promising research tradition in cognitive science. "There are a number of different frameworks in the running in cognitive science today" (p. 26), including "orthodox computationalism, connectionism, neuroscience" (p. 12) and a variety of others. Much the same approach could be used on the notions of representation exploited in these other traditions, though the results might well turn out quite different. "[T]o suppose that [these other research traditions] all make use of the same notion of representation seems naive" (p. 12). If we ask what each of these frameworks takes mental representation to be, "we are not likely to get a univocal answer" (p. 26).

This pluralistic picture is one I vigorously endorse. It adds an important dimension to the account of theories of mental representation that I have been sketching in this section. For if different paradigms within cognitive science use different notions of representation, then there isn't going to be *a* theory of mental representation of the sort we have been discussing. There will be *lots* of theories. Moreover, it makes no sense to ask which of these theories is the right one, since they are not in competition with one another. Each theory aims to characterize a notion of representation exploited in some branch of cognitive science. If different branches of cognitive science use different notions of representation, then there will be a variety of correct accounts of mental representation. Of course it might be thought that the various branches of cognitive science are themselves in competition, and that the correct theory of mental representation is the one that describes the notion of mental representation exploited by the correct cognitive science. But I see no reason to suppose that there is a unique correct framework for theories in cognitive science. There are lots of phenomena to explain, and lots of levels at which illuminating and scientifically respectable explanations can be given. Thus I am inclined to be a pluralist in this domain as well.

This is not the place for a detailed discussion of Cummins's account of the notion of mental representation, as it is used in computational theories of cognition. But there are a few themes in Cummins's work that I want to pursue a bit further, since they will lead us back to the question of how theories of mental representation are supposed to function in the debate over eliminativism.

5 Theories of Mental Representation and the Eliminativism Debate

As Cummins sees it, the notion of mental representation that he is trying to describe abstracts from both the history of the system, and "the actual items in a system's current environment" (p. 81). "According to computationalism, cognitive systems are individuated by their computational properties" (p. 82). And a pair of systems can have the same computational properties, even though they differ in history, in environment, and even in physical makeup. The taxonomy generated by this notion of mental representation is *individualistic*: if a pair of organisms or systems have the same physical makeup, then their representational states represent the same thing. However, following Putnam, Burge, and others, Cummins also maintains that the taxonomy of intentional states exploited by folk psychology is *anti-individualistic*: "beliefs and desires cannot be specified in a way that is independent of environment" or history (p. 140). What Cummins concludes from all of this is that beliefs, desires, and the rest of the intentional states of commonsense psychology are not among the items recognized by the computational theory of cognition. "What the anti-individualist arguments of Putnam and Burge prove from the point of view of the [computational theory of cognition] is that beliefs and desires aren't psychological states in the sense of 'psychological state' of interest to the CTC" (p. 140).

It looks as if what we have here is the beginnings of an argument for eliminativism in which both sorts of theories of mental representation that we have been sketching play a role. In outline, the argument works like this: first describe the notions of mental representation exploited by commonsense psychology and by computational theories of cognition. Next, compare the two. If they are significantly different, then the representational states of commonsense psychology are not part of the ontology of computational theories. Of course, this sort of argument won't make the eliminativist's case if it is restricted to the computational theory of cognition, since as we've lately noted, contemporary cognitive science is a variegated discipline, and there are lots of other research traditions around. So to develop a plausible defence of eliminativism, this argument would have to be repeated for each of the viable research traditions in the cognitive science marketplace. As an alternative to this case-by-case approach, the eliminativist could try to compress the process by showing that there are some features that any scientifically respectable notion of mental representation will have to have, and then arguing that these features are not endorsed by the account of mental representation implicit in folk psychology.[7]

However, even if all this goes well for the eliminativist, it is not clear that he will have made his case. To see why, let's go back to Cummins's contrast between beliefs, as they are construed in commonsense psychology, and the representational states of the computational theory of cognition. According to Cummins, commonsense psychology views beliefs anti-individualistically: they can't be specified in a way that is independent of environment. The psychological states posited by computational theories of cognition, by contrast, are individualistically individuated: they can be specified independent of environment. From this Cummins seems to conclude that the ontology of commonsense psychology is different from the ontology of the computational theory. The two theories are talking about different things. And Cummins is not alone in reasoning in this way. I have myself offered a similar argument in a variety of previous publications, as have some other authors (See Stich, 1978 and 1983, part II, and Stack, 1980). But despite having such distinguished advocates, it is not at all clear that the premises of the argument support its conclusion. What the premises do entail is that folk theory and computational theories make different and incompatible claims about the states they talk about. But that surely is not sufficient to show that they are talking about different things. If it were it would be all but impossible for theorists to disagree. Could it not be the case that folk psychology and computational theories are talking about exactly the same things, and that folk psychology is just wrong about them?

What is really at issue here is the question of what determines the reference of the terms used in a theory. Those with eliminativist sympathies often write as though they accepted some version of the description theory of reference.[8] But this is a doubly dubious doctrine for eliminativists to adopt. One danger is that naive versions of the description theory tend to trivialize eliminativism. If minor disagreements between what common sense says about mental states and what cognitive science says about them are sufficient to show that common sense and cognitive science are positing different entities, then of course eliminativism is correct. But who cares? No one ever thought that commonsense psychology would turn out to be right about everything. Indeed, if we grant that minor theoretical differences always engender different ontologies, and if we assume that later theories are typically closer to the truth than earlier ones, we end up with a quite mad view, a sort of *pan-eliminativism*. For surely it is very likely that *every* theory we now accept will undergo some improvements during the next century. If that's enough to show that the entities posited by current theories don't exist then *nothing* we now believe in exists!

A second concern about the description theory of reference is that even much more sophisticated versions of the theory may well be wide of the mark. And if they are, then no interesting ontological conclusions can be drawn from the fact that folk psychology and the cognitive sciences disagree about mental states. One philosopher who has seen this point very clearly is William Lycan. Here's how Lycan views the matter:

> I incline away from Lewis's Carnapian and/or Rylean cluster theory of the reference of theoretical terms, and toward Putnam's causal–historical theory. As in Putnam's examples of "water," "tiger," and so on, I think the ordinary word "belief" (qua theoretical term of folk psychology) points dimly toward a natural kind that we have not fully grasped and that only mature psychology will reveal. I expect that "belief" will turn out to refer to some kind of information-bearing inner state of a sentient being . . . but the kind of state it refers to may have only a few of the properties usually attributed to beliefs by common sense. Thus I think our ordinary way of picking out beliefs and desires succeeds in picking out real entities in nature, but it may not succeed in picking out the entities that common sense suggests that it does. (1988, p. 32)

As Lycan emphasizes, it is a consequence of this view that our commonsense theories may end up having been very wrong about the nature of beliefs and other representational mental states:

> I am entirely willing to give up fairly large chunks of our commonsensical or platitudinous theory of belief or of desire (or of almost anything else) and decide that we were just wrong about a lot of things, without drawing the inference that we are no longer talking about belief or desire. (1988, pp. 31–2)

Unfortunately, when the issue at hand is eliminativism, Lycan's line has much the same defect as naive versions of the description theory, though in the opposite direction. For on Lycan's view it is hard to see how *anything* could show that the posits of folk psychology are not part of the ontology of a given branch of cognitive science. Indeed, on Lycan's view, it is far from clear why we should not say that phlogiston really does exist. It's the stuff we now call "oxygen," and earlier theorists were "just wrong about a lot of things." So it seems that if we accept either the theory of reference that Lycan favors or the naive description theory, then the eliminativist's claim will be trivialized. On the description theory, eliminativism is trivially true; on the causal–historical theory, eliminativism is trivially false.

Where does all this leave us? If we want to construe eliminativism as an interesting doctrine, rather than one which is trivially true or trivially false, then our account of reference will have to be less restrictive than the naive description theory, and more restrictive than the causal–historical theory. And plainly we do want to construe eliminativism as an interesting doctrine, or so I used to think. Thus, when I first set out the argument that I've just sketched, my initial reaction was to hunt around for a more promising story about reference. However, I now think that was a serious mistake.

The problem is not that alternative accounts of reference are hard to find; quite the opposite. It's relatively easy to construct accounts of reference that appear to do just what we want. They are more restrictive than the causal–historical theory and less restrictive than the description theory. But this raises questions that should by now sound very familiar. Which of these theories of reference is the right one? And what counts as getting the theory right? Moreover, in light of the close connection between the notion of reference and the notion of mental representation, it is pretty clear that much of what was said about the latter notion in sections 3 and 4 could be repeated, with equal plausibility, about the former. If it can, then there isn't going to be any single, correct account of reference. Rather, there will be one account that describes our commonsense notion of reference (or several accounts, if there is more than one commonsense notion in circulation), and other accounts describing reference-like notions that may be of use in one or another project in psychology or linguistics or epistemology, or perhaps in some other discipline.

Now if all of this is right, some surprising conclusions follow. The first is that eliminativism cannot be viewed as a single thesis, nor even as a pair of theses as suggested in section 2. To see the point, consider the weaker of the two eliminativist theses distinguished earlier, the thesis which claims that the posits of commonsense psychology are not part of the ontology of cognitive science. If our recent reflections are on the right track, then this thesis makes no sense – it has no determinate truth conditions – unless it is tied to some specific account of reference. So if there are many perfectly correct accounts of reference, then there are many different readings of the "weak" eliminativist thesis. Moreover, it is plausible to suppose that on some of these readings the eliminativist's claim will turn out to be true, while on others it will turn out to be false. But if this is right, then it is far from clear that any reading of the eliminativist thesis is all that interesting a claim. Before we realized that any intelligible version of the doctrine had to be relativized or indexed to a theory of reference, it was perhaps plausible to claim that if eliminativism was true, then some grave intellectual catastrophe would ensure. And that, surely, is more than enough to make the doctrine interesting. But once we've seen the need to index the doctrine to some particular theory of reference, things look rather different. For surely no one is prepared to claim that eliminativism, no matter what theory of reference it is relativized to, will bring the intellectual roof down. Of course, one still might maintain that there is some particular theory of reference such that if eliminativism, indexed to that theory, is true, then worrisome consequences will ensue. And for all I know this might be right. But if it is right, it certainly isn't obvious; it is a claim that needs an argument. And I haven't a clue how that argument might go. So until we get some enlightenment on the matter, I think it is reasonable to suspect that the interest of eliminativism has been very much exaggerated.

6 Eliminativism and the Naturalism Constraint

Recall that on Fodor's view the "deepest motivation" for eliminativism, or "intentional irrealism", is the suspicion that "the intentional can't be *naturalized*" (1987, p. 97). Presumably the implicit argument for irrealism that Fodor has in mind has the structure sketched in the previous section: to be exploited in a respectable scientific theory a concept must be naturalizable. So if intentional notions can't be naturalized, then they can't be exploited in any respectable scientific theory. Fodor's own theory of content is largely motivated by the hope that this suspicion can be laid to rest. In this last section I want to consider a pair of questions about all of this. First: what would it take to allay the concern that "the intentional can't be naturalized," and how might a theory of mental representation of the sort we have been considering play a role in this process? Second: just how bad would it be if the project fails and we discover that we can't naturalize intentional notions?[9]

The answer to the first question seems clear enough, at least in outline. To put to rest the fear that the intentional can't be naturalized, we have to give a naturalistic account of a notion of mental representation that is (or might be) exploited in cognitive science, and with which the common-sense notion of mental representation may plausibly be identified. However, this answer raises a pair of problems. The first is simply a version of the problem that we were wrestling with in the previous section: What does it take to justify the cross-theoretic identification of a pair of theoretical concepts? On my view, there is no determinate answer to this question. But I have already said my piece on that topic, and won't reopen the issue here. The second problem is one that has been lurking in the shadows since the early pages of this paper, when the issue of "naturalizing" mental representation was first raised: what does it take for an account of mental representation to be *naturalistic?* Though I know of no one who has offered a detailed answer to this question, the literature strongly suggests that those who want a naturalistic account of mental representation want something like a definition – a set of necessary and sufficient conditions – couched in terms that are unproblematically acceptable in the physical or biological sciences.

Whether an appropriately naturalistic account of mental representation can be given is, of course, very much an open question. My own guess, for what little it's worth, is that the project is quite hopeless. However, in contrast with Fodor and many others, I am inclined to think that very little hangs on the matter. Fodor suggests that if we can't give a naturalistic account of mental representation, then there will be no place for the notion in serious science. And if that's the case, then the eliminativists will have won a major battle. Indeed, perhaps they will have won the war. But this suggestion strikes me as quite wrongheaded. To see why, we need only consider a few examples. Let's begin with the notion of a phoneme. What is it to be a /p/ or a /b/? If you want a naturalistic answer, one which gives necessary and sufficient conditions in physical or biological terms, then I'm afraid you're going to be disappointed. For despite many years of sophisticated research, there is currently no naturalistic answer available (for useful overviews, see Fry, 1979, and Pickett, 1980). Of course that situation might change. Phoneticians may come up with a naturalistic account of what it is for a sound sequence to be a /p/. But then again the current situation might not change. If it does not, this is surely no reason to become a phoneme-eliminativist and deny the existence of phonemes. Much the same point could be made about lots of other notions of unquestionable scientific utility. There is no naturalistic account of grooming behavior in primate ethology. Nor is there a naturalistic account of attack behavior in stickleback ethology. But surely it would be simply perverse to deny the existence of grooming behavior, simply because we can't define it in the language of physics and biology. Suitably trained observers can detect grooming behavior (or phonemes) with impressively high intersubjective reliability. And that, I would urge, is more than enough to make those notions empirically respectable. To demand more – in particular to demand that the notions in question can be "naturalized" – seems unmotivated and silly. The situation for *mental representation* looks entirely parallel. There may, perhaps, be good reasons to be an eliminativist. But the fact that mental representation can't be naturalized is not one of them.[10]

Notes

Earlier versions of this paper have been presented at the Royal Irish Academy, at MIT, at Northwestern University, and at the Universities of Bielefeld, Colorado, Gothenberg, Konstanz, Montreal, South Carolina and Syracuse. Comments and criticism from these audiences have been helpful in more ways than I could possibly record. I am grateful to Eric Margolis for help in tracking down some of the references. Parts of section 6 appeared in Stich (1991).

1 For causal co-variation theories, see Dretske, 1988; Fodor, 1987; and Fodor, 1990a. For teleological theories, see Fodor, 1990b; Millikan, 1984; and Papineau, 1987. For functional role theories, see Block 1986; Field, 1977; and Loar, 1981. For a theory inspired by the causal theory of reference, see Devitt and Sterelny, 1987. For a single factor theory, see Harman, 1986. For a multiple factor theory, see McGinn, 1982. For narrow theories, see Devitt, 1990 and Fodor, 1987. For a wide theory, see Burge, 1979.

2 For some not entirely satisfactory discussion of the point, see Stich (1983, Ch. 11, §1).

3 For a rather different story about the mechanism underlying our ability to attribute mental states by characterizing their content, see Gordon, (1986) and Goldman, (1989). For an extended critique of the Gordon–Goldman view, see Stich and Nichols, (forthcoming).

4 It is worth nothing that on several occasions Fodor has claimed that he would be satisfied with sufficient conditions "for one bit of the world to be about (to express, represent, or be true of) another bit," even if they are not necessary (Fodor, 1987, p. 98). See also Fodor 1990a, p. 52 ff.).

But, as noted in Jones, Mulaire, and Stich, (1991), if we read him literally, then it is hard to believe that this is what Fodor really wants. For providing conditions that are merely sufficient is just too easy.

If x is Fodor's most recent utterance of "Maria Callas" (or: if x is the concept that underlies that utterance) then x represents Maria Callas.

If y is Fodor's most recent utterance of "Meaning Holism is a crazy doctrine" (or the thought that underlies it) then y is about Meaning Holism, and y is true iff Meaning Holism is a crazy doctrine.

There are two sufficient conditions, and for a few pennies each I will be happy to provide indefinitely many more.

5 As Rosch frequently notes, her work in this area was inspired by Wittgenstein's *Philosophical Investigations*.

6 For an excellent review of the literature on prototype and exemplar theories, see Smith and Medin 1981.

7 This is, in effect, the strategy I tried in Stich, (1978). Still another strategy would be for the eliminativist to argue that one or another of the competing research traditions in cognitive science is not a serious contender, and thus need not be considered.

8 Lycan (1988) correctly characterizes the "doxastaphobe's" argument as follows:

Typically their arguments take the form: "Common sense characterizes beliefs [say] as having each of the following properties: F, G, H, . . . But nothing that will be mentioned by any respectable future psychology will have all or even very many of those properties; therefore, beliefs will not figure in a mature psychology." (p. 4)

9 For a more detailed treatment of the issues discussed in this section, see Stich and Laurence (forthcoming).
10 After this paper was written I was delighted to discover that Michael Tye had independently reached very similar conclusions on the basis of very similar arguments. An extremely interesting paper in which Tye develops these themes, "Naturalism and the mental," appeared later in the year.

References

Barsalou, L. (1987) "The instability of graded structure: implications for the nature of concepts," in U. Neisser (ed.) *Concepts and Conceptual Development: Ecological and Intellectual Factors in Categorization*, Cambridge: Cambridge University Press.

Block, N. (1986) "Advertisement for a semantics for psychology," in *Midwest Studies in Philosophy*, vol. 10, pp. 615–78.

Burge, T. (1979) "Individualism and the mental", in *Midwest Studies in Philosophy*, vol. 4, pp. 73–121.

Cummins, R. (1989) *Meaning and Mental Representation* Cambridge, Mass.: Bradford Books/MIT Press.

Devitt, M. 1990: "A narrow representational theory of the mind," in W. G. Lycan (ed.) *Mind and Cognition: a Reader*, Oxford: Blackwell, pp. 371–98.

Devitt, M. and Sterelny, K. (1987) *Language and Reality: an Introduction to the Philosophy of Language*, Cambridge, Mass.: Bradford Books/MIT Press.

Dretske, F. (1988) *Explaining Behavior: Reasons in a World of Causes*, Cambridge, Mass.: Bradford Books/MIT Press.

Field, H. (1977) "Logic, meaning and conceptual role," *Journal of Philosophy* 74, pp. 379–409.

Field, H. (1986) "Critical notice: Robert Stalnaker, *Inquiry*," *Philosophy of Science* 53, pp. 425–8.

Fodor, J. (1981) "Introduction Some notes on what linguistics is about," in N. Block (ed.) *Readings in Philosophy of Psychology*, vol. 2, Cambridge, Mass.: Harvard University Press, pp. 197–207.

Fodor, J. (1987) *Psychosemantics: the Problem of Meaning in the Philosophy of Mind*, Cambridge, Mass.: Bradford Books/MIT Press.

Fodor, J. (1990a) *A Theory of Content and Other Essays*, Cambridge, Mass.: Bradford Books/MIT Press.

Fodor, J. (1990b) "Psychosemantics, or: Where do truth conditions come from?" in W. G. Lycan (ed.) *Mind and Cognition: a Reader*, Oxford: Blackwell, pp. 312–37.

Fry, D. B. (1979) *The Physics of Speech*, Cambridge: Cambridge University Press.

Giere, R. N. (1988) *Explaining Science: a Cognitive Approach*, Chicago: University of Chicago Press.

Glymour, C., Kelly, K., Scheines, R., and Sprites, P. (1987) *Discovering Causal Structure: Artificial Intelligence for Statistical Modeling*, Orlando, Fla.: Academic Press.

Goldman, A. I. (1989) "Interpretation psychologized," *Mind and Language* 4, pp. 161–85.

Gordon, R. M. (1986) "Folk psychology as simulation," *Mind and Language* 1, pp. 158–71.

Harman, G. (1986) "Wide functionalism," in S. Schiffer and S. Steele (eds) *Cognition and Representation*, Boulder, Colo.: Westview Press, pp. 11–20.

Jones, T., Mulaire, E., and Stich, S. (1991) "Staving off catastrophe: a critical notice of Jerry Fodor's *Psychosemantics*," *Mind and Language* 6, pp. 58–82.

Langley, P., Simon, H., Bradshaw, G., and Zytkow, J. (1987) *Scientific Discovery: Computational Explorations of the Creative Process*, Cambridge, Mass.: MIT Press.

Loar, B. (1981) *Mind and Meaning*, Cambridge: Cambridge University Press.

Loewer, B. (1987) "From information to intentionality," *Synthese* 70, pp. 287–317.

Lycan, W. G. (1988) *Judgement and Justification*, Cambridge: Cambridge University Press.

McCloskey, M. (1983) "Naive theories of motion," in D. Gentner and A. L. Stevens (eds.) *Mental Models*, Hillsdale, NJ: Erlbaum.

McCloskey, M., Caramazza, A., and Green, B. (1980) "Curvilinear motion in the absence of external forces: naive beliefs about the motion of objects," *Science* 210 (4474), pp. 1139–41.

McGinn, C. (1982) "The structure of content", in A. Woodfield (ed.) *Thought and Object: Essays on Intentionality*, Oxford: Clarendon Press, pp. 207–58.

Millikan, R. G. (1984) *Language, Thought and Other Biological Categories: New Foundations for Realism*, Cambridge, Mass.: Bradford Books/MIT Press.

Murdock, G. P. (1980) *Theories of Illness: a World Survey*, Pittsburgh, Pa..: University of Pittsburgh Press.

Murphy, G. and Medin, D. (1985) "The role of theories in conceptual coherence," *Psychological Review*, 92(3), pp. 289–316.

Nersessian, N. J. (1992) "How do scientists think? Capturing the dynamics of conceptual change in science," in R. N. Giere (ed.) *Cognitive Models of Science* (*Minnesota Studies in the Philosophy of Science*, vol. 15), Minneapolis, Minn.: University of Minnesota Press, pp. 3–44.

Papineau, D. (1987) *Reality and Representation*, Oxford: Blackwell.

Pickett, J. M. (1980) *The Sounds of Speech Communication: a Primer of Acoustic Phonetics and Speech Perception*, Baltimore, Md.: University Park Press.

Ramsey, W., Stich, S., and Garon, J. (1990) "Connectionism, eliminativism and the future of folk psychology," *Philosophical Perspectives*, 4, pp. 499–533.

Rips, L. (1989) "Similarity, typicality, and categorization," in S. Vosniadou and A. Ortony (eds) *Similarity and Analogical Reasoning*, Cambridge: Cambridge University Press.

Sklar, L. (1974) *Space, Time and SpaceTime*, Berkeley, Calif.: University of California Press.

Smith, E. and Medin, D. (1981) *Categories and Concepts*, Cambridge, Mass.: Harvard University Press.

Sober, E. (1984) *The Nature of Selection: Evolutionary Theory in Philosophical Focus*, Cambridge, Mass.: Bradford Books/MIT Press.

Stack, M. (1980) "Why I don't believe in beliefs and you shouldn&t," unpublished paper delivered at annual meeting of the Society for Philosophy and Psychology.

Stich, S. (1978) "Autonomous psychology and the belief–desire thesis," *The Monist* 61, pp. 573–91.

Stich, S. (1983) *From Folk Psychology to Cognitive Science: the Case against Belief*, Cambridge, Mass.: Bradford Books/MIT Press.

Stich, S. (1991) "Do true believers exist?" *Proceedings of the the Aristotelian Society*, suppl. vol. 65, pp. 229–44.

Stich, S. and Laurence, S. (forthcoming) "Intentionality and naturalism".

Stich, S. and Nichols, S. (forthcoming) "Folk psychology: simulation or tacit theory?", *Mind and Language*.

Thagard, P. (1988) *Computational Philosophy of Science*, Cambridge, Mass.: Bradford Books/MIT Press.

Tye, M. (1992) "Naturalism and the mental," *Mind* 101 (403) (April), pp. 421–41.

Part IV
Beyond Reductive Naturalism

15
Analytical Philosophy and the Nature of Mind: Time for Another Rebirth?

John J. Haldane

I

One of the most significant aspects of postwar analytical philosophy, as that "school" developed in Great Britain and then spread throughout (and beyond) the English-speaking world, was the renaissance of philosophy of mind. This rebirth owed a great deal to the intellectual midwifery of Gilbert Ryle (1949) at Oxford and Ludwig Wittgenstein (1953) at Cambridge. In their rather different ways both of these philosophers were concerned to espouse versions of what might be termed "humanistic personalism." They both aimed to show that the subjects of psychological states and of intentional actions are nothing other than living, active human beings, standardly operating within social contexts and in accord with generally intelligible principles of reasoning and behavior.

Given these personalistic origins, it is ironic that the current state of analytical philosophy of mind is one in which the most favored models of mentality are scientific and Cartesian ones. That is to say, models which regard minds as organic computational machines, or as occult subjects located within and controlling gross material bodies. Clearly those who find depth, and truth, in the Wittgensteinian approach are not likely to be sympathetic to much contemporary, philosophical psychology, but will regard it as having failed to learn the lessons of the earlier attacks on Cartesianism and as being in the grip of a scientistic worldview. Finding themselves in a minority they might then look elsewhere for support, hoping to show that opposition to scientific and Cartesian ways of thinking is by no means philosophically eccentric. Perhaps, then, this partly explains the increasing British and North American interest in "continental" thought, particularly as it bears (as most of it does) on the nature of human beings. Husserl, Heidegger, Merleau-Ponty and Sartre are obvious enough subjects for the attention which they are now receiving from this quarter (see, e.g. Caws, 1979, Cooper, 1990; Dreyfus, 1991; Dreyfus and Hall, 1982; Mulhall, 1990).

A further reason why one might look beyond current orthodoxies is that their doctrinal assumptions are very narrowly drawn. Indeed, anyone who reads extensively within contemporary analytical philosophy of mind and reflects upon what he as she has been studying is likely to feel the discomfort of intellectual claustrophobia. For nothwithstanding that the subject is very widely and actively pursued its content is remarkably confined. The boundaries of possibility are taken to stand close to one another and the available options are correspondingly few and, I believe, unappealing. They are, basically, one or another form of *physicalism*, and one or another form of *dualism*.

Even this characterization suggests a wider range of possibilities than is actually favored. Most contributors to contemporary discussions assume some version of *property dualism*, the main point of difference being over the question of how the relevant properties (and perhaps all properties) are to be regarded, i.e. as created or discovered, as reducible or as *sui generis*, and so on. Some authors, John Searle for example, regard mental properties as real and as physical properties of the brain (1984). Others, such as Richard, Swinburne (1986), also view them as real but argue that they are entirely distinct from anything material. A third party agrees that *if* there were irreducible mental features then they could not be physical, but preferring to maintain the integrity of physical science they take this to imply the nonexistence of distinctly psychological characteristics. They then try to show that the psychological can be reduced to the physical, or argue that if reductionism should fail then so much the worse for our ordinary ways of thinking about ourselves as minded agents.

Quite recently, and rather against the tendencies of the 1960s and 1970s, there has been something of a revival of realist versions of dualism, though the small, frail, and uncertain offspring do not match the robust products of Platonic, Augustinian, and Cartesian conceptions. The more marked trend, however (in accord with the general nominalist movement of postwar philosophy) has been towards various forms of *antirealism*. Two such approaches in philosophy of mind are especially prominent nowadays and correspond to similar traditions in metaethics, namely *relativism* and *error theory* (the view that while our beliefs about some subject matter could be objectively true, in fact none are). A commonly held version of the former, which again is easily described by way of its parallel application in ethics, is *projectivism*. According to this, we are (for whatever reason) disposed to ascribe to human beings, and to some other things (including animals and perhaps machines), a range of characteristics which they do not *in fact* possess. As one might say, following David Hume (in *A Treatise of Human Nature*, Book III, part I),

> Take any bodily behaviour allowed to be an utterance, examine it and its causes in all lights, and see if you can find that matter of fact, or real existence, which you call *meaning*. In whichever way you take it, you find only bodily movements. There is no other matter of fact in the case. The meaning entirely escapes you, as long as you consider the object. You never can find it, till you turn your reflection into your own breast, and find a response, which arises in you, towards this behaviour.

Many people who hold this sort of view, such as Daniel Dennett (1987), are projectivists only in respect of certain classes of phenomena. They advocate realism with regard to constitutive features of the foundation upon which the response-dependent characteristics are imposed. Indeed, the very metaphor of projection seems to require realism at some level; for it does not seem possible that what faces us is simply layer upon layer of projections, images all the way through. On the other hand, there are those, including Hilary Putnam who think that the conjunction of projectivism and realism, with regard say to psychology and physiology respectively, fails to register the full implication of at least some of those considerations which might have moved one in the direction of projectivism in the first instance (Putnam, 1988). It is often supposed, for example, that no coherent account can be given of the idea that objects are possessed of properties independently of our conception or experience of them; or similarly that it makes no sense even to think of the world as delineated apart from particular theories or practices within which talk of things and their characteristics features. Thus, some hold that any *philosophical* distinction between the real and the projected is misconceived. For present purposes it will be sufficient (though not uncontroversial) to characterize views of this sort as instances of wholesale *conceptual relativism*. On this account one need not accord priority to one domain over another (though one is not necessarily prohibited from doing so). It is easy to see, therefore, why those who take everyday psychology seriously, but who are repelled by ontological dualism, are attracted to some version of this view.

In contrast to accounts which regard the subject matter of everyday psychology as partly (or wholly) constituted by our affective responses and

practical interests, advocates of *error theories* consider psychological concepts as products of mistaken explanatory hypotheses and insist that there
are simply no phenomena to which they are properly applicable: there are
no intentional states or processes. In view of this conclusion one might
suppose, with Paul Churchland (1984, 1988) for example, that *eliminativism* is the only reasonable option. However, one could concede that
notwithstanding the vacuity of everyday (and most theoretical) psychology,
we cannot or should not abandon our erroneous assumptions. This outlook
has about it something of Greek tragedy, as it conceives our condition to
be one of incurable delusion. For various reasons which I have set out at
length elsewhere and will not now repeat, I regard eliminativism and error
theory as entirely misconceived and ultimately unintelligible[1] I am in
sympathy with their proponents to this extent, however: if projectivism or
total conceptual relativism are the best that can be hoped for by way of
preserving our common view of ourselves as persons, then it would be
better to say that, after all, our self-conception is a delusion – for all that
it may be inescapable.

One reason for being suspicious of these forms of antirealism is that they
embody a general doctrine of *compatibilism* which suffers from the same
weakness as the more specific versions introduced in connection with
freedom and determinism. The latter claim that the idea that action is
unconditioned by prior causes is an illusion, but also maintain that even
though what we do is the result of earlier events over which we had no
control, we may nonetheless regard ourselves as agents. Given the metaphysics of the projectivist, for example, we are invited to believe that while
an event may be wholly determined in its causes it may be conceived of in
a fashion which allows it to be a free action. Certainly it is believable that
what is determined may be *thought of* as being free, but thinking does not
make it so, and in the circumstances this belief would be false. Of course,
the projectivist may reply that on his view our taking something to have a
psychological character may be sufficient for its possessing it, for according to his view responses *constitute* the phenomena. But then I think we
would do better to view things as they really are and say that so far as what
occurred is concerned it was determined, notwithstanding that we may
regard it in ways that take no account of this.

Considering these rejections of relativism and error theory, one might
now expect some enthusiasm for recent versions of *realist* property
dualism. Once again, however, I cannot see that these come close to being
coherent, never mind convincing. Admittedly they accord reality where
other views elevate delusion, but they give no intelligible account of how
mental properties are related to physical ones; more precisely, they give no
adequate account of how the two sets of properties are integrated. Some
authors take the view that the two sets cannot be brought together in any

way that accords with such common assumptions as that thought may be causally efficacious, and so they retreat to some form of *epiphenomenalism*, to the idea, that is, that mental events are inert by-products of neurophysiological activity. It is difficult to see that this is anything other than a defeat so far as concerns the attempt to give account of ourselves in accord with the testimony of experience and reflection. If the existence of psychological phenomena makes no difference to the course of events, then we are more than half way in to the position occupied by the error theorist. But this conclusion, like that of the unrestricted error theory itself, is so far at odds with the evidence which continues to motivate philosophy of mind that it is barely intelligible as an answer to the question: what is our nature as thinkers and agents?

Moreover, current versions of property dualism are wont to combine it with substance monism of a physicalist type. This encourages an emphasis on "our" in the previous question, for reflection suggests that there is a continuing psychophysical subject of thought and action. The neo-dualist is apt to cite the human body or some part of it, i.e. the brain, as being that with which this subject is associated, but these suggestions are fraught with conceptual and epistemological difficulties and we are no nearer to understanding how subjectivity could be a characteristic of an entity whose substantial identity is given by its physical nature.

II

So far I have offered a catalogue of failures. This invites the question: How, then, should analytical philosophy proceed in the task of understanding mind and its relation to matter? Here I would urge the value of looking to other streams in the tradition of western philosophy. Earlier I mentioned "continental" authors who in one or another way trace their concerns back to the highly innovative studies of the Austrian philosopher Franz Brentano. It was he who introduced the idea that what distinguishes the mental is *intentionality*: all mental phenomena have content, or are "about" something or other, even where what they intend does not exist outside of the thinker's awareness (Brentano, 1973). Until quite recently the study of intentional acts was largely the preserve of those who followed Husserl's programme of *phenomenology*. Now, however, intentionality is at the centre of analytical philosophy of mind and this shift has resulted in new and productive ways of thinking about the nature of the psychological.

What I would like to see next, however, is the incorporation of a tradition of philosophical inquiry that lies behind that of Husserl and Brentano. The latter's "introduction" of intentionality was in fact the reintroduction of an idea made much of within neo-Aristotelian scholastic psychology (with which Brentano, as a sometime seminarian, was familiar). Developing remarks made by Aristotle in *de Anima*, Aquinas, and others spoke of thoughts as involving intentional being (*esse intentionale*) and related the possibility of this mode of existence to the nature of the intellect as an active power of living human beings. This suggests a way of understanding mind which connects to a general account of our nature as animals of a certain sort, and promises the possibility of a wide-ranging philosophical anthropology that is neither mechanistic nor ethereal but shares something of the viewpoints of the personalisms of Wittengenstein and Husserl (for further discussion see Haldane, 1988, 1991, 1993a).

When reviewing the currently favoured options in philosophy of mind I remarked that most projectivists and (realist) property dualists are inclined to be monistic with respect to the ground or bearer of psychological attributes. This monism is materialistic in the sense nowadays intended by the term "physicalism." When reading the work of philosophers of these sorts, and indeed most other writers in the field, it is difficult to resist the ironic thought that, to some degree or another, they are working under the influence of corrupted versions of two Aristotelian ideas. The first is the *substance–attribute* distinction, the second the *form–matter* one.

It is sometimes said, for example in connection with discussions of the doctrine of transubstantiation, that the medieval scholastics thought of properties as being metaphysical "skins" enveloping the objects which possess them. This is historically quite inaccurate and badly misrepresents the view they actually held and had derived from their reading of Aristotle. From Locke onwards, however, there has been a growing tendency, especially among English-speaking philosophers, to think about substances and properties in something like the object–envelope way.

Given the materialist presumption, one might more aptly liken the supposed relationship to that between an object and skins or coatings which cover its surface. Just as one may add further layers and the character of the surface will change in various ways depending partly on the nature of the previous surface; so, in this way of thinking, properties are laid (by Nature) one upon another atop an underlying bearer, and the character of any given layer is determined in part by what lies beneath it. This simple picture best makes sense of much of the contemporary discussion of *supervenience*, especially in connection with the psychological aspects of human beings. It is as if there is a *something* covered in a chemical coating which contributes to but does not exactly determine the character of the animalistic coat, which in turn affects the psychological layer settled upon it. Put another, but no more satisfactory, way, the psychological "super-venes" upon the biological which "supervenes" upon the chemical. (Here the etymology suggests that the term fits exactly the relationship it is now employed to describe, one layer "coming upon" another).

I shall not dwell upon what is wrong with this picture nor the current uses of the idea of supervenience. It is worth remarking, however, that had they been able to make sense of them Aristotle and Aquinas would very likely have been amused. Certainly this way of regarding the substance–attribute relation is not at all what they had in mind. For them, to be a substance is to be a kind of thing some of the characteristics of which are (metaphysically) constitutive of it but others of which, including, for example, location and volubility, may be possessed at one time but not at another. Clearly, in the Aristotelian tradition it makes no sense, save in special cases, to think (even metaphorically) of characteristics, whether essential or accidental ones, as lying in "layers" over the surface of the things which possess them.

A further mark of the difference between a sophisticated neo-Aristotelean such as Aquinas and many contemporary writers is revealed by the ways in which each speaks of matter. Possibly both might say that a human being is materially composed but what this would be likely to mean in the mouth of each is importantly different. I said earlier that, as currently employed, the substance–attribute distinction suggests that if one could uncover the underlying bearer of the psychological, biological, and chemical layers exhibited by a human being one would be left with a "something." The question, "What?" might now be met with the answer, "a lump or other quantity of matter." This way of speaking reveals that the original *philosophical* concept of matter as co-relative with form or nature, has undergone a change leaving in its place (or, more confusingly, lying along side it) an *empirical* notion. For Aquinas, by contrast, matter is best thought of (when philosophical questions are at issue) not as a kind of experientially encounterable stuff but as a metaphysical aspect of substances, be they countable things or measurable quantities of certain kinds. The only sense in which it is unarguably true for Aquinas that a human being is materially constituted is that the substance, i.e. the individual, is an actual living nature operating in various ways – as opposed, that is, to a mere possibility of a life which we might envisage if invited to consider human nature as such.

Conceived of in the abstract, matter is the potentiality for the instantiation of form, and form is the actualizing principle, that which makes something to be the kind of thing it is. Neither matter nor form can exist outside the individual substance whose concrete existence they mutually determine. Consider in this connection the following passage from Aquinas' discussion of the metaphysics of the creation (from *Summa Theologial*, Ia, q. 66, a.1, ad 1):

> As to formation, the argument is clear. For if formless matter preceded in duration, then it already existed; for this is implied by duration; since the

goal of creation is the actuality of being. But act itself is form. To say, then, that matter preceded, but without form, is to say that being existed actually, yet without act, which is a contradiction in terms. Nor can it be said that it possessed some common form, on which afterwards supervened the different forms that distinguish it . . . Hence we must assert that primary matter was not created altogether formless, nor under any one common form, but under distinct forms.

In the metaphysical sense matter is the potentiality for the instantiation of form. (This claim is comparable to the idea that space is the condition of the existence of material objects.) Clearly, then, it does not follow from this alone that every individual substance which realizes this potentiality is material in the modern sense. This being so we might entertain the prospect that empirical matter involves but one mode of potentiality and that the same form or determining principle may be realized in distinct (but related) ways corresponding to different species of possibility. And furthermore that it may be realized in each of these simultaneously (this idea is discussed in Haldane, 1989, 1991, 1993b).

This is racing ahead into unfamiliar territory and is likely to involve a multitude of philosophical problems; but what it suggests is that in the effort to understand how there can be thinking acting subjects it may be worthwhile to return to the ideas of an earlier tradition which, for all its innovations, is still largely unknown to analytical philosophers. It would be gratifying if this return to the past were to result in a further renaissance in the philosophy of mind.

Notes

This paper draws material from my essay "Incarnational anthropology", in Haldane (1991).

1 See my (1993a) "Folk psychology and the explanation of human behaviour: understanding folk", a reply to Paul Churchland (1988) "Folk psychology and the explanation of human behavior." Our debate has since continued: see P.M. Churchland (1993) "Theory, taxonomy and methodology: a reply to Haldane's 'Understanding folk,' ," and J. Haldan (1993c) "Theory, realism and common sense: a reply to Paul Churchland."

References

Brentano, F. (1973) *Psychology from an Empirical Standpoint*, ed. L. McAlister, London: Routledge & Kegan Paul.

Caws, P. (1979) *Sartre*, London: Routledge & Kegan Paul.

Churchland, P. M. (1984) *Matter and Consciousness: a Contemporary Introduction to the Philosophy of Mind*, Cambridge, Mass.: Bradford Books/MIT Press.

Churchland, P. M. (1988) "Folk psychology and the explanation of human behaviour," *Proceedings of the Aristotelian Society*, suppl. vol. 62, pp. 209–21; reprinted 1993 in S. M. Christensen and D. R. Turner (eds) *Folk Psychology and the Philosophy of Mind*, Hillsdale, NJ: Erlbaum.

Churchland, P. M. (1993) "Theory, taxonomy and methodology: a reply to Haldane's 'Understanding folk,' " *Proceedings of the Aristotelian Society* 93, pp. 313–19.

Cooper, D. E. (1990) *Existentialism: a Reconstruction*, Oxford: Blackwell.

Dennett, D. C. (1987) *The Intentional Stance*, Cambridge, Mass.: Bradford Books/MIT Press.

Dreyfus, H. (1991) *Being-in-the-World: a Commentary on Heidegger's Being and Time, Division I*, Cambridge, Mass.: MIT Press.

Dreyfus, H. and Hall, H. (eds) (1982) *Husserl, Intentionality, and Cognitive Science*, Cambridge, Mass.: Bradford Books/MIT Press.

Haldane, J. (1988) "Psychoanalysis, cognitive psychology and self-consciousness," in P. Clark and C. Wright (eds) *Mind, Psychoanalysis and Science*, Oxford: Blackwell, pp. 113–39.

Haldane, J. (1989) "Brentano's problem," *Grazer Philosophische Studien* 35.

Haldane, J. (1991) "Incarnational authorpology," in D. Corkburn (ed.) *Human Beings (Royal Institute of Philosophy Supplement* 29), Cambridge: Cambridge University Press, pp. 191–211.

Haldane, J. (1993a) "Folk psychology and the explanation of human behaviour: understanding folk," *Proceedings of the Aristotelian Society*, suppl. vol. 62, pp. 223–54; reprinted 1993 in S. M. Christensen and D. R. Turner (eds) *Folk Psychology and the Philosophy of Mind*, Hillsdale, NJ: Erlbaum.

Haldane, J. (1993b) "Mind–world identity theory and the anti-realist challenge," in J. Haldane and C. Wright (eds) *Realism, Representation and Projection*, Oxford: Oxford University Press.

Haldane, J. (1993c) "Theory, realism and common sense: a reply to Paul Churchland," *Proceedings of the Aristotelian Society* 93, pp. 321–7.

Hume, D. (1978) *A Treatise of Human Nature*, ed. L. A. Selby Bigge and P. H. Nidditch, Oxford: Clarendon Press.

Mulhall, S. (1990) *On Being in the World: Wittgenstein and Heidegger on Seeing Aspects*, London: Routledge.

Putnam, H. (1988) *Representation and Reality*, Cambridge, Mass.: Bradford Books/MIT Press.

Ryle, G. (1949) *The Concept of Mind*, London: Hutchinson.

Searle, J. (1984) *Minds, Brains and Science*, Cambridge, Mass.: Harvard University Press and Harmondsworth: Penguin Books.

Swinburne, R. (1986) *The Evolution of the Soul*, Oxford: Clarendon Press.

Wittgenstein, L. (1953) *Philosophical Investigations*, trans. G. E. M. Anscombe, Oxford: Blackwell.

16
The Mind–Body Problem

Brian O'Shaughnessy

There is not just one mind–body problem, there are many such problems. They mostly arise around the various relations holding between the mind and the body, for example, the ontological and the epistemological relations. In this paper I will offer a few comments concerning the first or ontological issue, though I shall have little to say concerning the theory that mental phenomena are identical with cerebral phenomena (the identity theory). For much of the time I will confine my comments to areas in which I have actually carried out philosophical investigation: notably, the fields of action and epistemology.

1 Ontology and Identity

(1) To begin with, a few words on issues of identity and ontology. I will try briefly to chart some of the relations holding between the following four fundamental items: animal, animal body, animal mind, animal brain (including, of course, the human kind). Thus, what is the relation between the animal and its body? Evidently an intimate relation, but not, I think, one of identity. One simple consideration comes to our aid in discussing such questions: survival conditions. Animals cease to exist upon death, but the animal body survives permanently defunct (and typically also "on the way out"). Whereas a dead body, like a dead tree or a dead cell or amoeba, is a real being, a dead duck is no more, is entirely and eternally in the past. Now this swift demonstration of nonidentity scarcely proves distinctness – which, on the face of it, looks highly improbable. A simple considera-

tion confirms this "intuition." A rigorous logically sufficient condition of animal existence is a state of life in an animal body; and such a logical bond can scarcely link distinct existents. In any case, since the animal occupies a position in physical space and time, and must on that account be presumed to be endowed with physical matter, it seems almost certain that it shares the matter and physical parts of its body.

So much for the relation between animal and body. The next relation concerns that quintessentially important bodily organ, the brain. Thus, what is the nature of the relation between animal and brain? It is, I think, very similar to the relation charted above, and is like it in being a relation which conjoins nonidentity with nondistinctness. This should emerge in the discussion which follows. But the first thing to note is, that whereas no empirical investigation was needed for us to know that the life of the body and the life of the animal were one and the same, and therefore that the body *was* the seat of the life that gave us being, it had to be established by empirical means that the brain *was* the organ of mentality. This fact certainly constitutes a difference, and an interesting one at that, between the relation in which we stand to our bodies and to our brains. It implies that in a certain limited sense it is a mere contingency that the brain is the site of mentality – as it is scarcely contingency that the body sustains the animal in being. But in fact the difference is not really of great significance, the reason being that the contingency is merely epistemological in type. People need not know what the brain is, but can scarcely fail to know what the body is, since they can scarcely fail to know that its death is its owner's death. So we stand in two diverse epistemological relations, on the one hand to our brains, on the other hand to our bodies. But epistemology is something other than nature, and of little relevance to questions of nature and identity. For the animal brain could not be what it is, and alive and functioning, without the simultaneous existence of mental phenomena and therefore also without the simultaneous existence of its animal owner.

From these few observations we may conclude that empirical investigation has disclosed that a living brain is a rigorous sufficient, and presumably also necessary condition of animal existence. This demonstrates the nondistinctness of animal and brain. Meanwhile we know that the brain is like the body in being able to survive the demise both of its life and its owner; this demonstrates nonidentity. So far the relation matches that of animal and body. But they differ as relations in a few minor respects. After all, the brain is merely a part of the body. To be sure, it is a special and indeed essential, indeed *the* essential part, for whereas an animal can survive the removal or destruction of its foot, it cannot survive the destruction or death of its brain. Therefore the animal is not merely nondistinct from its brain, it is necessarily nondistinct. The brain is the essential seat of the animal's life, and therefore the essential seat of its death.

(2)　So far we have been concerned with the relations between three self-subsistent entities, between three substances: animal, body, brain. What are we to say of the fourth member of the original list, the animal mind? Is this likewise a substance? Surely not. A mind exists when a brain is *in one state*, namely life; it fails to exist when that state fails to inhere in the brain. In any case, a mind is constituted of phenomena which are *predicated* of the substance, animal; this is sufficient to ensure its nonsubstantiality. While the mind is systemic in character – being composed of a perceptual-system, a belief-system, a value-system, a conative or motor system, character traits, and the like (all in turn systemically related) – that systematicity is insufficient to realize substantiality. Now this is not because the mind depends for its existence, and internally so, upon a substance, namely the brain; after all, the same is true of the animal itself – which is nonetheless a substance. It is because the mind is exclusively constituted of phenomena and traits which are as such predicated of the animal owner: intelligence, generosity of temperament, a batch of memories, and so on.

How does this nonsubstantial item relate to the being which owns it, the animal? What is the relation between mind and animal? The mind or mentality is an essential endowment of animality, indeed is a necessary and sufficient condition of animal existence; but, not being a substance, it stands in a relation of nonidentity with the animal of which it is predicated. Since it depends for its existence upon the physical state of the animal, the mind of the animal is in a certain sense dependent upon the animal; but since its existence is a necessary condition of animal existence, the dependence is mutual (albeit of a different order in each case). What of the relation of mind to brain? It is a relation of nonidentity, since the brain is a substance and the mind not, and the brain survives the mind. And it is a relation of essential dependence, since the state of life in the brain is a rigorous necessary and sufficient condition of the existence of a mind. Now this last consideration seems to me to be a clue to the nature of mind. Might the mind be identified with the life of the brain? We have just seen that they rigorously necessitate, and are rigorous sufficient conditions of one another. Tentatively then I propose this theory: namely, that the mind of an animal *is* the life of its brain. It is true that the theory leaves hanging in mid-air the nature of "the life of the brain," for example, its relation to cerebral states. However, I think we may safely assume that some physically realizable state or another is a rigorous sufficient condition of brain life. Since the death of an animal is a physical phenomenon, the life and therefore also the mind of the animal must, I think, be physical in nature.

Finally, a word on the relation of mind to body. This seems easy enough to state in the above very general terms. Plainly, it is a relation of nonidentity, and once again for the reason of survival: typically, the body out-exists the mind. Also, it is a relation to total and essential dependence, necessitating a condition of life in *the* essential organ of the body, namely the brain. Accordingly, the mind must be the life of the (unique) essential body-organ, the essential subsector of the life of the animal body. Perhaps this *is* "the mind–body relation" (ontological variety)! Now once again this relation of total dependence is counterbalanced by a converse relation of total dependence – of a different kind. Animal bodies *as such* are bodies of beings with life and minds, so that the body stands in a relation of essential dependence to mind and life. It is not as if animal bodies came first in evolutionary development, and then acquired the subsequent and inessential traits of life and being-of-an-animal and of-a-mind-possessor. It misunderstands the nature of the dependence of the mind on the body, to suppose that things might have been like this. Necessarily, animal body and animal mind and animal life came into being at exactly the same rate. The life of the animal "up-lifts" organized matter, just as much as organized matter "sustains" that life.

2 Epistemology

The epistemological mind–body problem comes to our notice when we examine the various possible epistemological relations that can hold between an animal and its own body, which is to say, between certain mental cognitive phenomena and its body. Only some of these are of a particular or special philosophical interest. Thus there is nothing distinctive about the visual relation, except that we see from a point in the body: one catches sight of one's own limbs in exactly the same sense and same way that one sees any other object. And the same is true of the tactile relation: one feels one's own brow exactly as one might feel the brow of another. So there is neither a special seeing or touching of one's body. Indeed, we relate in general epistemologically to some parts of the body as we do to anything else in physical nature, for example, to some of our own internal organs. Nevertheless, one body region is epistemologically privileged so far as we are concerned, and the privilege is in this region manifest in special modes of knowing. The region I am thinking of consists in the spatial disposition of our limbs and of our body as a whole. And the special means of discovery is that which normally obtains as we are aware of the spatial disposition of limbs we are intentionally moving. While it would be possible to discover some of these spatial dispositions visually or tactually, it would be both unnecessary and unnatural. Normally one is aware of these properties of one's limbs in a mode that is special, and that is unique to one's own body. We stand in this special epistemological relation to no other object in the world. This may not be an a priori necessity, but it is nonetheless a fundamental fact about animal (including human animal) existence.

Is the relation perceptual in type? Do we normally *perceive* the disposition of our limbs? How do I know my arm is flexed? Certainly, it *seems* flexed, but is that enough to demonstrate perception? Whether or not it is depends upon whether the "seeming" in question is some kind of a cognitive attitude: whether it is, say, a believing or an inclination-to-believe or a "hunch", or whether it is instead something pre-cognitive. Then that it is no sort of cognitive attitude, is apparent from the fact that the "seeming" could in principle occur in a person who knew with absolute certainty that his arm was straight and not flexed. Instead, such "seeming" constitutes *data* which may or may not found or generate a cognitive attitude. Thus it is in normal conditions strong evidence that one's arm is flexed; indeed, it is one's usual way of knowing. When one remembers that the experience is caused by arm flexion, and caused in regular conditions of neuromuscular health, there can be no doubt that the relation is perceptual in character. That is, there is no doubt that an animal to whom it seems in this special way that one of its limbs lies in a certain posture is one who thereby is perceiving that posture of its limb.

It is perception. But it is a strangely immediate variety of peroeption. Indeed, it is so immediate and so certain that one is inclined to liken it to the relation in which we stand to our own sensations and thoughts (say). However, this must be a mistake. There can be no doubt that a variety of "priveleged access" obtains in these latter kinds of psychological case, and that significant error is in normal mental circumstances at the very least difficult to imagine. Nothing like this holds in the case of one's limbs. The facts to which one has this *special mode* of access are facts to which others have open and easy access, of a different yet equally authoritative kind; and while significant error in the first-person case is rare and mostly physically pathological, it is nonetheless perfectly easy to imagine such error in one whose mind is in a perfectly normal condition. Evidently, the immediacy encountered in this bodily case is different in kind from that holding in psychological cases. It is, in fact, unique.

The relation is immediate in the following respects. It is not causally immediate, since proprioceptive and kinaesthetic sensation, caused by the limb situation, typically have a role to play in the genesis of the perceptual experience. It is attentively immediate, and in a special, and total way. It is not just that representationalism breaks down completely in this variety of perception, so that no sensations, no structure of sensations, no limb movements of any kind, representationally "mirror" or "stand in for" the perceived item. Since representationalism is unpopular, this may cut little ice with many people. But it is immediate in another regard: namely in that no secondary quality attentively mediates the perception of one's body. One's limbs are not first and before all else perceived as warm/red/odorous/noisy: they are simply perceived as present *and* as spatially disposed in a certain way. This latter property is not absolutely unique to body-perception. Tactile perception is also immediate in this respect. However, tactile perception is mediated precisely by the variety of perception – namely, proprioception – under discussion. In a word, proprioception is totally attentively immediate. Absolutely nothing comes to the attention in and through which the attention manages to pass on to limb and its posture. The passage is absolutely immediate.

But the variety and extent of immediacy is not all that is unique in proprioception. It is unique in its independence of the will. Thus, one *does* nothing to be aware of one's body; it simply happens of its own accord, in a way that is in marked contrast to the use of the other senses, which to a degree much of the time are in accord with our will. To become aware of items in my environment I must look, listen, feel, or taste, but I more or less cannot get away from the awareness of my own body. This awareness dogs one, like a shadow. To be sure, I can concentrate my attention actively on to a leg's posture, or on to the disposition of the fingers of my hand; but even as I do this, I remain aware of my body as a whole, and of the distribution of my limbs, pretty much willy nilly. Nothing like this holds of the other modes of perception.

The last thing to be said about proprioception, which once again singles it out as unique amongst attentive perceptual phenomena, is its natural and unfailing recessiveness. When one perceives an item in the environment it is rather as if it comes forward out of a fog: clear, delineated, individuated – a figure on a ground of diminished individuation and muted intensity. It is quite other with proprioception. And it could not but be other. The body is *that through which* we engage practically and epistemologically with the items in our environment – even when, in reflexive and unnatural manner, one adopts to one's own body the kind of such relations that one naturally adopts to environmental items (e.g. in self-concernful physical action). It mediates our practical and perceptual contact with the rest of the world. It is for this reason that it has to be attentively recessive.

Consider a simple act like catching a ball. It is true that if one were not aware of one's hand and arm one would not know what to do with them and would not manage to catch the ball; but it is at the same time equally true that if we were aware of hand and arm posture *in the nonrecessive way* we are aware of the path of the ball, we would in an epistemological sense stand in our own way and likewise achieve nothing. While we are, and have to be, immediately and inactively aware of our bodies and their spatial properties if we are to act in our environments, the awareness in question has of necessity to lurk in the background, to play second and unobtrusive fiddle to the awareness of these environs. Only thus can it perform its natural function.

3 Action

(1) I shall not seriously argue pro or con the theory that identifies mental phenomena with cerebral phenomena. However, one or two factors point strongly in its favor. The first of these factors has been often enough remarked: namely, the causal interaction of mind and physical nature at large. That is, the fact that mental events are causally linked to the environment, as when the sight of a snake on a path causes one to jump out of its way. Here a physical item causally impacts upon the mind, generating belief and a state of alarm, which in turn generates act-desire and a bodily action that is manifest in the movement of one's legs. It is difficult to believe that the mental events of awareness, alarm, desire, and will (that lie causally sandwiched between the purely physical events of light falling on a retina and the resultant movement of one's legs) can themselves be of a wholly different and nonphysical order of being. How can they enter into regular and intelligible causal relations, and be at the same time so utterly and wholly unlike? While this scarcely proves the point at issue, it is a consideration of some weight.

The other – very simple – consideration which points to the same conclusion is the fact that mental events are situated in time, which is to say, *physical time* (a point which Descartes either ignored or undervalued). How can they be situated in physical time, without also being set in physical space? Maybe it is conceivable, but it is far from obvious that it is. But if mental events are indeed set in physical space, where else can that space be but somewhere in the brain? After all, a living and fully functioning brain is a strong sufficient condition of conscious mental events and experiences, while a merely living healthy brain is a strong sufficient condition of more enduring psychological characteristics like one's character or innate knowledge, etc. Do not these latter considerations strongly support the conclusion that, if mental events have a place in physical space, that space must be the space of the brain? Then it seems to me to be a small step to the conclusion that these brain-sited events must themselves be cerebral in character. Once again this is not a proof, for I have not shown that being in physical time is inconsistent with spacelessness, but once again it carries argumentative force.

(2)   A more limited approach that leads in the same direction is provided by the analysis of physical action. (And here I think we really do have proof, of a more limited conclusion.) I shall not much rehearse the arguments in favor of the analysis that I propose, except to note the following few points.

   (a)   When we physically act, we are always psychologically-immediately aware that – successfully or not – we have "done" something or another (whether it be merely to try to do whatever deed we embarked upon).

   (b)   Bodily actions like walking are not wholly distinct from the above event of which psychologically we were immediately aware as we walked.

   (c)   Walking (etc) at the very least includes leg movements.

   (d)   Successfully trying to walk *is* walking.

   The most debateable of these claims is (d), which I shall not here attempt to defend; (a) and (c) are more or less obvious. And a strong case can be made out for (b), which again I shall have to omit. Personally speaking, I have no doubt that all four claims are true. Then the conjunction of (a), (b), (c), (d), point to a theory of the following kind: namely, that a psychological event, of kind trying-to-walk, is identical with an event of which the physical event of leg movement is part. The conclusion is that physical actions are constituted out of purely physical events like leg movements, muscle contractions, neurological messages, and the like, and are at the very same time psychological events of the kind of willing or trying or endeavoring or attempting. Presumably, this one event must be at once psychological and physical in nature. It is revealed to be so, by the descriptions under which it falls. It is revealed to be psychological by falling under the description "trying to move a limb," and revealed to be physical by falling under a description which singles out all of the bodily events that are parts of the one act-event. But ontological status cannot be description-relative. Accordingly, this one event is at the same time psychological and physical in status. These two statuses are in no way at war with one another. On the contrary, they are in perfect harmony.

This is a kind of "identity theory," with a few differences. The differences are two. First, the mind–brain identity theory identifies absolutely all psychological events and states with physical cerebral events and states, whereas this theory restricts itself to *physical actions*. Second, the mind–brain identity theory identifies psychological events exclusively with *cerebral events*; but this theory identifies the psychological event of willing with a sequence of bodily events which encompass both cerebral events and a set of non-cerebral events which are its natural expression and development. Then bearing in mind that physical actions include not only the movements of particular limbs, but of the body as a whole – as when one dances or stands to attention or flexes one's torso – one could say that in a certain sense this theory amounts to a psychologization of the entire body! In any case, it constitutes support of a kind for the identity theory. The mind–brain identity theory is notoriously short of arguments, and some people embrace the doctrine out of little more than a pious regard or even reverence for the physical sciences. Indeed, so far as I know, no one has offered a really convincing philosophical argument for this undoubtedly *philosophical* theory. (Hence perhaps the tendency to gesture vaguely towards the advancing physical sciences as argument.) Then the argument advances above in favor of a double-aspect analysis of physical action amounts in my view to a serious philosophical argument for a non reductionist physicalist account of bodily actions. That is, for a subclass of psychological events.

4 Definitions

What can we say about the very nature of the main items under consideration, namely: animal, animal body, animal mind, and animal brain? Can we offer any kind of criterion or test, or perhaps more ambitiously a set of definitions, of these basic elements of our existence? Where it seems at all possible, I will try to offer definitions. Now a system of definitions cannot but employ certain primitive indefinables, out of which the concepts of the various *definienda* are assembled. The concepts that seem destined for that role in this particular enterprise are three: material object, life, and psychologicality. A word here about each, in reverse order. Despite the closeness of the tie between the mental and intentionality, the concept of psychologicality admits of no a priori – or, for that matter, a posteriori – definition partly because it is ultimate, partly because it is wholly pellucid, but also because it is transcendent of life-systems. The same is true of the concept of life, even though life has certain necessary properties: for example, inhering in select parcels of matter, typically being processive in nature, being capable under certain conditions of supporting psychologicality, etc. There really is no saying a priori what life in essence is, nor hope of ever discovering tight necessary and sufficient conditions for its presence. At best one can seek to devise deep scientific tests which might be expected to apply elsewhere than on our planet. Finally, despite the fact that matter has the necessary property of occupying space, I cannot see how a priori we can know what it is that, being matter, satisfies this property. Then it is out of these three primitive concepts that I hope to assemble at least some of the fundamentals under discussion.

Armed with such equipment, the property of animality proves easy enough to define. It is a complex property, namely, that of being living and endowed with the capacity to support psychological phenomena, that is, living and endowed with a mind (howsoever primitive). I think this implies having actually occurrent mental characteristics or qualities. An animal must have some kind of mental nature, and cannot be a mere *tabula rasa*. Or rather, let us say that it cannot be endowed with no mental nature of any kind. Even a *tabula rasa* has passive causal powers: say, the capacity to experience sense impressions and act-desires, and possibly *not* the capacity to experience guilt or anguish (necessarily absent from the repertoire of any conceivable mosquito *tabula rasa*). In sum, an animal *is* a living – and therefore "enmattered" – entity, that is endowed with determinate psychological characteristics.

Earlier in this paper I examined the identity relations holding between the animal and its body. Those relations proved to be such that these two physical entities could be neither identical with nor wholly distinct from one another, and such that they shared of necessity the same matter and parts. We have just now offered some sort of account of what animality is. Can we do the same for the animal body? Can we say, in terms of the given concepts, just what the animal body is? No doubt the animal body is a subvariety of material object – but which subvariety? Is it perhaps a subvariety of living object? But it depends what a "living object" is. Is it an object that is living; or is it instead an object that is – something else? Since animal bodies can be dead, it must one presumes be "something else." But what? This raises a serious difficulty, if we are looking for a categorical property. What categorical property of objects is either identical with, or logically equivalent to, the property of being alive or dead? If we know of a physical entity that it can exist and be either alive or dead, what categorical property do we thereby know it to possess? Since it is a property that plants and animal bodies share, it cannot be a genus-property like being a plant. Then is it the property "vital"? But that seems to be no more than an *ad hoc* and vacuous reiteration of the disjunctive property, and it should in any case be such as to exclude animals (whose death signals extinction). What covering kind unites amoeba, and plant, and animal body – and excludes animal? I must admit that I am unable to think of any categorical property that satisfies this specification. And at this point one might understandably despair of defining the animal body, of saying what it is. However, this seems unsatisfactory, seeing that we managed to define the animal to which the body belongs. Then perhaps the problem stems from the fact that the concept of animal body is in some way *abstracted* from that of animal. This suggests that we look for its place in the vital system from which it is thus abstracted, as a guide to its nature. And I believe this to be a fruitful procedure. After all, the animal body has a natural function: a function which is uniquely its own, and definitional of its very nature. Thus, the animal body is that material object whose sole and primary function is to support the life and existence of its animal owner. Such a nature is perfectly consistent with being in such a defunct condition as to be irretrievably unable to perform that function. In any case, this tells us what the animal body *is*. It constitutes a definition. Finally, it can be expressed in terms of the three primitive indefinables. Thus, the animal body is that material object whose sole and primary function is to support the life and existence of the enmattered living entity with psychological characteristics to which it belongs.

I shall have little to say about the remaining two items, mind, and brain. The mind must be accounted a nonsubstantial entity, constituted entirely of systematically and causally interrelated and often enduring phenomena of type psychological, that occur in some one animal. This seems to be what it is. And the brain, any brain anywhere, any time, must be the bodily organ whose function it is to support a mind.

17
Functionalism, Identity Theories, the Union Theory

Ted Honderich

A person's mind includes a sequence of mental or conscious events: sensations, perceptions, thoughts, beliefs, emotions, desires, intentions, and the like. A person's mind may also be taken to include a set of dispositions to mental events, no doubt to all of the mentioned kinds of them. The dispositions, including a supposed sexy subset to which Freud paid attention, are neural, since there is not anything else they can be. That a neural structure (or anything else) is a disposition is merely the fact that it is persistent and the fact that it together with something else will or would make up a causal circumstance for a later event, say my conscious hope at this moment that this paper will persuade you of something.[1]

Hume has the fame of first seeing that there seems no reason to take a person's mind to be any more than the sequence of mental events – we could as well say mental states – and the set of dispositions.[2] (Of course there is the implicit fact that the sequence is internally related in several ways, most notably in that some of the events are memories of others; that is what makes it a single sequence.) Hume has the fame, more particularly, of noting that when we observe our mental lives, or better, when we recollect the moment just past of our mental lives, we never recollect anything but mental events. That is, we never recollect anything in any sense mental which is external to mental events, which thing possesses, underlies, or organizes them. A person is not such a mental entity, but, insofar as mental facts are concerned, just a single sequence of mental events. Hume's truth should neither be overlooked or taken for anything else. It is not a denial of the subjectivity of mental events, of which more in due course.

1 Functionalism

The mind–body problem is the problem of the relation of mental to simultaneous neural events. (It is not, as I understand it, the problem of the relation of mental events to their explanatory antecedents, including neural dispositions.) To deal with the mind–body problem we evidently need conceptions of both mental and neural events. What in general are mental or conscious events? What is their nature? In the past couple of decades, functionalism has seemed to be an answer offered to this question which is so fundamental to the philosophy of mind. Does functionalism really provide an answer, an adequate characterization of mental events in general?

There is a lot of loose talk in this neighbourhood, and much argument by slogan. There is also a lot of scientized reflection of uncertain philosophical virtue – by, as you might say, those with the policy of Penelope's wooers.[3] Also, if you are looking for something of which the thesis of variable or multiple realization is actually true, you could do worse than by starting with functionalism itself. So it will be as well to be definite about what *I* have in mind in speaking of functionalism. Let me first exclude some things.

Functionalism is not the banal assertion that (1) all mental events, however conceived, at least typically have certain causes and effects. Everybody believes something of that sort, save perhaps some remaining defenders of free will and a couple of epiphenomenalists. Nor is functionalism the assertion that (2) all mental events, conceived independently of their causes and effects, at least typically do have certain causes and effects. Perhaps most non-functionalist philosophers of mind accept something like this, while strict functionalists, as I shall call them, do not, since they deny the possibility of a conception of mental events independent of the causes and effects. Nor is functionalism to be taken as the somewhat stronger proposition of determinism that (3) all mental events, conceived independently of their causes and effects, do always and without exception have certain causes and effects. At least very many non-functionalists accept that, while strict functionalists do not, again because of the contained assumption of an independent conception.

Nor, to turn away from mental events in general, the genus, is functionalism to be understood as the proposition that (4) kinds or species of mental events, say beliefs or intentions, do have typical kinds or species of causes and effects. That is very true. Nor is functionalism the proposition, which I and many others accept, that (5) each of beliefs, intentions, and other kinds of mental events are to be understood or defined *partly* in terms of kinds of causes and effects. Who ever set out to understand desires wholly independently of action or behavior?

Another thing to be put aside is (6) the belief that kinds of mental events, as well as token mental events, can be successfully discriminated, individuated, or identified just by their causes and effects – where that is not a claim about their nature, or the whole of their nature. The belief is very likely true. With respect to events of *any* kind, what is more common than successful individuation by cause or effect or both?

Functionalism as I am understanding it is also not (7) just the program, obviously a fruitful one, of investigating, theorizing about, giving formal accounts of, and finding analogies to the causal sequences in which human mental events occur – the genus of them or its species. That program will contribute to any full account of mental events, but is not to be confused with something else. (8) Let me add, finally, that there are various theories and doctrines that fall under names got by adding a prefix to "functionalism." The prefixes include "classical," "metaphysical," "methodological," "machine," "homuncular," "wide," "narrow," "teleological," "sober," "weak," and so on. I am concerned only with any of these which is or approximates to functionalism as I am understanding it.

Functionalism as I am understanding it, which comes in two kinds, *purports to be a complete answer to the question of what mental events in general are.* That is, *it purports to give all of the common nature of mental events.* Does it? If so it will of course distinguish mental events from all else.

In strict functionalism, the first and most interesting of the two kinds, mental events at bottom are said to consist in no more than events which stand in certain causal relations.[4] That is, an event insofar as it is mental is at bottom no more than an event which stands in certain causal relations. We are to understand, certainly, that there is no further true and very different characterization of mental events, events insofar as they are mental. They have no further and very different mental character.

Mental events, more particularly, are in causal relations with (1) input, (2) what are called other "inner" events, and (3) output. That is the basic answer to the fundamental question of the philosophy of mind. Hence my wanting that glass of wine over there consists fundamentally in an event which was (1) an effect of such things as the glass of wine, (2a) also an effect of such things as an inner event having to do with my seeing the glass, (2b) a cause of other inner events, and (3) also the cause of such things as an arm-movement in the direction of the glass. This account of my wanting the glass of wine, already far from simple because of the occurrences of "such things as," can be enlarged by saying of the causal relata of the wanting that they stand in causal relations to other things than the wanting. We thus get a "holistic" account of the event, something in accord with "the holism of the psychological." But what we have in description of the mental event or the event as mental remains no more than causal relations.

All that is pretty vague, but here is no need to be more precise.

Shall we take it that strict functionalism asserts of the mental events of which we know most, our human mental events, that they have no other properties than the causal ones? Shall we take it, that is, whatever we say about how they are "realized" in our brains, that *they* do not have neural properties? Philosophers who do this evidently make their account of our minds, of our mental events, ethereal. Those of them who are fleeing traditional mystery about the mind, fleeing talk of ghostly stuff, succeed in making our mental events into *yet less* than ghostly stuff. It is perhaps not careless to say that these philosophers at least aspire to make our mental events into *no more than relations*. In defining strict functionalism, let us not take this disastrous path.

Let us rather follow other philosophers to be found in this neighbourhood and take it that in strict functionalism the mental events of which we know most, human mental events, are also neural events. This identity theory, which I shall take as contained in the functionalism in question, reduces to just the proposition that certain of our neural events have certain causes and effects. (The proposition both completes this functionalism's account of our mental events and serves as its solution to the mind–body problem insofar as we humans are concerned.) But it is noted that it is a possibility of some sort that events of other kinds than neural, say silicon events for a start, could stand in the same causal relations. Indeed, silicon events could have replaced our neural events without any repercussion for the given facts of mentality. The silicon events could have stood in the same causal connections. This is the proposition of variable realization or multiple realization, of which a great deal is made.

So much for how I understand functionalism and in particular strict functionalism. Supporters of strict functionalism typically pass by a basic and general objection to their conception of our mental events – often pass it by in the course of considering what seem to me lesser objections which are by-products of the basic and general one. Let us not follow them, but hesitate.

What we have at bottom is that human mental events insofar as they are mental consist in no more than events which are certain effects and causes: effects of input and other inner events, causes of other inner events and output. (Add more talk of causal relations if you like.) And, whatever might have replaced them, our human mental events are also neural. That is all there is to them. No matter what is taken to be essential to them, which of course is their causal connections, they are just neural events in certain causal connections. It is imperative to note that they are not made anything more than that by the proposition about variable realization or replaceability. *It* doesn't add anything more about *their* nature, constituents, or properties. Nothing at all.

Will it be said that talk of nature, constituents, and properties is obscure and doctrine-ridden? No doubt, and rightly, but the talk will have to be clarified in accordance with the sound idea that a thing's own nature, constituents, or properties do not include the thing's uniqueness or want of uniqueness in all or any respects. To discover that something is replaceable by something else is not to discover more of *its* nature. No question about it itself is answered by way of propositions about its uniqueness or replaceability. There seems even more reason to say this than to say the same about propositions about a thing's relations generally.

I suspect that in the haze of doctrine, many functionalists and their fellow travelers do not see that nothing is added to their account of our mental events as neural effects and causes by the proposition of variable realization.[5] They mistakenly suppose that by variable realization, by what they might call untying the mental from just the neural, or extending the mental beyond the neural, or indeed making the mental independent of the neural, they have given some place or recognition to an inescapable conviction about the mental, a conviction which is one part of or one thing expressed in our ordinary conception of our mental events. That conviction is simply that *our mental events have other or more than neural and causal properties.* More will be said of our ordinary conception of mental events in the second part of this paper, in another connection. That the given conviction is inescapable and part of the conception seems to me beyond doubt.

To speak differently, given that this functionalism reduces human mental events to neural events in certain causal connections, it shares the principal rebarbativeness of a family of doctrines including eliminative materialism and the earlier "nothing-but" materialism rejected by Davidson and almost everyone else – the materialism that issues in the declaration "Conceiving the *Art of the Fugue* was nothing but a complex neural event" (Davidson, 1980, p. 214). That family of doctrines includes a denial of our mental events as having other than or more than neural and causal properties. That *is* rebarbative, and no doubt strict functionalism taken as an account of our mental events will because of this basic and general objection follow behaviorism into the honorable past of the philosophy of mind.

The objection of rebarbativeness does not overlook differences between functionalism and members of the given family of doctrines. I am aware for a start that eliminative materialism may be said to deny, and to intend to deny, the existence of mental events, and that functionalism may be said to intend to save them, to offer an account of them, indeed to express our common conception of them. Only for eliminative materialism are our common mental categories like categories in witchcraft. The two doctrines are nevertheless alike in allowing to what we take to be our mental events only some or other neural and causal properties. It is for this reason that functionalism will follow behaviorism into the past.

This will happen, as it seems to me, as soon as the haze clears, despite the fact that it is not easy to construct a fundamental argument against strict functionalism.[6] This is so since it is difficult, perhaps impossible, to find a premise more secure than what we adversaries of this functionalism are asked to prove, that our mental events satisfy the inescapable conviction that they have other or more than neural and causal properties. This is annoying but not much of a weakness of our case, any more than it is a weakness of my belief that I am now in pain that I probably cannot construct an argument with a premise stronger than that belief. Hume, by the way, said exactly the same of arguing against someone who claims to perceive a self in addition to mental events. For Hume, there was nothing more secure than that there is no such perception to be had.

Consider a second functionalism, not strict. It is distinct from certain other philosophies of mind, indeed many, only in emphasis. Mental events in general are said to have their causal properties as their *essential* or *distinctive* properties, and of course are also said to have neural or silicon properties or the like. But it is now allowed that some mental events may have other properties, taken as needing less emphasis. They may have qualities spoken of in terms of "qualia," or "what something is like," or "what it is like to be something," or "raw feels." In particular some of our human mental events may have these additional properties.

This lenient functionalism, as implied, allows for some human mental events which *lack* the additional qualities. Thus it faces the general objection that in part it has the rebarbative character of eliminative materialism and the like. Its careless and curiously disjunctive conception of the other human mental events, which have or may have the additional properties, is in line with the thoughts of various defenders of mental events as ordinarily conceived. That careless conception and the thoughts from which it comes are in my judgment very useful but insufficient. They do not try to characterize directly and in a general way the nature of mental events. Be that as it may, however, the careless conception in assigning certain properties to some mental events *is* enough to stand in the way of the identity theory included in lenient functionalism as well as in strict functionalism.

We will be coming back to identity theories, and to what may be a proof of their failure – which proof I rely upon in what has just been said about lenient functionalism. As mentioned earlier, we shall also be considering our ordinary conception of our mental events, and what can be made of it. Certainly it is an attempt to characterize directly and in a general way the nature of our mental events. Consider now a more radical objection to strict functionalism, again overlooked by its proponents in their concern with this or that lesser difficulty. It is that this functionalism is incoherent.

As remarked above, any adequate account of mental events in general must distinguish them from all else. How does strict functionalism attempt this? How does it try to distinguish these events from others? We are told that at bottom they are events which have certain causes and certain effects. The identification of these mental events then plainly depends on the identification of the causes and effects. It depends in part on the identification of input and output events. For present purposes, we can restrict ourselves to input and output events, and leave aside other inner events.

Which are these input and output events? What distinguishes input events from others, and what distinguishes output events from others? Let us again think of humans. What distinguishes input events, such as an input event involving the glass of wine, from other environmental events which are causal with respect to humans, say one having to do with a flea of mine of which I am unaware? Clearly input events are not *all* the environmental-causal events. What distinguishes output events, such as the arm movement towards the glass, from other bodily events which are effects of internal human causes, say the bodily event which is unintended perspiration? Clearly output events are not all such bodily-effect events. To speak differently, functionalists are not and cannot be concerned with all the causal sequences which run through a body, but only some. They want the ones some of whose inner events are mental. How do they find them?

It is pretty clear how strict functionalism standardly proceeds. What it in fact does, unreflectively, is to take input as exactly environmental causes of mental events, *with the mental events understood in something other than the causal way*. Plainly they are conceived in our ordinary way. For a start, these mental events are conceived as having more than causal and neural properties. So with output. That is bodily effects of mental events, *with those mental events understood in something other than the causal way*. It is our ordinary way.

But then strict functionalism proceeds in this standard way on the basis of exactly what it denies, a true characterization of the nature of mental events themselves in terms of something other than their causal relations. It is incoherent in that it proceeds precisely on the basis of what it denies (cf. Lowe, sect. 4).

Will you say at this point that I have missed or obscured a simple point? Science has regularly been interested in and identified some class of events, say certain hereditary events, maybe having to do with eye color. It has taken this class of events to have a cause, and hypothesized about the nature of that cause. Often its nature has been discovered. This is how things went with the gene. Will you say that functionalism does just this sort of reputable thing?

That seems to me a confusion. The scientific procedure is not near to the standard procedure of functionalism. Functionalism begins, not with something analagous to hereditary events, already identified, but with something analagous to the gene, which it then uses to identify other events, and which it then claims to understand wholly in terms of those events. It denies that it presupposes and depends on a conception of something analagous to the gene, but, as said, it *does* use just that conception in order to specify the causal relata. That seems to me not good science but bad philosophy. If the science *was* analagous, and bad, it would proceed from the hereditary events to the gene, and then deny it used and depended on any other conception of the hereditary events but their being effects of the gene.

Is it necessary that strict functionalism proceeds in its standard way? Perhaps it can contemplate only two other options. It must (1) pick out a subclass of environmental-causal events or a subclass of bodily-effect events by means which make no reference at all to mental events, or (2) pick out the subclasses by means of a reference to mental events which does not render functionalism incoherent.

Perhaps some will be tempted to think that this functionalism can proceed in the first way. They will say something of the following sort. "Well, can't we just start by specifying a class of environmental causes straight off, including causes of receptor-events in eyes and ears, and specifying a class of bodily effects straight off, say limb movements and speech-productions – and then say mental events are what come in the middle? How does that presuppose an idea of mental events which makes the whole thing incoherent?'

There is a plain reply, that the procedure *does* depend on the fatal idea, at the start. Specifying the subclass of environmental causes is and can only be done by choosing those that that have certain effects, mental events somehow conceived. Necessarily these mental events are conceived as other than just effects of environmental causes. So with specifying the right class of bodily effects. That is how the unnoticed flea and the perspiration get excluded, as they need to be.

Something else does not need to be added, but usefully can be. There is no special or intrinsic character had by some environmental causes and some bodily effects and such that the functionalist can somehow depend on this character to advance her enterprise. Special categories of environmental causes and bodily effects do not pick themselves out. One relevant fact here is that it is conceptually and nomically possible that *any* environmental cause and *any* bodily effect go with no mental event at all, however conceived. This is so of stimulation of the retinas and of an arm movement in the direction of a glass of wine or my lips producing the sounds in "Pass me that glass, sweetheart."

If the first option fails, what of the second? Can strict functionalism pick out subclasses of causal-environmental events and bodily-effect events by means of a reference to mental events which does not make it incoherent? Perhaps you will be tempted for a moment to the idea that functionalism can depend on this conception of mental events: those events to which we ordinarily but mistakenly or wholly unenlighteningly ascribe a certain character. This character will be the one spoken of in terms of "qualia," "what it is like to be something," and so on.

This option has several peculiarities, including its own fatal disability. It depends on the thought that we mistakenly or unenlighteningly characterize a certain set of events. But mistakenly or unenlighteningly characterizing a set of events requires that we must already have discriminated them. We must have a conception of them. This cannot be a conception that picks out nothing, or anything. Thus this line of functionalist thought also depends, at one remove, on exactly what it denies, a conception of mental events in terms of other than their causes and effects.[7]

Let me make one final remark here on something implicit in what has been said. If strict functionalism *did* have no conception of the genus mental events but the causal one, or no conceptions of such species as belief and intention but causal ones, all its propositions would have an analytic nature which they seem to lack – and which, I think, most functionalists must wish them to lack. For a start, "Mental events in general are those which have certain causes and effects" would be nothing other than the proposition, "Events which have certain causes and effects do have those causes and effects."

2 Identity Theories

It was said above that we have an ordinary conception of our mental events, a conception of their general nature, a conception which includes the conviction that they have other or more than neural and causal properties. It is a conception owed to direct reflection on all of them, and in particular to our capability of recalling any mental event just past. (That we can do this is surely beyond question. Whether this recalling was misdescribed by advocates of "introspection" is a question that can be put aside.) The conception is therefore owed to what can be called mental realism, the policy of reflecting directly on mental events in their reality rather than turning away to this or that more tractable fact pertaining to them, such as the logico- linguistic features of sentences about them (see, e.g., Davidson, 1980, pp. 209–12) or their causal relations, or whatever else.

When I recall my experience or mental event a moment ago of seeing the line of trees out the window, I recall a content. It is not the trees, since if my visual cortex and a good deal more of my brain had been the same, but those trees had not existed, I would have had the same experience with the same content. This content is for me very certainly not just a bare causal term, like something-I-know-not-what in a mechanism about which I know only what affects it and what it affects. Indeed, it seems that contents can exist for me without my knowing their causal relations. Further, as hardly needs to be added, the content I recall is for me not at all a neural fact – and hence not something only causal and neural.

The idea of content is already the idea of something necessarily in relation to something else. That the idea of content is in this way relational is owed to the recallable fact of something distinct from content but also, as we can say, within the experience or mental event. It is another component. This other thing, for various reasons, is not a person. Initially we are tempted, not only by tradition, to call it a subject. Even initially we can resist the temptation to make more of it than we can discern, more of it than a property of a mental event. We can have, I think, *no* view of it as a causal term, and certainly no view of it as neural.

As for the relation between subject and content in a mental event, it is difficult to resist an initial step of taking them to be in a way interdependent. No content without subject, and no subject without some or other content.

There is no doubt that such reflections as these rapidly issue in problems. One group of problems has to do with a content's standing in a second relation. This is its relation to an object – in the example, the content's relation to the trees. This relation, we naturally say in beginning, consists in a content's being an effect of and representative of the object. Trying to make some initial sense of representation, and the true thought that in standard representation we need to be aware of what does the representing, may result in further reflections on the relation between content and what was called subject. It may result in the conclusion that this relation is certainly *not* one such that the subject is standardly aware of the content – aware of it in the way that I am aware of the trees. This is a denial of contents as subjective objects of awareness, which is to say as sense data and the like.[8]

An attempt to understand the second part of the content–object relation in terms of the second – to understand representation in terms of the causal relation – may also force reflection on the subject–content relation, and indeed issue in the conclusion that even restrained talk of a subject is perhaps dispensable. The question arises, at any rate, of whether we should try to restrict ourselves just to some notion of nonstandard awareness of content.

A further group of problems has to do with another of our convictions, so far unmentioned. It is the conviction of the givenness of objects, the givenness of the world. It includes a denial of *any* kind of awareness of content as against object, an understanding of content as the presentation of object, and a rejection of global skepticism about the world. The denial of any kind of awareness of content makes for yet more difficulty about what was initially called the subject–content relation.

I wish to propose but one proposition in connection with this brisk and less than perfectly comprehensible summary, or rather, in connection with the reflections summarized.[9] It is a proposition which concedes and does not seek to avoid the great difficulties faced in thinking directly about the mental. The proposition is that the reflections have a distinctive subject matter, certainly not only causal or neural, whose existence is undeniable. It is a subject matter which determines agreement or disagreement with the admittedly deflationary course of reflections. The subject matter exists as the subject matter of those deflationary reflections, and certainly does not evaporate in the course of them. Mental events have distinctive properties or a distinctive character, badly understood but undeniable.

In sum, each mental event has what can be called, a little grandly, a character of interdependent duality, a duality of two interdependent parts. Put into somewhat philosophical language, this is our ordinary conception of our mental events. (The duality, as will be noted, has nothing to do with mind–brain dualism.) As we can say briefly and less grandly, each mental event has a character of subjectivity.

So – we can at least begin to characterize the general nature itself of mental events. And we need to. To flee the obscurity, to eschew mental realism, is to fail to enter into what has first claim on the name of philosophy of mind. It is to fail to deal with its fundamental question. Giving up on mental realism also makes any true solution to the mind–body problem highly unlikely. If we have no decent sense of the nature of mind, what will keep us from mistaken views of its relation to body?

What is that relation? How are properly conceived mental events related to neural events, in particular events within a human central nervous system? Neural events are electrochemical events. *Their* nature is becoming increasingly well known. It is evidently unlike the nature of mental events just indicated.

Let me note, however, that neural events are not effectively characterized as physical events. They are not thereby distinguished from mental events, and, as might also be said, they are too much distinguished from them. There is a basic conception of what is physical, having to do in part with extension in space and time, which conviction does not have the disability of being relativized to contemporary science, future science, or completed science. There seems to me no serious objection to regarding mental events as physical events according to the basic conception. That is not to say that their mental properties are electrochemical, or that the mind–body problem is resolved or made much easier. It is made *somewhat* easier by the fact that the mental and neural realms are allowed to have something in common: physicality.

The various sciences which together make up neuroscience may be said now to have established a general proposition to which empirical philosophers and commonsensical persons have long been inclined. That is the proposition that every mental event is *intimately* related to a neural event, in a kind of necessary connection with it. Just as there are no ghosts, which is to say no minds or persons floating free of bodies, so there are no ghostly mental events either. To speak of a neural event, of course, is not necessarily to speak of anything simple, anything owed to outmoded doctrines of brain localization.

The proposition of psychoneural intimacy by itself rules out some philosophical theories about mind and brain. (It rules out, for example, the central idea of dualist interactionism. That idea is that sometimes an earlier mental event, somehow independent of the brain, causes a later neural event, and sometimes an earlier neural event causes a later mental event as independent.) The proposition of psychoneural intimacy, for good or ill, has as a natural product the theory, or rather the family of theories, to the effect that each mental event is *identical* with a neural event. Such mind–brain theories, identity theories, have had a certain dominance which they may now be losing. They are, I think, open to a certain refutation.

The refutation depends, first, on what has already been asserted, that mental events have a certain distinctive character, different from that of neural events.[10] The refutation depends, second, on taking a certain clear view of what must be meant by asserting of one event e_1 that it was numerically identical to another, e_2. What must be meant is that the one event had all and only the properties of the other, or that the referent of "e_1" had all and only the properties of the referent of "e_2". This view of identity, owed to Leibniz, is distinct from much else, including a good deal about theoretic reduction, bridge laws, and the like, which in fact does not serve the purposes of identity theorists. In fact, much that is said of theoretic reduction and the like is more in accord with something to which we will come, the union theory.

Third, the refutation depends on asking a certain question of any identity theory: what properties does the theory take a mental event to have had?

There are two possible answers. If the answer given is that the mental event had only mental properties, as ordinarily or realistically conceived, then a certain intolerable conclusion follows. The neural event to which it was identical also had only such mental properties. The given answer mentalizes the brain. Similar reasoning shows the absurdity of answering, to a related question, that the neural event had only neural properties. In this case the mind is neuralized. These intolerable conclusions, what can be called true identity theories, might be said to respect the proposition of psychoneural intimacy. That is little consolation.

There are other identity theories, so called, which may result partly from seeing the absurdity of true identity theories. At any rate, they clearly intend something different. In answer to the question of what properties were had by the mental event, they answer that it had both mental and neural properties. This enables them to avoid mentalizing the brain or neuralizing the mind. This also makes them into something very different from true identity theories. They are dualistic identity theories. They involve a dualism of properties. But that is not what is most important.

One of two things that are important has to do with a further feature or features which these theories have, and a certain general requirement essential to thinking of mind and brain.[11] First the general requirement.

(1) We find it impossible to believe that mental events or mental facts, these being conceived in the ordinary way, are not part of the explanations of our actions. Such mental events or facts *are* inelimin-able parts of the explanations of actions, and also of later mental events. This requirement that we put on theories of mind and brain can be called the "proposition of mental indispensability," or indeed the "proposition on the falsehood of epiphenomenalism." Certainly it is not inconsistent with neuroscience.

Dualistic identity theories, as I am understanding them, have the further feature that they assign causal efficacy to only the neural properties of mental events. In part, as it seems to me, this move is owed to a misconception of neuroscience. They also have the further feature that they assert only the relation of identity with respect to the neural and the mental properties of a mental event. What this comes to, evidently, is that all that they assert of the neural properties and the mental properties is that they were properties of the one event. It is denied, or not asserted, that the neural and mental properties were in nomic or lawlike connection. For this reason such theories are also spoken of as token-identity theories, as against type-identity theories.[12]

Dualistic identity theories, despite strenuous attempts to be in accord with it, therefore run afoul of the proposition of mental indispensability. The mental properties of an event are given no causal role with respect to later mental events and actions. They are no more given a causal role than the color of something is given a causal role by the fact that the weight of the thing has such a role.[13] It may be thought that they could still satisfy the mentioned proposition if they were to allow for nomic connection between mental and neural properties, but this they do not do.[14]

(2)   The second important thing to be noted about dualistic identity theories is that contrary to natural expectation they also fail to satisfy the proposition of psychoneural intimacy. It seems easy to think that anything calling itself an identity theory must satisfy the proposition, but this is not so. The identity theories we are considering are merely to the effect that a mental property is a property of an event which also has a neural property. That by itself is far from giving us what the proposition of psychoneural intimacy requires, which is some kind of necessary connection between the mental and the neural. A mental property is made no more intimate with a physical than my height with my politics.

Still, it is not possible in this paper to do more than sketch a central part of the proposed refutation of identity theories. Without attempting more, I now turn to what seems to me a superior proposal about the mind–body problem.

3 The Union Theory

An arguable solution to the mind–body problem must be a product of at least the several requirements or constraints that have been mentioned. It must proceed from an adequate conception of the mental, as functionalism does not. It must be in accordance with psychoneural intimacy and also mental indispensability, which is not the case with the dualistic identity theories.

The theory of psychoneural union, or the union theory, consists in three parts, the first being a certain hypothesis. That hypothesis, the hypothesis of psychoneural nomic correlation or just the correlation hypothesis, has to do with a mental event and a simultaneous neural event. It is to the effect that they stand in a certain connection. The hypothesis is this:

> For each mental event of a given type there exists some simultaneous neural event of one of a certain set of types. The existence of the neural event necessitates the existence of the mental event, the mental event thus being necessary to the neural event. Any other neural event of any of the mentioned set of types will therefore stand in the same relations to another mental event of the given type.[15]

The hypothesis relates mental events only to neural events, and for that reason alone is different from the idea of functionalists about the variable realization of mental events not only in our central nervous systems, but in silicon and whatever else. The hypothesis *does* specify a many–one relation, but this holds between just the neural realm by itself and the mental. It specifies this many–one relation rather than a one–one relation since it appears to be a fact that different types of neural events can go with but one type of mental event.[16]

The correlation hypothesis depends on an explication of nomic relations, and in particular the relation of two events such that the first necessitates the second and the second is necessary to the first. What the relation comes to, in my view, is that certain conditional statements are true. For one thing to necessitate another is for it to be true, roughly, that since the first occurred, then, whatever else had been happening, the second would still have occurred. The hypothesis, since it concerns simultaneous events, may with reason be said *not* to take the neural event as causal with respect to the mental, or of course the mental event as causal with respect to the neural. The hypothesis asserts more than the supervenience of the mental on the physical, since supervenience as usually understood falls short of being nomic connection.[17]

What the correlation hypothesis comes to in part, informally speaking and by way of an example, is that my thought of Lublin a moment ago stood in a certain tight relation with a certain neural event, and if another event of exactly that type occurs, I or somebody else will be thinking of Lublin in exactly the same way.

There is nothing in the mentioned fairly standard explication of nomic elations which stands in the way of such relations holding between mental and neural events, as the hypothesis supposes. Further, there is very impressive neuroscientific evidence for the hypothesis. In my estimate the evidence is overwhelming. Even if philosophical objections to the hypothesis did not seem open to good rejoinders, as they do, the evidence could be taken to overbear the objections.[18] To speak too quickly, if there is a contest between a philosophical doctrine of the mental which stands in the way of its being in nomic connection with the neural, and, on the other hand, neuroscientific evidence that the mental is in nomic connection with the neural, it is the doctrine that must give way.

The second part of the union theory has to do with the causation of a mental event and the simultaneous neural event. (The causation is sometimes or often or perhaps nearly always a matter of the neural dispositions mentioned in passing at the start of this paper.) If we consider such a pair of events, as it seems to me, we must conclude that they constitute not two effects but one. This is only initially surprising, and clearly they must be so regarded. The argument rests in part on the idea that since a mental event, as just asserted, is necessary to the simultaneous neural event, it cannot be that the neural event is by itself necessitated by some prior causal circumstance. There can be no prior causal circumstance, something akin to a causally sufficient condition, for the neural event alone. If there were such a guaranteeing thing, the neural event would not have the simultaneous mental event as a necessary condition. It would not be dependent upon it.

The union theory in its third part is simply that each of a mental event and the simultaneous neural event may be causal with respect to an ensuing action or a later mental event. Each of the mental event and the neural event is within a causal circumstance for the action or later mental event.

The union theory, then, is that a mental event and the simultaneous neural event are nomically related, as specified by the correlation hypothesis, and that they constitute a single effect, and that each event may be causal with respect to an action or later mental event. (It is also true that the two events are in a less important sense a single cause.) The theory proceeds from an adequate conception of mental events. It will be evident that it is in accord with the proposition of psychoneural intimacy. This is a matter of its first two parts. It will be equally evident that in virtue of its third part it is in accord with the proposition of mental indispensability.

It is easy not to see clearly that the similarities and disimilarities which hold between mind–brain theories, and assumptions as to such similarities and dissimilarities, influence us too much. Let me then examine some assumptions. It may be supposed, first, that the union theory is properly spoken of as a dualism or dualistic while identity theories are not. In fact this is as good as a mistake.

Certainly there is every reason to regard the union theory as "more dualistic" than true identity theories, but they are open to the fatal objections noticed earlier and in any case are a minority of contemporary identity theories. Most contemporary identity theories, including the best-known one, Davidson's anomalous monism, are or appear to be dualistic identity theories. What these come to, when characterized as they were earlier, is the proposition that a mental *property* is a property of one event which also has a neural *property*. That is all that the talk of identity comes to. The union theory, in contrast, was expressed as the proposition that a mental and a simultaneous neural *event* are nomically connected, and a single effect, and that both *events* are causal with respect to actions and later mental events.

These ways of speaking produce the illusion that dualistic identity theories are "less dualistic" than the union theory. But it is no more than an illusion. There is no obstacle whatever in the way of stating the union theory in such a way that it disappears. What we can say is that the union theory comes to this: the mental and the neural properties of an event are nomically connected, and a single effect, and both properties are causal with respect to actions and later mental events. Both of dualistic identity theories and the union theory, if stated with full metaphysical or ontological propriety, would in my view be stated in terms of individual as against general properties of our central nervous systems. No doubt we should all go in for more metaphysical or ontological propriety.

Some readers may now wonder if the union theory is approximate to one of several sorts of identity theory famously discriminated by Davidson. He wrote,

> It may make the situation clearer to give a fourfold classification of theories of the relation between mental and physical events that emphasizes the independence of claims about laws and claims of identity. One the one hand there are those who assert, and those who deny, the existence of psycho-physical laws; on the other hand there are those who say mental events are identical with physical and those who deny this. Theories are thus divided into four sorts: *nomological monism*, which affirms that there are correlating laws and that the events correlated are one (materialists belong in this category); *nomological dualism*, which comprises various forms of parallelism, interactionism, and epiphenomenalism; *anomalous dualism*, which combines ontological dualism with the general failure of laws correlating the mental and the physical (Cartesianism). And finally there is *anomalous monism*, which classifies the position I wish to occupy. (Davidson, 1980, pp. 213–14)

There is much that might be said about this, in addition to what has been noticed already: that *anomalous monism* (or token-identity theory) appears to assert a dualism of properties, and hence is a dualistic identity theory, and that in general it is misleading to speak of the mental as against the physical rather than the mental as against the neural.

With respect to *nomological monism* (or type-identity theory) it is impossible that any consistent doctrine be monistic, in the strict sense of concerning but one thing and hence being a true-identity theory, and also include nomic or lawlike connection within itself. Nomic connection requires two things. But of course the label "nomological monism" can be and is used to cover the proposition of which we know, that a mental and a physical property are both properties of one thing, a dualistic identity theory.

Given this second usage, to come to the main question now under consideration, the union theory can of course be taken as approximate to nomological monism. Perhaps it is closest to that. However, it can also be taken as about as approximate to *nomological dualism*, although it is none of epiphenomenalism, interactionism, or parallelism. (The latter, I take it, cannot be what is usually often meant by "parallelism," which is the doctrine that the explanation of the correlation of mental and neural events is not within those events, a matter of *their* nomic connection, but a matter of God's ongoing control or whatever.) Nothing hangs on whether the union theory is assimilated to nomological monism or nomological dualism. Its name has the virtue of distinguishing it from other forms of both, and much else that is in some relation to it.

There is also a more general conclusion to be drawn from these reflections on Davidson's characterization. "Nomism" and "dualism" are no longer of much use, and need a long rest. The same is true of "identity theory."

As with any philosophical theory, the union theory's worth needs to be judged partly by its capability of resisting objections. Of course there are very many of these, deriving from a wide range of philosophical doctrines, commitments, and impulses. Let me finish by glancing at one objection.

The union theory is a paradigmatic instance of what is usually called individualism, as against anti-individualism or externalism. What this comes to, it might be said, is that the union theory offers explanations of the occurrence of a mental event wholly in terms of facts internal to the individual or person. These explanations are not partly in terms of facts external to the individual, facts of the individual's environment, in particular her linguistic environment.

But that characterization of the union theory may be unenlightening or misleading. Of course the union theory *does* consort perfectly with plain facts about the earlier explanatory role of environment with respect to mental events. We see, hear, and learn, with the eventual result that certain mental events occur. However, at the end of the story, there are sufficient explanations of those events within the individual.

As it seems to Tyler Burge, the individualism of the union theory is faulted by what is taken to be the provable proposition that there is no sufficient explanation of at least certain mental events within the individual. Given the different things meant by "arthritis" in two neurally identical but linguistically different worlds, a man's thought in one world that he has arthritis in his thigh may be false, and the neurally identical man's thought in the other world that he has arthritis in his thigh may be true, and the two thoughts may be different. If so, individualism and the union theory in particular are refuted (Burge, 1979, pp. 73–121).

One response to this doctrine has to do with its central proposition. That is somehow to the effect that mental events have a *dependency* on environment which is distinct from the standard dependency consistent with the union theory and much else: a special dependency somehow distinct from the standard dependency involving eyes, ears, and learning, however the special dependency may involve the standard dependency.

That special dependency remains obscure, true to its Hegelian ancestry. If it were to amount to no more than the fact that environmental facts enter into the *individuation* in a certain sense of mental events, then anti-individualism would be consistent with union theory. This is so since something can contribute to the individuation of something else without being at all explanatory of it – part of a full explanation of it. Effects and spatiotemporal location of something may contribute to its individuation. There are reasons for thinking, furthermore, that special dependency must indeed be conceived in terms of such individuation or something like it. Roughly speaking, all other alternatives are unbelievable or pretty much a mystery.[19]

Notes

1 This paper in its second and third sections is hardly more than a summary of what is laid out elsewhere, mainly in chs 1–6 of my (1988) *A Theory of Determinism: the Mind, Neuroscience, and Life-hopes*, and identically in a paperback of chs 1–6 of that book, *A Theory of Determinism: Mind and Brain* (1990). For a short, untechnical account, see chs 1–6 of my (1993a) *How Free Are You? The Determinism Problem*. For comments on earlier drafts of the present paper, I am really grateful to Jonathan Blamey, Tim Crane, John Heil, Jennifer Hornsby, O. R. Jones, E. J. Lowe, Paul Noordhof, Jane O'Grady, and Mike Targett. We are not all in agreement. Perhaps not in perfect mutual comprehension either.

2 David Hume, *A Treatise of Human Nature*, Book I, part IV, section 6.

3 "Those who study particular sciences and neglect philosophy are like Penelope's wooers, who made love to the waiting women" (Aristippus) in Bacon, *Apothogems*, no. 189.

4 I leave out complications having to do with logical or computational as against causal relations, which do not affect the issue.

5 Perhaps this is true of Kim Sterelny (1990). Others with iron stomachs do certainly see the fact. David Lewis (1966) did so in his early paper, "An argument for the identity theory."

6 The objection of rebarbativeness can be said to beg the question, and hence not to be "an argument." That shows that there is a role in inquiry for something other than "arguments," or, better, despite what I say in the text, that "arguments" can be too narrowly conceived.

7 There is also what may reduce to a variant of the second option, proposed to me by Paul Noordhof. It is that the functionalist can initially identify mental events as those events to which we have direct or introspective access, without saying anything of their nature. This needs more attention than I have room to give it here. So does what may be regarded as a general response to the incoherence objection by Tim Crane (1992, pp. 193–5) in his "Mental causation and mental reality."

8 On subjective objects of awareness, see my (1991) "Seeing qualia and positing the world."

9 The reflections in question are pursued in "Seeing things," forthcoming in *Synthese*. I refer to them partly for the additional reason that they may indicate that those who espouse mental realism are not necessarily inclined to free-and-easy or credulous thinking about the mind.

10 The proposition that mental events have this distinctive character of course makes pointless the identity theory within strict functionalism, which theory asserts that mental events are no more than neural events with certain causal roles.

11 As the diligent reader can work out, the identity theory within lenient functionalism is of this sort.

12 The names may be misleading. In an ordinary sense of "type," types of mental properties might go with types of neural properties without nomic connection. To assert mental properties are in nomic connection with neural properties is indeed to assert that types go with types, but to assert that types go with types is not necessarily to assert nomic connection.

13 For elaboration of my own view of this point, on which there is now some agreement, see the books mentioned in note 1 above and also Honderich (1982, 1984, 1993b).

14 In fact allowing for nomic connection, so long as only neural properties are allowed to be causal, will result in an inconsistent theory. See my discussion of neural causation with psychoneural correlation (Honderich, 1988 or 1990, pp. 154–7 in each case).

15 It may be useful to relate some usages. The genus mental events, as mentioned at the beginning of this paper, has in it the kinds or species which include beliefs generally and intentions generally. Each kind or species has in it a multitude of particular or token mental events. Each of these is of a type: the type which includes identical token events.

16 I now have some doubt that nomic connection between mind and brain must be one–many. There is something to be said for a one–one relation. What I have no doubt about is that the mind–brain connection is nomic.

17 However, see Davidson's (1993) recent and perhaps revisionary account of supervenience in "Thinking causes."

18 In particular I have in mind Davidson's (1980) objections to psychoneural nomic connection in "Mental events."

19 The argument is presented in my (1993b) "The union theory and anti-individualism."

References

Burge, T. (1979) "Individualism and the mental," in *Midwest Studies in Philosophy*, vol. 4, pp. 73–121.

Crane, T. (1992) "Mental causation and mental reality," *Proceedings of the Aristotelian Society* 92, pp. 185–202.

Davidson, D. (1980) "Mental events," in *Essays on Actions and Events*, Oxford: Clarendon Press.

Davidson, D. (1993) "Thinking causes," in J. Heil and A. Mele (eds) *Mental Causation*, Oxford: Clarendon Press, pp. 3–17.

Honderich, T. (1982) "The argument for anomalous monism," *Analysis* 42(1), pp. 59–64.

Honderich, T. (1984) "Smith and the champion of mauve," *Analysis* 44(2), pp. 86–9.

Honderich, T. (1988) *A Theory of Determinism: the Mind, Neuroscience, and Life-hopes*, Oxford: Clarendon Press.

Honderich, T. (1990) *A Theory of Determinism: Mind and Brain*, Oxford: Clarendon Press (pbk edn of first half of Honderich, 1988).

Honderich, T. (1991) "Seeing qualia and positing the world," in A. P. Griffiths (ed.) *A. J. Ayer: Memorial Essays*, Cambridge: Cambridge University Press, pp. 129–51.

Honderich, T. (1993a) *How Free Are You? The Determinism Problem*, Oxford: Oxford University Press.

Honderich, T. (1993b) "The union theory and anti- individualism," in J. Heil and A. Mele (eds) *Mental Causation*, pp. 137–59.

Honderich, T. (forthcoming) "Seeing things," *Synthese*.

Hume, D. (1978) *A Treatise of Human Nature*, ed. L. A. Selby-Bigge and P. H. Nidditch, 2nd edn, Oxford: Clarendon Press.

Lewis, D. (1966) "An argument for the identity theory," *Journal of Philosophy* 63, pp. 17–25; reprinted 1971 in D. M. Rosenthal (ed.) *Materialism and the Mind–Body Problem*, Englewood Cliffs, NJ: Prentice-Hall, pp. 162–71.

Lowe, E. J. (1991) "Real selves: persons of a substantial kind," sect, 4 in D. Cockburn (ed.) *Human Beings*, Cambridge: Cambridge University Press.

Sterelny, K. (1990) *The Representational Theory of Mind: an Introduction*, Oxford: Blackwell.

18
Nonreductive Materialism

Terence Horgan

I believe that all human behavior is susceptible in principle to neurobiological explanation. I deny, however, that this naturalist, or materialist, metaphysical claim forces us to choose between reductionism on the one hand, or unpalatable views like eliminativism or epiphenomenalism on the other hand. I advocate instead a nonreductive form of naturalism or materialism, a form that is robustly realist about mentality itself, about mental causation, and about mentalistic causal explanation. The position I favor makes three key claims. First, the mental and the neurobiological explanatory frameworks are compatible, rather than excluding each other. Second, although their compatibility does require that certain inter-level constraints be satisfied, it does *not* require that mentalistic psychology be reducible to neurobiology; indeed, psychology probably is not so reducible. Third, mentalistic causal explanations have an important kind of autonomy *vis-à-vis* neurobiological causal explanations. I will take up each of these claims in turn.

1 Causal Explanation and Multiple Explanatory Levels

In causal explanation the effect phenomenon e, described as instantiating a phenomenon type E, is shown to depend in a certain way upon the cause phenomenon c, described as instantiating a phenomenon type C. Often the dependence involves the fact that c and e are subsumable under a counterfactual-supporting generalization – either a generalization that directly links C to E, or else a more complicated generalization whose antecedent cites a combination of properties that includes C. But in order for the cited properties C and E to be genuinely explanatorily relevant to the causal transaction between c and e, it is not enough that c caused e and that c and e are subsumable under such a generalization. Rather, C and E must fit into a suitably rich pattern of counterfactual relations among properties.

It is important to understand how this feature is related to the structure of scientific laws. The generality of the fundamental laws of the natural sciences does not consist merely in their having the logical form, "All As are Bs.' It consists, rather, in the fact that they are systematic in scope and structure, so that a wide range of phenomena are subsumable under relatively few laws. One major source of their systematicity is that (1) the laws cite *parameterized* properties, namely quantitative magnitudes, where the parameters are numerical values that these magnitudes can take on when instantiated, and that (2) the laws contain universal quantifiers ranging over the values of these parameters (in addition to the universal quantifiers ranging over the non-numerical entities in a law's domain). Newtonian velocity, for example, is not a single property but an infinite array of determinate properties, one for each real value of V. The resultant generality of a physical law consists largely in the existence of a whole (typically infinite) set of specific nomically true principles, each of which is a specific instantiation of the law with specific numeric values "plugged in" for the quantitative parameters. Rich patterns of counterfactual dependence, of the sort that are a crucial feature of successful scientific explanation are reflected by the truth of such sets of specific law-instantiations.

On this general view, the explanatory relevance of a pair of properties C and E, instantiated respectively by a pair of causally related events or states c and e, consists largely in the fact that C and E fit into a suitable pattern of counterfactual relations. Accordingly, a single phenomenon can perfectly well be subject to a variety of different explanations, involving properties from a variety of different counterfactual relation patterns. Often several distinct patterns, all explanatorily relevant to a single phenomenon, will involve different levels in the hierarchy of the sciences, for example microphysical, neurobiological, macrobiological, and psychological.

Explanations at the level of intentional psychology evidently fare quite well, under this conception of explanatory relevance. Consider first commonsense psychology, so-called folk psychology. There are robust patterns of counterfactual dependence among the state types (including act types) posited by folk psychology – patterns systematizable via generalizations containing universal quantifiers ranging over suitable parameters. These parameters are not quantitative, but instead are *propositional* (or *intentional*); i.e., they are the kinds typically specified by "that" clauses. Take, for instance, explanations of actions on the basis of reasons. The intentional mental properties that constitute reasons (namely belief types, desire types, and other attitude types), in combination with act types, clearly figure in a rich and robust pattern of counterfactual dependence of actions upon reasons that rationalize them, a pattern undergirded by the following generalization:

> For any subject S, desire D, and action A, if S wants D and S believes that doing A will bring about D, then *ceteris paribus*, S will do A.

There also are rich patterns of counterfactual dependence among folk psychological mental states themselves, again undergirded by suitable *ceteris paribus* generalizations involving quantification over propositional/intentional parameters. Wanting, believing, etc. figure in these generalizations as vast (possibly infinite), highly structured, arrays of properties, a different specific property for each specific value of each propositional variable.

Theoretical intentional psychology, in order to be a viable scientific discipline, also will need to advert to rich patterns of counterfactual dependence over the state types it posits. So its laws too, if they are to have the kind of generality that is essential to science, will contain universal quantifiers ranging over its parameters.

2 Inter-level Constraints on Compatibility

What are the appropriate constraints on inter-level connections between distinct theories or explanatory frameworks, given the compatibilist conception of explanation just sketched, and given a broadly naturalist (or materialist, or physicalist) metaphysical orientation? In addressing this question one cannot simply proceed by first laying out the key theses of a naturalist/materialist metaphysics, and then reading off from these the appropriate inter-level constraints. For our notion of what constitutes naturalism or materialism is somewhat vague and inchoate. Articulating plausible inter-level constraints goes hand in hand with articulating a physicalistic metaphysical *Weltanshauung*. I propose four such constraints.

First is *compatibility with the causal explanatory adequacy of physics*. Metaphysical naturalism includes the view that physics is causally and explanatorily complete, within its own domain; i.e. every fact or phenomenon describable in the language of physics is fully explainable (to the extent that it is explainable at all) entirely on the basis of facts and laws of physics itself. There are no causal "gaps," in the nexus of physically describable events and processes, that get "filled in" by causes that are not themselves physically describable; and there are no explanatory gaps, *vis-à-vis* physical phenomena as physically described, that get filled in by higher level nonphysical explanations. Accordingly, inter-level connections among distinct theories or distinct explanatory frameworks must be consistent with the internal causal/explanatory completeness of physics.

Second is *physical supervenience.* Metaphysical naturalism also includes the view that the facts of physics synchronically fix, or determine, all the facts. One dimension of this supervenience idea is purely global, pertaining to physically possible worlds considered in their entirety:

> Any two physically possible worlds which are exactly alike physically are also exactly alike in all other respects.

A second, non-global, dimension pertains to individuals and their intrinsic properties:

> For any two individuals i and j, either in two distinct physically possible worlds or in a single such world, if i and j are exactly alike in all intrinsic physical respects then they are exactly alike in all other intrinsic respects.

And yet a third dimension pertains to individuals and their non-intrinsic properties – properties like propositional attitude state-types with wide content. It can be roughly characterized this way:

> For any two individuals i and j, either in distinct physically possible worlds or a single such world, if (1) i and j are exactly alike in all intrinsic physical respects, (2) i has a non-intrinsic property F, and (3) i and j are exactly alike with respect to all non-intrinsic physical features that are pertinent to i's possession of F, then j also possesses F.

Inter-level connections among distinct theories or distinct explanatory frameworks must be consistent with all three dimensions of physical supervenience.

Third is the *existence of physical causal mechanisms.* This constraint concerns causal explanations that cite properties from higher-level theories or explanatory frameworks. For any causal transaction where some higher level property F is cited as causally explaining the effect, there must be an *underlying mechanism* in virtue of which the transaction occurs – a mechanism involving a physical property (or a complex of physical properties) which, on the given occasion, *physically realizes* the property F. That is, causal transactions involving higher order properties must be grounded in causal mechanisms involving the nexus of physical causes and effects, mechanisms describable and explainable at the level of physics.

Fourth is the *noncoincidentality of higher-level generalizations*. In order for higher-level counterfactual relation patterns to have genuine causal/explanatory relevance to phenomena that exhibit higher-level properties, the higher-level generalizations that systematize those patterns must themselves be *noncoincidental*, when viewed from a lower level perspective. There is much still to be done philosophically in coming to understand what does, and does not, count as a generalization that is "merely coincidental." But let me mention one general line of thought, currently much in the air in philosophy of mind, which I find highly suggestive, especially in connection with laws and counterfactual relation patterns involving intentional mental states. The leading idea is that the tendency of a given kind of creature both (1) to instantiate certain higher level properties when it does, and (2) to satisfy the relevant higher level laws, is plausibly viewed as the product of nature's "design," through evolutionary natural selection. (In the case of wants, beliefs, and other intentional mental states, representational content and relational proper function are so intimately connected, presumably, that it is clearly no mere coincidence that attitude types and act types figure as they do in robust counterfactual patterns. On the contrary, the requirement that propositional attitudes should figure in such patterns is crucial to their relational proper function; it is their *raison d'être*, from the point of view of nature-as-designer.)

Notably absent from my list of proposed inter-level constraints is the requirement that higher-level laws, theories, or properties be *reducible* to lower-level ones. As I said at the outset, I deny that a naturalist/materialist position in metaphysics must embrace any such constraint. In particular, I deny that mentalistic psychology must be reducible to neurobiology; and in fact I very much doubt whether the former is *in fact* reducible to the latter. Reductionism will turn out to be false if it is physically possible for intentional mental state-types to be physically realized in a variety of different ways; and it seems very likely that that multiple physical realization is indeed physically possible, *at least* as between different physically possible species of cognizers (for instance, Martians vs. humans). Moreover, for all we now know (and I emphasize that we really *do not* now know), intentional mental states might turn out to be radically multiply realizable, at the neurobiological level of description, even in humans; indeed, even in individual humans; indeed, even in an individual human *given the structure of his nervous system at a single moment of his life.*

3 The Explanatory Autonomy of Psychology

Higher-level theoretical concepts typically are, as I shall put it, *strongly realization-neutral*. By this I mean that they are neutral both (1) about *how* they are realized at lower theoretical levels (and ultimately at the level of physics), and (2) about whether or not they are *uniquely* realized at lower levels (and ultimately at the physics level). Because of this feature, the integrity and applicability of special science concepts is not undermined if they turn out to be multiply realizable at lower theoretical levels of description (and ultimately at the level of physics).

Accordingly, multiple realizability also would not undermine the truth, or the explanatory potential, of higher-level theoretical generalizations either. When we explain a phenomenon by appeal to such a generalization, thereby fitting the phenomenon into a systematic pattern of counterfactual relations, it makes no difference *how* the abstract properties involved in this pattern are neurobiologically realized in humans, as long as they are realized somehow or other. Moreover, it makes no difference whether or not these properties are *uniquely* realizable in humans – as opposed to being either multiply realizable from one human to another, or even fully multiply realizable in each particular human.

Precisely because these things don't matter, psychological explanation has a degree of independence from neurobiological explanation. Thus the strong realization-neutrality of the properties figuring in psychological explanations is, I suggest, a feature that provides a robust form of explanatory autonomy for psychology.

Notes and References

Various aspects of the views summarized here are developed at greater length in Horgan (1993), and in the other papers listed below.

Horgan, T. (1981) "Token physicalism, supervenience, and the generality of physics," *Synthese* 49, pp. 395–413.

Horgan, T. (1982) "Supervenience and microphysics," *Pacific Philosophical Quarterly* 63, pp. 29–43.

Horgan, T. (1984) "Supervenience and cosmic hermeneutics," *Southern Journal of Philosophy* 22, Spindel Conference Supplement, pp. 19–38.

Horgan, T. (1987) "Supervenient qualia," *Philosophical Review* 96, pp. 491–520.

Horgan, T. (1989) "Mental quausation," *Philosophical Perspectives* 3, pp. 47–76.

Horgan, T. (1991) "Actions, reasons, and the explanatory role of content," in B. P. McLaughlin (ed.) *Dretske and His Critics*, Oxford: Blackwell, pp. 73–101.

Horgan, T. (1993) "Nonreductive materialism and the explanatory autonomy of psychology," in S. Wagner and R. Warner (eds) *Naturalism: a Critical Appraisal* South Bend, Ind.: University of Notre Dame Press.

Horgan, T. and Tienson, J. (1990) "Soft laws," in *Midwest Studies in Philosophy*, vol. 15, pp. 256–79.

19
The Myth of Nonreductive Materialism

Jaegwon Kim

I

Reductionism of all sorts has been out of favor for many years. Few among us would now seriously entertain the possibility that ethical expressions are definable, or reducible in some broader sense, in terms of "descriptive" or "naturalistic" expressions. I am not sure how many of us can remember, in vivid enough detail, the question that was once vigorously debated as to whether so-called "physical-object statements" are translatable into statements about the phenomenal aspects of perceptual experience, whether these are conceived as "sense data" or as some manner of "being appeared to." You may recall the idea that concepts of scientific theories must be reduced, via "operational definitions," to intersubjectively performable procedures whose results can be ascertained through observation. This sounded good – properly tough-minded and hard-nosed – but it didn't take long for philosophers and scientists to realize that a restrictive constraint of this sort was neither enforceable nor necessary – not necessary to safeguard science from the threat of metaphysics and pseudoscience. These reductionisms are now nothing but museum pieces.

   In philosophy of mind, too, we have gone through many reductionisms; some of these, such as logical behaviorism, have been defunct for many years; others, most notably the psychoneural identity theory, have been repeatedly declared dead; and still others, such as versions of functionalism, are still hanging on, though with varying degrees of difficulty. Perhaps as a result of the singular lack of success with which our earlier reductionist efforts have been rewarded, a negative image seems to have emerged for reductionisms in general. Many of us have the feeling that there is something rigid and narrow-minded about reductionist strategies. Reductionisms, we tend to feel, attempt to impose on us a monolithic, strait-jacketed view of the subject matter, the kind of cleansed and tidy picture that appeals to those obsessed with orderliness and discipline. Perhaps this impression has something to do with the reductionists' ritual incantations of slogans like "parsimony," "simplicity," "economy," and "unity," all of them virtues of a rather puritanical sort. Perhaps, too, reductionisms are out of step with the intellectual style of our times: we strive for patterns of life and thought that are rich in diversity and complexity and tolerant of disagreement and multiplicity. We are apt to think that the real world is a messy place and resists any simplistic drive, especially one carried on from the armchair, toward simplification and unification. In fact, the word "reductionism" seems by now to have acquired a negative, faintly disreputable flavor, – at least in philosophy of mind. Being a reductionist is a bit like being a logical positivist or member of the Old Left; an aura of doctrinaire naïveté hangs over such a person.

At any rate, reductionism in the mind–body problem has been out of fashion since the late 1960s; it has been about that long since the unexpectedly early demise of the psychoneural identity theory, a doctrine advertised by its proponents as the one that was in tune with a worldview adequately informed by the best contemporary science. Surprisingly, the abandonment of psychoneural reductionism has not led to a resurgence of dualism. What is curious, at least in terms of the expectations set by the earlier mind–body debates, is the fact that those who renounced reductionism have stayed with physicalism. The distinctive feature of the mind–body theories that have sprung up in the wake of the identity theory is the belief, or hope, that one can be an honest-to-goodness physicalist without at the same time being a reductionist. In fact, a correct and realistic view of science as it is practiced will show us, the new physicalists assure us, that as an account of the "cross-level" relation between theories, classical reductionism is untenable everywhere, not just about the psychophysical relation. The leading idea in all this has been the thought that we can assuage our physicalist qualms by embracing "ontological physicalism,"[1] the claim that all that exists in space-time is physical, but, at the same time, accept "property dualism," a dualism about psychological and physical attributes, insisting that psychological concepts or properties form an irreducible, autonomous domain. The issue I want to explore here is whether or not a robust physicalist can, consistently and plausibly, swear off reductionism, that is, whether or not a substantial form of physicalism can be combined with the rejection of psychophysical reduction.

To lay my cards on the table, I will argue that a middle-of-the road position of the sort just described is not available. More specifically, I will claim that a physicalist has only two genuine options, eliminativism and reductionism. That is, if you have already made your commitment to a version of physicalism worthy of the name, you must accept the reducibility of the psychological to the physical, or, failing that, you must consider the psychological as falling outside your physicalistically respectable ontology. Of course, you might decide to reconsider your commitment to physicalism; but I will not here consider what dualist alternatives there might be which are still live options for us. So if I am right, the choices we face concerning the mind–body problem are rather stark: there are three-dualism, reductionism, and eliminativism.

II

Pressures from two sources have been largely responsible, I believe, for the decline of reductionism in philosophy of mind, a decline that began in the late 1960s. One was Donald Davidson's "anomalism of the mental," the doctrine that there are no precise or strict laws about mental events (see Davidson, 1980). According to Davidson, the mental is anomalous not only in that there are no laws relating mental events to other mental events but none relating them to physical events either. This meant that no nomological linkages between the mental and the physical were available to enable the reduction of the former to the latter. The second antireductionist pressure came from a line of argument based on the phenomenon of "multiple realizability" of mental states which Hilary Putnam forcefully brought to philosophical attention, claiming that it directly refuted the reductive materialism of Smart and Feigl (see Putnam, 1975). Jerry Fodor and others have developed this idea as a general antireductionist argument, advancing the claim that the "special sciences," such as psychology, sociology, and economics, are in general irreducible to physical theory, and that reductive materialism, or "type-identity theory," is generally false as a theory about science (Fodor, 1974; see also Boyd, 1980). Earlier physicalists would have regarded the irreducibility as evidence showing the mental to be beyond the pale of a scientifically respectable ontology; that is, they would have inferred eliminativism from the irreducibility. This in fact was Quine's response to the problem of intentionality, as it is the response of some recent eliminativists (see, e.g., Churchland, 1981). But not for the latter-day physicalists: for them, the irreducibility only meant that psychology, and other special sciences, are "autonomous," and that a physicalist can, in consistency and good conscience, accept the existence of these isolated autonomous domains within science.

Let us begin with Davidson. As noted, the anomalism of the mental can be thought of as the conjunction of two claims: first, the claim that there are no purely psychological laws, that is, laws connecting psychological events with other psychological events, and second, the claim that there are no laws connecting psychological events with physical events. The second claim, which we might call "psychophysical anomalism," is what underlies Davidson's argument against reductionism. The argument is simple and direct: the demise of analytical behaviorism scotched the idea that the mental could be definitionally reduced to the physical. Further, psychophysical anomalism shows that a nomological reduction of the mental isn't in the offing either. The implicit assumption about reduction in this argument is one that is widely shared: reduction of one theory to another requires the derivation of the laws of the reduced theory from those of the reducer, and for this to be possible, terms of the first theory must be appropriately connected via "bridge principles," with those of the second. And the bridge principles must be either conceptually underwritten as definitions, or else express empirical lawlike correlations ("bridge laws" or "theoretical identities").[2]

This is all pretty straightforward. What was striking was the further philosophical conclusions Davidson inferred from these considerations. Far from deriving some sort of dualism, he used them to argue for a materialist monism. His argument is well known, but it bears repeating. Mental events, Davidson observed, enter into causal relations with physical events.[3] But causal relations must be backed by laws; that is, causal relations between individual events must instantiate lawful regularities. Since there are no laws about the mental, either psychophysical or purely psychological, any causal relation involving a mental event must instantiate a physical law, from which it follows that the mental event has a physical description, or falls under a physical event kind. From this it further follows that the event is a physical event. For an event is physical (or mental) if it falls under a physical event kind (or a mental event kind).

It follows then that all events are physical events – on the assumption that every event enters into at least one causal relation. This assumption seems entirely unproblematic, for it only leaves out events that are both *causeless* and *effectless*. If there are any such events, it is difficult to see how their existence can be known to us; I believe we could safely ignore them. So imagine a Davidsonian universe of events: all these events are physical events, and some of them are also mental. That is to say, all events have physical properties, and some have mental properties as well. Such is Davidson's celebrated "anomalous monism."

Davidson's ontology recognizes individual events as spatiotemporal particulars. And the principal structure over these events is causal structure; the network of causal relations that interconnect events is what gives intelligible structure to this universe of events. What role does mentality play, on Davidson's anomalous monism, in shaping this structure? The answer: None whatever.

For anomalous monism entails this: the very same network of causal relations would obtain in Davidson's world if you were to redistribute mental properties over its events any way you like; you would not disturb a single causal relation if you randomly and arbitrarily reassigned mental properties to events, or even removed mentality entirely from the world. The fact is that under Davidson's anomalous monism mentality does no causal work. Remember: on anomalous monism, events are causes or effects only as they instantiate physical laws, and this means that an event's mental properties make no causal difference. And to suppose that altering an event's mental properties would also alter its physical properties and thereby affect its causal relations is to suppose that psychophysical anomalism, a cardinal tenet of anomalous monism, is false.[4]

Anomalous monism, therefore, permits mental properties no causal role, not even in relation to other mental properties. What does no causal work does no explanatory work either; it may as well not be there – it's difficult to see how we could miss it if it weren't there at all. That there are in this world just these mental events with just these mental characteristics is something that makes no causal difference to anything. On anomalous monism, that an event falls under a given mental kind is a causally irrelevant fact; it is also something that is entirely inexplicable in causal terms. Given all this, it's difficult to see what point there is in recognizing mentality as a feature of the world. I believe that if we push anomalous monism this way, we will find that it is a doctrine virtually indistinguishable from outright eliminativism.

Thus, what we see is this: anomalous monism, rather than giving us a form of nonreductive physicalism, is essentially a form of eliminativism. Unlike eliminativism, it allows mentality to exist; but mentality is given no useful work and its occurrence is left wholly mysterious and causally inexplicable. This doesn't strike me as a form of existence worth having. In this respect, anomalous monism does rather poorly even in comparison with epiphenomenalism as a realism about the mental. Epiphenomenalism gives the mental a place in the causal network of events; the mind is given a well-defined place, if not an active role, in the causal structure of the world.

These observations highlight the importance of *properties*; for it is in terms of properties and their interrelations that we make sense of certain concepts that are crucial in this context, such as law, causality, explanation, and dependence. Thus, the anomalousness of mental properties has far-reaching consequences within Davidson's framework: within it, anomalous properties are causally and explanatorily impotent, and it is doubtful that they can have any useful role at all. The upshot is that we don't get

in Davidson's anomalous monism a plausible form of nonreductive physicalism; his anomalous monism comes perilously close to eliminativism.[5]

III

Let us now turn to the multiple realizability (or "compositional plasticity")
of psychological events and its implications for phychophysical reduction.
In a passage that turned out to have a profound impact on the discussions
of the mind–body problem, Putnam wrote,

> Consider what the brain-state theorist has to do to make good his claims.
> He has to specify a physical-chemical state such that *any* organism (not just
> a mammal) is in pain if and only if (a) it possesses a brain of a suitable
> physical-chemical structure; and (b) its brain is in that physical-chemical
> state. This means that the physical-chemical state in question must be a
> possible state of a mammalian brain, a reptilian brain, a mollusc's brain
> (octopuses are mollusca, and certainly feel pain), etc. At the same time, it
> must *not* be a possible (physically possible) state of the brain of any
> physically possible creature that cannot feel pain. Even if such a state can
> be found, it must be nomologically certain that it will also be a state of the
> brain of any extraterrestrial life that may be found that will be capable of
> feeling pain before we can even entertain the supposition that it may *be* pain.
> (Putnam, 1975, p. 000)

This paragraph helped bring on an unexpectedly early demise of the
psychoneural identity theory of Smart and Feigl and inspired a new theory
of the mental, functionalism, which in spite of its assorted difficulties is
still the most influential position on the nature of the mental.[6] Putnam's
basic point is that any psychological event-type can be "physically realized"
or "instantiated" or "implemented" in endlessly diverse ways, depending
on the physical-biological nature of the organism or system involved, and
that this makes it highly implausible to expect the event to correlate
uniformly with, and thus be identifiable with, some "single" type of neural
or physical state. This idea has been used by Fodor to formulate a general
antireductionist argument, whose gist can be quickly summarized.

As we have seen, reduction of one theory to another is thought to
require the derivation of the laws of the reduced theory from the laws of
the reducer via "bridge laws." If a predicate of the theory being reduced
has a nomologically coextensive predicate in the reducing theory, the univer-
sally quantified biconditional connecting the two predicates will be
available for use as a bridge law.[7] Let us say that the vocabulary of the
reduced theory is "strongly connected" with that of the reducing theory if
such a biconditional bridge law correlates each predicate of the former

with a predicate of the latter. It is clear that the condition of strong connectibility guarantees reduction (on the assumption that the theory being reduced is a true theory). For it would enable us to rewrite basic laws of the target theory in the vocabulary of the reducer, using these biconditional laws in effect as definitions. Either these rewrites are derivable from the laws of the reducing theory, or else they can be added as additional basic laws. In the latter case, the reducer theory has been expanded; but that does not diminish the ontological and conceptual import of the reductive procedure.

But what multiple realization puts in doubt, according to the antireductionist, is precisely the strong connectibility of mental predicates *vis-à-vis* physical-neural predicates. For any psychological property, there is in principle an endless sequence of nomologically possible physical states such that, though each of them "realizes" or "implements" it, none of them will by itself be coextensive with it. Why can't we take the *disjunction* of these physical states as the physical coextension of the mental property? Putnam somewhat disdainfully dismisses this move, saying only that "this does not have to be taken seriously" (Putnam, 1975, p. 437). I think there are some complex issues here about disjunctive predicates vs. disjunctive properties, complexity of predicates vs. that of properties, etc.; but these are likely to be contentious issues that can only distract us at present.[8] So let us go along with Putnam here and disregard the disjunctive solution to the multiple realization problem.

In rejecting the disjunction move, however, Putnam appears to be assuming this: *a physical state that realizes a mental event is at least nomologically sufficient for it.* For if this assumption were rejected, the disjunction move couldn't even get started. This generates laws of the form $P_i \rightarrow M$, where M is a mental state and P_i is a physical state that realizes it. Thus, where there is multiple realization, there must be psychophysical laws, each specifying a physical state as nomologically sufficient for the given mental state. Moreover, Putnam's choice of examples in the quotation above, which are either biological species or determinate types of physical structures ("extraterrestrials"), and his talk of "species-specificity" and "species- independence" (1975, p. 437) suggest that he is thinking of laws of a somewhat stronger form, "$S_i \rightarrow (M \leftrightarrow P_i)$", which, relative to species or structure Si, specifies a physical state, Pi, as both necessary and sufficient for the occurrence of mental state M. A law of this form states that any organism or system, belonging to a certain species, is such that it has the given mental property at a time if and only if it is in a certain specified physical state at that time. We may call laws of this form "species-specific biconditional laws."

In order to generate laws of this kind, biological species may turn out to be too wide; individual differences in the localization of psychological functions in the brain are well known. Moreover, given the phenomena of learning and maturation, injuries to the brain, and the like, the neural structure that subserves a psychological state or function may change for an individual over its lifetime. What is important then is that these laws are relative to physical-biological structure-types, although for simplicity I will continue to put the matter in terms of species. The substantive theoretical assumption here is the belief that for each psychological state there are physical-biological structure types, at a certain level of description or specification, that generate laws of this form. I think an assumption of this kind is made by most philosophers who speak of multiple realizations of psychological states, and it is in fact a plausible assumption for a physicalist to make.[9] Moreover, such an assumption seems essential to the very idea of a physical realization; what else could "physical realization" mean?

So what I am saying is this: the multiple realization argument perhaps shows that the strong connectibility of mental properties *vis-à-vis* physical properties does not obtain; however, it *presupposes* that *species-specific strong connectibility* does hold. Merely to defeat the antireductionist argument, I need not make this second claim; all I need is the weaker claim that the phenomenon of multiple realization is *consistent* with the species-specific strong connectibility, and it seems to me that that is plainly true.

The point of all this is that the availability of species-specific biconditional laws linking the mental with the physical breathes new life into psychophysical reductionism. Unlike species-independent laws, these laws cannot buy us a *uniform* or *global* reduction of psychology, a reduction of every psychological state to a uniform physical-biological base across all actual and possible organisms; however, these laws will buy us a series of species-specific or local reductions. If we had a law of this form for each psychological state-type for humans, we would have a physical reduction of human psychology; this reduction would tell us how human psychology is physically implemented, how the causal connections between our psychological events and processes work at the physical-biological level, what biological subsystems subserve our cognitive capacities and functions, and so forth. This is reduction in a full-blown sense, except that it is limited to individuals sharing a certain physical-biological structure. I believe "local reductions" of this sort are the rule rather than the exception in all of science, not just in psychology (see Enc, 1983). In any case, this is a plausible picture of what in fact goes on in neurobiology, physiological psychology, and cognitive neuroscience. And it seems to me that any robust physicalist must expect, and demand, the possibility of local reductions of psychology just in this sense.[10]

Thus, the conclusion we must draw is that the multiple realizability of the mental has no antireductionist implications of great significance; on the contrary, it entails, or at least is consistent with, the local reducibility of psychology, local relative to species or physical structure-types. If psychological states are multiply realized, that only means that we shall have multiple local reductions of psychology. The multiple realization argument, if it works, shows that a global reduction is not in the offing; however, local reductions are reduction enough, by any reasonable scientific standards and in their philosophical implications.

IV

Some have looked to the idea of "supervenience" for a formulation of physicalism that is free of reductionist commitments. The promise of supervenience in this area appears to have been based, at least in part, on the historical circumstance that some prominent ethical theorists, such as G. E. Moore and R. M. Hare, who constructed classic arguments against naturalistic reductionism in ethics, at the same time held the view that moral properties are "supervenient" upon descriptive or naturalistic properties. So why not think of the relation between psychological and physical properties in analogy with the relation, as conceived by these ethical theorists, between moral and descriptive properties? In each instance, the supervenient properties are in some substantive sense dependent on, or determined by, their subvenient, base properties and yet, it is hoped, irreducible to them. This was precisely the line of thinking that appears to have prompted Davidson to inject supervenience into the discussion of the mind–body problem. He wrote

> Although the position I describe denies there are psychophysical laws, it is consistent with the view that mental characteristics are in some sense dependent, or supervenient, on physical characteristics. Such supervenience might be taken to mean that there cannot be two events alike in all physical respects but differing in some mental respects, or that an object cannot alter in some mental respect without altering in some physical respect. Dependence or supervenience of this kind does not entail reducibility through law or definition: if it did, we could reduce moral properties to descriptive, and this there is good reason to *believe* cannot be done. (1980, p. 214)

Although Davidson himself did not pursue this idea further, many other philosophers have tried to work this suggestive idea into a viable form of nonreductive materialism.

The central problem in implementing Davidson's suggestion has been that of defining a supervenience relation that will fill the twin requirements he set forth: first, the relation must be nonreductive; that is, a given domain can be supervenient on another without being reducible to it.

Second, the relation must be one of dependence: if a domain supervenes on another, there must be a sturdy sense in which the first is dependent on the second, or the second determines the first. But it has not been easy to find such a relation. The main difficulty has been this: if a relation is weak enough to be nonreductive, it tends to be too weak to serve as a dependence relation; conversely, when a relation is strong enough to give us dependence, it tends to be too strong – strong enough to imply reducibility.

I will not rehearse here the well-known arguments pro and con concerning various supervenience relations that have been proposed. I will instead focus on one supervenience relation that has seemed to several philosophers[11] to hold the most promise as a nonreductive dependency relation, namely "global supervenience." The generic idea of supervenience is that things that are indiscernible in respect of the "base" (or "subvenient") properties cannot differ in respect of the supervenient properties. Global supervenience applies this consideration to "worlds," giving us the following formulation of psychophysical supervenience:

> Worlds that are indiscernible in all physical respects are indiscernible in mental respects; in fact, physically indiscernible worlds are one and the same world.

Thus, any world that is just like this world in all physical details must be just like it in all psychological respects as well. This relation of supervenience is appropriately called "global" in that worlds rather than individuals within worlds are compared for discernibility or indiscernibility in regard to sets of properties. What is it for two worlds to be physically, or mentally, indiscernible? For simplicity let us assume that the same individuals exist in all the worlds.[2] We may then say that two worlds are indiscernible with respect to a set of properties just in case these properties are distributed over individuals in the same way in the two worlds.

It can be shown that, as hoped, the global supervenience of the mental on the physical does not entail the existence of psychophysical laws; at least, not in a straightforward way (see Kim, 1987). Thus, global supervenience is consistent with the nomological irreducibility of the mental to the physical. The only question then is whether it yields an appropriate relation of dependency between the mental and the physical, one that is strong enough to qualify it as a physicalism. The answer, I will argue, is in the negative.

We may begin by observing that the global supervenience of the mental permits the following: imagine a world that differs from the actual world in some minute physical detail. We may suppose that in that world one lone hydrogen atom somewhere in deep space is slightly displaced relative to its position in this world. This world with one wayward hydrogen atom could, consistently with the global supervenience of the mental, be as different as you please from the actual world in any mental respect (thus, in that world nothing manifests mentality, or mentality is radically redistributed in other ways). The existence of such a world and other similarly aberrant worlds does not violate the constraints of global supervenience; since they are not physically indiscernible from the actual world, they could, under global supervenience, differ radically from this world in psychological characteristics.[13]

If that doesn't convince you of the weakness of global supervenience as a determination or dependency relation, consider this: it is consistent with global supervenience for there to be two organisms in our actual world which, though wholly indiscernible physically, are radically different in mental respects (say, your molecule-for-molecule duplicate is totally lacking in mentality). This is consistent with global supervenience because there might be no other possible world that is just like this one physically and yet differing in some mental respect.[14]

It seems to me that indiscernibility considerations at the global level, involving whole worlds, are just too coarse to give us the kind of dependency relation we should demand if the mental is truly dependent on the physical. Like it or not, we treat individuals, and perhaps also aggregates of individuals smaller than total worlds, as psychological units, and it seems to me that if psychophysical determination or dependence means anything, it ought to mean that the psychological nature of each such unit is wholly determined by its physical nature. That is, dependency or determination must hold at the local as well as the global level.

Moreover, talk of whole worlds in this connection, unless it is anchored in determinative relations obtaining at the local level, has little verifiable content; it is difficult to see how there can be empirical evidence for the global supervenience thesis that is not based in evidence about specific psychophysical dependencies – dependencies and correlations between specific psychological and physical properties. In fact, it seems to me that we must look to local dependencies for an *explanation* of global supervenience as well as its evidence. Why is it the case that no two worlds can exist that are indiscernible physically and yet discernible psychologically? Or why is it the case that "physical truths determine all the truths" (see Hellman and Thompson, 1975; Post, 1987), as some prefer to put it? I think this is a legitimate question to raise, and as far as I can see the only answer, other than the response that it is a brute, unexplainable metaphysical fact, is in terms of local correlations and dependencies between specific mental and physical properties. If the global supervenience of the mental on the physical were to be proposed as an unexplainable fact that we must accept on faith, I doubt that we need to take the proposal seriously.

Specific psychophysical dependencies holding for individuals, and other proper parts of the world, are both evidence for, and an explanatory ground of, global supervenience.

The trouble is that once we begin talking about correlations and dependencies between specific psychological and physical properties, we are in effect talking about psychophysical laws, and these laws raise the specter of unwanted physical reductionism. Where there are psychophysical laws, there is always the threat, or promise, of psychophysical reduction. We must conclude that supervenience is not going to deliver to us a viable form of nonreductive materialism.

V

So far I have reviewed three influential formulations of nonreductive materialism: Davidson's anomalous monism, the Putnam–Fodor doctrine of psychological autonomy, and supervenient physicalism, and found each of them wanting either as a materialism or as a antireductionism. In this final section, I want to advance a direct argument to show why the prospects for a nonreductive physicalism are dim.

Let us first of all note that nonreductive physicalism is not to be a form of eliminativism; that is, it acknowledges the mental as a legitimate domain of entities. What sort of entities? Here let us, for convenience, make use of the Davidsonian scheme of individual events, thinking of mentality to be exhibited as properties of these events. Thus, as a noneliminativist, the nonreductive physicalist believes that there are events in her ontology that have mental properties (e.g. being a pain, being a belief that snow is cold, etc.). I argued earlier, in discussing Davidson's anomalous monism, that if your noneliminativism is to be more than a token gesture, you had better find some real causal work for your mental properties. The fact that a given event is a mental event of a certain kind must play some causal-explanatory role in what other events occur and what properties they have. Thus, I am supposing that a nonreductive physicalist is a mental realist, and that to be a mental realist, your mental properties must be *causal properties* – properties in virtue of which an event enters into causal relations it would otherwise not have entered into.

Let me now make another assumption: psychophysical causation takes place; that is, some mental events cause physical events. For example, a sudden sharp pain felt in my hand causes a jerky withdrawal of the hand. It is true that in a Davidsonian domain, all events are physical; that is, every event has some physical property. But when I say that mental events cause physical events, something stronger is intended, namely that an event, *in virtue of its mental property*, causes another event to have a certain physical property. I believe that this assumption will be granted by most of us; it will be granted by anyone who believes that at least sometimes our limbs move because we have certain desires and beliefs.[15] When I walk to the water fountain for a drink of water, my legs move in the way they do in part because of my desire for water and my belief that there is water to be had at the water fountain.

There is a further assumption that I believe any physicalist would grant. I call this "the causal closure of the physical domain." Roughly, it says this: Any physical event that has a cause at time *t* has a physical cause at *t*. This is the assumption that if we trace the causal ancestry of a physical event, we need never go outside the physical domain. To deny this assumption is to accept the Cartesian idea that some physical events have only nonphysical causes, and if this is true there can in principle be no complete and self-sufficient physical theory of the physical domain. If the causal closure failed, our physics would need to refer in an essential way to nonphysical causal agents, perhaps Cartesian souls and their psychic properties, if it is to give a complete account of the physical world. I think most physicalists would find that picture unacceptable.

Now we are ready to derive some consequences from these assumptions. Suppose that a certain event, in virtue of its mental property, causes a physical event. The causal closure of the physical domain says that this physical event must also have a physical cause. We may assume that this physical cause, in virtue of its physical property, causes the physical event. The following question arises: What is the relationship between these two causes, one mental and the other physical? Each is claimed to be a cause of the physical effect. There are two initial possibilities that we can consider.

First, when we are faced with two purported causes of a single event, we could entertain the possibility that each is only a partial cause, the two together making up a full or sufficient cause, as when a car crash is said to be caused by the driver's careless braking and the icy condition of the road. Applied to our case, it says that the mental cause and the physical cause are each only a partial cause, and that they together make up one sufficient cause. This seems like an absurd thing to say, and in any case it violates the causal closure principle in that it regards the mental event as a necessary constituent of a full cause of a physical event; thus, on this view, a full causal story of how this physical event occurs must, at least partially, go outside the physical domain.

Could it be that the mental cause and the physical cause are each an independent sufficient cause of the physical effect? The suggestion then is that the physical effect is overdetermined. So if the physical cause hadn't occurred, the mental cause by itself would have caused the effect. This picture is again absurd: from what we know about the physiology of limb movement, we must believe that if the pain sensation causes my hand to withdraw, the causal chain from the pain to the limb motion must somehow make use of the causal chain from an appropriate central neural event to the muscle contraction; it makes no sense to think that there was an independent, perhaps telekinetic, causal path from the pain to the limb movement. Moreover, the overdetermination idea seems to violate the causal closure principle as well: in the counterfactual situation in which the physical cause does not occur, the closure principle is violated. For the idea that the mental and the physical cause are each an independent sufficient cause involves the acceptance of the counterfactual that if the physical cause had not occurred, the mental cause would have occurred and caused the physical effect. This is in violation of the causal closure principle.

These two ways of looking at the situation are obvious nonstarters. We need a more plausible answer to the question: How are the mental cause and the physical cause of the single physical effect related to each other? Given that any physical event has a physical cause, how is a mental cause *also* possible? This I call "the problem of causal-explanatory exclusion," for the problem seems to arise from the fact that a cause, or causal explanation, of an event, when it is regarded as a full, sufficient cause or explanation, appears to *exclude* other independent purported causes or causal explanations of it.[16]

At this point, you might want to protest: Why all this beating around the bush? Why not just say the mental cause and the physical cause are one and the same? Identification simplifies ontology and gets rid of unwanted puzzles. Consider saying that there are in this glass two distinct substances, H_2O and water; that is, consider saying that water and H_2O co-occur everywhere as a matter of law but that they are distinct substances nonetheless. This would invite a host of unwanted and unnecessary puzzles: given that what is in the glass weighs a total of ten ounces, how much of the weight is to be attributed to the water and how much to the H_2O? By dropping a lighted match in the glass, I extinguish it. What caused it? Was it the water or the H_2O? Were they each only a partial cause, or was the extinguishing of the match overdetermined? The identification of the water with the H_2O puts all these questions to rest in a single stroke: there is here one thing, not two. The identity solution can work similar magic in our present case: the pain *is* a neural state – here there is one cause, not two. The limb motion was caused by the pain, that is to say, by a neural state. The unwanted puzzles vanish.

All this is correct. But what does the identity solution involve? Remember that what is for us at issue is the causal efficacy of mental properties of events *vis-à-vis* their physical properties. Thus, the items that need to be identified are properties; that is, we would need to identify mental properties with physical properties. If this could be done, that would be an excellent way of vindicating the causal powers of mentality.

But this is precisely the route that is barred to our nonreductivist friends. The identification of mental properties with physical properties is the heart of reductionist "type physicalism." These property identities would serve as bridge laws *par excellence*, enabling a derivational reduction of psychology to physical theory. The identities entail psychophysical correlations of biconditional form, stable over possible, or nomologically possible, worlds, and this, we have been told, is excluded by Davidson's mental anomalism and Putnam's multiple realization argument. So the identity solution is out of the question for the nonreductive materialist. Is there any other way to respond to the causal exclusion problem, a way that falls short of identifying mental with physical attributes?

There is one, but it isn't something that would be palatable to the nonreductivist. I believe that the only way other than the identity solution is to give a general account of causal relations involving macro-events as "supervenient causal relations," causal relations that are supervenient on micro-causal processes. You put a kettle of water on the stove and turn on the burner; and soon the water starts to boil. Heating the water caused it to boil. That is a causal relation at the macro-level. It is natural to think of this causal relation as supervenient on certain underlying causal processes at the micro-level. The heating of water supervenes on the increasing kinetic energy of water molecules, and when their mean kinetic energy reaches a certain level, water molecules begin to move in turbulence, some of them being ejected into the air. Boiling is a macro-state that supervenes on just these micro-processes. A sharp pain causes an anxiety attack five seconds later. What's going on? Again, it is tempting, and natural, to think thus: the pain is supervenient on a certain underlying neural activity, and this neural event causes another neural event to occur. The anxiety attack occurs because it is supervenient on this second neural event.

The general model of supervenient causation applied to macro-causal relations is this: macro-event m is a cause or effect of event E in virtue of the fact that m is supervenient on some micro-event, n, which is a cause or effect of event E.[17] The suggestion then is that we use this model to explain mental causation: a mental event is a cause, or an effect, of another event in virtue of the fact that it is supervenient on some physical event standing in an appropriate causal relation to this event. Thus, mental properties are seen as deriving their causal potential from the physical properties on which they supervene. That is the main idea.

But what sort of supervenience relation is involved in this picture? Global supervenience we considered above obviously will not do; it does not give us a way of speaking of supervenience of specific mental properties on specific physical properties, since it only refers to indiscernibility holding for worlds. Supervenient causation in my, sense requires talk of specific mental properties supervening on specific physical base properties, and this is possible only if there are laws correlating psychological with physical properties. This is what I have called elsewhere "strong supervenience," and it can be argued plausibly that supervenience of this strength entails the possibility of reducing the supervenient to the subvenient.[18] I will spare you the details here, but the fact that this form of supervenience directly involves psychophysical laws would be enough to give pause to any would be nonreductive physicalist. I am not entirely certain that this supervenience solution will suffice; that is, I am not certain that anything short of the identity solution will resolve the exclusion problem. However, I believe that it is the only alternative to explore if, for whatever reason, you are unwilling or unable to go for psychophysical attribute identities. But I doubt that this solution will be found acceptable by the nonreductivist any more than the identity solution.

If nonreductive physicalists accept the causal closure of the physical domain, therefore, they have no visible way of accounting for the possibility of psychophysical causation. This means that they must either give up their antireductionism or else reject the possibility of psychophysical causal relations. The denial of psychophysical causation can come about in two ways: first, you make such a denial because you don't believe there are mental events; or second, you keep faith with mental events even though you acknowledge that they never enter into causal transactions with physical processes, constituting their own autonomous causal world. So either you have espoused eliminativism, or else you are moving further in the direction of dualism, a dualism that posits a realm of the mental in total causal isolation from the physical realm. This doesn't look to me much like materialism.

Is the abandonment of the causal closure of the physical domain an option for the materialist? I think not: to reject the closure principle is to embrace irreducible nonphysical causes of physical phenomena. It would be a retrogression to Cartesian interactionist dualism, something that is definitive of the *denial* of materialism.

Our conclusion, therefore, has to be this: nonreductive materialism is not a stable position. There are pressures of various sorts that push it either in the direction of outright eliminativism or in the direction of an explicit form of dualism.

Notes

My thanks to Richard Brandt, Sydney Shoemaker, and Ernest Sosa for helpful comments on earlier versions, and to David Benfield, Barry Loewer, and Brian

McLaughlin for discussing with me some of the topics of this paper. The paper was originally the presidential address before the Eighty-seventh Annual Central Division Meeting of the American Philosophical Association in Chicago, Illinois, April 28, 1989.

1 Throughout I will be using "physicalism" and "materialism" (and their cognates) interchangeably; similarly, "mental" and "psychological."

2 The classic source on reduction is Ernest Nagel (1961) *The Structure of Science*, ch. 11.

3 Actually the argument can proceed with a weaker premise to the effect that mental events enter into causal relations, either with physical events or with other mental events.

4 Davidson (1980) says in "Mental events" that he believes in the "supervenience" of the mental on the physical, and this does introduce a constraint on the distribution of physical properties when the distribution of mental properties is altered. This, however, does not detract substantively from the point being made here. For one, it remains true, on the notion of supervenience Davidson favors (which corresponds to "weak supervenience"; see his "Replies to Essays X–XII" (Davidson, 1985) that the removal of *all* mental properties from events of this world would have no consequence whatever on how physical properties are distributed over them. For another, the supervenience of the mental is best regarded as an independent thesis, and my present remarks only concern the implications of anomalous monism. I consider the supervenience view below in section IV.

5 Davidson's overall views of the mental are richer and more complex than the present discussion might seem to indicate. I believe that they contain some distinctly dualistic elements; for a discussion of this aspect of Davidson, see Kim (1985). There have been some interesting recent attempts, which I cannot discuss here, to reconcile anomalous monism with the possibility of mental causation; see, e.g., Ernest LePore and Barry Loewer (1987) Brian McLaughlin (1989); Terence Horgan (1989).

6 Putnam himself has abandoned functionalism; see Putnam (1988, chs 5 and 6).

7 There are some complex logical and ontological details we are leaving out here. See, for details, Robert L. Causey (1977).

8 Note also that derivational reduction does not *require* strong connectibility; any set of bridge laws, of whatever form and strength, will do as long as it enables the required derivation. But this obviously depends on the strength of the two theories involved, and there seems to be little of interest that is sufficiently general to say about this. There are also philosophical considerations for thinking that biconditionals and attribute identities are important in reduction. Cf. Lawrence Sklar (1967).

9 Ned Block says, "Most functionalists are willing to allow . . . that for each type of pain-feeling organism, there is (perhaps) a single type of physical state that realizes pain in that type of organism" (1980, p. 172). Such a law would have exactly the form under discussion.

10 This point, and some related points, are elaborated in my "Disunity of psychology as a working hypothesis?" (forthcoming).

11 Including Terence Horgan 1982 in his "Supervenience and microphysics"; John Haugeland (1982) in "Weak supervenience"; John Post (1987) in *The Faces of Existence*; and Bradford Petrie (1987) "Global supervenience and reduction". The model-theoretic notion of determination worked out by Geoffrey Hellman and Frank Thompson (1975) in "Physicalism: ontology, determination, and reduction", is closely related to global supervenience.

12 Even with this simplifying assumption certain complications arise; however, we may disregard them for the present purposes. For further details see Kim (1988).

13 This particular difficulty can be largely met by formulating global supervenience in terms of *similarity* between worlds rather than indiscernibility. See Kim (1987).

14 This shows that global supervenience is consistent with the failure of "weak supervenience". See Kim (1987).

15 For a forceful statement of this point see Fred Dretske (1988).

16 This idea is developed in greater detail in Kim (1989).

17 For critical discussions of this model, see Brian McLaughlin (1984); Peter Menzies (1988; pp. 560–74).

18 I am putting the point somewhat tentatively here because it involves several currently contentious issues. For a general argument for this point, see Kim (1984, esp. section III; 1992). However, this argument makes use of infinite disjunctions and conjunctions (actually, infinite disjunctions are all one needs; see Kim, 1992). If the argument is found objectionable because of this feature, it could be supplemented with an argument modeled on my argument in section iii above against the Putnam–Fodor antireductionist thesis. This means that the supervenience relation needed for the model of supervenient causation sketched here must require that each supervenient property have a *nomologically coextensive base property relative to the given physical structure*. There are, I believe, plausible considerations in favor of this stronger supervenience relation as a basis for the concept of supervenient causation (or the reduction of causal relations); however, I cannot go into the details here.

References

Block, N. (ed.) (1980) "Introduction: what is functionalism?", in *Readings in Philosophy of Psychology*, vol. 1, Cambridge, Mass.: Harvard University Press.

Boyd, R. (1980) "Materialism without reductionism: what physicalism does not entail," in N. Block (ed.) *Readings in Philosophy of Psychology*, vol. 1, Cambridge, Mass.: Harvard University Press.

Causey, R. L. (1977) *Unity of Science*, Dordrecht: Reidel.

Churchland, P. M. (1981) "Eliminative materialism and the propositional attitudes," *Journal of Philosophy* 78, pp. 67–90.

Davidson, D. (1980) [1970] "Mental events," in *Essays on Actions and Events*, Oxford: Clarendon Press.

Davidson, D. (1985) "Replies to Essays X–XII," in B. Vermazen and M. B. Hintikka (eds) *Essays on Davidson: Actions and Events*, Oxford: Clarendon Press, pp. 242–52.

Dretske, F. (1988) *Explaining Behavior: Reasons in a World of Causes*, Cambridge, Mass.: Bradford Books/MIT Press.

Enc, B. (1983) "In defense of the identity theory," *Journal of Philosophy* 80, pp. 279–98.

Fodor, J. (1974) "Special sciences, or the disunity of science as a working hypothesis," *Synthese* 28, pp. 97–115.

Haugeland, J. (1982) "Weak supervenience," *American Philosophical Quarterly* 19, pp. 93–103.

Hellman, G. P. and Thompson, F. W. (1975) "Physicalism: ontology, determinism, and reduction," *Journal of Philosophy* 72, pp. 551–64.

Horgan, T. (1982) "Supervenience and microphysics," *Pacific Philosophical Quarterly* 63, pp. 29–43.

Horgan, T. (1989) "Mental quausation," *Philosophical Perspectives* 3, pp. 47–76.

Kim, J. (1984) "Concepts of supervenience," *Philosophy and Phenomological Research* 45, pp. 153–76.

Kim, J. (1985) "Psychophysical laws," in E. LePore and B. P. McLaughlin (eds) *Actions and Events: Perspectives on the Philosophy of Donald Davidson*, Oxford: Blackwell.

Kim, J. (1987) " 'Strong' and 'global' supervenience revisited," *Philosophy Phenomological Research* 48, pp. 315–26.

Kim, J. (1988) "Supervenience for multiple domains," *Philosophical Topics* 16, pp. 129–50.

Kim, J. (1989) "Mechanism, purpose, and explanatory exclusion," *Philosophical Perspectives* 3, pp. 77–108.

Kim, J. (19)

Kim, J. (1992) "Supervenience as a philosophical concept," *Metaphilosophy* 21, pp. 1–17.

LePore, E. and Loewer, B. (1987) "Mind matters," *Journal of Philosophy* 84, pp. 630–42.

McLaughlin, B. P. (1984) "Event supervenience and supervenient causation," *Southern Journal of Philosophy* 22, Spindel Conference Supplement on Supervenience, pp. 71–91.

McLaughlin, B. P. (1989) "Type epiphenomenalism, type dualism, and the causal priority of the physical," *Philosophical Perspectives* 3, pp. 109–35.

Menzies, P. (1988) "Against causal reductionism," *Mind* 97, pp. 551–74.

Nagel, E. (1961) *The Structure of Science*, New York: Harcourt, Brace & World.

Petrie, B. (1987) "Global supervenience and reduction," *Philosophy and Phenomenological Research* 48, pp. 119–30.

Post, J. F. (1987) *The Faces of Existence*, Ithaca, NY: Cornell University Press.

Putnam, H. (1975) [1967] "The nature of mental states," in *Philosophical Papers*, vol. 2, *Mind, Language, and Reality*, Cambridge: Cambridge University Press.

Putnam, H. (1988) *Representation and Reality*, Cambridge, Mass.: Bradford Books/MIT Press.

Sklar, L. (1967) "Types of inter-theoretic reduction," *British Journal for the Philosophy of Science* 18, pp. 109–24.

20
Mind Matters

Ernest LePore and Barry Loewer

Who knows what I want to do?... Isn't it all a question of brain chemistry, signals going back and forth, electrical energy in the cortex?... Some minor little activity takes place somewhere in this unimportant place in one of the brain hemispheres and suddenly I want to go to Montana or I don't want to go to Montana. Maybe it's just an accidental flash in the medulla and suddenly there I am in Montana and I find out I really didn't want to go there in the first place... It's all this activity in the brain and you don't know what's you as a person and what's the brain and what's some neuron that just happens to fire or just happens to misfire...

Don DeLillo, *White Noise*

Consider the following, admittedly imprecise claims:

1 The mental and the physical are distinct.
2 The mental and the physical causally interact.
3 The physical is causally closed.

Much can be said in favor of each of these. In support of (1) we can point to the failure of attempts to reduce the phenomenal and the intentional to the physical, and to arguments from Descartes to Donald Davidson which purport to show that such reductions are, in principle, impossible. (2) is supported by our everyday experience and by various theories of perception and action. (3) means that every physical event or fact has, in its causal history, only physical events and facts. Both (3) and its cousin,

3′ All causation is reducible to, or grounded in, physical causation, where 'grounded' means, roughly, that causal relations supervene on noncausal physical facts and laws, have seemed to many philosophers to be supported by the development of the sciences.

The trouble is that it seems (1), (2), and (3) are incompatible. To be a bit more definite, consider their application to events. (1) then says that no mental event is a physical event; (2), that some mental events cause physical events and vice versa; and (3), that all the causes of physical events are physical events. The inconsistency is obvious. If mental events are distinct from physical events and sometimes cause them, then obviously the physical is not causally closed. The dilemma posed by the plausibility of each of these claims and by their apparent incompatibility is, of course, the mind–body problem.[1]

Our primary concern here is how Davidson's[2] account of the relation between the mental and the physical, which he calls "anomalous monism" (AM), attempts to resolve the dilemma. AM consists of the following three theses:

4   There are no strict psychophysical or psychological laws and in fact all strict laws are expressed in a purely physical vocabulary (the anomalousness of the mental).
5   Mental events causally interact with physical events.
6   Event c causes event e only if there is a strict causal law which subsumes c and e (entails that c causes e) (the nomological character of causality).

(4) is a version of (1). It is commonly held that a property expressed by M is reducible to a property expressed by P (where M and P are not analytically connected) only if there is an exceptionless bridge law that links them.[3] So it follows from (4) that (intentional) mental and physical properties are distinct.[4] (6) says that c causes e only if there are singular descriptions D of c and D' of e and a strict causal law L such that L and "D occurred" entail "D caused D'" (Davidson, 1980, p. 158). (6) and the second part of (4) entail that physical events have only physical causes and that all event causation is physically grounded.[5]

The notion of a law being "strict" figures prominently both in Davidson's affirmation of the distinctness of the mental and the physical and in his account of causation. Davidson's notion of a strict law is best explained by contrast with non-strict laws. A non-strict law is a generalization that contains a *ceteris paribus* qualifier that specifies that the law holds under "normal or ideal conditions," where the relevant notions of normal or ideal are specified by the theoretical context of the law. The generalizations one finds in the special sciences are mostly of this kind. In contrast, a strict law is one that contains no *ceteris paribus* qualifiers; it is exceptionless not just *de facto* but as a matter of law. A non-strict law may be improved upon by explicitly including some of its *ceteris paribus* conditions in its antecedents. Davidson's view is that psychophysical laws of the form whenever a person is in physical state *P*, then he is in intentional state *M* are *essentially* non-strict. That is, no matter how many conditions are added to the antecedent, short of trivializing the generalization, it will not be strict.[6]

Given the parallel between (4) and (6), and between (1) and (3), it may seem that the former are also incompatible. But they are not. Davidson shows that they all can be true if (and only if) mental events are identical to physical events (1980, p. 215). Let us say that an event *e* is a physical event just in the case when *e* satisfies a basic physical predicate (that is, a physical predicate appearing in a strict law). Since only physical predicates (or predicates expressing properties reducible to basic physical properties) appear in strict laws, it follows that every event that enters into causal relations satisfies a basic physical predicate. So, those mental events which enter into causal relations are also physical events.

AM is committed only to a partial endorsement of (1). The mental and physical are distinct insofar as they are not linked by strict law – mental properties are not reducible to physical properties – but they are not distinct insofar as mental events are physical events. This being so, one might wonder whether AM also only partially endorses claims (2) and (3). In fact, Davidson's views have been criticized precisely on the point of (2). Ernest Sosa writes, "I conclude that . . . anomalous monism is [not] really compatible with the full content of our deep and firm conviction that the mind and body each acts causally on the other" (1984, p. 278). Ted Honderich goes even further, charging that AM is really a form of epiphenomenalism: "I went on . . . to claim that [AM] was epiphenomenalist; it did not make the mental as mental an ineliminable part of the explanation of actions" (1984, p. 88).

If Honderich means that Davidson's views are committed to epiphenomenalism with respect to mental events, he is clearly mistaken, since, according to AM, mental events do cause other events. They *are* physical events and so can, like any event, have consequences. It is rather that, on AM, as he puts it, the mental *as* mental – some writers use the expressions "*qua* mental" and "in virtue of being mental" – is causally irrelevant. In defense of Davidson, one might reply that, although it is correct to say it is not *c* as mental that causes *e*, this has nothing to do with any epiphenomenalism on the part of the mental, but simply reflects the fact that it is not events *as* mental or *as* physical or *as* anything else which cause other events. Causation is a relation between events, not between events *as* *F*s. It seems to Davidson's critics, however, to make sense to distinguish some features of an event as causally relevant and others as causally irrelevant. It is this distinction which underlies the locution that it is *c as F* (not *as F'*) that causes *e* (to be *G*). Sosa and Fred Dretske illustrate their understanding of the distinction in the following passages:

> A gun goes off, a shot is fired and it kills someone. The loud noise is the shot. Thus if the victim is killed by the shot it is the loud noise that kills the victim . . . In a certain sense the victim is killed by the loud noise. Not by the loud noise as a loud noise but only by the loud noise as a shot, or the like . . . The loudness of the shot has no causal relevance to the death of the victim. Had the gun been equipped with a silencer the shot would have killed the victim just the same (Sosa, 1984, pp. 277–8).

> Meaningful sounds, if they occur at the right pitch and amplitude, can shatter glass, but the fact that these sounds have a meaning is irrelevant to their having this effect. The glass would shatter if the sounds meant something completely different or if they meant nothing at all (Dretske, 1989, p.00)

Sosa, Honderich, Kim, Dretske, (among others)[8] think that, once we have made the distinction between the causally relevant and irrelevant features of an event, we will see that it is a consequence of AM that mental features are never causally relevant. Why is the causal irrelevance of the mental supposed to be entailed by AM? Kim reasons as follows:

> Consider Davidson's account: whether or not a given event had a mental description . . . seems entirely irrelevant to what causal relations it enters into. Its causal powers are wholly determined by the physical description or characteristic that holds for it; for it is under its physical description that it may be subsumed under a causal law. And Davidson explicitly denies any possibility of a nomological connection between an event's mental description and its physical description that could bring the mental into the causal picture (1984, p. 267).

The argument is that, since, according to AM, *c* causes *e* only if there is a strict law that subsumes *c* and *e* and since strict laws contain only physical (never mental) predicates, it follows that the mental features of events *c* and *e* are irrelevant to whether they are causally connected. The physical features of events suffice to fix, given the strict laws, *all* causal connections. Mental features neither suffice nor are required to fix causal connections. The argument is powerful. The conclusion the authors draw from it is that on AM *the mind does not matter*; that a neural event has a certain intentional content is as irrelevant to its effect as the fact that the sounds are meaningful is to the sounds causing the glass to break.

But is this criticism of AM correct? We claim that it is not, and that it rests on a simple, but perhaps not obvious, confusion. The confusion is between two ways in which properties of an event c may be said to be causally relevant and irrelevant. Consider the following locutions:

1 Properties F and G are relevant$_1$ to making it the case that c causes e, and

2 c's possessing property F is causally relevant$_2$ to e's possessing property G

We will say that (1) holds iff c has F and e has G, and there is a strict law that entails Fs cause Gs. It is in this sense that it is c's having F and e's having G "make it the case" that c causes e. Relavance$_2$ is a relation among c, one of its properties F, e, and one of its properties G. It holds when c's being F brings it about that e is G. We shall argue that those who charge AM with epiphenomenalism are guilty of confusing relevance$_1$ with relevance$_2$.

None of the authors we have been considering defines the sense of causal relevance they have in mind when they accuse AM of rendering the mental causally inefficacious. Their discussions, though, do suggest a *test* for causal irrelevance. Recall Sosa's remark that "had the gun been equipped with a silencer it would have killed the victim just the same" and Dretske's remark that "the glass would shatter if the sounds meant something completely different." So it may be that Sosa and Dretske (and others) think that AM entails the causal irrelevance of the mental, because they think that it entails the falsity of such mentalistic counterfactuals as: if Fred had not believed that Jerry would attend the conference, he would not have come.

In view of this counterfactual test for causal relevance$_2$, we suggest that the authors who propose it may have in mind the following characterization of causal relevance$_2$.[9]

(1) c's being F is causally relevance$_2$ to e's being G iff
  (a) c causes e.
  (b) Fc and Ge.
  (c) $-Fc > -Ge$
  (d) Fc and Ge are logically and metaphysically independent.[10]

Condition (d) is intended to exclude cases in which the connection between F and G is conceptual/metaphysical rather than causal, e.g. c's being the cause of e is causally relevance$_2$ to e's being caused by c, when c does cause e.

The heart of our response to the claim that AM is committed to epiphenomenalism is this: AM entails that mental features are causally relevance$_1$, but does not entail that they are causally relevance$_2$. Before arguing these claims, we need to discuss the interpretation of the counter-factual:

(Q)   If event c were not F, then event e would not be G.

We will adopt the Lewis–Stalnaker account of counterfactuals,[11] according to which $A > B$ is true iff B is true at all the worlds most similar to the actual world at which A is true (or A is true at no such world). We will suppose that an event e that occurs at the actual world may occur or have counterparts that occur at others; "c" and "e" are to be understood as rigid designators of events. In evaluating (Q), we need to look at the most similar worlds to the actual world at which c fails to be F. c may fail to be F at w either by existing there and not being F or failing to occur at w (or have a counterpart) at all. (Q) is true just in the case when the most similar worlds at which counterparts to c fail to have F or at which c fails to have a counterpart are such that counterparts to e fail to have G or e fails to have a counterpart.

The irrelevance$_1$ of the mental follows immediately from the definition of relevance$_1$ and from AM's (4) and (6). The relevance$_1$ of psychological predicates, however, is perfectly compatible with the truth of counterfac-tuals $-Fc > -Ge$, where F and G are predicates that do not occur in strict laws. That is, the set of strict laws and basic physical facts do not by themselves settle the truth values of counterfactuals.

We can see that this is so as follows: consider the set of worlds W at which all the strict laws hold. (This set includes the actual world α.) Until a *similarity order*, $\geqslant \alpha$, is placed on W, the truth values of almost all counterfactuals are indeterminate. Only those counterfactuals $A > B$ such that the strict laws and noncounterfactual statements true at α entail $A \to B$ or $-(A \to B)$ have determinate truth values, since any similarity ordering $\geqslant \alpha$ will make the former true and the latter false. This is just the lesson of Nelson Goodman's (1983) failed attempts to analyze counter-factuals in terms of laws. What Goodman found is that laws and noncounterfactual truths are themselves not sufficient to settle the truth value of any but a limited set of counterfactuals. It follows that the truth of counterfactuals of the sort needed to establish causal relevance$_2$ (since neither they nor their negations are entailed by the strict physical laws and noncounterfactual truths) are compatible with AM.

Of course, it is one thing to show that mentalistic counterfactuals are compatible with AM. It is quite another thing to produce an account of what makes these counterfactuals true and also show that this account is compatible with AM. The question of what makes counterfactuals true is a general one which concerns all counterfactuals and not just mentalistic ones. We shall briefly address it toward the end of our discussion.

To this point, we have shown that, if (I) supplies sufficient conditions for causal relevance$_2$, then there is no incompatibility between AM and the causal relevance$_2$ of the mental.[12] This is important, since, as we have seen, many of Davidson's critics seem to think there is such an incompatibility. There are two further related questions we need to address. One is whether causal irrelevance$_1$ alone is sufficient to sustain a charge of epiphenomenalism. A second is whether there are some further conditions on (I) such that, once added, AM does entail the causal relevance$_2$ of the mental.

Why would anyone think that irrelevance$_1$ of the mental entails epiphenomenalism? Honderich formulates a principle he calls "the principle of the nomological character of causally relevant properties," according to which c's having F is causally relevant to e's having G, iff there is a law of the form Fs cause Gs (1982, p. 62). If one thinks, as Honderich does, that AM implies that psychological predicates never appear in causal laws, then one might conclude that psychological features have no causal role to play and indeed that psychology could not be a science. But, as Davidson has been careful to observe (1980, p. 240), there may very well be psychological and psychophysical causal laws that support counterfactuals and other subjunctive conditionals; it is just that such laws cannot be *strict*. If Honderich intends for the principle of nomological relevance to include non-strict as well as strict laws, then AM is compatible with the causal relevance (in Honderich's sense) of psychological properties. If he intends for the principle to include only strict laws, then it is an unacceptable principle. It is implausible that there are any strict laws linking "is a match striking" with "is a match lighting." So, on the strict law construal of Honderich's principle, being a match striking is not causally relevant to the match's lighting. On this construal, Honderich's principle would render virtually all properties of events causally irrelevant$_2$. This certainly seems wrong.

In arguing that AM entails the causal irrelevance of the mental, some authors have suggested a strengthened account of causal relevance$_2$. For example, Sosa writes

> I extend my hand because of a certain neurological event. That event is my sudden desire to quench my thirst. Thus, if my grasping is caused by that neurological event, it's my sudden desire that causes my grasping ... Assuming the anomalism of the mental, though extending my hand is, in a certain sense, caused by my sudden desire to quench my thirst, it is not caused by my desire qua desire but only by desire qua *neurological* of a certain sort ... [T]he being a desire of my desire has no causal relevance to my extending my hand (if the mental is indeed anomalous): *if the event that is in fact my desire had not been my desire but had remained a neurological event of a certain sort, then it would have caused my extending my hand just the same* (1984, pp. 277–8, our emphasis).

This passage suggests the following as a sufficient condition for causal irrelevance$_2$:

(II) c's being F is causally irrelevant$_2$ to e's being G, if there is a property $F*$ of c such that $(F*c \ \& - Fc)$ holds nonvacuously.

Even when $-Fc > -Ge$ holds, there may be a property $F*$ of c such that $(F*c \ \& -Fc) > Ge$. In this case, it may seem that it is in virtue of c's being $F*$, not F, that e is G. When this holds, we will say that $F*c$ "screens off" Fc from Ge. Converting (II) into a necessary condition for causal relevance$_2$ and adding it to (I), we obtain the following proposal:

(III) c's being F is relevant$_2$ to e's being G iff the conditions in (I) are satisfied and there is *no* property $F*$ of c such that $(F*c \ \& -Fc) > Ge$ holds nonvacuously.

Sosa seems to think that it follows from AM that c's being a certain neural state, Nc, screens off c's being a desire to quench thirst, Mc, from e's being an extending of the hand, Be. More generally, he seems to think that neural properties screen off intentional mental properties. Presumably, Sosa thinks that this follows from AM, because he thinks there are strict laws connecting neural properties with behavioral properties. Since mental properties are not reducible to neural properties, it follows that there are physically possible worlds in which Nc, Mc, and in *all* such worlds Be.

It is not at all clear that there are strict laws connecting neural properties with mental properties (and so that AM *entails* that the neural property screens off the mental property), but it does seem that, as a matter of fact in a case like Sosa's, the neural property does screen off the mental property. The worry then is that, if (II) is kept as a condition on causal irrelevance$_2$, then the causal irrelevance$_2$ of the mental will follow from AM after all.[13]

In response to this, notice first that (II)'s rendering the mental causally irrelevant$_2$ is independent of AM, at least to the extent that the problem-creating counterfactual, $(Nc \ \& -Mc) > Be$, holds whether or not there is a strict law linking N with B. So anyone who adopts (II) as a condition on causal irrelevance$_2$ will be committed to the causal irrelevance$_2$ of the mental in this case. But it seems to us that (II) is not a correct condition on irrelevance$_2$. It renders even properties connected by strict law causally irrelevant$_2$. To see this, consider the neural event c and the behavioral event e in Sosa's example. c possesses basic physical property P and mental property M (being a desire to quench his thirst), and e possesses the property B (being a certain movement of the hand). Assuming a strict law between P and B, it follows that:

(S) $(-Mc \,\&\, Pc) > Be$.

So, P screens off M from B. Now consider the counterfactual:

(T) $(-Pc \,\&\, Mc) > Be$.

It can be shown that (T) is compatible with AM *and* (S). Furthermore, it is plausible that (T) is in fact true. If c had been a desire to quench thirst but had not been P, it would have had some other property $P*$. Furthermore, c still would have resulted in an e that has the property B. That is, in the closest possible world in which Sosa desires to quench his thirst but this desire is not a P, it still causes him to extend his hand. Supporting this claim there may be a law, though not strict, to the effect that, when someone experiences a sudden desire to quench his thirst and believes there is a glass of water in front of him which he can reach by extending his hand, then, *ceteris paribus*, his hand will extend. When we consider the possibility that c is M but not P, this law "takes over" so that c still causes an event that is B. Here is a nonpsychological example which will, perhaps, help elucidate our claim.

Consider the event of hurricane Donald striking the coast causing the streets to be flooded. That event is identical to the event of certain air and water molecules moving in various complex ways. Call the property of consisting of molecules moving in such ways P. It is perfectly possible for the following counterfactual to be true: if hurricance Donald had not had property P (that is, if a hurricane as much like Donald as possible, though without P, had occurred), then it still would have caused the streets to be flooded. Indeed, it would have had some property $P*$ sufficiently similar to P, and $P*$ events (under the relevant conditions) cause floodings. The result is that Donald's being a hurricane would be said to be causally irrelevant to its flooding the streets. We think that examples such as this one show that (III) is too strong a requirement on casual relevance$_2$.[14]

A fully adequate account of causal relevance$_2$ should show how mentalistic counterfactuals are grounded. What is it about Sosa, his situation, etc., that makes it true that, if he had not experienced a sudden desire to quench his thirst, he would not have extended his hand? We do not have such an account, but we do want to suggest an approach that fits within the framework of AM. As we have observed already, the existence of non-strict psychophysical and psychological laws is compatible with AM. A non-strict law is one which has a *ceteris paribus* qualifier. The interesting thing about such laws is the ways in which they can support counterfactuals. We will illustrate this by building upon a suggestion by Lewis (1975). Let R, W, and B be the statements that a red block, a white block, and a blue block are placed in front of Donald and S_r, S_w and S_b be the statements that Donald sees a red block, a white block, and a blue block. We will suppose, as is plausible, that there are non-strict laws of the form:

(L) If X and C, then S_x,

where C are conditions like lighting is good, Donald is awake and paying attention, and so on. Even with such conditions added, the law is a *ceteris paribus* one and, if AM is correct, it will be impossible to add explicit conditions that turn it into a strict law. When the laws (L) hold, we will say that the statements describing what Donald sees depend nomically on the statements describing the blocks in front of him. Call conditions C counterfactually independent of the family of statements $\{R, W, B\}$, if C would continue to hold no matter which member of $\{R, W, B\}$ is true. Lewis shows that, if C and the *ceteris paribus* conditions associated with (L) are counterfactually independent of $\{R, W, B\}$, then S_x will depend counterfactually on X. That is, each of the counterfactuals, $R > S_r$, $W > S_w$, $B > S_b$ will be true. If we further assume that a block which has one of three colors will be placed in front of Donald (and that this statement is also counterfactually independent of (R, W, B)), then the statement $-X > -S_x$ will also be true. Suppose a red block is placed in front of Donald, and this event causes the event of his seeing a red block. It will follow that, if the first event had not been a placing of a red block, then the second event would not have been Donald's seeing a red block. As Lewis points out, this "grounding" of counterfactuals in laws fails to *reduce* counterfactuals to laws, since the assumption of counterfactual independence is essential. It does show, however, how laws, including *ceteris paribus* laws, can support counterfactuals. The program for a psychology compatible with AM is the discovery and the systematization of such non-strict laws (at various levels) connecting psychological and behavioral properties.

We have seen that AM attempts to resolve the mind–body problem by endorsing (2), (3), and (3′), denying (1) with respect to events, and affirming (1) with respect to properties. Davidson is silent on (2) and (3) with respect to properties, leading to the accusation that AM is committed to epiphenomenalism. We rebutted this charge by showing that AM is compatible with there being counterfactual dependencies between events in virtue of their mental properties. To do this is to affirm (2) with respect to properties but, of course, to deny (3) with respect to properties. An event's physical features may counterfactually depend on another event's mental features. But, interestingly, we need not deny (3′) for our account of causal relevance₂. It may be that all counterfactuals *supervene* on basic physical truths and strict laws. That is, if two possible worlds are exactly alike with respect to basic physical facts and strict laws, they are exactly alike with respect to counterfactuals. This fairly strong physicalism still allows sufficient autonomy of the mental so that it is not reducible to the physical and it has a genuine explanatory and causal role to play.

Notes

Thanks are due to Jonathan Adler, John Biro, Paul Boghossian, Donald Davidson, Fred Dretske, Ray Elugardo, Jerry Fodor, Richard Foley, Terry Horgan, Brian McLaughlin, Alexander Rosenberg, Stephen Schiffer, and John Searle.

1 Similar characterizations of the mind–body problem can be found in J. L. Mackie (1979) and Anthony Skillen (1984).

2 This view is given in three places in Davidson's (1980) *Essays on Actions and Events*: at the beginning and end of "Mental Events," pp. 208, 223; and in "Psychology as philosophy," p. 231. Where nothing else is said, all page references in the text of our paper are to this book.

3 Davidson's argument against psychophysical laws is restricted to laws whose psychological predicates express propositional attitudes.

4 We shall typically speak of features, aspects, and properties of events. For present purposes, however, unless we indicate otherwise, what we say can be recast in terms of events satisfying descriptions or predicates.

5 Davidson never provides an example of a strict causal law. And there are some philosophers who think his account of causation is much too stringent, because there may be too few strict causal laws. (The best candidates for such laws are basic laws of quantum mechanics.) It is not our aim here to defend Davidson's metaphysical account of causation.

6 For an explication and defense of Davidson's arguments for the impossibility of strict psychophysical laws, see Jaegwon Kim (1985) and also the introduction by McLaughlin in the same volume. Cf. also LePore and Loewer, "Davidson and the anomalousness of the mental" (forthcoming).

7 For similar characterizations and examples of causal relevance, see Ted Honderich (1982, p. 61); John Searle (1983, pp. 155–7); Elizabeth Anscombe (1975, p. 78); and Peter Achenstein (1977, pp. 368).

8 Others who have argued that AM is epiphenomenalist include: F. Stoutland (1976, p. 307); Dagfinn Føllesdal (1985, p. 315); Mark Johnston (1985, p. 423); and Skillen (1984, p. 520).

9 While many philosophers appeal to the notion of causal relevance, it is far from clear that there is a single or well-characterizable notion that underlies the locution that c *qua* F causes e to be G. We are here interested only in sketching enough of an account to refute the charge that AM is committed to epiphenomenalism. Anyone interested in a thorough explication of causal relevance would have to show how to accommodate familiar difficulties involving preemption, overdetermination, and so on. But these are problems which confront every account of causation and we will not discuss them here.

10 c's being F and e's being G are metaphysically independent, iff there is a possible world in which c (or a counterpart of c) is F but e (or a counterpart of e) fails to occur or fails to be G and vice versa.

11 See David Lewis (1973) and Robert Stalnaker (1968). There are differences between the two accounts irrelevant to our discussion.

12 Although there is a tradition in the philosophy of action arguing that there are conceptual connections between propositional attitudes and actions, this does not entail that particular propositional attitude properties are conceptually connected. For example, suppose that John believes that Mary is across the street and, for this reason, waves his hand. Let c be John's thought, e his action, F the property of his believing Mary is across the street, and G the property of being a waving hand. Clearly, we can have c's being F causally relevant$_2$ to e's being G, since c's being F can obtain without e's being G and vice versa in some metaphysically possible world.

13 Jerry Fodor has argued that a taxonomy of propositional attitude states in terms of their truth conditions is not a taxonomy in terms of causal powers. See his *Psychosemantics* (1987); ch. 2. Condition (III) may be involved in the view of some philosophers that scientific psychology requires a notion of narrow content. Thus Fodor seems to hold that Oscar's belief that water quenches thirst is not causally relevant$_2$ to Oscar's behavior, since, if Oscar were in the same neural state as he is in but had not believed that water quenches his thirst, he would have behaved identically. The antecedent of this counterfactual is thought to be metaphysically possible for Putnamian reasons: if Oscar has lived in an environment containing XYZ and not H_2O his neural state would have been a belief that twin-water quenches thirst. One might conclude that, if we want a notion of content such that propositional attitudes are causally relevant$_2$ in virtue of their contents, then we need a notion of content which makes propositional attitudes supervene on neural states.

14 It may be that there is some account of causal relevance$_2$ midway in strength between (I) and (III) which captures what some of Davidson's critics have in mind. We leave to them the task of formulating it and attempting to demonstrate that AM entails the irrelevance$_2$ of the mental so characterized.

References

Achenstein, P. (1977) "The causal relation," in *Midwest Studies in Philosophy*, vol. 4, pp. 369–86.

Anscombe, G. E. M. (1975) "Causality and determination," in E. Sosa (ed.) *Causation and Conditionals*, London: Oxford University Press, pp. 63–81.

Davidson, D. (1980) *Essays on Actions and Events*, Oxford: Clarendon Press.

Dretske, F. (1989) "Reasons and causes," *Philosophical Perspectives* 3, pp. 1–15.

Fodor, J. A. (1987) *Psychosemantics: the Problem of Meaning in the Philosophy of Mind*, Cambridge, Mass.: Bradford Books/MIT Press.

Føllesdal, D. (1985) "Causation and explanation: a problem in Davidson's view on action and mind," in E. LePore and B. P. McLaughlin (eds) *Actions and*

Events: Perspectives on the Philosophy of Donald Davidson, Oxford: Blackwell, pp. 311–23.

Goodman, N. (1983) *Fact, Fiction, and Forecast*, 4th edn, Cambridge, Mass.: Harvard University Press.

Honderich, T. (1982) "The argument for anomalous monism," *Analysis* 42(1), pp. 59–64.

Honderich, T. (1984) "Smith and the champion of mauve," *Analysis* 44(2), pp. 86–9.

Johnston, M. (1985) "Why having a mind matters," in E. LePore and B. P. McLaughlin (eds) *Actions and Events: Perspectives on the Philosophy of Donald Davidson*, Oxford: Blackwell, pp. 408–26.

Kim, J. (1984) "Epiphenomenal and supervenient causation," in *Midwest Studies in Philosophy*, vol. 9, pp. 257–70.

Kim, J. (1985) "Psychophysical laws," in E. LePore and B. P. McLaughlin (eds) *Actions and Events: Perspectives on the Philosophy of Donald Davidson*, Oxford: Blackwell, pp. 369–86.

LePore, E. and Loewer, B. (forthcoming) "Davidson and the anomalousness of the mental," in J. Tomberlin (ed.) *Philosophical Perspectives on the Philosophy of Mind*.

Lewis, D. (1973) *Counterfactuals*, Oxford: Blackwell.

Lewis, D. (1975) "Causation," in E. Sosa (ed.) *Causation and Conditionals*, London: Oxford University Press, pp. 180–91.

Mackie, J. L. (1979) "Mind, brain and causation," in *Midwest Studies in Philosophy*, vol. 4, pp. 19–29.

McLaughlin, B. P. (1985) "Introduction," in E. LePore and B. P. McLaughlin (eds) *Actions and Events: Perspectives on the Philosophy of Donald Davidson*, Oxford: Blackwell.

Searle, J. (1983) *Intentionality: an Essay in the Philosophy of Mind*, Cambridge: Cambridge University Press.

Skillen, A. (1984) "Mind and matter: a problem that refuses dissolution," *Mind* 93, pp. 514–26.

Sosa, E. (1984) "Mind-body interaction and supervenient causation," in *Midwest Studies in Philosophy*, vol. 9, pp. 271–82.

Stalnaker, R (1968) "A theory of conditionals," in N. Rescher (ed.) *Studies in Logical Theory*, Oxford: Blackwell.

Stoutland, F. (1976) "The causation of behavior," *Acta Philosophica Fennica* 28 (1–3) (*Essays on Wittgenstein in Honor of G. H. von Wright*), pp. 286–325.

Part V
Subjectivity, Incorrigibility, and Dualism

21
What's Wrong with the Philosophy of Mind?

John Searle

1 The Solution to the Mind–Body Problem and Why Many Prefer the Problem to the Solution

The famous mind–body problem, the source of so much controversy over the past two millennia, has a simple solution. This solution has been available to any educated person since serious work began on the brain nearly a century ago, and, in a sense, we all know it to be true. Here it is: mental phenomena are caused by neurophysiological processes in the brain and are themselves features of the brain. To distinguish this view from the many others in the field, I call it "biological naturalism." Mental events and processes are as much part of our biological natural history as digestion, mitosis, meiosis, or enzyme secretion.

Biological naturalism raises a thousand questions of its own. What exactly is the character of the neurophysiological processes and how exactly do the elements of the neuroanatomy – neurons, synapses, synaptic clefts, receptors, mitochondria, glial cells, transmitter fluids, etc. – produce mental phenomena? And what about the great variety of our mental life: pains, desires, tickles, thoughts, visual experiences, beliefs, tastes, smells, anxiety, fear, love, hate, depression, and elation? How does neurophysiology account for the range of our mental phenomena, both conscious and unconscious? Such questions form the subject matter of the neurosciences, and as I write this, there are literally thousands of people investigating these questions.[1] But not all the questions are neurobiological.

Some are philosophical or psychological or part of cognitive science generally. Some of the philosophical questions are: what exactly is consciousness and how exactly do conscious mental phenomena relate to the unconscious? What are the special features of the "mental," features such as consciousness, intentionality, subjectivity, mental causation; and how exactly do they function? What are the causal relations between "mental" phenomena and "physical" phenomena? And can we characterize those causal relations in a way that avoids epiphenomenalism?

There is a great deal to say about these questions, but at this point I want to note a remarkable fact. I said that the solution to the mind–body problem should be obvious to any educated person, but at present in philosophy and cognitive science many, perhaps most, of the experts claim to find it not at all obvious. In fact, they don't even think the solution I have proposed is true. If one surveys the field of the philosophy of mind over the past few decades one finds it occupied by a small minority who insist on the reality and irreducibility of consciousness and intentionality and who tend to think of themselves as property dualists, and a much larger mainstream group who think of themselves as materialists of one type or another. The property dualists think that the mind–body problem is frightfully difficult, perhaps altogether insoluble.[2] The materialists agree that if intentionality and consciousness really do exist and are irreducible to physical phenomena, then there really would be a difficult mind–body problem, but they hope to "naturalize" intentionality and perhaps consciousness as well. By "naturalizing" mental phenomena, they mean reducing them to physical phenomena. They think that to grant the reality and irreducibility of consciousness and other mental phenomena commits one to some form of Cartesianism, and they do not see how such a view can be made consistent with our overall scientific world picture.

I believe that both sides are profoundly mistaken. They both accept a certain vocabulary and with it a set of assumptions. I intend to show that the vocabulary is obsolete and the assumptions are false. It is essential to show that both dualism and monism are false because it is generally supposed that these exhaust the field, leaving no other options. Most of my discussion will be directed at the various forms of materialism because it is the dominant view. Dualism in any form is today generally regarded as out of the question because it is assumed to be inconsistent with the scientific worldview.

So the question I want to pose is: What is it about our intellectual history and environment that makes it difficult to see these rather simple points that I have made about the "mind–body problem"? What has made "materialism" appear to be the only rational approach to the philosophy of mind? This paper is about the current situation in the philosophy of mind, and this one might have had the title, "What is wrong with the materialist tradition in the philosophy of mind."

Seen in perspective, the last fifty years of the philosophy of mind, as well as cognitive science and certain branches of psychology, present a very curious spectacle. The most striking feature is how much of mainstream philosophy of mind of the past fifty years seems obviously false. I believe there is no other area of contemporary analytic philosophy where so much is said that is so implausible. In the philosophy of language, for example, it is not at all common to deny the existence of sentences and speech acts; but in the philosophy of mind, obvious facts about the mental, such as that we all really do have subjective conscious mental states and that these are not eliminable in favor of anything else, are routinely denied by many, perhaps most, of the advanced thinkers in the subject.

How is it that so many philosophers and cognitive scientists can say so many things that, to me at least, seem obviously false? Extreme views in philosophy are almost never unintelligent; there are generally very deep and powerful reasons why they are held. I believe one of the unstated assumptions behind the current batch of views is that they represent the only scientifically acceptable alternatives to the antiscientism that went with traditional dualism, the belief in the immortality of the soul, spiritualism, and so on. Acceptance of the current views is motivated not so much by an independent conviction of their truth as by a terror of what are apparently the only alternatives. That is, the choice we are tacitly presented with is between a "scientific" approach, as represented by one or another of the current versions of "materialism," and an "antiscientific" approach, as represented by Cartesianism or some other traditional religious conception of the mind. Another odd fact, closely related to the first, is that most of the standard authors are deeply committed to the traditional vocabulary and categories. They really think there is some more or less clear meaning attaching to the archaic vocabulary of "dualism," "monism," "materialism," "physicalism," etc., and that the issues have to be posed and resolved in these terms. They use these words with neither embarrassment nor irony. One of the many aims I now have is to show that both these assumptions are mistaken. Properly understood, many of the currently fashionable views are inconsistent with what we know about the world both from our own experiences and from the special sciences. To state what we all know to be true, we are going to have to challenge the assumptions behind the traditional vocabulary.

Before identifying some of these incredible views, I want to make an observation about presentational style. Authors who are about to say something that sounds silly very seldom come right out and say it. Usually a set of rhetorical or stylistic devices is employed to avoid having to say it in words of one syllable. The most obvious of these devices is to beat around the bush with a lot of evasive prose. I think it is obvious in the writings of several authors, for example, that they think we really don't have mental states, such as beliefs, desires, fears, etc. But it is hard to find passages where they actually say this straight out. Often they want to keep the commonsense vocabulary, while denying that it actually stands for anything in the real world. Another rhetorical device for disguising the implausible is to give the commonsense view a name and then deny it by name and not by content. Thus, it is very hard even in the present era to come right out and say, "No human being has ever been conscious." Rather, the sophisticated philosopher gives the view that people are sometimes conscious a name, for example, "the Cartesian intuition," then he or she sets about challenging, questioning, denying something described as "the Cartesian intuition." Again, it is hard to come right out and say that no one in the history of the world ever drank because she was thirsty or ate because he was hungry; but it's easy to challenge something if you can label it in advance as "folk psychology." And just to give this maneuver a name, I will call it the "give-it-a-name" maneuver. Another maneuver, the most favored of all, I will call the "heroic-age-of-science" maneuver. When an author gets in deep trouble, he or she tries to make an analogy with his or her own claim and some great scientific discovery of the past. Does the view seem silly? Well, the great scientific geniuses of the past seemed silly to their ignorant, dogmatic, and prejudiced contemporaries. Galileo is the favorite historical analogy. Rhetorically speaking, the idea is to make you, the skeptical reader, feel that if you don't believe the view being advanced, you are playing Cardinal Bellarmine to the author's Galileo (see for example, P. S. Churchland, 1987). Other favorites are phlogiston and vital spirits, and again the idea is to bully the reader into supposing that if he or she doubts, for example, that computers are actually thinking, it can only be because the reader believes in something as unscientific as phlogiston or vital spirits.

2 Six Unlikely Theories of Mind

I will not attempt to provide a complete catalogue of all the fashionable, implausible materialist views in contemporary philosophy and cognitive science, but will list only half a dozen to give the feel of the thing. What these views share is a hostility toward the existence and mental character of our ordinary mental life. In one way or another they all attempt to downgrade ordinary mental phenomena such as beliefs, desires, and intentions and to cast doubt on the existence of such general features of the mental as consciousness and subjectivity.[3]

First, perhaps the most extreme version of these views is the idea that mental states, as such, don't exist at all. This view is held by those who call themselves "eliminative materialists." The idea is that, contrary to a widely held belief, there really aren't any such things as beliefs, desires, hopes, fears, etc. Early versions of this view were put forth by Feyerabend (1963) and Rorty (1965).

A second view, often used to support eliminative materialism, is the claim that folk psychology is – in all probability – simply and entirely false. This view has been advanced by P. M. Churchland (1981) and Stich (1983). Folk psychology includes such claims as that people sometimes drink because they are thirsty and eat because they are hungry; that they have desires and beliefs, that some of these beliefs are true, or at least false; that some beliefs are better supported than others; that people sometimes do something because they want to do it; that they sometimes have pains; and that these are often unpleasant. And so – more or less indefinitely – on. The connection between folk psychology and eliminative materialism is this: folk psychology is supposed to be an empirical theory and the entities it "postulates" – pains, tickles, itches, and so on – are supposed to be theoretical entities on all fours, ontologically speaking, with quarks and muons. If the theory goes, the theoretical entities go with it: to demonstrate the falsehood of folk psychology would be to remove any justification for accepting the existence of the folk psychological entities. I sincerely hope I am not being unfair in characterizing these views as implausible, but I have to confess that that is how they strike me. Let me continue the list.

A third view of this same type holds that there is nothing specifically *mental* about the so-called mental states. Mental states consist entirely in their causal relations to each other and to the inputs and outputs of the system of which they are a part. These causal relations could be duplicated by any system that had the right causal properties. Thus a system made of stones or beer cans, if it had the right causal relations, would have to have the same beliefs, desires, etc., as we do, because that is all there is to having beliefs and desires. The most influential version of this view is called "functionalism," and it is so widely held as to constitute a contemporary orthodoxy.

A fourth implausible view, and indeed the most famous and widely held of the current catalogue, is the view that a computer could have – indeed must have – thoughts, feelings, and understanding solely in virtue of implementing an appropriate computer program with the appropriate inputs and outputs. I have elsewhere baptized this view "strong artificial intelligence," but it has also been called "computer functionalism."

A fifth form of incredibility is to be found in the claim that we should not think of our mental vocabulary of "belief" and "desire," "fear" and "hope," etc., as actually standing for intrinsically mental phenomena, but rather as just a manner of speaking. It is just a useful vocabulary for explaining and predicting behavior, but not to be taken literally as referring to real, intrinsic, subjective, psychological phenomena. Adherents of this view think that the use of the commonsense vocabulary is a matter of taking an "intentional stance" toward a system.[4]

Sixth, another extreme view is that maybe consciousness as we normally think of it – as inner, private, subjective, qualitative phenomena of sentience or awareness – does not exist at all. This view is seldom advanced explicitly.[5] Very few people are willing to come right out and say that consciousness does not exist. But it has recently become common for authors to redefine the notion of consciousness so that it no longer refers to actual conscious states, that is, inner, subjective, qualitative, first-person mental states, but rather to publicly observable third-person phenomena. Such authors pretend to think that consciousness exists, but in fact they end up denying its existence.[6]

Sometimes mistakes in the philosophy of mind produce mistakes in the philosophy of language. One, to my mind, unbelievable thesis in the philosophy of language, which comes from the same stable as the examples we have just been considering, is the view that where meaning are concerned, there just aren't any facts of the matter in addition to patterns of verbal behavior. On this view, most famously held by Quine (1960), there just isn't any fact of the matter about whether when you or I say "rabbit" we mean rabbit, undetached part of a rabbit, or stage in the life history of a rabbit.[7]

Now what is one to do in the face of all this? It is not enough for me to say that it all seems implausible; rather, I think a philosopher with patience enough and time should sit down and do a point by point, line by line refutation of the whole tradition. I have tried to do that with one specific thesis in the tradition, the claim that computers have thoughts and feelings and understanding solely in virtue of instantiating a computer program (the "right" computer program with the "right" inputs and outputs) (Searle 1980). This view, strong artificial intelligence, is an attractive target because it is reasonably clear, there is a simple and decisive refutation, and the refutation can be extended to other versions of functionalism. I have also tried to refute Quine's thesis of indeterminacy (Searle 1987), which I believe also lends itself to a frontal assault. With some of the views, however, the situation is much messier. How, for example, would one go about refuting the view that consciousness does not exist? Should I pinch its adherents to remind them that they are conscious? Should I pinch myself and report the results in the *Journal of Philosophy*?

To conduct an argument in the traditional sense, it is essential that there be some common ground. Unless the participants agree on the premises, there is no point in trying to derive a conclusion. But if somebody denies the existence of consciousness from the very start, it is difficult to know what the common ground in the study of mind would be. On my view, if your theory results in the view that consciousness does not exist, you have simply produced a *reductio ad absurdum* of the theory, and similarly with many other views in contemporary philosophy of mind.

Several years of debating these issues, both in public forums and in print, have convinced me that quite often the fundamental issues in the debate do not rise to the surface. If you debate with people, for example, about strong artificial intelligence or the indeterminacy of translation, the sheer implausibility of such theories is disguised by the apparently technical character of the arguments bandied back and forth. Worse yet, it is hard to get the assumptions that lead to these theories out in the open. When, for example, somebody feels comfortable with the idea that a computer would suddenly and miraculously have mental states just in virtue of running a certain sort of program, the underlying assumptions that make this view seem possible are seldom stated explicitly. So, in this discussion I want to try an approach different from direct refutation. I am not going to present one more "refutation of functionalism"; rather, I want to begin the task of exposing and thereby undermining the foundations on which this whole tradition rests. If you are tempted to functionalism, I believe you do not need refutation, you need help.

The materialist tradition is massive, complex, ubiquitous, and yet elusive. Its various elements – its attitude toward consciousness, its conception of scientific verification, its metaphysics and theory of knowledge – are all mutually supporting, so that when one part is challenged, the defenders can easily fall back on another part whose certainty is taken for granted. Here I speak from personal experience. When you offer a refutation of strong AI or of the indeterminacy thesis or of functionalism, the defenders do not feel it necessary to try to meet your actual arguments, because they know in advance that you must be wrong. They know that the materialist tradition – which they often mistakenly call "science" – is on their side. And the tradition is not just part of academic philosophy. If you hear lectures in cognitive science or read popular articles on artificial intelligence, you will encounter the same tradition. It is too large to summarize in a paragraph or even a chapter, but I believe that if I continue to allow it to unfold itself, the reader will have no difficulty recognizing it.

Before beginning an assault on the foundations, I need to specify certain elements of the structure a little more precisely and to say something about its history.

3 The Foundations of Modern Materialism

By "the tradition," I mean in large part the cluster of views and methodological presuppositions that centers on the following (often unstated) assumptions and theses:

1   Where the scientific study of the mind is concerned, consciousness and its special features are of rather minor importance. It is quite possible, indeed desirable, to give an account of language, cognition, and mental states in general without taking into account consciousness and subjectivity.[8]

2   Science is objective. It is objective not only in the sense that it strives to reach conclusions that are independent of personal biases and points of view, but more important, it concerns a reality that is objective. Science is objective because reality itself is objective.

3   Because reality is objective, the best method in the study of the mind is to adopt the objective or third-person point of view. The objectivity of science requires that the phenomena studied be completely objective, and in the case of cognitive science this means that it must study objectively observable *behavior*. As far as a mature cognitive science is concerned, the study of the mind and the study of intelligent behavior (including the causal foundations of behavior) are pretty much the same study.

4   From the third-person, objective point of view, the only answer to the epistemological question: How would we know about the mental phenomena of another system? is: We know by observing its *behavior*. This is the only solution to the "other minds problem."

Epistemology plays a special role in cognitive science because an objective science of cognition must be able to distinguish such things as cognition, intelligent behavior, information-processing, etc., from other natural phenomena. A basic question, perhaps the basic question, in the study of the mind is the epistemological question: How would we know whether or not some other "system" has such-and-such mental properties? And the only scientific answer is: by its behavior.

5   Intelligent behavior and causal relations to intelligent behavior are in some way the essence of the mental. Adherence to the view that there is an essential connection between mind and behavior range all the way from the extreme version of behaviorism that says there isn't anything to having mental states except having dispositions to behavior, to the functionalists attempt to define mental notions in terms of internal and external causal relations, to Wittgenstein's (1953, § 580) puzzling claim, "An 'inner process' stands in need of outward criteria."[9]

6   Every fact in the universe is in principle knowable and understandable by human investigators. Because reality is physical, and because science concerns the investigation of physical reality, and because there are no limits on what we can know of physical reality, it follows that all of the facts in the universe are knowable and understandable by us.

7   The only things that exist are ultimately physical, *as the physical is traditionally conceived*, that is, as opposed to the mental. This means that in the traditional oppositions – dualism versus monism, mentalism versus

materialism – the right-hand term names the correct view; the left-hand term names the false view.

Already it should be clear that these views hang together; because reality is objective (point 2), it must be ultimately physical (point 7). And the objectivist ontology of points 2 and 7 leads naturally to the objectivist methodology of points 3 and 4. But if the mind really exists and has an objective ontology, then it appears its ontology must be in some sense behavioral and causal (point 5). This, however, forces epistemology to the front of the stage (point 4), because it now becomes crucially important to be able to distinguish the behavior of those systems that lack mental states from those that really have mental states. From the fact that the reality is ultimately physical (point 7), and the fact that it is completely objective (point 2), it is natural to assume that everything in reality is knowable by us (point 6). Finally, one thing is obvious: there is no place – or at least very little place – for consciousness in this overall picture (point 1).

In a fuller treatment I would hope to show that each of these points is, at best, false, and that the total picture they present is not only profoundly unscientific, it is incoherent.

4 Historical Origins of the Foundations

Historically, how did we get into this situation? How did we get into a situation where people can say things that are inconsistent with obvious facts of their experiences?

What one wants to know is: what is it about the history of contemporary discussion in the philosophy of mind, psychology, cognitive science, and artificial intelligence that makes such views conceivable, that makes them seem perfectly respectable or acceptable? At any given time in intellectual history we are, all of us, working within certain traditions that make certain questions seem the right ones to ask and certain answers seem the only possible answers. In contemporary philosophy of mind, the historical tradition is blinding us to the obvious facts of our experiences, giving us a methodology and a vocabulary that make obviously false hypotheses seem acceptable. The tradition has risen from its early crude behaviorist beginnings more than a half century ago through "type–type" and "token–token" identity theories to the present sophisticated computational models of cognition. Now what is it about the tradition that makes it so powerful in such a counterintuitive way? I wish I understood these matters well enough to give a full historical analysis, but I fear I have only a few guesses and suggestions to make about the nature of the symptoms. It seems to me that there are at least four factors at work.

First, we have a terror of falling into Cartesian dualism. The bankruptcy of the Cartesian tradition, and the absurdity of supposing that there are two kinds of substances or properties in the world, "mental" and "physical," is so threatening to us and has such a sordid history that we are reluctant to concede anything that might smack of Cartesianism. We are reluctant to concede any of the commonsense facts that sound "Cartesian," because it seems that if we accept the facts, we will have to accept the whole of Cartesian metaphysics. Any sort of mentalism that recognizes the obvious facts of our existence is regarded as automatically suspect. At the most extreme, some philosophers are reluctant to admit the existence of consciousness because they fail to see that the *mental* state of consciousness is just an ordinary biological, that is, *physical*, feature of the brain. Perhaps even more exasperatingly, they are aided in this error by those philosophers who cheerfully acknowledge the existence of consciousness and in so doing suppose they must be asserting the existence of something nonphysical.

The view that consciousness, mental states, etc., exist, in the most naive and obvious sense, and play a real causal role in our behavior has nothing special to do with Cartesian dualism. After all, one does not have to read the *Meditations* to be conscious that one is conscious or that one's desires, as mental phenomena, conscious or unconscious, are real causal phenomena. But when one reminds philosophers of these "Cartesian intuitions," one is immediately accused of Cartesianism. I have, personally speaking, been accused of holding some crazy doctrine of "property dualism" and "privileged access," or believing in "introspection" or "neovitalism" or even "mysticism," even though I have never, implicitly or explicitly, endorsed any of these views. Why? Partly, no doubt, it is just intellectual carelessness (or perhaps even worse) on the part of the commentators, but there is also something deeper involved. They find it difficult to see that one could accept the obvious facts about mental states without accepting the Cartesian apparatus that traditionally went along with the acknowledgment of these facts. They think the only real choices available are between some form of materialism and some form of dualism. One of my present aims is to show that this conception is mistaken, that one can give a coherent account of the facts about the mind without endorsing any of the discredited Cartesian apparatus.

Second, along with the Cartesian tradition we have inherited a vocabulary, and with the vocabulary a certain set of categories, within which we are historically conditioned to think about these problems. The vocabulary is not innocent, because implicit in the vocabulary are a surprising number of theoretical claims that are almost certainly false. The vocabulary includes a series of apparent oppositions: "physical" versus "mental," "body" versus "mind," "materialism" versus "mentalism," "matter" versus "spirit." Implicit in these oppositions is the thesis that the same phenomenon under the same aspects cannot literally satisfy both terms. Sometimes the semantics and even the morphology seems to make this opposition explicit, as in the apparent opposition between "materialism" and "immaterialism." Thus we are supposed to believe that if something is mental, it cannot be physical; that if it is a matter of spirit, it cannot be a matter of matter; if it is immaterial, it cannot be material. But these views seem to me obviously false, given everything we know about neurobiology. The brain causes certain "mental" phenomena, such as conscious mental states, and these conscious states are simply higher-level features of the brain. Consciousness is a higher level or emergent property of the brain in the utterly harmless sense of "higher level" or "emergent" in which solidity is a higher level emergent property of H_2O molecules when they are in a lattice structure (ice), and liquidity is similarly a higher-level emergent property of H_2O molecules when they are, roughly speaking, rolling around on each other (water). Consciousness is a mental, and therefore physical, property of the brain in the sense in which liquidity is a property of systems of molecules. If there is one thesis that I would like to get across in this discussion, it is simply this: the fact that a feature is mental does not imply that it is not physical; the fact that a feature is physical does not imply that it is not mental. Revising Descartes for the moment, we might say not only "I think, therefore I am" and "I am a thinking being," but also *I am a thinking being, therefore I am a physical being*.

But notice how the vocabulary makes it difficult, if not impossible, to say what I mean using the traditional terminology. When I say that consciousness is a higher level physical feature of the brain, the temptation is to hear that as meaning physical-as-opposed-to-mental, as meaning that consciousness should be described *only* in objective behavioral or neuro-physiological terms. But what I really mean is consciousness *qua* consciousness, *qua* mental, *qua* subjective, *qua* qualitative is *physical*, and physical *because* mental. All of which shows, I believe, the inadequacy of the traditional vocabulary.

Along with the apparent oppositions are names that apparently exhaust the possible positions one can occupy: there is monism versus dualism, materialism and physicalism versus mentalism and idealism. The eagerness to stick with the traditional categories produces some odd terminology, such as "property dualism," "anomalous monism," "token identity," etc. My own views do not fit any of the traditional labels, but to many philosophers the idea that one might hold a view that does not fit these categories seems incomprehensible.[10] Perhaps worst of all, there are several nouns and verbs that look as if they had a clear meaning and actually stood for well-defined objects and activities: "mind," "self," and "introspection" are obvious examples. The contemporary cognitive science vocabulary is no better. We tend to assume uncritically that expressions such as "cognition," "intelligence," and "information-processing" have clear definitions and actually stand for some natural kinds. I believe such assumptions are mistaken. This point is worth emphasizing: "intelligence," "intelligent behavior," "cognition," and "information-processing," for example, are not precisely defined notions. Even more amazingly, a lot of very technical sounding notions are poorly defined: notions such as "computer," "computation," "program," and "symbol," for example. It does not much matter for most purposes in computer science that these notions are ill-defined (just as it is not important to furniture manufacturers that they do not have a philosophically precise definition of "chair" and "table" either); but when cognitive scientists say such things as that brains are computers, minds are programs, etc., then the definition of these notions becomes crucial.

Third, there is a persistent objectifying tendency in contemporary philosophy, science, and intellectual life generally. We have the conviction that if something is real, it must be equally accessible to all competent observers. Since the seventeenth century, educated people in the West have come to accept an absolutely basic metaphysical presupposition: *Reality is objective.* This assumption has proved useful to us in many ways, but it is obviously false, as a moment's reflection on one's own subjective states reveals. And this assumption has led, perhaps inevitably, to the view that the only "scientific" way to study the mind is as a set of objective phenomena. Once we adopt the assumption that anything that is objective must be equally accessible to any observer, the questions are automatically shifted away from the subjectivity of mental states toward the objectivity of the external behavior. And this has the consequence that instead of asking the questions, "What is it to have a belief?", "What is it to have a desire?", "What is it like to be in certain sorts of conscious states?", we ask the third-person question, "Under what conditions would we from outside *attribute* beliefs, desires, etc., to some *other* system?" This seems perfectly natural to us, because, of course, most of the questions we need to answer about mental phenomena concern other people and not just ourselves.

But the third-person character of the epistemology should not blind us to the fact that the actual ontology of mental states is a first-person ontology. The way that the third-person point of view is applied in practice makes it difficult for us to see the difference between something really having a mind, such as a human being, and something behaving *as if* it had a mind, such as a computer. And once you have lost the distinction between a system's really having mental states and merely acting as if it had mental states, then you lose sight of an essential feature of the mental, namely that its ontology is essentially a first-person ontology. Beliefs, desires, etc., are always *somebody*'s beliefs and desires, and they are always potentially conscious, even in cases where they are actually unconscious.

I am here trying to diagnose a historically conditioned pattern of investigation that makes the third-person point of view seem the only scientifically acceptable standpoint from which to examine the mind. It would take an intellectual historian to answer such questions as when did the "Under-what-conditions-would-we-attribute-mental-states?" question come to seem the right question to ask? But the intellectual effects of its persistence seem clear. Just as Kant's commonsense distinction between the appearances of things and things in themselves eventually led to the extremes of absolute idealism, so the persistence of the commonsense question "under what conditions would we attribute mental states?" has led us into behaviorism, functionalism, strong AI, eliminative materialism, the intentional stance, and no doubt other confusions known only to experts.

Fourth, because of our conception of the history of the growth of knowledge we have come to suffer from what Austin called the *ivresse des grands profondeurs*. It does not seem enough somehow to state humble and obvious truths about the mind; we want something deeper. We want a theoretical discovery. And of course our model of a great theoretical discovery comes from the history of the physical sciences. We dream of some great "breakthrough" in the study of the mind, we look forward to a "mature" cognitive science. So the fact that the views in question are implausible and counterintuitive does not count against them. On the contrary, it can even seem a great merit of contemporary functionalism and artificial intelligence that they run dead counter to our intuitions. For is this not the very feature that makes the physical sciences so dazzling? Our ordinary intuitions about space and time or, for that matter, about the solidity of the table in front of us, have been shown to be mere illusions replaced by a much deeper knowledge of the inner workings of the universe. Could not a great breakthrough in the study of the mind similarly show that our most firmly held beliefs about our mental states are equally illusory? Can we not reasonably expect great discoveries that will overthrow our commonsense assumptions? And, who knows, might not some of those great discoveries be made by some of us?

5 Undermining the Foundations

One way to state some of the salient features of my argument is to state them in opposition to the seven principles I mentioned earlier. To do this, I need first to make explicit the distinctions between ontology, epistemology, and causation. There is a distinction between answers to the questions, What is it? (ontology), How do we find out about it? (epistemology), and What does it do? (causation). For example, in the case of the heart, the ontology is that it is a large piece of muscle tissue in the chest cavity; the epistemology is that we find out about it by using stethescopes, EKGs, and in a pinch we can open up the chest and have a look; and the causation is that the heart pumps blood through the body. With these distinctions in mind, we can go to work.

(1) *Consciousness does matter.* I believe that there is no way to study the phenomena of the mind without implicitly or explicitly studying consciousness. The basic reason for this is that we really have no notion of the mental apart from our notion of consciousness. Of course, at any given point in a person's life, most of the mental phenomena in that person's existence are not present to consciousness. In the formal mode, most of the mental predicates that apply to me at any given instant will have conditions of application independent of my conscious states at that moment. However, though most of our mental life at any given point is unconscious, I argue that we have no conception of an unconscious mental state except in terms derived from conscious mental states. If I am right about this, then all of the recent talk about mental states that are in principle inaccessible to consciousness is really incoherent.

(2) *Not all of reality is objective; some of it is subjective.* There is a persistent confusion between the claim that we should try as much as possible to eliminate personal subjective prejudices from the search for truth and the claim that the real world contains no elements that are irreducibly subjective. And this confusion in turn is based on a confusion between the epistemological sense of the subjective–objective distinction, and the ontological sense. Epistemically, the distinction marks different degrees of independence of claims from the vagaries of special values, personal prejudices, points of view, and emotions. Ontologically, the distinction marks different categories of empirical reality. Epistemically, the ideal of objectivity states a worthwhile, even if unattainable goal. But ontologically, the claim that all of reality is objective is, neurobiologically speaking, simply false. In general mental states have an irreducibly subjective ontology.

   If I am right in thinking that consciousness and subjectivity are essential to the mind, then the conception of the mental employed by the tradition is misconceived from the beginning, for it is essentially an objective, third-person conception. The tradition tries to study the mind as if it consisted of neutral phenomena, independent of consciousness and subjectivity. But such an approach leaves out the crucial features that distinguish mental from nonmental phenomena. And this more than any other reason accounts for the implausibility of the views I mentioned at the beginning. If you try to treat beliefs, for example, as phenomena that have no essential connection with consciousness, then you are likely to wind up with the idea that they can be defined solely in terms of external behavior (behaviorism), or in terms of cause and effect relations (functionalism), or that they do not really exist at all (eliminative materialism), or that talk of beliefs and desires is just to be constructed as a certain manner of speaking (the intentional stance). The ultimate absurdity is to try to treat consciousness itself independently of consciousness, that is, to treat it solely from a third-person point of view, and that leads to the view that consciousness as such, as "inner," "private" phenomenal events, does not really exist.

Sometimes the tension between the methodology and the absurdity of the results becomes visible. In recent literature, there is a dispute about something called "qualia" and the problem is supposed to be, "Can functionalism account for qualia?" What the issue reveals is that the mind consists of qualia, so to speak, right down to the ground. Functionalism can't account for qualia because it was designed around a different subject matter, namely attributions of intentionality based on third-person evidence, whereas actual mental phenomena have to do not with attributions but with the existence of conscious and unconscious mental states, both of which are first-person, subjective phenomena.

(3) *Because it is a mistake to suppose that the ontology of the mental is objective, it is a mistake to suppose that the methodology of a science of the mind must concern itself only with objectively observable behavior.* Because mental phenomena are essentially connected with consciousness, and because consciousness is essentially subjective, it follows that the ontology of the mental is essentially a first-person ontology. Mental states are always somebody's mental states. There is always a "first person," an "I," that has these mental states. The consequence of this for the present discussion is that the first-person point of view is primary. In the actual practice of investigation, we will of course study other people, simply because most of our research is not on ourselves. But it is important to emphasize that what we are trying to get at when we study other people is precisely the first-person point of view. When we study *him* or *her*, what we are studying is the *me* that is him or her. And this is not an epistemic point.

In light of the distinctions between ontology, epistemology, and causation, if one had to summarize the crisis of the tradition in one paragraph, it would be this:

The subjectivist ontology of the mental seems intolerable. It seems intolerable metaphysically that there should be irreducibly subjective, "private" entities in the world, and intolerable epistemologically that there should be an asymmetry between the way that each person knows of his or her inner mental phenomena and the way that others from outside know of them. This crisis produces a flight from subjectivity and the direction of the flight is to rewrite the *ontology* in terms of the *epistemology* and the *causation*. We first get rid of subjectivity by redefining the ontology in terms of the third-person, epistemic basis, behavior. We say, "Mental states just are dispositions to behavior" (behaviorism), and when the absurdity of that becomes unbearable we fall back on causation. We say, "Mental states are defined by their causal relations" (functionalism), or "Mental states are computational state" (strong AI).

The tradition assumes, falsely in my view, that in the study of the mind one is forced to choose between "introspection" and "behavior." There are several mistakes involved in this, among them:

(4) *It is a mistake to suppose that we know of the existence of mental phenomena in others only by observing their behavior.* I believe that the traditional "solution" to the "problem of other minds," though it has been with us for centuries, will not survive even a moment's serious reflection. I have more to say about these issues elsewhere, but at present just this: if you think for a moment about how we know that dogs and cats are conscious, and that computers and cars are not conscious (and by the way, there is no doubt that you and I know both of these things), you will see that the basis of our certainty is not "behavior," but rather a certain causal conception of how the world works. One can see that dogs and cats are in certain important respects relevantly similar to us. Those are eyes, this is skin, these are ears, etc. The "behavior" only makes sense as the expression or manifestation of an underlying mental reality, because we can see the causal basis of the mental and thereby see the behavior as a manifestation of the mental. The principle on which we "solve" the problem of other minds, I shall argue, is not: same-behavior- ergo-same-mental-phenomena. That is the old mistake enshrined in the Turing test. If this principle were correct, we would all have to conclude that radios are conscious because they exhibit intelligent verbal behavior. But we do not draw any such conclusion, because we have a "theory" about how radios work. The principle on which we "solve the other minds problem" is: same-causes-same-effects, and relevantly-similar-causes-relevantly-similar-effects. Where knowledge of other minds is concerned, behavior *by itself* is of no interest to us; it is rather the combination of behavior with the knowledge of the causal underpinnings of the behavior that form the basis of our knowledge.

But even the foregoing seems to me to concede too much to the tradition, because it suggests that our basic stance toward dogs, cats, radios, and other people is epistemic; it suggests that in our everyday dealings with the world we are busy "solving the other minds problem" and that dogs and cats are passing the test and radios and cars failing. But that suggestion is wrong. Except in odd cases, we do not solve the other minds problem, because it does not arise. Our background capacities for dealing with the world enable us to cope with people in one way and cars in another, but we do not in addition generate a hypothesis to the effect that this person is conscious and that car is not conscious, except in unusual cases.

In the sciences, epistemic questions do of course arise, but epistemic questions are no more essential to understanding the nature of the mind than they are to understanding the nature of the phenomena studied in any other discipline. Why should they be? There are interesting epistemic questions about knowledge of the past in history, or knowledge of unobserved entities in physics. But the question "*How* is the existence of the phenomena to be verified?" should not be confused with the question "*What* is the nature of the phenomena whose existence is verified?" The crucial question is not "Under what conditions would we *attribute* mental states to other people?" but rather, "What is it that people *actually have* when they have mental states?" "What are mental phenomena?" as distinct from "How do we find out about them and how do they function causally in the life of the organism?"

I do not want this point to be misunderstood: I am not saying that it is easy to find out about mental states, and that we don't have to worry about epistemic questions. That's not the point at all. I think that it is immensely difficult to study mental phenomena, and the only guide for methodology is the universal one: use any tool or weapon that comes to hand, and stick with any tool or weapon that works. The point I am making here is different: the epistemology of studying the mental no more determines its ontology than does the epistemology of any other discipline determine its ontology. On the contrary, in the study of the mind as elsewhere, the whole point of the epistemology is to get at the pre-existing ontology.

(5) *Behavior or causal relations to behavior are not essential to the existence of mental phenomena.* I believe that the relation of mental states to behavior is purely contingent. It is easy to see this when we consider how it is possible to have the mental states without the behavior, and the behavior without the mental states. Causally we know that brain processes are sufficient for any mental state and that the connection

between those brain processes and the motor nervous system is a contingent neurophysiological connection like any other.

(6) *It is inconsistent with what we in fact know about the universe and our place in it to suppose that everything is knowable by us.* Our brains are the products of certain evolutionary processes, and as such they are simply the most developed in a whole series of evolutionary paths that include the brains of dogs, baboons, dolphins, etc. Now, no one supposes that, for example, dogs can be brought to understand quantum mechanics; the dog's brain is simply not developed to that extent. And it is easy to imagine a being that is further developed along the same evolutionary progression than we are, that stands to us roughly as we stand to dogs. Just as we think that dogs cannot understand quantum mechanics, so this imaginary evolutionary product would conclude that though humans can understand quantum mechanics, there is a great deal that the human brain cannot grasp.[11] It's a good idea to ask ourselves, who do we think we are? And at least part of the answer is that we are biological beasts selected for coping with hunter-gatherer environments, and as far as we know, we have had no significant change in our gene pool for several thousand years. Fortunately (or unfortunately), nature is profligate, and just as every male produces enough sperm to repopulate the earth, so we have a lot more neurons than we need for a hunter-gatherer existence. I believe that the phenomenon of surplus neurons – as distinct from, say, opposed thumbs – is the key to understanding how we got out of hunter-gathering and produced philosophy, science, technology, neuroses, advertising, etc. But we should never forget who we are; and for such as us, it is a mistake to assume that everything that exists is comprehensible to our brains. Of course, methodologically we have to act as if we could understand everything, because there is no way of knowing what we can't: to know the limits of knowledge, we would have to know both sides of the limit. So potential omniscience is acceptable as a heuristic device, but it would be self-deception to suppose it a fact.

Furthermore, we know that many beings on our earth have neurophysiological structures that are different enough from ours for it to be literally unknowable to us what the experiences of those beings are really like.

(7) *The Cartesian conception of the physical, the conception of physical reality as* res extensa, *is simply not adequate to describe the facts that correspond to statements about physical reality.* When we come to the proposition that reality is physical, we come to what is perhaps the

crux of the whole discussion. When we think of the "physical," we think perhaps of things like molecules and atoms and subatomic particles. And we think that they are physical, in a sense that is opposed to the mental, and that things like sensations of pain are mental. And if we are brought up in our culture, we also think these two categories must exhaust everything that exists. But the poverty of these categories becomes apparent as soon as you start to think about the different kinds of things the world contains, that is, as soon as you start to think about the facts that correspond to various sorts of empirical statements. So if you think about balance-of-payments problems, ungrammatical sentences, reasons for being suspicious of modal logic, my ability to ski, the state government of California, and points scored in football games, you are less inclined to think that everything must be categorized as either mental or physical. Of the list I gave, which are mental and which are physical?

There are at least three things wrong with our traditional conception that reality is physical. First, as I have noted, the terminology is designed around a false opposition between the "physical" and the "mental," and as I have already claimed, that is a mistake. Second, if we think of the physical in Cartesian terms as *res extensa*, then it is obsolete even as a matter of physics to suppose that physical reality is physical on this definition. Since relativity theory, we have come to think of, for example, electrons as points of mass/energy. So on the Cartesian definition of "physical," electrons would not count as physical. Third, and most important for our present discussion, it is a very deep mistake to suppose that the crucial question for ontology is, "What sorts of things exist in the world?" as opposed to, "What must be the case in the world in order that our empirical statements be true?"

Noam Chomsky once said (in conversation) that as soon as we come to understand anything, we call it "physical." On this view, trivially, anything is either physical or unintelligible. If we think of the makeup of the world, then of course everything in the world is made of particles, and particles are among our paradigms of the physical. And if we are going to call anything that is made up of physical particles physical; then, trivially, everything in the world is physical. But to say that is not to deny that the world contains points scored in football games, interest rates, governments, and pains. All of these have their own way of existing: athletic, economic, political, mental, etc.

The conclusion is this: once you see the incoherence of dualism, you can also see that monism and materialism are just as mistaken. Dualists asked,

"How many kinds of things and properties are there?" and counted up to two. Monists, confronting the same question, only got as far as one. But the real mistake was to start counting at all. Monism and materialism are defined in terms of dualism and mentalism, and because the definitions of dualism and mentalism are incoherent, monism and materialism inherit that incoherence. It is customary to think of dualism as coming in two flavors, substance dualism and property dualism; but to these I want to add a third, which I will call "conceptual dualism." This view consists in taking the dualistic concepts very seriously, that is, it consists in the view that in some important sense "physical" implies "nonmental" and "mental" implies "nonphysical." Both traditional dualism and materialism presuppose conceptual dualism, so defined. I introduce this definition to make it clear why it seems to me best to think of materialism as really a form of dualism. It is that form of dualism that begins by accepting the Cartesian categories. I believe that if you take those categories seriously – the categories of mental and physical, mind and body – as a consistent dualist, you will eventually be forced to materialism. Materialism is thus in a sense the finest flower of dualism; a discussion of its difficulties and recent history is undertaken elsewhere.

Notes

1 Or at least they are investigating the preliminaries of such questions. It is surprising how little of contemporary neuroscience is devoted to investigating, e.g., the neurophysiology of consciousness.
2 The best-known proponent of this view is Thomas Nagel (1986), but see also Colin McGinn (1991).
3 I will confine my discussion to analytic philosophers, but apparently the same sort of implausibility affects so-called Continental philosophy. According to Dreyfus (1991), Heidegger and his followers also doubt the importance of consciousness and intentionality.
4 The best-known exponent of this view is Daniel Dennett (1987).
5 But for an explicit statement, see Georges Rey (1983).
6 In different ways, I believe this is done by Armstrong (1968, 1980), and Dennett (1991).
7 Another form of incredibility, but from a different philosophical motivation, is the claim that each of us has at birth all of the concepts expressible in any words of any possible human language, so that, for example, Cro-Magnon people had the concepts expressed by the word "carburetor" or by the expression "cathode ray oscillograph." This view is held most famously by Fodor (1975).
8 Howard Gardner, in his comprehensive summary of cognitive science (1985), does not include a single chapter – indeed not a single index entry – on consciousness. Clearly the mind's new science can do without consciousness.

9 On my view, an inner process such as feeling a pain, for example, does not "stand in need" of anything. Why should it?

10 Oddly enough, my views have been confidently characterized by some commentators as "materialist," by some others, with equal confidence, as "dualist." Thus, for example, U. T. Place writes, Searle "presents the materialist position" (1988, p. 208), while Stephen Stich writes, "Searle is a property dualist" (1987, p. 133).

11 A closely related point is made by Noam Chomsky (1975).

References

Armstrong, D. M. (1968) *A Materialist Theory of the Mind*, London: Routledge & Kegan Paul.

Armstrong, D. M. (1980) *The Nature of Mind and Other Essays*, Brisbane: University of Queensland Press.

Chomsky, N. (1975) *Reflections on Language*, New York: Pantheon Press.

Churchland, P. M. (1981) "Eliminative materialism and the propositional attitudes," *Journal of Philosophy* 78, pp. 67–90.

Churchland, P. S. (1987) Reply to McGinn, Letters to the Editor, *Times Literary Supplement*, March 13.

Dennett, D. C. (1987) *The Intentional Stance*, Cambridge, Mass.: Bradford Books/MIT Press.

Dennett, D. C. (1991) *Consciousness Explained*, Boston, Mass.: Little, Brown.

Dreyfus, H. (1991) *Being-in-the-World: a Commentary on Heidegger's Being and Time, Division I*, Cambridge, Mass.: MIT Press.

Feyerabend, P. K. (1963) "Mental events and the brain," *Journal of Philosophy* 60, pp. 295–6.

Fodor, J. A. (1975) *The Language of Thought*, New York: Crowell.

Gardner, H. (1985) *The Mind's New Science: a History of the Cognitive Revolution*, New York: Basic Books.

McGinn, C. (1991) *The Problem of Consciousness: Essays Towards Resolution*, Oxford: Blackwell.

Nagel, T. (1986) *The View from Nowhere*, New York: Oxford University Press.

Place, U. T. (1988) "Thirty years on: is consciousness still a brain process?" *Australasian Journal of Philosophy* 66, pp. 208–19.

Quine, W. V. O. (1960) *Word and Object*, Cambridge, Mass.: MIT Press.

Rey, G. (1983) "A reason for doubting the existence of consciousness," in R. J. Davidson, G. E. Schwartz, and D. Shapiro (eds) *Consciousness and Self-Regulation*, vol. 3, New York: Plenum, pp. 1–39.

Rorty, R. (1965) "Mind-body identity, privacy and categories," *Review of Metaphysics* 29(1), pp. 24–54.

Searle, J. R. (1980) "Minds, brains, and programs," *Behavioral and Brain Sciences* 3, pp. 417–24.

Searle, J. R. (1987) "Indeterminancy, empiricism, and the first person," *Journal of Philosophy* 83(3), pp. 123–54.

Stich, S. (1983) *From Folk Psychology to Cognitive Science: the Case against Belief*, Cambridge, Mass.: Bradford Books/MIT Press.
Stich, S. (1987) Review of J. R. Searle, *Minds, Brains and Science, Philosophical Review* 96, pp. 129–33.

22
The Token-identity Thesis

John Foster

I

What is the relationship between mind and body? In this paper, I want to examine a position which is currently very popular, though in my view mistaken.[1] The position is known as the "token–identity thesis," and it claims that each mental event is (i.e. is identical with) a physical event. Almost invariably, the thesis is held in a more specific form, which takes the relevant physical events to be neural events in the subject's brain.

In formulating the thesis as the claim that each mental *event* is (is identical with) a physical (neural) *event*, I am using the term "event" in a slightly broader than usual sense. We normally only speak of something as an event if it involves some change in the condition of the world at the time, or over the period, of its occurrence. But as I am here using the term, we can speak of the event of something's being in a certain state at a certain time, without any implication that this event marks any alteration in the object's condition relative to the preceding period. Thus we can speak of the event of someone's holding a certain belief at a certain time (without the implication that he has just acquired it) and we can speak of the event of someone's being in a certain neural state at a certain time (without the implication that he has just come into it). Although a departure from ordinary usage, this broad use of the term has become the standard philosophical practice in this area, and it is for this reason that I adopt it in the present discussion.

In adopting this broad use, we must be careful not to confuse the *event* of something's being in a certain state with the corresponding *state of affairs*. States of affairs are individuated more finely than events. Thus if the properties of being *F* and being *G* are distinct, then, for any object *x* and time *t*, the states of affairs of *x*'s being *F* at *t* and *x*'s being *G* at *t* must also be distinct; but the corresponding events may be the same. For example, if someone is holding an object which is both round and brown, the state of affairs of his holding something brown is different from that of his holding something round. But there is only one concrete event.

II

The token-identity thesis, as I have said, is currently very popular. The main reason for this is that it seems to permit a more plausible account of the causal relations between mind and body than any which is available if the thesis is rejected. There are two related aspects to this. First, if we suppose that mind and body are ontologically separate, so that mental items do not occur within the framework of the physical world, there is the problem of how we can make sense of the claim, which it would be difficult to deny, that there is causal traffic between them. How can we think of the mind and the body as coming into causal contact unless the events which take place in them are located in the same spatiotemporal system? Second, the impressive progress of physical science makes it natural to assume that any physical event, to the extent that it can be causally explained at all, can be causally explained in purely physical terms: in terms of prior physical events and conditions and physical laws. And it seems that once this assumption has been made we would be obliged to identify mental events with physical events in order to allow them the causal efficacy which we believe them to possess. Clearly, these are points which anyone trying to discredit the identity thesis needs to take into account, though since there is not the space to do this here, I shall just refer the reader to the relevant discussion in my *The Immaterial Self* (1991, ch. 6).

Whatever arguments the identity theorist can develop in support of his position, they will not be effective if the position itself is incoherent. And it is here that we encounter the most fundamental issue. Can we really make sense of the psychophysical identities which the theorist is postulating? Can we understand what it would be for the event of someone's being in pain to be the very same as the event of his neurons firing in a certain way, or for the event of someone's believing that cats are carnivorous to be the very same as the event of his brain containing a certain neuronal network? The prima-facie problem is obvious. Mental and neural events seem to be events of quite different kinds – events with quite different intrinsic natures, needing to be specified in quite different terms. Are we not obliged to say that the events are different simply because their natures are different, in the way that cabbages are different from kings and lumps of chalk are different from lumps of cheese?

Of course, there is no difficulty as such in the notion of the same concrete event being an instance of different event-types. The event of someone's holding something brown may be the same as the event of his holding something round; the event of someone's pressing a switch may be the same as the event of his turning on the light; the event of someone's moving a piece of wood from one square on a board to another may be the same as the event of his checkmating his opponent. All these cases are unproblematic, because we can see exactly how each of the event-types leaves room for, and combines with, the other. Thus we know that an event of holding something brown will qualify as an event of holding something round if the object held has both attributes; we know that an event of pressing a switch will qualify as an event of turning on the light if it has the appropriate electrical and photic effects; we know that, in the context of chess, the movement of a piece will qualify as an event of checkmate if it conforms to certain rules and creates a position of a certain kind. The problem in the case of the alleged psychophysical identities is that there seems to be no analogous way of understanding how the event-types fit together, of comprehending how the psychological and physical descriptions home in on the same target. Suppose, for example, we are considering the alleged identity of a pain-event P, occurring in Smith's mind at t, with a neural event N (e.g. some firing of the C-fibers), occurring in Smith's brain at t. Our conception of P in terms of its psychological (introspectively manifest) character seems to offer no clue as to how it could also have a neural character, and our conception of N in terms of its physical (scientifically discoverable) character seems to offer no clue as to how it could also have an experiential character. Nor, on the face of it, does there seem to be any way of combining these different conceptions in the framework of some richer perspective in which the coincidence of their objects is made clear. Thus once we have envisaged something as a pain, we seem to have no way, other then by merely stipulating that it is a neural item, of making it clear to ourselves how this same thing could be available for inspection by a physiologist. And once we have envisaged something as an event of C-fiber firing, we seem to have no way, other than by merely stipulating that it is a mental item, of making it clear to ourselves how this same thing could be accessible to introspection. In short, it seems that we can form no conception of what it would be for the relevant psychological and physical event-types to be coinstantiated other than a purely formal one – the formal grasp of what it means to say that there is something which is an instance of both.

The difficulties for the identity theorist become even more manifest when we consider the modal properties of mental and neural events. Let us continue to focus on the example of *P* and *N*. We have a strong initial intuition that, whatever its relations with the physical world, *P* is *essentially* a pain-event, that it would be logically impossible for *P* to occur without possessing its pain-experiential character. At the same time, we have the equally strong intuition that, whatever its relations with *P*, *N* is *not* essentially a pain-event. For we can surely envisage a counterfactual situation in which exactly the same neural event occurs in Smith's brain at *t* (its identity as *N* being fixed by its physical properties, its brain location, and its causal origins), but in which, with a suitable change in psychophysical law, Smith does not have a pain-experience at *t*. But if we retain both these intuitions, we are forced to conclude that *P* and *N* are numerically distinct. For, between them, the two intuitions entail that there is a property (that of being essentially a pain-event) which is true of *P* but not of *N*. Moreover, it seems that the same considerations will preclude psychophysical identity in each case. For, given any mental event *x* and neural event *y*, we have the same two initial intuitions that *x*'s psychological character is essential to *x* but not to *y*.

This, in effect, is Saul Kripke's argument against token identity (see Kripke, 1980, pp. 146–7). The argument is not, as it stands, conclusive, since the identity theorist might still be able to find some way of discrediting one of the modal intuitions on which it is based. Thus, in the case of *P* and *N*, he might be able to show that, despite initial appearances, the pain-event does not possess its pain-experiential character essentially. Or alternatively, he might be able to show that, despite initial appearances, we cannot envisage a counterfactual situation in which the neural event occurs without Smith's being in pain. In the present context, the point of introducing the argument is to bring out the full measure of the prima-facie problem which the identity theorist faces. If the theorist is to retain his position, he must show us how to make sense of the postulated identities; and this means, in particular, showing us how we can discard one of the two modal intuitions which jointly entail that the relevant events are distinct.

III

There are just three ways in which the identity theorist could try to meet this challenge. In this section, I shall consider the two most familiar.

One way in which the theorist might try to make sense of his position would be by endorsing some kind of conceptual (analytical) reduction of the mental to the nonmental. That is, he might claim that the mental predicates we assign to mental events can be defined, or analyzed, in purely nonmentalistic terms, in such a way as to make it clear how mental events can be neural. There are various possibilities here, but undoubtedly the most plausible reductionist strategy, or at any rate the least implausible, would be to endorse some form of functionalism. Thus, in the case of *P* and *N*, the identity theorist might explain his position like this: "The intrinsic character of *N* – what *N* is like in itself – is to be specified in purely physical terms. But *N* also qualifies as a mental event (as an event of Smith's being in pain) in virtue of the characteristic functional role which events of this intrinsic physical type play in Smith's causal system; for example, the fact that such events tend to be brought about by certain forms of bodily stimulation or injury, the fact that such events tend to produce certain kinds of semi-automatic response, like shrieking and wincing, and the fact that such events tend to serve as a negative reinforcement of response-types that induce them. There is thus no problem in understanding how *P* and *N* can be identical. The psychological specification of *P* is to be construed as a specification of its functional character (more precisely, the functional role of things of its intrinsic type) and thus leaves room for a physicalistic account of its intrinsic nature. The physical specification of *N* is a specification of its intrinsic nature and thus leaves room for an additional psychological specification in functionalist terms. Nor will there be any problem over Kripke's modal intuitions. It may not be entirely clear what functional properties, if any, are essential to *N*. But once this has been settled, one or other of the two modal intuitions will be discredited. Most likely we will decide that it is logically possible for *N* to occur without having that functional character required for its qualification as a pain-event, and, on this basis, conclude that *P* itself (= *N*) only possesses its pain-experiential character contingently.'

There is no denying that if psychological predicates could be defined in functional terms, then the token-identity thesis would be unproblematic – and indeed irresistible. However, it seems to me that the functionalist account is vulnerable to a number of objections. One objection is that, however the account is developed, we can envisage situations in which something – for example, a man-made machine – satisfies all the functional requirements for possessing a mind without actually possessing one. Another objection (the converse of the first) is that we can envisage situations in which something – for instance, someone who lacks a motor-output system altogether – possesses a mind but fails to satisfy the functional requirements for possessing one. But I think the most decisive objection is made by the so-called "knowledge-argument" (see Foster, 1991, ch. 3, sect. 4). Thus consider the case of someone who is congenitally blind and so not equipped to acquire a knowledge of the psychological character of visual experience from his own case. Such a person could, in principle, acquire a complete knowledge of the functional role of visual experience in the causal system of the sighted; and if functionalism were true, this knowledge should suffice for a full knowledge of the psychological character of such experience. But it is clear that it would not. It is clear that, even with this functional information, the blind person would remain ignorant of the nature of visual experience *qua experience*: he would not be able to discover the character of such experience as introspection reveals it; he would not be able to tell what it is like, subjectively, for the sighted to see. This objection not only refutes the functionalist account, but also refutes *any* conceptual reduction of the mental to the nonmental. For it is clear that no information about visual experience formulated in nonmentalistic terms would suffice to convey to the blind subject the experiential knowledge which he lacks.

A second way in which the token–identity theorist might try to make sense of his position would be by embracing the thesis of *type* identity. The *token*-identity thesis merely claims that each mental event is identical with some neural event. The *type* identity thesis endorses this claim, but claims, in addition, that each psychological type of mental event is identical with some physical type of neural event, so that the psychological character of any mental event is, or is an aspect of, its intrinsic physical character. If acceptable, this further claim would immediately eliminate any problem over token identity. There would be no more difficulty in understanding how a mental event could be identical with a neural event than in understanding how a neural event could have the appropriate physical character. Nor would there be any difficulty in discarding one of Kripke's modal intuitions. Presumably, each relevant neural event would possess essentially those physical properties which give it its psychological character, so that we cannot, after all, envisage a possible world in which N occurs without the occurrence of a pain.

But the problem now for the identity theorist is how to make sense of the further claim. Obviously, he does not want to say that the psychological specification of a mental event is itself neurophysiological, since that would be plainly false. Thus a psychological description of Smith's pain-experience at t would not allow us to deduce anything about what is going on in his brain, specified in purely physical terms; nor would a neurophysiological description of the state of his brain tell us anything about the character of his experience, specified in psychological terms. Presumably, then, the identity theorist will see the identity of a given psychological type with a given physical type as something which is to be established *empirically*, like the identity of water with H_2O and the identity of heat with kinetic energy. What allows us to equate water with H_2O is that our ordinary, pre-scientific concept of water identifies it by such things as its sensible appearance, its observable forms and sources, and its observable powers and propensities, factors which do not purport to reveal its real essence. The concept picks out water as that kind of stuff, whatever it is, which satisfies certain observational requirements, leaving room for science to determine what the real nature of the stuff which satisfies these requirements is. In an analogous way, the identity theorist will say that our ordinary concept of a given psychological type identifies it in a way which does not reveal its real essence, and so leaves room for the neurophysiologist to specify this essence in physical terms. In its development, this position tends to have a close affinity with functionalism; for the theorist will usually suppose that it is by (or predominantly by) reference to their functional properties that our ordinary concepts identify the relevant types.[2]

This approach to the problem is ingenious, but for a number of reasons it fails. To begin with, it is very implausible to suppose that each psychological type, as identified by our ordinary criteria, will turn out to be invariably associated with the same neurophysiological type across all subjects and times, and that each relevant neurophysiological type will be likewise invariably associated with the same psychological type. Moreover, even if by chance they obtain, such associations would surely be only contingent: they would not have the necessity (i.e. the preservation-through-all-possible-worlds character) required for strict identity.[3] But perhaps the most crucial point is that, like the functionalist account, the type identity thesis fails to do justice to the character of conscious experience as introspection reveals it. Take again the case of pain (though any other type of experience would serve equally well). The type identity theorist thinks that pain could turn out to be a purely physical state, because he thinks that our ordinary, pre-scientific concept of pain is, as one might put it, *topic-neutral*: a concept which fails to reveal the real essence of pain and so leaves it available for neurophysiological specification. But this topic-neutrality claim is plainly false. Part, and indeed the central core, of our ordinary concept is drawn from our direct acquaintance with pain through introspection; and what introspective awareness reveals is the nature of pain as such. What, after all, are the alternatives? We cannot say that introspection merely reveals the functional role of pain, since, in analogy with the case of the congenitally blind subject, someone who had no experience of pain could not derive a knowledge of its introspectible character from its functional specification. Nor can we press a distinction between the introspective appearance of pain and its real nature, in the way that we can distinguish the sensible appearance of a physical item from its real nature. For to speak of the introspective appearance of pain is just to speak of how it subjectively feels to the subject who is in pain, and the character of this feeling is none other than the essence of pain-experience itself. In any case, even if our concept of pain allowed us to draw this distinction, the introspective appearance of pain would itself remain a mental phenomenon whose real nature could only be specified in psychological terms.

IV

There is still one final way in which the token identity theorist might try to make sense of his position. The failure of conceptual reductionism and type identity commits him to conceding that the psychological character of a mental event is something *sui generis*, something which cannot be specified or conceived of in any but mentalistic terms. But in making this concession, the theorist is not committed to regarding the psychological as metaphysically fundamental. For he could still insist that each mental event derives its psychological character from certain other facts about it, facts which only concern its status as a physical event. In other words, he could say that, while the psychological character of a mental event cannot be redescribed nonmentalistically (either by conceptual reduction or type identity), its possession of this character is wholly constituted by, and nothing over and above, its possession of certain other properties which *can* be specified nonmentalistically and which belong to it as something physical. We may call this position *metaphysical* mental reductionism, to distinguish it from the conceptual form of reductionism we have already considered. The point of the label "metaphysical" is that this new form of reductionism involves recognizing different metaphysical levels of reality. It involves saying that there is a metaphysically fundamental reality which is wholly nonmental, and that there is a metaphysically derivative reality of mental facts, which have their own *sui generis* character, but are wholly sustained by (derive their obtaining from) the nonmental facts in the fundamental reality. In practice, metaphysical mental reductionists take the fundamental reality to be purely physical.

The crucial question now is: how, without falling back on some sort of conceptual reduction or type identity, could the theorist defend his claim that mental events derive their psychological character from these more fundamental facts? Well, I think his best chance is to appeal to an analogy.

Consider the following three claims:

1 Physical objects have color, and color which is visible to us in appropriate conditions.
2 Science has shown that color-appearance is to be ultimately explained in terms which do not involve any explicit ascription of color to the objects in question, in terms of such facts as the arrangement of surface atoms, the effects of this arrangement on the reflection and absorption of light, the effects of photic input on the human nervous system, and the effects of neural processes on human experience.
3 Physical color is something *sui generis*: statements ascribing colors to physical objects cannot be conceptually reduced to statements of a

radically different (not color-ascriptive) kind (e.g. to statements which say how the objects are disposed to look); nor can an object's color (being something sensible) be identified with some aspect of its scientifically specifiable nature, such as that microstructural property on which its disposition to color-appearance is grounded.

Considered on its own, each of these claims is likely to strike us as very plausible, if not clearly correct. Yet the three together appear to be in conflict. For granted that physical color is *sui generis*, the scientific explanation of color-appearance seems to show that physical objects either have no color at all or have colors which, being irrelevant to color-appearance, are entirely invisible to us. However, there *is* a way of reconciling the claims, namely by adopting a form of metaphysical reductionism. Thus we could draw a distinction between the metaphysically fundamental reality, which is as science describes it, and a metaphysically derivative reality, in which physical objects are visibly colored. We could say that physical objects possess visible color, and in a way which cannot be re-expressed (whether by conceptual reduction or scientific specification) in non-color-possessive terms, but that their possession of color is wholly constituted by, and nothing over and above, the scientifically discovered facts which account for their color-appearance. Of course, because this postulated reduction is metaphysical, rather than conceptual, there would be no question of a *deductive* step of inference from the statements recording the fundamental facts to those recording the color-facts which they sustain. For this reason, the sustainment would have to be, from an epistemic standpoint, "retrospective": one which we were only equipped to recognize by having independent knowledge of the two sets of facts it relates. We would have to begin by accepting (on the basis of our ordinary visual experience) that objects are visibly colored, and then go on to establish the derivative status of their possession of color by establishing the scientific explanation of their color-appearance.

This approach to the case of physical color is attractive, because it is the only way of reconciling the three claims which we are inclined to accept. I think the metaphysical *mental* reductionist would do best to try to defend his position in a broadly similar way. Thus he should represent his position as the only way of reconciling three claims which appear to be in conflict but which are all correct. The first is the claim that there are mental states and activities, and ones whose psychological character is known to the subject through introspection. This he would take to be obvious. The second is the claim that the fundamental facts are exclusively physical. This he would accept either on the basis of some scientifically motivated argument, or because he finds philosophical difficulties in any alternative, or both. The third is the claim that the psychological character of the mental is something *sui generis*: something which cannot be redescribed in nonpsychological terms. This he would accept in deference to the philosophical objections to conceptual reductionism and type identity. The reductionist should insist that each of these claims is true; and he should then point out that, taken together, they oblige us to accept that mental facts are sustained and wholly constituted by physical facts in the way he envisages. As in the case of color, the postulated sustainment would have to be merely retrospective. The reductionist would have to concede that a knowledge of the physical facts on its own would not suffice to establish the obtaining of the mental facts they sustain; he could only claim that, knowing the mental independently, we can establish that they are physically sustained by establishing that the physical facts alone are fundamental.

This sounds promising. But in fact the supposed analogy with the case of color breaks down at a crucial point. In the latter case, the postulated fundamental reality, though devoid of physical color, does include, in a scientifically elaborated form, all the facts which concern physical-color appearance: facts such as that objects with the appropriate microstructural properties are disposed to reflect certain wavelengths of light, that light of certain wavelengths, entering the eye, produces certain effects on the human nervous system, and that certain processes in the human nervous system give rise to certain kinds of color-experience. From these facts, it is not possible to deduce that objects are colored, but it is possible to deduce that they will appear colored in certain ways to the human observer who views them in certain conditions. This is of crucial importance to the success of the reductionist enterprise. For granted that physical color exists, is *sui generis*, and is visually accessible to us, it is precisely the fact that science fully accounts for the visual phenomena, without attributing colors to the objects themselves, which justifies us in according physical color its derivative status. Without this non-color-ascriptive explanation of color appearance, there would be simply no rationale for construing the physical color-facts as constituted by more fundamental physical and psychophysical facts rather than as an autonomous ingredient of the fundamental reality. But this aspect of the color-case is entirely missing in the case of the mind. The fundamental reality which the metaphysical mental reductionist postulates is wholly nonmental. But just because of this, a description of what obtains in that reality can provide no information about the facts of introspective appearance. We cannot deduce, from such a description, anything about how things are mentally; and *a fortiori*, just because introspection is a form of mentality, we cannot deduce anything about how things introspectively seem to subjects in respect of their mentality. But this means that we have no way of understanding how the mental facts could be nonmentalistically constituted. Since there is no deductive inference from the nonmental to the mental, it is only if we independently take the mental facts for granted that we can have any chance of representing them as constituted by the nonmental facts in question. But once we have taken them for granted, we cannot avoid according them a metaphysically fundamental status unless the specification of the nonmental facts provides the ultimate explanation of why it ordinarily seems to us that these mental facts obtain. And the specification of the nonmental facts cannot provide this explanation without losing its nonmentalistic character.

This leads on to a further objection to the metaphysical reduction of the mental. In any cases where we exclude some domain of putative facts from the metaphysically fundamantal reality there must always be the option of adopting a nihilist rather than a reductive view of the domain in question. Thus if we decide that the fundamental reality is devoid of physical color then we have at least the option of denying the existence of physical color altogether and of interpreting color-appearance as a kind of systematic illusion created by the effects of colorless physical objects on human experience. Likewise, if we decide that the fundamental reality is devoid of *physical* facts or of *moral* facts, we have the option of rejecting these facts altogether and explaining away the factors which ordinarily incline us to accept them. Now (as Descartes so clearly saw (e.g. in *Meditations* II)) what is distinctive about the mental case is that this nihilist option is not available. We cannot coherently deny the existence of mentality altogether, not just because our own mentality is directly evident to us through introspection, but because any attempt to represent our introspective beliefs as erroneous would still be an acknowledgement that we have them, and also because there is no way of advancing the nihilist claim without representing it as expressing one's own intellectual view of the matter. But granted that the nihilist option is not available – that we have no way of conceiving of the actual world as devoid of mentality – then the metaphysically reductionist option is not available either. For if we could coherently take the *fundamental* reality to be wholly nonmental there would be no absolute bar to our adopting an ontologically austere view, which refused to give recognition to any category of putative facts which that reality excluded and which were not deducible from it. In other words, the absoluteness of our commitment to the obtaining of mental facts obliges us to regard them as metaphysically fundamental.

V

It seems to me, then, that, like conceptual reductionism and the type-identity thesis, metaphysical mental reductionism fails. Since these three approaches are the only ones by which the defender of the token identity thesis could try to make sense of his position, I conclude that the thesis is untenable and that mental events are nonphysical. I also think we can use this conclusion as a basis for establishing a further dualist position, namely that mental events occur in the biographies of nonphysical mental subjects. But I shall not try to defend this further (Cartesian) position here (but see Foster, 1991, ch. 7).

Notes

1 For a more detailed discussion of the issues, see Foster (1991).
2 Even in this form, however, the position does not qualify as functionalist in the strict sense; for it represents the psychological types, not as themselves functional types, but as physical types which our ordinary concepts pick out in functional terms.
3 On the necessity of identity, see Kripke (1980, Lectures II and III).

References

Foster, J. (1991) *The Immaterial Self: a Defence of the Cartesian Dualist Conception of the Mind*, London: Routledge.
Kripke, S. A. (1980) *Naming and Necessity*, Oxford: Blackwell (first published 1972 in D. Davidson and G. Harman (eds) *Semantics of a Natural Language*, Dordrecht: Reidel, pp. 253–355, 763–9).

23
Body and Soul

Richard Swinburne

All theories of the mind–body problem in the history of thought seem to me all to be variants of four main positions. I shall describe these, and defend one of them.[1] But first, I must introduce some terminology. (For a full exposition and justification of my view of the relation of mind to body see Swinburne, 1986.)

I understand by a substance a thing, a component of the world which interacts causally with other components of the world and which has a history through time. Tables and chairs, stars and galaxies, neurones, sacs of transmitter chemical, and persons are substances. Substances have (monadic) properties, such as being square or yellow, having a mass of two pounds, or such-and-such an electric potential. They also have polyadic properties, or relations to other substances, such as being taller than, or lying between. "Taller than" is a relation which relates two substances; "lying between" is a relation which relates three substances. (One object lies between a second object and a third object.) I shall understand by an "event" the instantiation of a property (either a monadic property or a relation) in a particular substance or particular substances at particular times, such as this tie being now green, or this neurone firing at 3 p.m.; or John being taller than James last year; or Birmingham now lying between Oxford and Manchester. Events are states of substances. The history of the world is just the sequence of all the events of which have happened. If you know all the events which have happened (which properties were instantiated in which substances when), you know all that has happened.

Properties and events may be physical or mental. I understand by a "physical property" one such that no one subject is necessarily better placed to know that it is instantiated than is any other subject. Physical properties are public; there is no privileged access to them. Thus having a mass of ten pounds, being eight feet tall, and being square are all physical properties. So too are the typical properties of neurones in the brain: being in such-and-such an electrical state or releasing a transmitter chemical. Anyone who chooses can find out as surely as can anyone else whether something is eight feet tall, or in a certain electrical state. Physical events are those which involve the instantiation of physical properties. "Mental properties," as I shall understand the term, are ones to which one subject has privileged access, which he is necessarily in a better position to know about anyone else. It looks as if such properties as being in pain or having a red afterimage, are mental, for any person in whom they are instantiated does seem necessarily to be better placed to know about them that does anyone else. It looks too as having a belief or a desire or a thought or a purpose are also mental properties. 'Mental events' are events which involve the instantiation of mental properties (e.g. John being in pain at midday yesterday).

The first position on the mind–body problem, which I shall call hard materialism, claims that the only substances are material objects, and persons (including human beings) are such substances. A person is the same thing as what is loosely called his body (and his brain is the same thing as his mind). The only events which occur, the only things that happen in the world, are physical events, namely ones which consist in the instantiation of physical properties in material objects. There are no mental events in the sense in which I have analyzed this notion, for there are no events distinct from physical events to which the subject has privileged access. My being in pain or having an afterimage may seem to be mental events, but really they are not – according to the hard materialist; really they are just brain events or patterns of public behavior.

Now hard materialism seems to me obviously wrong. There really are events which humans experience and which in consequence they can know about better than does anyone else who studies their behavior or inspects their brain. My sensations, for example – my having a red afterimage or a smell of roast beef, or my feeling a pain – are such that, while I can learn about them in the same ways as others do (by inspecting my brain-state or studying a film of my behavior), I have an additional way of knowing about them other than those available to the best student of my behavior or brain: I actually experience them. Consequently they must be distinct from brain events, or any other physical events.

The second position, which I shall call soft materialism (it is sometimes called 'property dualism'), agrees with hard materialism that the only substances are material objects, but it claims that some of these have mental properties which are distinct from physical properties. Persons are material objects; again, a person is the same thing as his body, and his brain is the same thing as his mind. But persons (and their brains) have, as well as physical properties, also mental properties, such as feeling tired and having a visual sensation of such and such a color and shape, whereas most substances such as tables and chairs, galaxies and electrons, have only physical properties. Mental events – e.g. my having a pain now – are different from brain-events; they are not physical events; but they are caused by and often themselves cause brain events.

The basic difficulty however with soft materialism, as with hard materialism, is that there seem to be more truths about the world than the doctrine says that there can be. Soft materialism says that you have told the whole story of the world when you have said which material objects exist and which properties (mental and physical) they have. However, full information of this kind would still leave you ignorant of whether some person continued to live a conscious life or not. Knowledge of what happens to bodies and their parts will not show you for certain what happens to persons. Let me illustrate this with the example of brain transplants. The brain consists of two hemispheres, and a brain stem. There is good evidence that humans can survive and behave as conscious beings if much of one hemisphere is destroyed. Now suppose my brain (hemisphere plus brain stem) were divided into two, and each half brain taken out of my skull and transplanted into the empty skull of a body from which a brain has just been removed; suppose further there to be added to each half-brain from some other brain (e.g. the brain of my identical twin) whatever other parts (e.g. more brain stem) are necessary in order for the transplant to take and for there to be two living persons with lives of conscious experiences. If this operation were done and we then had two living persons, both with lives of conscious experiences, which would be me? Probably both would to some extent behave like me and make my memory claims; for behavior and speech depends, at any rate in very large part, on brain-states, and there is very considerable overlap between the "information" carried by the two hemispheres which gives rise to behavior and speech. But both persons would not be me. For if they were both identical with me they would be the same person as each other (if *a* is the same as *b*, and *b* is the same as *c*, then *a* is the same as *c*) and they are not. They now have different experiences and lead different lives. There remain three other possibilities: that the person with my right half-brain is me, or that the person with my left half-brain is me, or that neither is me. Maybe neither future person is me; it may be that cutting the brain stem creates a new person, so that the whole process creates two new conscious persons, neither of whom is me. Perhaps I am the left half-brain person, or maybe it is the right-brain person who is me. Even if one subsequent person resembles the earlier me more in character and memory claims than does the other, that one may not be me. Maybe I've survived the operation but am changed in character and have lost much of my memory as a result of it, in consequence of which the other subsequent person resembles the earlier me more in his public behavior than I do. And even if the fourth answer, that they are both to some extent me were (despite its apparent incoherence) correct, neither science nor philosophy can show that to us, for certain, for all the evidence which could ever be obtained would be compatible with the other possibilities as well.

Reflection on this thought experiment shows that however much we know about what has happened to my brain (and other parts of my body), we don't necessarily know what has happened to me. It is clearly a crucial factual matter whether I have survived an operation. (Only someone under the strong grip of a philosophical dogma could deny that.) It follows that there must be more to me than my brain, a further essential immaterial part whose continuing in existence makes the brain (and so body) to which it is linked my brain (and body), and to this something I give the traditional name of "soul." I am my soul plus whatever brain (and body) it is connected to. Normally my soul goes when my brain goes, but in unusual circumstances (such as when my brain is split) it is uncertain where it goes.

Nor is it necessary for my survival that any part of my brain survive; it suffices that the immaterial part survive. The stronger argument is to be found in embryo in Descartes. This argument claims that it is logically possible that I who am now conscious might continue to exist if all my body were suddenly destroyed. By the "logical possibility" of my continuing to exist without my body I mean that there is no internal contradiction in this supposition (e.g. it is not like "he is both over six feet and under five feet tall at the same time"). And surely it must be that the religious believer who claims that he will live after the destruction of his body does not contradict himself; we can understand the claims that he is making because it is a coherent one. It then argues that if anything is to continue to exist over time, some part of it must continue to exist – and that is surely true of anything. My desk cannot continue to exist if every part of it is destroyed – and so on. So, the argument concludes, if it is to be logically possible that I survive when all my body is destroyed, there must now already exist another part of me (an immaterial part) whose survival guarantees my survival – and that is what I am calling the soul. As this argument has often wrongly been accused of various fallacies, I set it out in rigorous logical form in an appendix.

So the rejection of soft materialism has led to substance dualism, the view that there are two separate parts to a human being: body and soul, two connected substances. The connection consists in bodily events (instantiations of physical properties in a material object) causing mental events (instantiations of mental properties in the essential part of the person), and mental events causing bodily events. But substance dualism divides into two different positions. The stronger position, which I call hard dualism, holds that the soul has a necessary immortality. If you separate it from the body, it will, on this view, continue to exist "under its own steam"; it is indestructible. I see no reason for holding that position; it seems to me that the arguments of Plato and many later philosophers in favor of this view are simply fallacious. Rather I advocate the wider position, which I call soft dualism. This holds that during normal earthly life the soul is dependent for its functioning (i.e. having a mental life) on the functioning of the body; at death, when the body ceases to function, the soul does too. But it is a separate thing which a God if he chooses can make to function again (with or without a new body).

Appendix

Formal Version of Descartes's Argument
I use the usual logical symbols: "&" as "and," " – " as "not," ◊ as "it is logically possible." My definitions are:

$p =$ "I am a conscious person and I exist in 1990."
$q =$ "My body is destroyed in the last instant of 1990."
$r =$ "I have a soul in 1990."
$s =$ "I exist in 1991."
x   ranges over all consistent propositions compatible with (p & q) and describing 1990 states of affairs.
"(x)"   is to be read in the normal way as "for all propositions x."

The argument may now be set out as follows:

Premise 1:   p
Premise 2:   (x) ◊ (p & q & x & s)
premise 3:   – ◊ (p & q & –r & s)

Premise 2 says that it is possible that I survive into 1991, given that I am conscious in 1990, even if my body is totally destroyed and whatever else might be the case in 1990, compatible with these last two suppositions. I understand by my body all the physical part of me, and by my soul any nonphysical part of me. Then premise 3 is simply a consequence of the general metaphysical truth that a substance cannot continue to exist if no part of it continues to exist.

It follows form premise 2 and premise 3 that –r is not within the range of x. But since –r describes a 1990 state of affairs, it follows that it is not compatible with (p & q).

Hence (p & q) entails r. But the addition to p of q, which describes what happens to my body at the end of 1990 can hardly affect whether or not p entails r. So I conclude that p by itself entails r. Hence, from Premise 1, r.

Reference

Swinburne, R. (1986) *The Evolution of the Soul*, Oxford: Clarendon Press.

24
The Ineffable Soul

Zeno Vendler

(1) I have often been accused, as if it were a sin, of being a dualist. I plead not guilty. Does it mean, then, that I am a materialist? God forbid! It would be a worse transgression.

Dualism, and I mean the Cartesian version, has at least an intuitive appeal. Not for nothing has it become, as Ryle pointed out, the "official doctrine." It agrees with the overwhelming conviction of mankind (supported by nearly all religions) that human beings consist of body and soul. I recently reflected with some amusement on the motto engraved in the coat of arms of the University of Oregon, in a place, that is, where inspiring pearls of wisdom are usually displayed. *Mens agitat molem* it says, nicely capturing the enduring dualist idea of the willing spirit dragging along the lazy flesh.

But, alas, conviction is not a proof. Common sense has been found wrong, and corrected by science, in many other matters; just think of the geocentric view of the cosmos, and our naive notions about Euclidean space and temporal simultaneity. Is it not possible, then, that science should provide a similar correction to our received opinions about body and soul?

The perhaps dominant view among philosophers in these days is that such a correction is underway. There is nothing in human experience that neuroscience cannot account for, and there is nothing the human intellect can do which a suitably powerful computer cannot. Thus there is no need for a soul, a principle distinct from the body; all human functions can be explained within the system of the exact sciences, ultimately reducible to physics and mathematics. This is the materialist position. The name is somewhat misleading: what is at issue is not what "stuff" we are made of, but whether there is anything in us that exceeds the explanatory power of "unified" science. Therefore "physicalism" or "scientism" would be better names, but I shall stick with with the older and more familiar one.

There are some less ambitious versions of the materialist position: functionalists and anomalous monists do not insist on reducing the mental to the physical. Nevertheless, more as a profession of faith rather than a result of cogent argument, most of them still maintain the primacy of the physical: it alone, they say, is fully explainable by science, thus it *must* underlie the mental superstructure understood in "loose" concepts (of "folk-psychology") which are not fit to be integrated into the scientific system. Hence the requirement: no change in the mental without a change in the physical, even if we cannot conceive the how . . .

In whatever form it is presented, I cannot accept the materialist view. And, curiously enough, my objections are not based on the so-called "higher" mental abilities we possess, but on the "lower" ones. Not on the powers of understanding, reasoning, or choice, but on the modest functions of sensation, feeling, and emotion. To put it in a nutshell: the chess-playing computer Deep Thought, or an improved successor, may one day beat Kasparov, but it will not enjoy doing so (Feng-hsiung Hsu, 1990).

It appears, then, that I am what some so charitably call a "qualia freak;" I believe that the elements of human consciousness, the buzzing-blooming confusion of our Humean selves are in principle beyond what science can explain. And here this is not just a matter of two incommensurate conceptual networks grappling with the same reality. In this case we have the emergence of an altogether new domain: content of experience, essentially subjective, thus inaccessible to any public, interpersonal, conceptual system. So even if functionalism and anomalous monism were successful in dealing with the higher functions of the mind, it would have no bearing on this other domain. Thoughts, beliefs, intentions, and the like do not "feel" like anything, and what I am after are precisely things felt or experienced. Indeed, as it is increasingly realized, these approaches spectacularly fail in dealing with qualia, forcing their proponents to ignore them altogether or, in a typical sour-grapes move, declare them insignificant.

Am I not then, after all, driven back into dualism? Did I not just imply a real distinction, if not between body and mind, then at least between the body according to science and the soul according to Hume? Obstinately, once more I reject the charge, being aware of course of the burden of defense and explanation I thereby assume. In trying to provide them I shall heavily rely on some conceptual tools offered by Wittgenstein on the one hand, and some medieval doctors, particularly St Thomas Aquinas, on the other. I shall use these notions as I have understood them, and found them helpful, without making any pretence of being a faithful interpreter of these authors.

(2) I shall begin with the distinction I attempted to draw above between the "higher" and the "lower" functions of the mind. A lovely text by Wittgenstein (and a peculiarity of the German language), allows me to be more precise. He says in § 154 of the *Philosophical Investigations*:

In the sense in which there are processes (including mental processes) which are characteristic of understanding, understanding is not a mental process. (A pain&s growing more or less; the hearing of a tune or sentence: these are mental processes). (Wittgenstein, 1953).

This is a puzzling text – but only in English. In German it makes perfect sense. The key word is *seelisch*, which is translated here as "mental." The translation is misleading, yet it is not the translator's fault. We do not have in English the exact equivalent of the German word *seelisch*. We have one for *Seele*: soul. But no adjectival form exists. On the other hand, the English words "mind" and "mental" do not have exact German equivalents: neither *Seele* and *seelisch*, nor *Geist* and *geistlich* quite do.

Now what exactly does *seelische Vorgänge* mean? Wittgenstein's examples are quite illuminating: the growing pain and the hearing of a melody. That is to say, things we experience (and often enjoy or have to endure). But we do not *experience* understanding, therefore it is not a *seelisch* process. Nor would be reasoning, deliberation, and the like. Yet in English there is nothing wrong with calling them all *mental* processes or, as in the case of understanding, mental achievements.

Now we understand, incidentally, the reason for Wittgenstein's warning prior to the text quoted: "Try not to think of understanding as a "mental process" [*seelischer Vorgang*] at all. For *that* is the expression which confuses you. Of course it does: it suggests that understanding is something you experience, like a stab of pain or a flash of light. Now I can formulate my claim more precisely: the mental, at least in the sense of the *seelisch*, is beyond the grasp of science, and indeed beyond the reach of any interpersonal conceptual system.

But I am not through yet with Wittgenstein's text. He admits that there are processes, including *seelisch* processes, characteristic of understanding, even if understanding itself is not such a process. Indeed it would be a grave mistake to divorce experience from thinking altogether. As it has been stressed by Aristotle and the Scholastics, we are no angels, thus "phantasms" accompany all our thoughts, place them in time, and make them our own. Thus it will not do to dismiss the flow of impressions as something insignificant even for the highest forms of thought.

Remember Kasparov and Deep Thought. Kasparov thinks as a human being does: while figuring out his next move a stream of images, words, accompanied by scraps of feelings and sensations, runs through his consciousness. None of these is his thinking, yet his thinking could not occur without them. Deep Thought's "thinking" is pure, free of such accoutrements. Deep Thought may have a mind, sort of, but unlike Kasparov, has no soul. Therefore, and here comes a move in a Thomistic–Wittgensteinian vein, it does not really think, does not really have a mind, simply because these terms acquire their meaning in the human context. Thus when we say that it thinks, or has a mind, we invoke the licence of analogy, much the same way as when we say, going in another direction, that God thinks, or has a mind. This point will gain in importance in the sequel.

(3)   I return to my main claim: the *seelisch* is beyond the grasp of science. This becomes quite obvious as we reflect upon the utter impotence of science to explain the qualitative features of our experience. Take two examples: color and pain. Concerning the former, physics has offered us a convincing account of the objective situation in terms of diverse frequencies of electromagnetic radiation. Neuroscience follows suit, and identifies the various mechanisms involved in the perception of color from the retina to the optic center in the brain. None of these processes give us any clue, however, what the colors look like. Accordingly, whereas it is easy to tell the difference between, say, red and blue light in terms of physics, there is no way to tell, in any terms, the difference between the experience (*Empfindung*) of perceiving red light and blue light. This is the reason why we resort to such desperate measures as saying, red is like the blare of a trumpet, or that blue is somehow more "serious" than pink.

And, of course, this is the reason why some philosophers worry about the possibility of inverted spectra. Wittgenstein mentions this in § 272 of the *Investigations*: "The assumption would thus be possible – though unverifiable – that one section of mankind had one sensation of red (*eine Rotempfindung*) and another section another." His point is that such a possibility would not affect the meaning of the word "red," since subjective experiences fall outside the language-game.

And, we may add, they fall outside science for exactly the same reason, as we are going to see. Incidentally, I myself do not worry about the possibility of inverted spectra, since I have a nice little transcendental argument excluding them (1984, pp. 30–1). Be that as it may, the present point is that no *scientific* demonstration can do the trick. Science may describe the neural state underlying the perception of a certain color in the greatest detail, but it cannot say anything about the relation between it and the experience itself, i.e., between the *körperlich* and the *seelisch*. Just compare these two explanations: "Red light is of lower energy than light of other colors, therefore it has much less effect on ordinary photographic plates than the others, so you can use it in darkrooms" and "Red light is of lower energy than light of other colors, therefore it looks red rather than green or blue." The second "explanation" is a joke.

The situation is exactly similar with respect to pain. Materialists claim that pain *is* the excitation of C-fibers or something like that. This simply cannot be the case. An angel, or an intelligent alien, might know as much physiology as the best scientist, or more. He might have, in other words, a comprehensive knowledge of the neural state in question. Yet, by that fact alone, he would have no idea at all what pain feels like, i.e., what pain really is. Because pain is, essentially, something felt. Worse: he would have no idea that there are such things as feelings accompanying some neural states. Wittgenstein remarks in § 283: "Only of what behaves like a human being can one say that it *has* pain." I extend the remark: "And only what *is* like a human being can one say of it that it has pain." Attribution of experience is not grounded in scientific inquiry, but in common nature and a shared way of life, which the angel, or the alien, would not have. Only what has a soul can see a soul in another. Finally, once more, the whole vocabulary of common speech, even if augmented with the terminology of neuroscience, is utterly incapable of describing what pain feels like or how, for instance, it differs from a tickle.

The impossibility of telling what red looks like, or what pain feels like, points to the fundamental reason for the failure of science to capture these sensations in its network. They are subjective experiences: they exist only for the subject that has them; their *esse* is indeed but *percipi*. Hence they are not in the publicly observable, interpersonal domain. Accordingly, as Wittgenstein pointed out, they cannot play a role in the public language-game: the beetle in the box cannot be exhibited (§ 293). Now science, like language, is an interpersonal enterprise; its domain is the publicly observable. Therefore it cannot reach something which is essentially private, as sensations and feelings are. Not even the scientist can peek into the box.

(4) Think of the following surrealistic experiment. Poor Job's skull is open, and any of his brain processes can be monitored through microscopes end electronic displays. And, by a clever arrangement of optical devices, he himself too can observe his own neural processes as much as the people around him. Now the investigator focuses on the appropriate C-fibers, and pinches him hard on the leg. The fibers begin to fire. "Ah, he is in pain," say the observers. Job, looking at the same displays, agrees: "Yes I am, and I feel it too." The point is that the second half of his remark is totally independent of what he observes, and what anyone can observe. Thus if you insist that the pain is the neural state, you have to grant at least that he has a privileged access to it, which does not show up in the neural connections, since they are observable to all.

But, obviously, this is a wrong way of describing the situation. Job has no "access" to his pain, he simply feels pain. Grammar tends to mislead us here into thinking that as, for instance, there is a difference between what one eats, the food, and the eating of it, so there is a difference between what one feels, the pain, and the feeling of it . . . No, the feeling itself is the pain. Consider the following correct analogies: having a rest, taking a nap, or giving a kick. Having a rest *is* resting, taking a nap *is* napping, and giving a kick *is* kicking. In the same way, feeling pain, or having pain, is simply hurting or being in pain. Pain, and other sensations, are not "things" in the world, or in the body, which could be located, identified and observed, or to which an "access" can be had. They are nothing in the physical world, yet something to a subject. In other words, they are "epiphenomena" which arise *for a subject* if certain neural conditions are fulfilled. Their *esse* is strictly *esse pro*, their existence is exhausted in being perceived.

Mirror images provide a good analogy (see Vendler, 1991). We see them, yet they are nothing in the physical world. The mirror image of my face appears behind the mirror, yet there is nothing there but bricks. The mirror image is there because I see it there, and not the other way around, namely, that I see it there because it is there. No wonder then that no one else can see the *same* mirror image. In a similar way, Job's pain is in his leg because he feels it there, and not the other way around, namely, that he feels it there because it is there. Like mirror images, pains, sensuous color, and other localized qualia are projected by a subject rather than "accessed."

Wittgenstein has a rather cute remark in 276. He speaks of our temptation to make a color impression (*Farbeindruck*): "It is as if we detached the color-*impression* from the object, like a membrane." Looking into a mirror the temptation is likely to gain force: there the "membrane" is already detached, it is not in its place! The temptation is to be resisted. Membranes are things in the world; color impressions, whether they are projected on their object or elsewhere, as in a mirror, are not.

(5) The private sensation of pain, like the beetle in the box, "has no place in the language-game at all" says Wittgenstein in 293, "not even as a *something*: for the box might even be empty." Thus *pain* is not a name of a thing, no matter how vaguely conceived. For, as he points out in § 261, the words " 'sensation' . . . 'has' and 'something' also belong to our common language" and are not applicable to essentially private things.

If it is not even something, then it must be nothing; so it seems that our recent discussion has been but much ado about nothing. Perhaps indeed the best policy is to say nothing about the qualia, since nothing *can* be said, thus the philosophers are right who deny or ignore them altogether. Whereof one cannot speak . . .

That of course won't do, and Wittgenstein is the first to admit it. We come to the crucial exchange in 304:

> But you will surely admit that there is a difference between pain-behavior accompanied by pain and pain-behavior without any pain.
> Admit it? What greater difference could there be?
> And yet you again and again reach the conclusion that the sensation (*Empfindung*) itself is a *nothing*.
> Not at all. It is not a *something*, but not a *nothing* either! The conclusion was only that nothing would serve just as well as something about which nothing could be said.

The passage teaches us several things. First, Wittgenstein is not a behaviorist. Pain does not consist in mere behavior. Second, he is not a reductive materialist. If he were, then pain would be *something* to him (C-fiber firing or something similar). Third, the sensation of pain can be ignored in the task of understanding how language works: there a nothing would do equally well. Thus, if you like, he is a behaviorist in linguistics without, however, taking a metaphysical stand. One can put it in this way too: he draws attention to the fact that our language falls short of dealing with sensations. And, of course, this is right. I was harping on this point throughout the previous discussion: we cannot *say* what pain feels like, what red looks like; we cannot *tell* in words the difference between the perceptions of pain and tickle, or red and blue.

Sensations cannot be named, but can be imagined; they are beyond the grasp of words, but not beyond the reach of fancy. In § 302

Wittgenstein talks of imagining someone else's pain, and finds it difficult. "What I have to do is not simply to make a transition in imagination (*in der Vorstellung*) from one place of pain to another. As from pain in the hand to pain in the arm. For I am not to imagine that I feel pain in some region of his body (which would also be possible)." Accordingly, pains are by no means nothing: I can place them in the imagination here and there, even, maybe, beyond the confines of my body. And, for sure, imagining pain in this way does not merely consist in imagining pain behavior . . . The same is true of color: I can imagine this very table looking pink.

His use of the word *Vorstellung* in this text helps us to understand a sentence in § 300: "The image of pain certainly enters into the language-game in a sense; only not as a picture." This too sounds mysterious in English till we realize that "image" is *Vorstellung*, and "picture" is *Bild* in the original. *Vorstellung*, imagination, is something private, *Bild*, picture, is in the public domain. Thus we cannot have a *Bild* of pain: e.g. we cannot draw one; but we certainly have a *Vorstellung*. And this, of course, plays a role in understanding pain-talk. We are no robots . . .

(6) Sensation is not something, we cannot use our common words to talk about it, and we have no others. Are we to resort, then, to emitting the inarticulate sound Wittgenstein mentions in § 261? Not quite. For, after all, he himself talks about pain (the *Empfindung*) through page after page, and we understand (well, sort of) what he says or tries to say. And I myself did talk, quite a lot, about pain, color, and other qualia, and I hope you have understood some of it. So the inconceivable has been done. As Goethe says at the end of *Faust*:

> Das Unbeschreibliche,
> Hier ist's getan.

But how? And please keep the *Ewig-Weibliche* out of it.

Goethe's words occur in a theological context. And this reminds us that our problem, the problem of the ineffable, is by no means new. Medieval doctors encountered a similar difficulty in trying to talk about God, the angels, separate souls, and their activities in a language not quite up to the task. And some of them, particularly Thomas Aquinas, have succeeded in showing the way it can be done.

What was their problem, the one addressed in the various treatises *De Divinis Nominibus*? It can easily be summarized. According to the Aristotelean tradition, the proper object of the human understanding is the *quidditas rerum sensibilium*, the nature of sensible things. Therefore the meaning of our words is derived from their employment in talking about the physical world. Hence, according to their proper signification, our words are unsuitable to name or describe supersensible reality.

There is a way, however, to stretch the power of our words. And this is explained in the famous doctrine of analogy. It is a complex and beautifully worked out theory, which I cannot reproduce here in detail. Just some highlights.

True, we cannot say what God is, but we can suggest what he is like, and what he is not. We first have to deny all predicates that entail restrictions and imperfections, e.g. God is not a body, does not change, is not in time, etc. Then we may attribute predicates which do not imply imperfections: thus we say that God is a substance, a person, that he is wise, good, and so forth. But then we immediately have to remove the burden of imperfection still clinging to these terms owing to their origin, i.e. their normal employment in talking about the material world. God is a substance, but not subject to accidents; a person, but has no body; God is wise, but this does not mean that he is experienced and circumspect in his conduct; he is good, but not in the sense of being unselfish or law-abiding. Finally we reassert these predicates now purified of any stain and say that God is an infinite substance, super-wise, super-good, the source and exemplar of all these perfections in the visible world.

I quote a most potent text from Aquinas's *Questiones Disputatae de Potentia* (VII, 5, ad 2, my translation). He is commenting on a text by Dionisius:

According to the doctrine of Dionisius these things are said of God in three ways. First affirmatively, when we say God is wise; which we have to say of him because there is in him a likeness of the wisdom which derives from him; but because in God wisdom does not exist in the way we understand and describe it, it can be denied, saying that God is not wise. But since we do not deny wisdom of God because he falls short of wisdom, but because in him it exists in a way that exceeds what we mean by that word, and what we understand, we have to say that he is superwise. And so, through these three ways of expressing that God is wise, Dionisius perfectly explains how such things are attributed to God.

These three ways are often referred to as the *via analogica*, *via negativa*, and *via supereminentiae*.

It is to be regretted, by the way, that the philosophy of language practiced in this century has precious little to say on analogy, a fascinating topic which was so important to Aristotle and his medieval successors. Don't give up hope – we rediscovered metaphor; analogy may be the next . . .

(7)   God is wise, yet God is not wise . . . but he is wise in another way. Pain is not something, but not a nothing either. Perhaps it is something in another way . . . Let us try the *via analogica* and the *via negativa* in discussing sensations.

Pains are localized. I may feel pain in my foot, so it is there. But it is not there in the way the bones and muscles are there. Amputees may feel pain in their missing leg. Pains can move (think of shooting pains), yet this does does not mean that there is something there that really moves as, for instance, the blood moves in the veins. A pain is a process: it begins, waxes and wanes, and then it stops. But it is not a process that can be observed, not even by the person in pain. People have pains, but not in the way they have houses, limbs, abilities, and debts. Notice here, incidentally, the wide range of analogies the term *have* displays in its use. Pains are often caused by bodily injury, but not in the same sense as, say, the confluence of blood is caused by bodily injury. In the latter case there are two observable physical processes linked by causality, but not in the former. "This is the same pain I had an hour ago." How do you know? What are the identity conditions for pains? Who is to apply them? Can you go wrong? Pain is not a thing, a process, or a property – yet not a nothing either.

Colors too are perceived in a place. Yet they are not there as the surface molecules are there. Otherwise science would find them. And it does not. All it can find are particles selectively reflecting electromagnetic radiation, and these things do not reveal the qualia perceived. Mirror images are seen in color behind the mirror. Yet there is nothing there but the wall. Color is a property of objects, but not in the sense shape, mass, and electric charge are. If there were no perceivers, all these would remain. Sensuous color would not. Calling it a "secondary" quality is acknowledging that it is a property only in an analogous sense.

It is obvious that the same conclusions ought to hold of the totality of our inner life, Hume's "bundle" of perceptions in smooth transition from one moment to another: our soul, if you like, which is by no means the same thing as the body and its processes. Yet it is not another "thing" either. It is like a substance, for it changes in time, but it is not a substance since, as again Hume pointed out, there is nothing enduring in it that underlies the changes. And certainly it is not something that could be, scientifically or otherwise, detected or observed. It is nothing in the world, yet something *to* me, *to* you, and so forth; *esse pro*, as we said above. Consequently, when I imagine being you, I do not imagine being a body, for that cannot be done (try to imagine being a rock – or a computer), but being a subject enjoying or enduring the experiences appropriate to that body, as if it were *my* body. And in this way I can have a *Vorstellung*, but not a *Bild*, of another person's inner life.

From these reflections it is clear that I am not a materialist. The "soul," i.e. the totality of one's inner life is not in the public, observable domain, thus it lies beyond the reach of science. Am I, then, a dualist? I think it is equally obvious that I am not.

A dualist, to be worthy of the name, has to believe in two distinct things as explanatory principles in a certain domain of inquiry. Descartes, for instance, most emphatically believed in two distinct and complete substances causally interacting in man: body and soul. I do not. For there is no "genus" to which my bodily processes and my mental states belong, and there is no "genus" to which my body and my soul belong. And *two* is predicated on a set. And a set is defined by a genus (or a species) to which its members belong. And, as we have demonstrated, not even the universal "genus," something, is broad enough to accomodate my soul and my body. I speak faceticiously of course; Aristotle teaches us that something, i.e. being, is not a genus. And "not a nothing" is still less. To Descartes, however, substance is a bona fide genus. He could not be more explicit on this point; he says in the *Principles*: "The term 'substance' applies univocally to mind and body . . . these can be understood to fall under this common concept" (Descartes, 1985, p. 210). Thus believing in two substances makes him a true dualist. But, if you accuse me of dualism, you better tell me in two *whats* you think I believe.

Experiences, and the soul, are something only in an analogous sense; they are only *esse pro*. So they cannot share a genus with a genuine substance, the body, or its attributes and processes, which are genuine accidents. Sets don't straddle categories; one cannot count across them. Otherwise, if I have a hat, I would have at least two things: the hat and its shape. So I am not a dualist, neither a substance, nor a property dualist.

A final worry: but what about the "I" to whom all my experiences appear, and for whom they are *esse pro*? The Kantian "I" lurking behind the Humean self? Is that not a substance distinct from the body? No. I agree with Wittgenstein: "I" is not a name of anything, has no identity conditions, and is descriptively empty (§ 404–10). Yet I do not think it is a nothing either. But since it is the mere subject of experiences, its understanding will depend upon the analogy through which we understand those experiences themselves.

Since I hope to be absolved of the charge of dualism for the reasons just given, I shall be generous in turn and grant, for the very same reasons, that science does not *miss* anything in describing man and animals in purely materialistic terms. It is no more incumbent upon science to find a soul in the body than to find God in the world. True, science does not tell the whole story. But, alas, it is a story that cannot be *told* except *per speculum in aenigmate*.

References

Descartes, R. (1985) *The Philosophical Writings of Descartes*, vol. 1, trans. J. Cottingham, R. Stoothoff, D. Murdoch, and A. Kenny, Cambridge: Cambridge University Press.

Feng-hsiung Hsu. *et al.* (1990) "A grandmaster chess machine," *Scientific American* 263, pp. 44–50.

Vendler, Z. (1984) *The Matter of Minds*, Oxford: Clarendon Press.

Vendler, Z. (1991) "Epiphenomena," in A. P. Martinich and M. J. White (eds) *Certainty and Surface in Epistemolgy and Philosophical Method: Essays in Honor of Avrum Stroll*, Lewiston, Ut.: Edwin Mellen Press, pp. 101–14.

Wittgenstein, L. (1953) *Philosophical Investigations*, trans. G. E. M. Anscombe, Oxford: Blackwell.

25
On the Distinctness of the Mental and the Physical

George Myro

I

Leaping is physical, but thinking is mental. Most of us do both. These are facts which only a philosopher might be allowed to deny. I shall say something about such denials towards the end of the paper. But I should like to begin by considering: what are we to make of the facts?

We seem to have a prima-facie distinction between two types of phenomena – the mental and the physical – or rather, I think, a number of overlapping and crisscrossing distinctions in which notions of the mental or notions of the physical or both take a side. But there is a tradition in philosophy according to which there is one such distinction – between the mental and the physical – not necessarily coinciding with any of the prima-facie ones, which is of special philosophic interest. This is presumably because it offers us a deeper and more comprehensive glimpse into the nature of reality – or, if you prefer, into the nature of our conceptual scheme – perhaps by enabling us to explain or define other distinctions or other concepts, for example, the numerous prima-facie distinctions. When I henceforth speak of "*the* distinction between the Mental and the Physical," I shall have in mind this supposed one important distinction.

What we are to make of the facts, then, is this: we are to see whether we can discern in them the distinction between the Mental and the Physical. Naturally, we shall want to rehearse a little what this distinction is supposed to be.

It is supposed to be, I think, a distinction between two types of phenomena, that is, between the phenomenon-*types*. I use the word "phenomenon" as neutrally and noncommittally as possible to cover whatever it is we want to be talking about. In particular, I want to leave as open as possible the question as to what philosophical categories what we are talking about happens to belong to: whether we are talking about substances, attributes, abstract particulars, events, processes, facts, and so on – and, in a pinch, even whether we are talking about concepts. Whatever phenomena are supposed to be, the distinction is supposed to be between two *types* of them. By "type" I do not mean "class," but rather, "feature" (I am willing to say "attribute" or "property," if you are) by which phenomena may be classified. To say, then, that there is a distinction between two phenomenon-types is to say that there are two distinct features by which phenomena may be classified into classes, whether or not these classes overlap or even coincide. I think, for example, that fruits and vegetables are two types of botanical matter, although some vegetables are fruits; and that men and featherless bipeds are two types of zoological matter, even if all and only featherless bipeds are men. Thus the existence of the distinction between the mental and the physical is compatible with at least some versions of the so-called Identity Theory of the Mental and the Physical.

So we are to see whether there are two distinct features of phenomena: one in virtue of which phenomena can be classified as Mental – let us call this feature "Mentalness"; and one in virtue of which phenomena can be classified as Physical – let us call this feature "Physicalness."

A further point has to be made about the nature of the distinction. The two interesting features, Mentalness and Physicalness, are not supposed to be on a par with other features which phenomena may have. Rather, a phenomenon is supposed to possess the feature of Mentalness, for example, *in virtue of* possessing certain other features, and, furthermore, not in virtue of possessing such-and-such *enumerated* features, but rather in virtue of possessing features of a certain *type*. And the same goes, I think, for Physicalness. That is to say, the features Mentalness and Physicalness are to be understood in terms of the following definition-schemata:

$$\phi \text{ is Mental iff } (\exists F)\,(F(\phi) \ \& \ M\,(F)\,)$$
$$\phi \text{ is Physical iff } (\exists F)\,(F(\phi) \ \& \ P\,(F)\,)$$

The most controversy-generating point which has to be made about the nature of the distinction has to do with the features (of features) represented in the schematic definitions by "M" and "P," respectively. M-ness and P-ness are supposed to be *incompatible*: no feature can be both M and

P. And even more: *M*-ness and *P*-ness are supposed to be, so to speak, "hereditary." That is, any feature which is definable entirely in terms of (logical constants and) features which are *M* is itself *M*; and a feature definable entirely in terms of (logical constants and) features which are *P* is itself *P*. So it follows that no feature which is *M* is definable entirely in terms of (logical constants and) features which are *P*; and *mutatis mutandis* the same goes for a feature which is *P*.

I shall summarize this by saying that features which are *M* and features which are *P* are supposed to be *mutually irreducible*.

Finally, features which are *M* should be those which, intuitively, make a phenomenon "mental" – I shall say: "mentalistic features"; and features which are *P* should be those which make a phenomenon "physical" – I shall say: "physicalistic features."

I have tried to formulate a thesis which, I think, has often been implicit in philosophical theories and controversies. To show that this is so would require a detailed survey and analysis of the history of philosophy. But I should like to illustrate the applicability of my formulation to two philosophical theories.

Cartesian Dualism is the view that there are two distinct types of substances: thinking substances and extended substances. Here substances are to be put under the rubric of "phenomena." These phenomena, i.e. substances, have various features. Thinking substances have such features as various sorts of thinkings, experiencings, and willings; extended substances have such features as various shapes, sizes, and motions. The relevant features of thinking substances have in turn a feature, *M*-ness, namely the feature of being, so to speak, "accessible in a privileged way." I shall have a great deal to say about this feature. The relevant features of extended substances have an incompatible feature, *P*-ness, namely the feature of *not* "being accessible in a privileged way." The feature of "privileged accessibility" and its contradictory are, furthermore, "hereditary." And, finally, the two features are intended to pick out, respectively, features which are intuitively "mentalistic" and those which are intuitively "physicalistic." Thus Cartesian Dualism exemplifies the distinction between the Mental and the Physical, as I have formulated it.

To be sure, according to Cartesian Dualism, the two distinct types of phenomena-substances are also non-overlapping. But this is a claim over and above the implicit distinction between the Mental and the Physical. For this distinction leaves open the question whether the two types of phenomena overlap.

Thus, for example, the distinction is also implicit in a view which, in effect, commits itself to the overlap. The Strawsonian view about persons can be interpreted as the view that there are two types of basic particulars: those which have, if I may say so, "physicalistic" properties or features and those which have "psychologistic" properties or features. Persons – at least, as a rule – have both. Nevertheless, the two types of basic particulars are distinguishable with the aid of a distinction between the two types of properties or features. And it seems to me that the distinction between the latter is made in terms of something akin to "privileged accessibility" or absence thereof.

The second illustration is the so-called Thesis of Intentionality. According to one version of this thesis, phenomena such as thoughts, perceptions, and desires possess features – for example, the feature of being a thought about unicorns, or the feature of being a perception of a unicorn, or the feature of being a desire for a unicorn – which themselves all have a feature M-ness, namely intentionality. I shall not have anything further to say about what this feature (intentionality) is supposed to be. What is important for my purposes is that other features, such as the feature of being such-and-such a neurophysiological process or state, are supposed to possess a feature P-ness, namely non-intentionality. The feature of intentionality and its contradictory are supposed to be "hereditary". And, finally, the two features are intended to pick out, respectively, the features which are intuitively "mentalistic" and those which are intuitively "physicalistic." As far as I can see, the Thesis of Intentionality is compatible both with the assertion and the denial of at least some versions of the so-called Identity Theory of the Mental and the Physical. Nevertheless, within the Thesis of Intentionality is implicit the distinction between the Mental and the Physical which I have formulated.

Well, then, what are we to make of the facts with which I began this paper? Is there the distinction between the Mental and the Physical? I should like to argue that there is, and that the features M-ness and P-ness with the aid of which it is to be made are, respectively, "privileged accessibility" and absence thereof, in a sense to be elucidated by drawing inspiration from Descartes. But my argument will be incomplete in a certain respect (I will be unable to show that everything that we might want to regard as Mental has features which have "privileged accessibility"). (I also *suspect* that this way of formulating the distinction is intimately connected with the formulation of it by means of intentionality – but I promised to say nothing more about intentionality.)

I must make the following parenthetical remark at this point. In recent philosophical discussions two impingent questions have been largely debated: (1) whether there is something like "privileged access" (or a related feature, "privacy"), and (2) whether "privileged access" is adequate for the distinction between the Mental and the Physical. And often something like the following unfavorable answer has been propounded. To be sure, a person can be and often is cognizant of his own psychological states without having to perform the observations or theoretical computations which someone else would have to perform to become cognizant of these states. But this does not support the distinction between the Mental and the Physical. For we can explain how the very *same* phenomena and features of phenomena which require observations or theoretical computations on the part of an outside observer can give rise directly to cognitions in one's own case. My brief comment on this answer is that it focuses unduly on the mechanism of cognition and neglects the justification of such cognitions. I hope that the meaning of this brief saying will become apparent in the sequel.

II

I can tell that I am thinking, and what I am thinking, right off, but I have to look around me to tell whether I am leaping, and where. That doesn't sound right at all. And it isn't. But there is something right about it, as I shall try to show. I shall try to elucidate a sense of "privileged access" in which I do have such access to my thinking and I do not have such access to my leaping. In doing this I shall follow a line of reasoning initiated by Descartes.

Descartes reached the view that he was a combination of two substances, one a thinking one and the other an extended one, by thinking up an argument to show that there are two types of substances and then leaping to the conclusion that if there are two types of substances, there are two substances, one of each type. I shall not concern myself with the leap, and I have little sympathy with it.

What is Descartes' argument that there are two types of substances? In a nutshell, it is this: there are features of substances which are "indubitable": such features as thinking, doubting, understanding, conceiving, affirming, denying, willing, desiring, imagining, and perceiving. And there are features of substances which are "dubitable": such features as shapes, sizes, and motions. So there are two types of substances: substances which have "indubitable" features and substances which have "dubitable" features. I imagine that Descartes calls the former "thinking substances" because all the "indubitable" features entail what he calls "thinking," namely, consciousness; and all the "dubitable" features entail extension or occupation of space. The thesis has the form of the schema for the distinction between the Mental and the Physical – with "indubitable" replacing "*M*" and "dubitable" replacing "*P*".

But now, what about this "indubitability" and "dubitability"? Can we make sense of that? In the two cases in which Descartes carries out the reasoning fairly explicitly we can see what is involved. The two cases are "existence" and "thinking." There is some awkwardness about these two cases. It seems wrong to regard "existence" as a feature, and if we did, we might reach the unpalatable conclusion that since existence is M, i.e. "indubitable," every existing thing must belong to the type defined as: having a feature which is M. The awkwardness about "thinking" is that it is not clear what is meant. We might interpret it as meaning: thinking something or other. But we have the further problem that Descartes seems to mean by "thinking" something rather like consciousness, rather than thinking; and we mean by "thinking" a great many things. Nevertheless, in spite of the awkwardness, we can see, I think, what is supposed to be involved in "indubitability" and "dubitability."

Let us interpret "x thinks (at t) that p" as meaning: x is (at t) taking it to be the case that p – that is, what philosophers used to express by "x judges (at t) that p." And let us, in view of problems of referential opacity, interpret "x thinks (at t) y to be F" as meaning: x is (at t) taking y to be F. Now we can see in what sense one's existence and one's thinking are "indubitable" for one. For from one's thinking that one exists or that one thinks something or other it follows logically that what one thinks – namely, that one exists or that one thinks something or other – is true. That is, we can say that feature F-ness is *indubitable* for x (at t) if and only if

if x thinks (at t) x to be F then x is F

is logically true. Observe that leaping is *not indubitable* in this sense. For we can all easily construct hypothetical cases in which x thinks he is leaping while he in fact is not.

So the Cartesian argument for two types of features (those which are *indubitable* and those which are not) and, consequently, for two types of substances (those which have *indubitable* features and those which have *dubitable* features) is maintained.

But one may feel dissatisfied with the result. It seems too abstract and remote from the live issues of the connection between mental phenomena, on the one hand, and behavior and neurophysiological processes, on the other. And to a degree, I think, this feeling is just.

The dissatisfaction can reasonably take, I think, two lines of expression. First, one may say: very well, but what about specific mental phenomena, such as thinking that snow is white or thinking that there are unicorns, and the neurophysiological processes which are almost certainly involved in these, and the behavior which is in one way or another connected with them? What about their interrelationships? Second, one may say: very well, the formal conditions for the distinction between the Mental and the Physical have been satisfied, but what is the significance of the result? Suppose, for example, that the feature of thinking that one is in neurophysiological state S is the very same as (i.e. is logically equivalent to) or has as conjunct (i.e. entails) the feature of being in neurophysiological state S. It will follow that the feature of being in neurophysiological state S is *indubitable* in this sense. So what?

To allay these dissatisfactions I should like to do two things: (1) to broaden the notion of *indubitability* to that of *privileged accessibility*, which will be a feature of a much wider range of features than merely of "existence" and of thinking something or other; namely, it will be a feature of all the specific thinkings that so-and-so, and also of all the havings of such-and-such a sense-experience; (2) to argue that it would be unreasonable to suppose that an intuitively "physicalistic" feature could have the feature of *privileged accessibility*.

Descartes concentrated on being right. That is, he emphasized those features which are such that one must have them if one thinks that one has them. Evidently, for such features results of empirical inquiry of the standard sort are irrelevant for determining whether one has them or not. I want to concentrate on this more general type of features: features for which results of empirical inquiry of the standard sort are irrelevant for determining whether one has these features or not. And I think it is reasonable to maintain that whatever intuitively "physicalistic" features may be, they cannot be features such that results of empirical inquiry of the standard sort are irrelevant for determining whether or not one has these features.

What do I mean by saying that results of empirical inquiry of the standard sort are irrelevant for determining whether one has feature F? Unfortunately, I do not have an adequate definition of the phrase "result of empirical inquiry of the standard sort." But I mean by this phrase, roughly: a condition of having had sense-experiences reflection upon which which would rationally justify or warrant one in thinking something which is not entailed by one's having had those sense-experiences. I mean, even more roughly: having performed such observations or theoretical computations based on observations as entitle one to think that so-and-so is the case.

By saying that results of empirical inquiry of the standard sort are *irrelevant* for determining whether one has feature F, I shall mean that no such result can be reasonably regarded as being sufficient, or necessary, for one's being justified in thinking that one has or does not have feature F. I shall distinguish two senses of such irrelevance. In the *strong* sense, results of empirical inquiry of the standard sort cannot be regarded as being sufficient, or necessary, for one's being justified in thinking that one has or does not have feature F in *any* cases. In the *weak* sense, results of empirical inquiry of the standard sort cannot be regarded as being sufficient, or necessary, for one's being justified in thinking that one does or does not have feature F in *all* cases – nor, indeed, in *most* cases – that is, *as a rule*.

(Of course, I do not mean to suggest that when results of empirical inquiry of the standard sort are irrelevant for determining whether or not one has feature *F*, results of such inquiry are also irrelevant for other people's determining whether or not one has feature *F*, or for one's own determining whether or not one had feature *F* at other times.)

III

How can results of empirical inquiry of the standard sort be irrelevant for determining whether or not one has feature *F*? There are two ways (at least), one corresponding to the strong sense of irrelevance, and the other to the weak. I shall now discuss the first way.

The general idea, very crudely, is: results of empirical inquiry of the standard sort are irrelevant (in the strong sense) for determining whether or not one has feature *F* just in case *what* one happens to think can be used to determine correctly whether or not one has feature *F* and reliance on results of empirical inquiry of the standard sort would expose one to unnecessary risks of error.

Let me try to make this idea more precise. Let me say that the totality τ of what *x* thinks (at *t*) *epistemically refutes for x at t* the thought that *p* if and only if it is logically impossible that *x* should think at *t* τ together with *p* and that his thinking at *t* τ together with *p* should involve thinking *no more falsehoods* than his thinking at *t* τ without *p*.

For example, for any choice of *q*, any totality τ which contains *q* *epistemically refutes for x at t*: *x* does not think at *t* that *q* – for it is impossible to add this thought to τ without adding a falsehood.

Let me further say that the totality τ of what *x* thinks (at *t*) *epistemically guarantees for x at t* the thought that *p* if and only if it is logically impossible *x* should think at *t* τ together with *p* and that his thinking at *t* τ together with *p* should involve thinking *no more truths* than his thinking at *t* τ without *p*.

For example, for any choice of *q*, any totality τ which does not contain *q* *epistemically guarantees for x at t*: *x* does not think at *t* that *q* – for it is impossible to add this thought to τ without adding a truth.

Indeed, we can see that any totality which does contain *q* both *epistemically refutes for x at t*: *x* does not think at *t* that *q*, and *epistemically guarantees for x at t*: *x* thinks at *t* that *q*. And any totality which does not contain *q* both *epistemically refutes for x at t*: *x* thinks at *t* that *q* – and *epistemically guarantees for x at t*: *x* does not think at *t* that *q*.

Now I take it to be a true principle that as long as *x* thinks something which *epistemically refutes q* for him at that time, nothing can fully justify or warrant him in adding *q* to his thoughts. For it is logically impossible that such an addition should fail to be an addition of falsehood.

And I further take it to be a true principle that as long as x thinks something which *epistemically guarantees q* for him at that time, nothing other than mere reflection can be required for him to be justified or warranted in adding q to his thoughts. For it is logically impossible that such an addition should fail to be an addition of a truth.

But then it follows, for any choice of q, that if x thinks (at t) that q, then nothing can justify his thinking (at t) that he does not think (at t) that q, and nothing other than mere reflection can be required to justify him in thinking (at t) that he does think (at t) that q. And it also follows that if x does not think (at t) that q, then nothing can justify his thinking (at t) that he does think (at t) that q, and nothing other than mere reflection can be required to justify him in thinking (at t) that he does not think (at t) that q.

In particular, then, no result of empirical inquiry of the standard sort can either justify or be required for justifying x in thinking at t either that he does or that he does not think at t that q. That is, results of empirical inquiry of the standard sort are irrelevant for x for determining whether or not x has the feature: thinking that q, for every choice of q.

If we say that x has privileged access to feature F if and only if results of empirical inquiry of the standard sort are irrelevant for x for determining whether or not x has feature F, then we may conclude that one has privileged access to any feature of the sort: thinking that q – for any choice of q. Furthermore, since, for any intuitively "physicalistic" feature F, results of empirical inquiry of the standard sort *are* relevant for determining whether or not one has that feature F – so that one does not have privileged access to that feature F – we may conclude that: thinking that q – for any value of q – is not a "physicalistic" feature. Thus we are at least not prevented from equating "privileged accessibility" with M-ness in the definition which supplies the distinction between the Mental and the Physical.

Observe that one does not have privileged access, in the sense explained, to one's leaping. There is nothing which one might think to which one could not add the hypothesis that one is leaping, or its contradictory, without adding something which is bound to be true or bound to be false. Thus standard empirical results are always relevant. We can all construct hypothetical cases in which someone may justifiably infer that he is in some peculiar hallucinatory state in which it seems to him that he is leaping whereas in fact he is not, or the other way around.

What goes for leaping, goes for all intuitively "physicalistic" features. This places limits on attempts to equate thinking that q with being in some behavioral, dispositional, neurophysiological, behavior-explaining, or Turing-machine-like state S. For, surely, for all such states results of empirical inquiry of the standard sort *are* always relevant for determining whether or not one is in those states.

Let me make the point by resurrecting the second objection to the Cartesian argument based on "indubitability," which I discussed earlier. One may be tempted to argue thus. Suppose that the feature of thinking that *q just is* the feature of being in state S. Then it follows that whenever one thinks that q, one cannot add to one's thoughts the thought that one is in state S without adding a truth, or the thought that one is not in state S without adding a falsehood. And whenever one fails to think that q, one cannot add to one's thoughts the thought that one is in state S without adding a falsehood, or the thought that one is not in state S without adding a truth. So it follows, on the supposition, that one has privileged access to the feature of being in state S. But how does this prevent the feature of being in state S from being an intuitively "physicalistic" feature?

The reply is: whatever words are being used to express the feature, it has been conceded that the feature is such that *no* possible results of empirical inquiry of the standard sort can in all rationality be allowed to influence one's decision as to whether or not one has that feature. And I submit that such a feature cannot be regarded as "physicalistic" in any sense other than that one chooses to use words to express this feature which *would* be appropriate to a feature which is "physicalistic."

All this is not to say that thinking that q cannot be identified with some "physicalistic" state S. But this will amount to saying that there is a phenomenon which has both the feature of being the state of thinking that q and the feature of being state S. The two features will remain distinct. And so will the two features: being in the state of thinking that q – and – being in state S. And one will have privileged access to one of these two features but not to the other.

(A parenthetical remark. Suppose it is granted that the case has been made for saying that features of the sort: thinking that q – are accessible in a privileged way, and no intuitively "physicalistic" features are so accessible. What about intuitively "mentalistic" features *other* than those of the sort: thinking that q? I believe that the notion (feature) of "privileged accessibility" can be broadened or generalized by following Descartes in supposing: (1) that all intuitively "mentalistic" features are species or "modes" of *consciousness* (in a sense which will have to be adequately explained); (2) that being conscious of ϕ in "mode" μ is to be analyzed as being conscious of (the ordered couple, say) of μ-ness and ϕ; (3) that "epistemic refutation" and "epistemic guaranteeing" are to be more broadly defined in terms of the totality of what one is *conscious* of, rather than merely the totality of what one is thinking. I believe that it will then follow that one has "privileged access" to whatever one is conscious of in whatever "mode." But the plausibility of this procedure will depend on the initial sympathy which one may have with it, and this approach will have to be defended by independent arguments.)

IV

I proceed now to an independent argument to show that one has privileged access, in the *weak* sense, to features of the *sort*: having such-and-such a sense-experience. Here my argument will be much more loose and depend on assumptions, though, I hope, reasonable ones.

The first is that there are such things – features – as: having such-and-such a sense-experience. I cannot say a great deal in support of this assumption or even in explanation of the phrase "having such-and-such a sense-experience." I can give an example: having an experience of seeing a red tomato two feet directly in front of one on a uniform field of blue. I have in mind the phenomena which have occasioned philosophic talk of sense-data and sensings. But I must steer clear of the controversy which pervades this subject. I shall assume that one can have an experience of seeing a red tomato whether one actually sees one (but not always then) or whether one merely seems to see one, as in illusions and hallucinations. I shall avoid making any judgments as to whether there are such things as experiences, sense-data, or any "objects" towards which one stands in relation when one has such-and-such a sense-experience. I shall avoid making any judgments as to the nature of the terminology which one might use to report that one is having such-and-such a sense-experience. All these important, interesting, and difficult questions I must pass by. Nevertheless, I hope that I have given you a good enough idea of what I mean by the phrase "having such-and-such a sense-experience."

The second assumption has to do with the connection between our concepts and our sense-experiences. It has been sometimes thought that the connection is quite rigid: that the applicability of our concepts is definable or at least specifiable entirely in terms of our having such-and-such sense-experiences. I think that the connection is much more flexible than that, but that, nevertheless, a connection of a logical sort is involved. Very roughly, I take it to be a conceptual truth that, at least for a very wide range of concepts, to have a concept is to regard having sense-experiences of various sorts as relevant to – in the sense of contributing to the justification or warranting of – one's application or withholding of the concept. As you already know, I hold that one need not regard sense-experiences as relevant in *every* case. And I further hold that the manner in which sense-experiences are to be regarded as relevant in any given case depends largely on the beliefs that one has about the world and one's situation in the world. I mean that, for example, to have a concept of a color is to regard experiences of seeing colors as relevant to determining whether something has that color. But the way in which such experiences are regarded as relevant in a given case will depend on one's beliefs about, for example, the lighting conditions. And whether and in what manner one regards experiences of watching meter-readings as relevant to determining the color of something will depend on one's beliefs about spectrographic matters. What I am saying is that, given the beliefs one has, one must be able to determine which sense-experiences would support and which would undermine the applicability of the concept.

Since the beliefs one has help to determine whether given sense-experiences are to be regarded as supporting or undermining, it seems natural to suppose that the beliefs do this in virtue of implying – in some sense, perhaps probabilistically – that if the concept is truly applicable then one should be having sense-experiences of a certain sort, or that if the concept is truly inapplicable then one should be having sense-experiences of a certain other sort, or, perhaps, converses of these. In general, I am inclined to subscribe to the view that sense-experiences support beliefs when those beliefs explain those sense-experiences.

I also take it that to regard sense-experiences as supporting or undermining is to tend to accept or reject beliefs according to whether one does or does not have such sense-experiences.

Putting all this together, let me state my second assumption in the following convenient form. It is a conceptual truth that it is a necessary condition of x's having a concept of feature F that in general and by and large the following should be the case: when x believes that he stands in relation R to feature F, then, first, if x is not unaware that his beliefs imply that if he should be standing in relation R to feature F, he would be having sense-experiences E, then x is having sense-experiences E, and, second, if x is not unaware that his beliefs imply that if he should be standing in relation R to feature F, he would not be having sense-experiences E', then x is not having sense-experiences E'.

For example, a necessary condition of x's having a concept of an aroused lion is that when x believes that there is an aroused lion in the next room then, first, if x is not unaware that it follows from his beliefs that if there were an aroused lion in the next room, he would be having a sense-experience of hearing certain roaring sounds, then x is having a sense-experience of hearing such roaring sounds, and, second, if x is not unaware that it follows from his beliefs that if there were an aroused lion in the next room, he would not be having the sense-experience of hearing a rehearsal of a violin sonata from that direction, then he is not having that sense-experience.

Now I am ready to state my argument.

Let us take as the value of "F" the feature of having sense-experience E, and as the value of "R" simply the relation of having that feature. Since the conditional, if x has E, then x has E, follows from any beliefs whatsoever, which is a fact of which it is difficult to be unaware, it follows from the principle that I have enunciated that it is a conceptual truth that if one has the concept of having sense-experience E then in general and by and large when one believes that one has sense-experience E, one does in fact have sense-experience E. And if we similarly take as the value of "R" the relation of not having the feature E, it follows from the principle which I have enunciated that it is a conceptual truth that in general and by and large when one believes that one does not have sense-experience E, one does in fact not have sense-experience E.

What this shows is that the general and by and large infallibility concerning one's own sense-experiences, which has seemed evident to many philosophers, is a conceptual truth and a consequence of the very conditions for having concepts.

But now if it is a conceptual truth that one must in general and by and large be right in one's beliefs concerning whether or not one has such-and-such sense-experiences, it follows that results of empirical inquiry of the standard sort cannot be regarded as *systematically* relevant for determining whether or not one is having such-and-such a sense-experience – in the following sense. Whatever such results might be in each of the set of cases in which one had beliefs concerning whether or not one had such-and-such a sense-experience, these results could not be regarded as justifying the conclusion that one was wrong in all or even most of these cases.

This shows that one cannot equate the feature of having such-and-such a sense-experience with any intuitively "physicalistic" feature. For any such feature F, results of empirical inquiry of the standard sort might justify the conclusion that one did not have this feature F in all or most of those cases in which one believed that one had such-and-such a sense-experience, and that one did have this feature F in all or most of those cases in which one believed that one did not have such-and-such experience. If we did equate the feature F with the feature of having such-and-such a sense-experience, the results in question would have to be regarded as justifying the conclusion that one was wrong in all or at least most cases about whether or not one had such-and-such a sense-experience. And such a conclusion could not possibly be true.

Let us observe that the feature of leaping differs in this respect from the feature of having such-and-such a sense-experience. It might be thought that if someone was very frequently wrong in his remarks about whether he was leaping or not – I mean that any candidate for such a remark which we might choose would very frequently turn out to be wrong – then it would follow that he did not have the concept of leaping. But this would not be quite right. It would be a reasonable inference but only under the assumption that his sense-experiences were correlated with objective states of affairs in the normal way. We can all construct hypothetical cases in which someone has a sequence of non-veridical sense-experiences of leaping and not leaping such that his remarks are in harmony with his sense-experiences but not with the objective states of affairs. The point is precisely that whether or not one has a concept depends on how one reacts to one's sense-experiences, rather than on how one's reactions are correlated with objective states of affairs.

V

A few final words about philosophical denials of the facts with which I started. It is sometimes proposed that although many things can be shown about the concepts which we do actually have, such demonstrations cannot always be regarded as showing anything about the nature of reality, on the grounds that the concepts which we do actually have are inappropriate to the facts. For example, it is sometimes suggested that our concepts of thinking and having sense-experiences are inappropriate to the facts in somewhat the way in which concepts of ghosts or will-o'-the-wisps are inappropriate to the facts. Now the proposal is itself rather unclear. Are we to suppose that what is proposed is that no one ever thinks or has sense-experiences? Is this compatible with allowing that there might have been someone who thought and had sense-experiences? Finally, it is not easy to see how the proposal can be coherently made. For isn't it part of the thesis that a concept is inappropriate to the facts that people have thought something which is not or could not be supported by sense-experience? Perhaps these questions can be answered, but it is not easy to see how they would be.

What I want to do now is to be sympathetic to the proposal and to suppose that many changes in concepts will or might occur and that concepts which we do actually have will or might be abandoned. But I think that there are limits to such sympathy. We cannot accept proposals which we cannot understand. And we cannot suppose that someone is making a proposal which we do not understand if we cannot understand how what he is doing could be making a proposal. These limits are not limitations. It is not that there might be something which we cannot think; rather what there might be is not merely what we can think but also what we can think coherently. When someone is prophesying and we show his prophecy to be incoherent, we are not making a counter-prophecy; we are not really saying that what he says will happen won't happen. We are rather saying that he is not saying anything, and that's why he is not saying anything which will happen.

26
In Defense of a Dualism

Richard Warner

The traditional doctrine of incorrigibility recognizes a fundamental epistemological difference between the mental and the physical. That is the spirit of the doctrine; the doctrinal letter is that beliefs about mental items are immune to error while beliefs about physical items enjoy no such immunity. The letter is false. To take something (e.g. a sensation) to be of a certain kind (e.g. a pain) is to commit oneself to the claim that the thing is relevantly similar to other things of that kind, and the relevant similarity may be *merely* apparent, even in the case of pain. I defend the spirit, not the letter. Incorrigibility is, of course, just one of the traditional doctrines that asserts an essential epistemological difference between the mental and the physical. The reason for singling it out is that the other doctrines – such as privacy or privileged access – identify a distinctive feature of the mental only if those claims incorporate or imply incorrigibility (see Rorty, 1970).

My defense of incorrigibility – of the spirit – rests on the claim that a *certain kind* of mistake, possible in the recognition of physical things, is not possible in the case of – certain – mental items. I will not try to say which mental items; I will focus exclusively on the example of pain. To illustrate the kind of mistake in question, suppose your ability to recognize foxes is completely unimpaired, and that, as a result of using this ability, you believe a particular item to be a fox. You might be mistaken; the "animal" might be a hologram, for example. Mistakes of this sort are impossible in the case of pain. Suppose your ability to recognize pain is completely unimpaired, and, as a result of using that ability, you believe you are in pain. Given that your ability is unimpaired, your belief *must* be true. This is a modal property of pain. No physical thing has this property.

So I claim; roughly speaking, that is Impairment is just one of three possible ways in which you could end up with a false belief, but, for now, talk of impairment captures the intuitive idea.

To distinguish the two kinds of mistake is to recognize a dualism, a dualism between the mind-independent and the mind-dependent. An item is mind-independent just in case it's being the way it is does not, in any essential way, depend either on our beliefs about it, or on the way in which we form those beliefs. Therefore: *Fs* (things, properties, events, whatever) are mind-independent only if there is no necessary connection of the sort just described between the exercise of the ability to recognize *Fs* and the truth of the resulting belief that a given item is (an) *F*. Such a connection makes being (an) *F* depend, in an essential way, on beliefs about whether something is (an) *F*. Pain is not mind-independent, given, of course, the necessary truth of your unimpaired belief that you are in pain. In contrast, foxes, chairs, and mountains, for example, certainly are mind-independent.

But how can defending *this* dualism count as defending the spirit behind the traditional incorrigibility doctrine? That doctrine recognizes a difference between the mental and the physical, not the mind-independent and the mind-dependent. The answer is that certain mental phenomena are clearly mind-dependent while the physical – on the prevailing philosophical conception[1] – is the exemplar *par excellence* of the mind-independent. It would, however, be a mistake to insist that the traditional dualism of the mental and physical coincides with the distinction between mind-independent and mind-dependent. Not all mind-dependent items are mental;[2] and not all physical phenomena are fully mind-independent.[3]

1 Recognitional Abilities

Careful reflection on certain features of our everyday epistemological practices reveals the dualism between the mind-dependent and the mind-independent. Current discussions of the mind–body problem typically pay scant attention to such practices, and this is a serious mistake. The traditional incorrigibility doctrine rightly drew attention to these practices.

We can begin with a few general remarks about recognitional abilities. The ability to recognize *Fs* is the capacity reliably to form true beliefs as to whether or not a given item is an *F*. I will, because it is natural and convenient, talk of the exercise of a recognitional ability; however, I do not mean to imply that the activation of the ability is always or even usually under one's voluntary control. An ability, e.g. to recognize foxes by sight, may be causally and non-voluntarily activated by a fox's coming into view. Such non-voluntary activation counts as an exercise.

Our focus is on the ability *non-inferentially* to recognize pain. I begin with an example. Suppose you have a pounding headache; imagine that it feels as if someone were pounding with a hammer on the inside of your forehead. You say, "My head hurts," expressing your belief that you are in pain. The belief is a manifestation of your ability reliably to form true beliefs as to whether you are in pain; that is, you form the belief as a result of exercising your ability to recognize pain. The belief does not result from any inference.[4] In particular, you do not first note how your head feels and then infer, relying on the qualities the feeling manifests, that the feeling is a feeling of pain. This should be obvious to anyone who reflects in an unbiased way on the experience of, for example, having a pounding headache. But it is easy for philosophical theorizing to bias reflection here, for it is natural to think that there are, as it were, two sides to recognition here: the feeling of pain, and the belief that arises in the presence of the feeling, the belief that one is in pain. If we think this, we may slip into thinking that one can – and may even typically – reach the belief the one is in pain by inference from the feeling.

A crude – very crude – empiricist picture of recognition provides a philosophical justification for such a position. On this picture, recognition is a matter of inspecting a feeling present to consciousness for the marks and features that indicate that, e.g., the concept pain applies. To think this way, however, is to presuppose far too sharp a distinction between feeling and believing. Typically, when you feel pain, the sensory and the cognitive are mixed together in the state of "feeling pain." The belief and the feeling arise together in a single state of "feeling pain," a state with both sensory and cognitive content. "The feeling" and "the belief" occur simultaneously; one does not arrive at the belief by first inspecting the feeling for certain marks and features.

Thus, to have the ability non-inferentially to recognize pain is to have the ability reliably to form true *non-inferential feeling-beliefs* about whether one is in pain. This is not, of course, to deny that one can feel pain without believing that one does.[5] I am focusing on cases, like the pounding headache case, in which one exercises one's ability non-inferentially to recognize pain. In such cases, one believes – non-inferentially – that one is in pain. I also do not deny that *sometimes* we proceed in roughly the way our crude empiricist model describes. We sometimes do inspect feelings for marks and features that indicate that we are in pain. An example is in order.

Suppose dentistry is for you an ordeal of fear and anxiety. As you sit in the dentist's chair, your attention is agonizingly riveted on what the dentist is doing and on what you are feeling. You see the sharp prong of the hard silver instrument as it approaches your mouth; you feel it scrap on your teeth and hear the peculiar sound it makes. Suddenly, one of these sounds lasts longer than the others as the instrument abruptly slides off your tooth. You feel it strike the soft surrounding tissue, and you protest,

"That hurt!" You should be completely anesthetized, so the dentist is perplexed. After some apologetic and reassuring words to the effect that it will never happen again, the dentist, to test the anesthesia, probes the tissue once more. Calmer now, you all you feel is a non-painful sensation of pressure; moreover, you recognize your present sensation as qualitatively identical to the sensation you felt before. The reason you thought that previous sensation painful was that, in your anxiety, you would have taken virtually any sudden, unexpected sensation to be a pain. When you said, "That hurt!", you exercised your ability non-inferentially to recognize pain, but your anxiety impaired the ability, and the impairment explains the false belief. When the dentist probes the second time, we can imagine that you proceed as the crude empiricist model describes. You refrain from forming any belief as to whether the second sensation is a pain until you have carefully and self-consciously inspected the feeling.

The point to emphasize is that such self-conscious attention is the exception. Typically, the exercise of a recognitional ability produces a belief without anything like the inspection the empiricist model imagines. It is a philosophical mistake (an all too common one) to take, without further argument, what we do self-consciously in the exceptional case as a model of what happens unselfconsciously in the run of the mill case.

2 The Kinds of Mistake

The key to seeing that the body is not mind-independent lies in distinguishing two ways in which one may fail to know: failures due to lack, impairment, or negligent use of a recognitional ability; and failures that arise from other sources.[6] My claim is that, where one's belief results (or, in the case of lack, is taken by the believer to result) from exercising the ability to recognize by inner feeling the position of one's limbs, failures to know that one's limb is in a certain position can arise only from the first source. To distinguish the two ways in which one may fail to know, let us focus initially on a belief, not about the position of one's limbs, but about an ordinary mind-independent object. Suppose that you see – or, at least, think you see – that the animal in the field is a fox; and so you claim to know, by sight, that it is a fox. Now, it really is a fox, a paradigm fox in fact, in plain view in good light. Even in such conditions, you may fail to know. There are three cases to distinguish.

(1) Lack of Ability

Ignorant of the color, size, and shape of a fox, you do not have the ability to recognize a fox by sight; so, since it is by sight that you claim to know, you do not know that the animal is a fox. You believe the animal is a fox because you mistakenly believe you have the ability to recognize foxes by sight. You have the mistaken belief because, for a joke, we told you that the only small, pointy-eared animals around were foxes, when in fact the area is full of small, pointy-eared dogs.

(2) Impaired Ability

In this case, you have the ability to recognize foxes by sight; however, the ability is impaired. It is important to distinguish two subcases.

Distortions You do not have your glasses on; or you have been drugged so that your vision is blurred; or you are so anxiety-ridden that your vision blurs, and so on. In these cases, the item in your visual field – the item you take to be the fox – does not determinately look like a fox; at best, it looks like a blurry fox; at worst, it looks like a blurry indeterminate something. If your ability is sufficiently impaired in this way, you do not know that the animal is a fox.

The empiricist picture of recognition sketched earlier exerts its full appeal here, for it provides a ready explanation of why distortions impair. Recall that, on this picture, recognition by sight is a matter of inspecting the item present in the visual field for the marks and features that indicate that, e.g., the concept *fox* applies. Sufficient distortion means that the relevant marks and features will not adequately reveal themselves. Despite the appeal, this view of recognition is as wrong for visual perception as it is for pain, for visual recognition is, like the recognition of pain, typically non-inferential. Typically, a fox's coming into view causes the non-inferential belief that a fox is present by activating the ability to recognize foxes by sight.[7]

But then why are distortions impairments? It is important to remember that we are focusing on a situation in which a paradigm fox is in plain view in good light. Thus the input to the visual system is in no way defective. In such a case, distortion signals a malfunction in the processing of visual information. Talk of information-processing is appropriate here because having a non-inferential recognitional ability is a matter of having a certain psycho*physiological* endowment; it is a matter of one's nervous system working in a way that reliably leads to certain beliefs. The system can malfunction to such a degree that an exercise of the recognitional ability will not allow one to determine *with any reliability* whether a fox is present. In such a case, the belief that results from exercising the ability will not qualify as knowledge.

Inner illusions In this sort of case – which, for want of better, I have called "inner illusions" – the item in your visual field determinately looks like something other than what it in fact is. For example, suppose you have taken a drug that affects your nervous system's processing of perceptual information in a way that makes foxes look exactly like dogs.

Note that on the crude empiricist view there is no reason to think of an inner illusion as an impairment of a recognitional ability; rather, in the case of an inner illusion, recognition proceeds by inspecting the inner illusion for certain marks and features, and this inspection can proceed in an entirely *un*impaired way even in the presence of the inner illusion. If a further counterexample to this view is needed, inner illusions certainly provide one, for the drug clearly does impair your ability to recognize foxes by sight. To have that ability is to be a reliable detector of foxes; and, if foxes look exactly like dogs to you, you cannot reliably detect foxes. Having the ability to recognize foxes by sight is, as we noted above, a matter of having a certain psychophysiological endowment, the human system of visual perception realized in our psychology and physiology; the drug that makes foxes look exactly like dogs impairs the physiological processes that subserve that recognitional ability. Compare what we may call an "outer illusion": a hologram of a fox, a hologram indistinguishable by sight from a real fox. The presence of such a hologram does not alter the way you process perceptual information. It provides an input that is processed in the normal way. What the hologram example shows is that you can be fooled into thinking a hologram is a fox even with a perfectly intact recognitional ability. The drug, by contrast, alters the normal physiological processes that subserve the recognitional ability.

A final qualification: there is, of course, no sharp distinction between inner illusions and distortions. Is the following example an inner illusion or a distortion? I am looking at a fox, but the fox as presented in my visual field looks more like a blurry dog than anything else. It is pointless to look for a non-arbitrary answer here; rather, there is a continuum of cases, and we are merely labelling one end "distortions" and the other end "inner illusions."[8]

(3) Negligently Used Ability

One acts negligently if one acts without due care. The level of care due is a function of one's goals in acting and of what one knows, or should know.[9] For example, suppose that Jones is a forest ranger whose job it is to scan the forest for smoke from fires. As Jones knows, or should know, his vision is so blurred that he cannot tell the difference between a smoke cloud and a normal cloud. Nonetheless, relying on his impaired ability to recognize smoke clouds by sight, Jones decides, wrongly, that a certain cloud is just a normal cloud, not a smoke cloud. Given his goal of detecting fires, and given what he knows (or should know), Jones acts negligently.[10] Note that where the relevant knowledge is lacking, so is negligence. Suppose you have taken – but have no reason to think you have taken – a drug that makes dogs look exactly like foxes; it need not be at all negligent for you to rely on your ability to recognize foxes by sight in forming the belief that a certain item is a fox. This is a case of impairment, not of negligence.

The forest ranger case is of course a case of both, and if all cases of negligence were also cases of impaired abilities, we would have no reason to have a separate category. But one can also negligently rely on an *un*impaired ability. Suppose you, I, and Jones are about to go in search of foxes to photograph (conscience-stricken hunters that we are, we have given up our guns for cameras). Swearing you to secrecy, I tell you that, for a joke on Jones, I placed holograms of foxes in many different spots. The holograms are indistinguishable by sight from real foxes and are sufficiently numerous that it would be negligent to try to identify foxes by visual means alone. Nonetheless, you see and photograph what you take to be a fox, ignoring, in the excitement of the moment, the possibility that it might be a hologram. It was negligent of you to proceed in this way, given your goal of photographing only *known* foxes.

I should emphasize that the distinction between negligence and impairment is not always clear. Consider another negligence example: you merely glance for a second at the animal, not nearly long enough to see what you need to see to determine if it is a fox. You are sufficiently experienced in visual recognition that you know, or at least you should know, that you are not looking long enough accurately to determine whether the animal is a fox. Nonetheless, you negligently form the belief that it is a fox. Given the way in which you employ (or try to employ) your recognitional ability, you do not know that the animal is a fox. The point is that this example could also be plausibly described as a case of impairment. We can think of your carelessness as impairing your ability; for example, your brief glance produced only a distorted item in your visual field. What this shows is that we cannot insist on too sharp a distinction between impairment cases and negligence cases. Again, there is a continuum of cases, and we are merely labeling one end "impairment" and the other end "negligence." Doing so promotes clarity by allowing us explicitly to mark epistemological differences among the cases at the extreme ends of the continuum.

Cases (1) to (3) are exhaustive of the ways in which failures to know can be laid at the door of recognitional abilities. If you have the unimpaired and non-negligently employed ability to recognize foxes by sight, how could you fail to know because of something wrong with the recognitional ability? By hypothesis there is nothing wrong.

The fox case also illustrates the distinction – crucial for our purposes – between failures to know due to lack, impairment, or negligent use of a recognitional ability; and, failures that arise from other sources. As an example of the latter sort of failure, suppose you exercise your unimpaired, non-negligently employed ability to recognize foxes by sight; as a result, you form the belief that a certain item is a fox. In response, I tell you that earlier, as a practical joke, I placed holograms of foxes in various spots; the holograms are indistinguishable by sight from real foxes. I ask you how you know that the apparent fox is not just a hologram. You are at a loss to answer, revealing that you do not know that the object is a fox.[11] Nonetheless, your recognitional ability is entirely in order. It is unimpaired: you are not drunk, drugged, hypnotized, fatigued, or any such thing; and, it is non-negligently employed: you have not been inattentive, careless, or any such thing. The problem is not your ability; it is the holograms.

Some may object that all the example shows is that you lack the ability to recognize foxes by sight: if you really had it, you would be able to tell a fox from a hologram. This objection overlooks the fact that one can have the ability to recognize *Fs* without having the ability to recognize *Fs* in all circumstances. Suppose, as we are about to go out fox hunting, I ask you, "Can you recognize a fox when you see one?" Your "yes" answer means that, in normal circumstances, you are a reliable detector of foxes. Your inability to distinguish the real foxes from the holograms does not show that you lack the ability you attribute to yourself. Lack, after all, is a relative notion, relative to some conception of completeness. The relevant conception in the example is "reliable detection in normal circumstances." This is the ability that human beings typically have, and (part of) the explanation of your failure to know is that the object of perception has an aspect (its being a hologram) that a perceiving subject – even one in complete possession of the relevant recognitional ability – may fail to detect.

Of course, some will still be skeptical that I have adequately distinguished between failures to know because of lack, impairment, or negligent use of recognitional abilities, and failures to know arising from other sources. In drawing the distinction, I merely relied on examples, and some will – no doubt – doubt that it is possible to provide a principled account of why the examples divide up along the lines laid down. I have answered this skeptical challenge elsewhere (Warner, 1993b), and will not repeat that answer here. My goal here is to make the distinction as intuitively compelling as possible by carefully delineating certain features of our everyday epistemological practices. I will have achieved this goal if the main objection of naturalistically inclined philosophers is that I failed to draw the distinction in a principled way. That would make the battleground just what I think it should be: the character of our everyday epistemological practices.

3 A Qualified Incorrigibility Thesis

Now let us return to pain. We can state the crucial claim more precisely:

(∗) Necessarily if, as a result of the non-negligent exercise of the unimpaired ability non-inferentially to recognize pain, one believes that one is in pain, then, one is in pain.[12]

We can think of (∗) as asserting a qualified incorrigibility for the belief that one is in pain.

Note that (∗) does not mention *knowledge*; it merely asserts that the belief must be true. This may seem odd, for in formulating (∗) we relied on a distinction between two ways in which one may fail to know: failures due to lack, impairment, or negligent use of a recognitional ability; and failures that arise from other sources. Shouldn't (∗) be formulated in terms of knowledge? But this is not necessary. Ordinarily, when you satisfy the conditions of (∗) you do know that you are in pain. You qualify as knowing whenever you are sufficiently justified in thinking that your belief results from the properly employed, unimpaired ability. In such a case, you are justified in thinking things that, if true, mean your belief cannot be false.[13] So, by focusing on true belief in (∗), we have not really abandoned our original focus on knowledge.

Is (∗) true? It may seem easy to describe a counterexample to (∗). Recall the anxiety version of the dentist example where you mistakenly believe a sensation of pressure to be a pain. I claimed that your anxiety impaired your ability to recognize pain. But why view the matter this way? Why not think that your ability to recognize pain is unimpaired and properly employed? To make the point more graphically, suppose – to engage in some neurological science fiction – that your anxiety operates this way. Let N be neural activity sufficient for the occurrence of pain. N includes a sequence of neural events $e_1 \ldots e_n$ involving interactions between the brain stem and the frontal cortex. Suppose that occurrence of $e_1 \ldots e_n$ alone, without the rest of N, is sufficient to cause one to believe that one is in pain, and imagine that your anxiety in the dentist case causes the sequence $e_1 \ldots e_n$ to occur even though the rest of N does not occur. The result is that you believe you are in pain even though you are not. What appears to be pain is really just a kind of hallucination, an anxiety-produced "neural hologram," as it were. The hallucination consists in the occurrence of the sensation of pressure in conjunction with $e_1 \ldots e_n$. After all, the objection goes, the combination of the sensation with $e_1 \ldots e_n$ is surely as much like pain as a hologram of a fox is like a fox. Why not think the "neural hologram" makes your belief false even though your ability is unimpaired and properly employed?

The reply is easy. The example does nothing to show (∗) is false, for even if we grant that "neural holograms" of pain are possible, they are clearly *inner illusions*, and, as such, qualify as an impairments of the ability. This is a sufficient reply, but there is a philosophically much more interesting reply as well: namely, in the case of pain, "neural holograms" – and more generally inner illusions – are simply impossible. I have argued this point elsewhere (Warner, 1993a) and will not repeat the argument here.

The point to note instead is that (∗) does not stand alone. Similar assertions hold, not just for other mental items, but also for certain beliefs about logical relations (see Warner, 1989), certain beliefs about the location and movement of parts of the body (see Warner, 1993b), and certain beliefs about the reasons for action.[14] Mind-dependence is not confined to the mental. It is a far more general phenomenon, a phenomenon that the complacent naturalism of our day denies. From the dualist perspective developed here, naturalism is the mistaken, and hence doomed project of showing that all apparently mind-dependent phenomena are really mind-independent phenomena.

Of course, my negative pronouncement on naturalism turns on the status of (∗) as a *necessary* truth. Or, to be more exact, (∗) is, on my view, a priori; adequate reflection reveals its necessity. So a full defense of (∗) requires answering skepticism about the a priori. Dualism and a priori are intimately intertwined issues. My goal here has been to defend the dualist strand.

Notes

1 This is not a conception I endorse; I criticize it in Warner (1993b).
2 It follows from my argument in Warner (1989) that first-order logical relations are mind-dependent.
3 The body is clearly physical, but it is not fully mind-independent, as I argue in Warner (1993b).
4 Some like to say the *nervous system* makes inferences even when those processes are totally inaccessible to introspection. This is quite mistaken. Inference, and reasoning in general is a purposive activity. When we engage in reasoning, we do so – typically at least – with the intention of producing reasons where the reasons are relevant to some end in view. We could not have such an intention if we did not have cognitive access to at least some of the thoughts and beliefs that comprise the premises of our reasonings. To lack such access would be to lack access to the reasons that give the reasoning its point; to lack such access is to be unable to engage in the purposive activity of reasoning.

5 I do not think one can, but there is no need to argue that here.

6 Austin (1979, pp. 79–80) draws a similar, if not entirely explicit, distinction.

7 Of course, we may sometimes proceed as the empiricist model suggests. If I am racing my sailboat in the fog, and I discern an indistinct reddish item sticking up out of the water, I may, after careful inspection and reflection, infer that it is the racing mark that I am supposed to round.

8 In discussing impairments, we have focused on cases in which there is an actual item perceived, the fox in the examples. If we remove this restriction, we can think of dreams as impairments of recognitional abilities. In my dream it may seem to me exactly as if I see a fox; this is an impairment of my ability to recognize foxes, for when I am dreaming in this way, I am not a reliable detector of foxes. One of the errors Descartes makes in the First Meditation is to treat dreams as if they left recognitional abilities intact. Descartes should not ask, "How do I know I am not dreaming?", but instead, "How do I know that my recognitional abilities are not impaired by a dream?" The issue is whether it makes sense to suppose that a dream could impair *all* the recognitional abilities by which I might come to have knowledge of the external world.

9 The analogy with negligence in tort law is, of course, intentional.

10 This is a little fast. Negligence is a more contextual matter than these remarks suggest. Jones might, for example, be the only forest ranger available and thus *have* to decide whether the cloud is a smoke cloud. In such as situation, it need not be negligent for him to rely on his recognitional ability. I have suppressed the contextual aspect of negligence in the interests of ease of exposition.

11 You fail to know because I have given you good reason to think that what you see might be a hologram; having been given such a reason, to know that what you see is a fox, you have to know that it is not a hologram. The reason you fail to know is not that to know that p (that the animal is a fox) one must know whatever is entailed by p (that it is not a hologram). Indeed, it is probably not true that to know that p one must know everything entailed by p; see, e.g., Robert Nozick (1981, ch. 3). However, to know that p one must know that not-q, in those cases in which q and p cannot both be true, and one has (at least in light of certain considerations) good reason to think q might be true. See Austin (1979).

12 There are counterexamples if the ability is not non-inferential. (See Warner, 1993a).

13 Of course, the issues here lead into questions about Cartesian skepticism; see note 8.

14 I argue for this claim in (Warner, forthcoming).

References

Austin, J. L. (1979) "Other minds," in *Philosophical Papers*, ed. J. O. Urmson and G. J. Warnock, Oxford: Oxford University Press, pp. 76–116.

Nozick, R. (1981) *Philosophical Explanations*, Cambridge, Mass.: Harvard University Press.

Rorty, R. (1970) "Incorrigibility as the mark of the mental," *Journal of Philosophy* 67 (12), pp. 399–424.

Warner, R. (1989) "Why is logic a priori?", *The Monist* 72, pp. 40–51.

Warner, R. (1993a) "Incorrigibility," in H. Robinson (ed.) *Objections to Physicalism* Oxford: Clarendon Press.

Warner, R. (1993b) "Is the body a physical object?", in S. Wagner and R. Warner (eds) *Naturalism: a Critical Appraisal*, South Bend, Ind.: Notre Dame University Press.

Warner, R. (forthcoming) "Incommensurability as a jurisprudential puzzle," *Chicago-Kent Law Review*.

27
The Rejection of the Identity Thesis

George Bealer

The identity thesis, let us agree, is the doctrine that every mental property (e.g. being in pain) is identical to a first-order physical property (e.g. having firing C-fibers).[1] Prevailing opinion seems to be that the identity thesis is false. The most popular arguments for this opinion are the multiple-realizability argument and the Nagel–Jackson knowledge argument.[2] I will try to show that these arguments are unsatisfactory as they stand and that their problems are incurable. For better arguments, opponents of the identity thesis must look to the history of philosophy, specifically to two closely related arguments traceable to the writings of Descartes: the modal argument and the certainty argument. Although these arguments are also unsatisfactory as they stand, I will try to show that (unlike their more fashionable cousins) they can be successfully reformulated. But to refute the identity thesis in its full generality, we shall have to weave them together into a single new argument. The result will have striking implications concerning the nature of the mind–body relation.

A unifying theme of the paper is that each of the four arguments is plagued by doubts that originate in scientific essentialism, the doctrine (popularized by Saul Kripke and Hilary Putnam) that there are a posteriori necessities (e.g. water = H_2O). If scientific essentialism suitably generalizes beyond physical property identities, then each of the four arguments is at best inconclusive. True, Saul Kripke has tried to save the modal argument from this kind of aggressive scientific essentialism, but I will argue that Kripke's defense (and much of the discussion of it) is misconceived.

1 The Modal and Multiple-realizability Arguments

The weakest version of the modal argument is this:

> It is possible that someone could be in pain and not have firing C-fibers.
>
> If the property of being in pain = the property of having firing C-fibers, then it is necessary that, for all x, x is in pain if and only if x has firing C-fibers.
>
> Therefore, the property of being in pain $\neq$ the property of having firing C-fibers.[3]

The argument is valid, and the second premise is undeniable. So the soundness of the argument comes down to the first premise. This premise is intuitive, so why not accept it straight off? Scientific essentialism is the main source of doubt.[4] After all, we could give a formally analogous argument for the conclusion that the property of being water $\neq$ the property of being H_2O. The first premise of this argument would be: it is possible that there could be a sample of water that is not a sample of H_2O. At least initially this seems intuitive. However, scientific essentialists have given powerful arguments that this premise (and in turn, the conclusion) is false. What is or is not possible regarding water cannot be decided a priori by our modal intuitions; empirical science is required. The worry is that perhaps scientific essentialism can be generalized from physical properties such as the property of being water to mental properties such as the property of being in pain. Until this question of the scope of scientific essentialism is settled, the soundness of the modal argument is in doubt.

I said that this version of the modal argument is weak. To see why, notice that it does not refute the identity thesis in its full generality. After all, the conclusion of the argument is consistent with the thesis that having firing C-fibers is a *sufficient condition* for being in pain. So identity theorists are free to maintain that being in pain is identical to the disjunctive property formed from the property of having firing C-fibers and the other (perhaps infinitely or indefinitely many) first-order physical properties that are sufficient for pain. Alternatively, identity theorists are free to maintain that being in pain is identical to some first-order physical property that is common to the first-order physical properties that individually are sufficient for pain. To rule out such theses, the first premise of the modal argument must be strengthened. For example, the new premise might be: it is possible for there to be someone who feels pain but does not have firing C-fibers *and* someone who has firing C-fibers but does not feel pain.[5] (This challenges the thesis that having firing C-fibers is a sufficient condition for being in pain.) Alternatively, the new premise might be something like: it is possible for there to be a being that feels pain but has no body.[6] (This premise challenges the thesis that the envisaged disjunctive property is a necessary condition for being in pain.) But, as with the weak modal premise, these stronger modal premises are called into question by scientific essentialism.

The multiple-realizability argument is also designed to refute the identity thesis in its full generality.[7] One common formulation of it resembles the weak modal argument in that its first premise is a generalization on the latter's modal premise. The new premise is that there are infinitely many, or indefinitely many, possible physical "realizations" of pain: C-fibers, silicon fibers, etc. Because this is a modal premise, however, scientific essentialism raises the same doubt about it as about the first premise in the weak modal argument.

This formulation has a further problem. As with the first premise of the weak modal argument, this new premise does not, by itself, prevent the property of being in pain from being identical to the disjunctive property formed from the infinitely many (or indefinitely many) possible "realizations" of pain. Because the aim of the multiple-realizability argument is to refute the identity thesis in its full generality, there is a need for special auxiliary premises (which are not needed for any of the modal arguments). But these auxiliary premises turn out to be problematic in their own right. For example, one familiar version uses an auxiliary premise to the effect that, if there is no *finite* first-order physical definition of a given property, the property is not a first-order physical property (see Fodor, 1965, pp. 171 ff., esp. p. 174; Putnam, 1975b, pp. 414ff. and 1975a, p. 299). (For alternative auxiliary premises, see (1)–(3) in the next paragraph.) But there are counterexamples. Suppose that the primitive general term "H" was introduced with the following reference-fixing remark: "H is a property with a rigid extension, and something has H iff it is a space-time point occupied by some subatomic particle." Intuitively, H is not a second-order physical property; it certainly has no noncircular finite second-order physical definition. But it would be very odd to say that H is not a physical property. So we seem forced to the view that H is a first-order physical property, but one that has an *infinitary* definition: Hu iff$_{\text{def}}$ $u = x_1 y_1 z_1 t_1$ or $u = x_2 y_2 z_2 t_2$ or . . .[8] Hence, a counterexample. (If one replaces "finite" with "explicitly stateable," "humanly recognizable," etc., there are even more counterexamples.) The larger point is that unstateability by finite beings does not, in general, establish ontological conclusions.

There are also nonmodal formulations of the multiple-realizability argument. The main premise is that a mental property like being in pain *actually* has very diverse physical "realizations." The auxiliary premises are (something like) the following: (1) if a property has very diverse physical "realizations," any first-order physical definition of it must be disjunctive; (2) "natural" (as opposed to *ad hoc* "Cambridge") properties do not have disjunctive definitions, and (3) mental properties like being in pain are "natural" properties.[9] There are many problems with this argument. First, its main premise is subject to a genuine (*vs.* merely skeptical) problem of other minds as it applies to creatures in species physiologically very unlike ours (e.g. fish). Are we sure that what they feel is really pain, sure enough to base the rejection of the identity thesis on it? Naturally, advocates of the nonmodal formulation have their answers ready, but the debate threatens to end in a stalemate. At this point, the most convincing – and least vulnerable – move would be to observe that, surely, it is at least *possible* that physiologically very dissimilar creatures could feel pain. But this is a modal premise, which takes us back to a modal formulation. A second drawback is that the auxiliary premises invoke a metaphysical framework ("natural" as opposed to "Cambridge" properties) which seems to many people (not me) to be as controversial as the identity thesis itself. Another problem is that (1) is open to counterexamples: a property like being 100 degrees Celsius has very diverse "realizations," and yet it has a nondisjunctive definition.[10] Premise (2) is also open to doubt. "Definition-by-cases" is a standard method of definition in logic, mathematics, philosophy, and science, and such definitions are standardly written out in the form of disjunctions. It is implausible to claim that every property requiring that kind of definition is a "Cambridge" property.[11] A final problem is that some identity theorists could invoke a sophisticated scientific essentialist point to deny (3). Specifically, they could draw a parallel between "pain" as it applies to physiologically diverse species and "jade" as it applies to chemically diverse compounds (see, e.g. Kim, 1992). If there is no shared "natural" property in the latter case, how can we be sure that there is in the former? Again, stalemate threatens. The most convincing, and least vulnerable, response is to retreat to the very weak modal premise that, surely, it is at least *possible* that some common "qualitative feel" could be shared by creatures in physiologically diverse species. But as soon as modal premises are invoked, the scientific essentialist worry re-emerges.

The conclusion is that the multiple-realizability argument requires auxiliary premises that are quite problematic; in addition, it runs into the scientific essentialist worry. The modal argument, both weak and strong, also runs into that worry. But at least it is free of problematic auxiliary premises.

2 The Certainty and Knowledge Arguments

The certainty argument is roughly this: I am certain that I am in pain, but I am not certain that I have firing C-fibers; therefore, pain and firing C-fibers are not identical.[12] A mirror image of the certainty argument is the knowledge argument, which goes roughly as follows: suppose that I know all of a being's physical properties; it does not follow that I would thereby be in a position to know its mental properties; therefore, the physical properties and the mental properties are different.[13] (Note the structural similarity between the knowledge argument and G. E. Moore's "open-question argument" which is associated with the "naturalistic fallacy.") The knowledge argument is thus "bottom–up" whereas the certainty argument is "top–down."

According to traditional logical theory, the above version of the certainty argument is ambiguous, having both an intensional ("opaque") reading and an extensional ("transparent") reading. On the intensional reading, the argument is invalid. (Analogy: I am certain that I have pain; I am not certain that I have the experience under discussion in lecture three of *Naming and Necessity*; therefore, pain ≠ the experience under discussion in lecture three of *Naming and Necessity*. On the intensional reading of this argument, the premises are true but the conclusion false.) Alternatively, on its extensional reading, the above version of the certainty argument is equivalent to: pain is such that I am certain that I have it; firing C-fibers are such that I am not certain that I have them; therefore, pain ≠ firing C-fibers. This argument is valid, but to know the second premise, I would already have to know that pain ≠ firing C-fibers, the very thing the argument is supposed to show. So on its extensional reading the argument is question-begging.[14]

To save the certainty argument from these difficulties, let us try shifting to an *intensional-abstraction* formulation. Consider the following modal argument form: (a) $\Box Fx$; (b) $\neg\Box Gx$; therefore, being $F \neq$ being G. Arguments with this form are valid despite the fact that "F" and "G" occur intensionally. Now consider the intensional-abstraction formulation of the certainty argument:

1 I am absolutely certain that I am in pain.

2 I am not absolutely certain that I have firing C-fibers.

3 Therefore, being in pain ≠ having firing C-fibers.

In view of the above, we know that the mere fact that "am in pain" and "have firing C-fibers" occur intensionally does not explain what is wrong with this argument. Mere intensionality is not the problem. To see the real problem, contrapose (2) and (3) (i.e. interchange the (2) and (3) and change their signs). The new argument is formally equivalent to the original. The problem is that this new argument has the same form as the standard propositional-attitude version of the *paradox of analysis*. For example,

> I am absolutely certain that computable functions are computable functions.
> Being a computable function = being a recursive function.
> Therefore, I am absolutely certain that computable functions are recursive functions.

This argument is invalid. The first premise is true, as is the second: being a computable function is the same thing as being a recursive function. (If not, what is it? Substitute your favorite definition. Or is computability an undefinable primitive?! If so, choose a definable property.) But the conclusion is false: I am *not* absolutely certain that all computable functions are recursive. Because the argument is invalid and because the intensional-abstraction formulation of the certainty argument is formally equivalent, it is invalid as well. This is the real problem.

Let us look more closely at the propositional-attitude version of the paradox of analysis. The puzzle it raises is this: if being a computable function is just being a recursive function, then since I am certain that computable functions are computable functions, how could I fail to be certain that computable functions are recursive? The standard informal explanation is this: I am not certain of how to *define* what it is to be a computable function. That is, I am not certain that a function is computable iff$_{def}$ it is recursive. Of course, it is difficult to devise an intensional logic that adequately captures these phenomena. But this does not belie the phenomena.

The intensional-abstraction formulation of the certainty argument is formally equivalent to the propositional-attitude version of the paradox of analysis and is therefore invalid. Identity theorists who accept scientific essentialism should diagnose the situation thus. Being in pain is in fact having firing C-fibers. Nevertheless, I can be certain that I am in pain and not certain that I have firing C-fibers. The reason is that I do not know the relevant definition: x is in pain iff$_{def}$ x has firing C-fibers. Of course, this definition is a *scientific definition*, (akin to the scientific definition of water: x is water iff$_{def}$ x is H_2O) whereas we previously considered a mathematical definition (f is computable iff$_{def}$ f is recursive). But this difference has no bearing on the argument's form and resulting invalidity. In fact, scientific definitions are just that much harder to know than mathematical definitions, for they are essentially a posteriori. The force of this criticism is undeniable.[15]

The same criticism can be made of the Nagel–Jackson knowledge argument: it is formally equivalent to a propositional-attitude version of the paradox of analysis and, hence, is invalid. Identity theorists may agree with Jackson (Nagel *mutatis mutandis*) that there are things that Mary does not know about color experience before her release.[16] (Mary is a neurophysiologist who has been confined to a black and white environment; she knows every physical fact relevant to experiencing red but never experiences red until she is released.) The identity theorists' explanation can be that Mary does not know the relevant scientific definition. If she did, she would have all the information needed to know everything relevant there is to know about experiencing red. She cannot know this definition, however, without having experienced red and having used such experience evidentially; indeed, the need for such experience is (part of) what makes the definition essentially a posteriori. Because her ignorance of the definition is entirely consistent with the thesis that experiencing red is identical to a physical property, the knowledge argument is thus no threat to the identity thesis.

With respect to knowing what it is like to experience red, identity theorists might prefer a slightly more complex story: suppose upon her release Mary exclaims, "So *this* is what it is like to experience red." Four items are open to scientific definition: the relation holding between u and v such that u experiences v; the relation holding between x and y such that x is what y is like; red; and *this*. From these scientific definitions – plus physical facts relating the right-hand sides of these definitions to one another – one can deduce the new fact which Mary discovers, namely, that *this* is what it is like to experience red.

Are these scientific definitions (u experiences v iff$_{def}$ ... ; etc.) *physical facts*? The question is terminological. Identity theorists are free to answer that they are *not* physical facts but rather *definitional facts*, namely, facts of scientific definition. In turn, they may hold that, although before her release Mary knows every *physical* fact about experiencing red, she does not know every fact about experiencing red: specifically, she does not know these definitional facts and various physical-cum-definitional facts, which are logical consequences of the physical facts plus these definitions. On this view, *all* the facts are either physical, definitional, or physical-cum-definitional. This is all that identity theorists ever wanted to claim.[17]

3 An Attempted Reformulation of the Certainty and Knowledge Arguments

We have seen that both the certainty argument and the knowledge argument are invalid as they stand. Can they be reformulated? A first start would be to "modalize" them. Recall the standard informal explanation of the propositional-attitude version of the paradox of analysis. Someone can fail to be certain that computable functions are recursive functions, for the person can fail to know how to define computability. Given that one can fail to know this, by what means does one ever know it? One way is through the testimony of an authority. Another way is to engage in a priori research. It is possible to arrive at a correct definition of computability using reason alone: by eliciting a priori intuitions about what would and would not count as a computation in various possible cases; by subjecting those intuitions to a priori dialectical critique; by constructing an a priori mathematical theory that systematizes the surviving intuitions; finally, by giving a priori proofs of relevant supporting theorems about computability.

This suggests a modalized version of the certainty argument:

1 It is possible for someone to know a priori whether or not being F = being G.

2 It is possible for someone to know that he is F solely by virtue of the fact that he currently is F.

3 *If* it is possible for someone to know a priori that being F = being G, and it is possible for someone to know that he is F solely by virtue of the fact that he currently is F, *then* it is possible for someone to know that he is G solely on the basis of reason and the fact that he currently is F.

4 It is *not* possible for someone to know that he is G solely on the basis of reason and the fact that he currently is F.

Therefore, being $F \neq$ being G.

This *is* a valid argument. To see this, suppose that being F = being G. Then, (1) would imply that it is possible for there to be someone who knows a priori that being F = being G. From this, (2), (3), and *modus ponens*, it follows that it is possible for there to be someone who knows that he is G solely on the basis of reason and the fact that he currently is F. But this contradicts (4). Given that the supposition that being F = being G yields a contradiction, being $F \neq$ being G.

The idea is to let $\ulcorner F \urcorner$ be "pain" and $\ulcorner G \urcorner$ be "firing C-fibers." On this understanding, (2), (3), and (4) are acceptable, as we will now explain. (2) is intuitively obvious. It says that one can know that one is in pain solely by virtue of the fact that one is currently in pain. (Notice that "know" has replaced "is certain" in the present formulation, so in contrast to the original formulation there is now no commitment to Cartesian infallibility, indubitability, or incorrigibility.)[18] (3) is intuitively obvious. It says that, if it is possible for someone to have a certain kind of a priori knowledge and someone to have a certain kind of introspective knowledge, then it is possible for someone to have both kinds of knowledge and to use them to derive an immediate logical consequence. (4) is similarly unproblematic. When we say that a person uses only reason and the fact that he is currently in pain, we mean to rule out that the person has had any prior exposure to physiological theory, its instruments, or its terminology. We also mean to rule out that the person is making any evidential use of the following: sensory facts besides the fact that he is in pain, memories of sensory facts, previously learned empirical theories, testimony of others, and so forth. Understood this way, (4) is intuitively obvious: if a person meets all these requirements, plainly the person could not on that slender basis know that he possesses firing C-fibers.[19] Given that (2), (3), and (4) are acceptable, the correctness of the argument comes down to (1). Unfortunately, there is a problem with this premise.

Our earlier discussion shows that (1) would be true if $\ulcorner F \urcorner$ were "computable function" and $\ulcorner G \urcorner$ were "recursive function." However, given scientific essentialism, (1) would be false if $\ulcorner F \urcorner$ were "water" and $\ulcorner G \urcorner$ were "H_2O." For, given scientific essentialism, it is *essentially* a posteriori that being water = being H_2O. Hence, if "pain" and "firing C-fibers" are like "computable function" and "recursive function," the modalized version of the certainty argument goes through. On the other hand, if they are like "water" and "H_2O," it fails. So, once again, the correctness of an initially promising argument comes down to the question of the scope of scientific essentialism.

Now just as we have "modalized" the original certainty argument in an effort to avoid the problem raised by propositional-attitude versions of the paradox of analysis, we can do the same for the Nagel–Jackson knowledge argument. But the result is the same. If scientific essentialism generalizes from terms like "water" to terms like "pain," this modalized knowledge argument would also be in doubt.

4 Kripke's Defense of the Modal Argument

I now turn to this question of the scope of scientific essentialism (SE). The arguments supporting SE rely on intuitions: without them SE would be unjustified. Consider the famous twin-Earth intuition: if all and only samples of water here on Earth are in fact composed predominantly of H_2O and if, traveling to another planet, we were to find samples of a stuff that is macroscopically like water but composed of XYZ ($\neq H_2O$), those samples would, intuitively, not be water. Suppose that this and kindred intuitions are correct, and suppose that all and only samples of water are as described. Then, we may conclude that in all actual and counterfactual situations something would be composed of water if and only if it were composed predominantly of H_2O. In turn, we may conclude that, necessarily, water = H_2O.

But there is a problem. Before the advent of SE, we had a host of anti-SE intuitions, for example, the intuition that it could have turned out that some samples of water contained no hydrogen. What are we to make of the conflict between pro- and anti-SE intuitions?

Proponents of SE have two responses. First, they could simply declare that anti-SE intuitions are mistaken whereas their own pro-SE intuitions are correct. However, critics of SE could simply meet this response by stating that things are the other way around. The result would be a complete stalemate. To avoid this stalemate, proponents of SE must turn to the second response. According to it, widespread conflict among our intuitions is only an appearance. All, or at least most, of our intuitions are correct. Despite their correctness, however, many are *misreported*. When we try carefully to rephrase our (apparently) anti-SE intuitions to make them consistent with our pro-SE intuitions, we succeed. But when we try to rephrase the latter to make them consistent with the former, we fail. Accordingly, the stalemate is broken in favor of SE.

Kripke and other scientific essentialists have in fact used two rephrasal strategies to defend SE. The first turns on an alleged pragmatic equivocation in the kind of possibilities at issue. When we report our pro-SE intuitions (e.g. twin-Earth intuitions), what we say is strictly and literally true, and what we are reporting are ordinary possibilities. But when we report our apparently anti-SE intuitions, we confuse ordinary possibility with the possibility of a certain kind of epistemic situation. For example, when we say "It could have turned out that some samples of water contained no hydrogen," what we say is strictly and literally false. The intuition is true but incorrectly reported. The correct report would be something like this: "It is possible for there to be a population of speakers in an epistemic situation qualitatively identical to ours and they use the expression 'water' to refer to something other than water or they use the term 'hydrogen' to refer to something other than hydrogen." As Kripke remarks in connection with the Hesperus–Phosphorus case,

> Now this seems very strange because in advance, we are inclined to say, the answer to the question whether Hesperus is Phosphorus might have turned out either way. (1980, p. 103)
>
> And so it's true that given the evidence that someone has antecedent to his empirical investigation, he can be placed in a sense in exactly the same situation, that is a qualitatively identical epistemic situation [to ours], and call two heavenly bodies "Hesperus" and "Phosphorus," without their being

identical. So in that sense we can say that it might have turned out either way. (1980, pp. 103–4)

Generalizing from these examples, we arrive at the following schema for applying this sort of rephrasal strategy: ⌜It could have turned out that A⌝ is to be rephrased as ⌜It is possible that a population of speakers in an epistemic situation qualitatively identical to ours would make a true statement by asserting ⌜A⌝ with normal literal intent⌝.[20] Consider our intuition that it could have turned out that there were samples of water containing no hydrogen. The rephrasal comes out true because in the envisaged population of speakers "water" might not name water but rather XYZ or "hydrogen" might not name hydrogen but rather X. When rephrased thus, the original apparently anti-SE intuition is plainly consistent with the thesis that, necessarily, water = H_2O.

For the second rephrasal strategy, it is best simply to quote Kripke:

> In the case of some necessary *a posteriori* truths, however, we can say that under appropriate qualitatively identical evidential situations, an appropriate corresponding qualitative statement might have been false. The loose and inaccurate statement that gold might have turned out to be a compound should be replaced (roughly) by the statement that it is logically possible that there should have been a compound with all the properties originally known to hold of gold. The inaccurate statement that Hesperus might have turned out not to be Phosphorus should be replaced by the true contingency mentioned earlier in these lectures: two distinct bodies might have occupied, in the morning and the evening, respectively, the very positions actually occupied by Hesperus–Phosphorus–Venus.
>
> I have not given any general paradigm for the appropriate corresponding qualitative contingent statement. Since we are concerned with how things might have turned out otherwise, our general paradigm is to redescribe both the prior evidence and the statement qualitatively and claim that they are only contingently related. In the case of identities, using two rigid designators, such as the Hesperus–Phosphorus case above, there is a simpler paradigm which is often usable to at least approximate the same effect. (1980, pp. 142–3)

Kripke's "simpler paradigm" goes as follows. Suppose that ⌜R_1⌝ and ⌜R_2⌝ are co-designating rigid designators whose designatum might have been fixed by the nonrigid (i.e. contingent) designators ⌜D_1⌝ and ⌜D_2⌝, respectively. When we report an apparently anti-SE intuition with ⌜It might have turned out that $R_1 \neq R_2$⌝, our intuition is correct, but it is to be rephrased as ⌜It is possible that $D_1 \neq D_2$⌝. On its standard narrow-scope reading, the latter sentence is consistent with the SE thesis that, necessarily, $R_1 = R_2$. For ⌜D_1⌝ and ⌜D_2⌝ are only contingently co-designating. For example, "It might have turned out that water $\neq H_2O$" might be rephrased as: "It is possible that the clear thirst-quenching stuff $\neq$ the such-and-such chemical compound." The latter is consistent with the thesis that, necessarily, water $= H_2O$, for there is a possible situation in which there could be a unique clear thirst-quenching stuff that is not a such-and-such chemical compound.

Although the two rephrasal strategies bear a superficial resemblance to one another, they are clearly not identical. For example, as indicated, there is at hand a rather precise rule for applying the first strategy; Kripke indicates that there is not at hand a precise rule for applying the second strategy.

This brings us to Kripke's modal argument against the identity thesis (1980, pp. 144–55). It is just a traditional modal argument together with an auxiliary argument to the effect that the *second* rephrasal strategy fails to deflate the modal intuition upon which the argument rests. Three points are in order.

1   The argument is plainly inadequate as it stands, for Kripke neglects one of his own rephrasal strategies, namely, the first one.

2   Kripke holds that the second strategy fails to deflate the indicated modal intuition, for any description $\ulcorner D_1 \urcorner$ that might serve to fix the reference of "pain" would, like "pain" itself, *rigidly* designate pain.[21] Specifically, every application of the second rephrasal strategy to the sentence "It is possible that pain $\neq$ firing C-fibers" only leads to a sentence (e.g. "It is possible that the feeling that feels like this $\neq$ firing C-fibers") that strictly and literally *entails* the original sentence. So the intuition retains its original force. But there are two errors in this reasoning. The first is in not recognizing that, depending on the circumstances, *nonrigid* designators $\ulcorner D_1 \urcorner$ could be used – and surely sometimes are used – to pick out pain. For example, "the feeling to which I am most averse" and "the feeling for which I have greatest spontaneous hate" pick out pain, but they do so only contingently. After all, they might have picked out nausea.[22] The second error, noted by Boyd (1980, p. 84) would arise even if one were to suppose with Kripke that each reference-fixing description $\ulcorner D_1 \urcorner$ that might replace "pain" is just another rigid designator for pain. For even then it would not follow that every application of the second rephrasal strategy to "It is possible that pain $\neq$ firing C-fibers" yields a rephrasal that entails the original sentence. To obtain a rephrasal that does not, one merely needs a nonrigid description $\ulcorner D_2 \urcorner$ that contingently fixes the reference, not of $\ulcorner R_1 \urcorner$, but of $\ulcorner R_2 \urcorner$; that is, one merely needs a nonrigid description $\ulcorner D_2 \urcorner$ that contingently fixes the reference, not of "pain," but of "firing C-fibers." And they are easy to find. Identity theorists thus have a way of honoring the original intuition used in the modal argument

without threatening their thesis that, necessarily, pain = firing C-fibers. By fixating on $\ulcorner R_1 \urcorner$ (i.e. "pain"), Kripke neglected to consider $\ulcorner R_2 \urcorner$ (i.e. "firing C-fibers").

3 Kripke's second rephrasal strategy is based on the thesis that, when we report an intuition with $\ulcorner$Possibly, $R_1 \neq R_2 \urcorner$, often the true thing we have in mind is strictly and literally reported with $\ulcorner$Possibly, $D_1 \neq D_2 \urcorner$, where $\ulcorner R_1 \urcorner$ and $\ulcorner R_2 \urcorner$ are names and $\ulcorner D_1 \urcorner$ and $\ulcorner D_2 \urcorner$ are descriptions. But Kripke, of all people, should not be proposing that, when we make use of proper-name sentence in ordinary conversation (even if the sentence happens to be of the form $\ulcorner$Possibly, $R_1 \neq R_2 \urcorner$), we have in mind something *descriptive*. After all, the situation is *phenomenologically and behaviorally indistinguishable* from situations in which we have in mind something *nondescriptive* (as, for example, when Kripke asserts his well-known thesis "If Hesperus = Phosphorus, then it is not possible that Hesperus ≠ Phosphorus"). For Kripke to deny this would be *ad hoc* and implausible. Hence, the rephrasal strategy itself is implausible. In fact, it can be shown that this rephrasal strategy does not even accomplish the goal of breaking the stalemate between our apparently conflicting pro- and anti-SE intuitions.[23] For one can wield it so as to sustain the original force of the latter and to deflate the original force of the former, thereby rendering our pro-SE intuitions consistent with traditional anti-SE. The following recipe provides one way of doing this. Adopt the traditional description theory of names. Hold that names occurring in reports of anti-SE intuitions *are* being used strictly and literally and that they express *nonrigid* descriptive content. Hold that names occurring in reports of pro-SE intuitions are *not* being used strictly and literally and that they are being used to express *rigid* descriptive content.[24] (This rigidity could, for example, be the result of implicitly understood actuality operators.) The rephrasal strategy can thus be used to affirm anti-SE just as effectively as it can be used to affirm pro-SE. Therefore, the stalemate is not broken.

In fairness, Kripke tells us that this rephrasal strategy does not always take the form of merely replacing a statement's rigid designators $\ulcorner R_1 \urcorner$ and $\ulcorner R_2 \urcorner$ with associated definite descriptions $\ulcorner D_1 \urcorner$ and $\ulcorner D_2 \urcorner$. He states that his "general paradigm is to redescribe both the prior evidence and the statement qualitatively and claim that they are only contingently related" (1980, p. 143). The above criticism, however, carries over *mutatis mutandis* to the proposed "qualitative redescriptions" of other statements that report anti-SE intuitions. Specifically, one can sustain the original force of our anti-SE intuitions and, by deft use of actuality operators, always deflate the original force of our pro-SE intuitions, thereby rendering them consistent with traditional anti-SE. So, the second rephrasal strategy, in its full original form, fails to break the stalemate in favor of SE. Of course, Kripke *is* on to something with his talk of "qualitative redescription of the prior *evidence*." The sound idea is this: it is possible for people in qualitatively the same epistemic situation as ours to be thinking and talking about different things from those we are thinking and talking about. But this is precisely the idea that drives the *first* rephrasal strategy. "Qualitative redescriptions of the original *statement*" are completely beside the point; indeed, they only create an opening for anti-SE to perpetuate the statement.

The conclusion should now be plain. To break the stalemate, scientific essentialists must forget the second rephrasal strategy and turn to (some form of) the first. When they do so the stalemate seems to be broken in their favor. According to this strategy, when one wishes to deflate the force of an intuition reported with ⌜Possibly A⌝, one rephrases that report with ⌜It is possible that a population of speakers in an epistemic situation qualitatively identical to ours would make a true statement by asserting ⌜A⌝ with normal literal intent⌝.[25] Because our anti-scientific-essentialists are traditional internalists, they are committed to holding that the meaning of ⌜A⌝ cannot differ across populations of speakers in qualitatively identical epistemic situations. Accordingly, they must hold that the rephrasal entails the original report. In particular, when the original intuition seems to have a pro-SE force, they are committed to holding that the rephrasal has that force as well.[26] By contrast, scientific essentialists are not traditional internalists, so they are free to hold that the meaning of ⌜A⌝ can differ across populations of speakers in qualitatively identical epistemic situations. So when the original intuition seems to have an anti-SE force, they are free to hold that that force is deflated upon rephrasal. The stalemate is thus broken in their favor.

The conclusion is that the cogent defense of SE rests on the first rephrasal strategy, not the second. But this conclusion shows that Kripke's defense of the modal argument (and the vast philosophical literature on Kripke's defense) is off the mark.

5 The Modal Argument Reformulated

Consider the cogent SE argument that being water = being H_2O. The argument consists of two steps. First, pro-SE intuitions supporting the identity are elicited: for example, the twin-Earth intuition regarding water and XYZ. Second, it is shown that the (first) rephrasal strategy can be used to deflate the force of our anti-SE intuitions but that, when anti-scientific-essentialists attempt to use it to deflate the force of our pro-SE intuitions (i.e. the intuitions elicited in step one), they fail. Because both steps evidently succeed, one may conclude that SE holds for "water." To show that it also holds for mental expressions like "pain" the identity theorist needs to go through both steps.

But the first step fails for expressions like "pain."[27] To see this, consider the "pain" analogue of the original twin-Earth argument. Suppose that on Earth all and only creatures that are in pain have firing C-fibers. Suppose that upon traveling to a twin-Earth, we find creatures that are macroscopically indistinguishable from the creatures on Earth. For example, our human Doppelgängers have everyday behavioral "input–output functions" that are the same as ours. Their "pain" behavior is exactly like ours. They utter "sentences" that, if they were English sentences, would attest to the dreadfulness of pain. Their "dentists" inject something they "call" "anesthetic." Their "torturers" are effective in eliciting "confessions." And so on. It turns out, however, that, whereas our pain – and our attendant pain behavior – co-occurs with the firing of C-fibers, the "pain" behavior of the creatures on twin-Earth co-occurs instead with the firing of C_t-fibers (which, unlike C-fibers, are not composed largely of hydrogen, oxygen, and carbon, but rather of X, Y, Z, and W). Now would we say that these creatures are in pain on the indicated occasions? Well, to be sure, we would not be *certain* that they are in pain; macroscopic behavioral criteria never entail that a mental predicate applies. Nevertheless, we would have very good evidence that they are in pain. But this is not the point. The point is that *it would not be counterintuitive to say that they are in pain*. Note the contrast. It would be counterintuitive to say that samples of XYZ on twin-Earth are samples of water. This intuition is the very foundation of the SE argument concerning water. The analogous intuition concerning pain is simply *missing*.[28] Accordingly, the foundation of the argument that SE generalizes from physical expressions like "water" to mental expressions like "pain" is simply missing. Without this foundation, the thesis that SE does so generalize is nothing but an article of faith.

This conclusion may be used to win a positive result. We have seen that in the case of terms like "water" there is a pending stalemate between pro-SE and anti-SE intuitions and that, to break the stalemate, scientific essentialists must then go on to apply the rephrasal strategy to reconcile the apparently conflicting intuitions. Now nearly all philosophers wish to rely evidentially on intuitions (this includes both parties in our debate over the soundness of the modal argument). As a consequence, we are committed to the technique of resolving pending stalemates by means of the rephrasal strategy. Otherwise, we would be forced to admit that a huge number of our intuitions are mistaken and, therefore, that the evidential weight of intuitions is questionable. But in the absence of a pending stalemate, there is no requirement to subject our intuitions to the rephrasal strategy; absent a pending stalemate, the presumption is that our intuitions are correct as reported. However, we have just seen that pro-SE intuitions concerning mental expressions like "pain" are missing. At the same time, we have a wealth of traditional anti-SE intuitions concerning expressions like "pain." So the sort of pending stalemate that threatens in the case of intuitions concerning expressions like "water" is absent in the case of intuitions concerning expressions like "pain." The presumption, therefore, is that the latter intuitions are correct as reported. However, one of these intuitions is the key modal premise in the weak modal argument, that is, the intuition reported with "It is possible for there to be something that has pain but lacks firing C-fibers." Therefore, the presumption is that this premise is correct as reported and, hence, that the argument goes through without further ado.

This is the first step in our defense of the weak modal argument. Now for the second. Suppose that the above assessment is mistaken and that there is a requirement to subject the argument's key modal intuition to the rephrasal strategy. Identity theorists who would undermine the argument by invoking SE must grant that this modal intuition is true but incorrectly reported and that, when the initial report is subjected to the rephrasal strategy, the resulting rephrasal is true. According to the rephrasal strategy, our true intuition is correctly reported by (something like) "It is possible that there could be a population of speakers in an epistemic situation qualitatively identical to ours who would make a true statement by asserting 'Something has pain but lacks firing C-fibers' with normal literal intent." If there were a population of speakers in an epistemic situation *qualitatively identical* to ours, they would use "something" to mean something; "has" to mean has; "lack" to mean lack; "pain" to mean pain. (If there is doubt about the last claim, let "pain" be replaced with the demonstrative "this" throughout the argument, and let it be understood that we are using "this" for a certain salient phenomenal quality to which each of us is attending during our present experiences of sharp pain. Then our counterparts in a population of speakers whose epistemic situation is *qualitatively identical* would have to be using "this" for an *identical quality*.)[29] Nevertheless, people in a qualitatively identical epistemic situa- tion could use "firing C-fibers" to refer to something *other than* firing C-fibers. (This is the echo of Boyd's criticism of Kripke.) For example, they could inhabit a possible world in which the following hold: except for the envisaged speakers, all apparently sentient beings are nonconscious automata; the speakers' term "firing C-fibers" refers paradigmatically to a certain silicon-based process that their scientists commonly observe in the "brains" of these automata; this process never occurs in any being that is conscious (i.e it never occurs in any of the speakers). In view of such possibilities, the rephrasal of the key modal intuition undermines the original force of that intuition.

This negative outcome is only temporary, however. The argument can be reformulated in such a way that its key modal premise does withstand the rephrasal strategy. The idea is to find a substantive *necessary condition* for having firing C-fibers that can be specified in terms whose basic semantic properties would remain the same for any population of speakers whose epistemic situation is qualitatively identical to ours. We already know that there are some terms like this. For example, any population of speakers whose epistemic situation is qualitatively identical to ours would use "has" to mean has and "pain" to mean pain. We are looking for a substantive necessary condition for having firing C-fibers that can be described exclusively in terms with this kind of semantic stability.

Surely there is a necessary condition that fills the bill. Our larger goal is to show that scientific essentialism does not generalize from items like water to items like pain. Suppose for reductio that it does. Then certainly it would generalize from items like water to items like C-fibers. Just as water has an essence discoverable by chemists, so C-fibers would have one discoverable by cell biologists. Now C-fibers are phylogenetically comparatively old unmyelinated neurons with a distinctive morphology: an item would not *be* a C-fiber unless it had certain specific kinds of nonconscious functionally related parts. How many such parts must C-fibers have? The count may be performed on a very small scale, perhaps even at a level of macromolecules. So the count can be very large, far exceeding anything the ancients would have dreamt. Suppose it is at least 74,985,263. Then it is necessary that an item is a C-fiber only if it has 74,985,263 or more nonconscious functionally related parts. In turn, it is necessary that a being x has been firing C-fibers only if x has some parts that have 74,985,263 or more functionally related nonconscious parts. This necessary condition has the desired semantic stability: any population of speakers in an epistemic situation qualitatively identical to ours would use "has some parts that have 74,985,263 or more functionally related nonconscious parts" the way we do. By "74,985,263," they would mean 74,985,263; by "function," function; by "relation," relation; by "non," non; by "conscious," conscious; and so on.[30]

Using these ideas, we may reformulate the weak modal argument thus:

1 It is possible that a being could have pain but lack parts that have 74,985,263 or more functionally related nonconscious parts.

2 If the property of being in pain = the property of having firing C-fibers, then necessarily, for all x, x is in pain iff x has firing C-fibers.

3 Necessarily, for all x, if x has firing C-fibers, x has some parts that have 74,985,263 or more functionally related nonconscious parts.

Therefore, the property of being in pain ≠ the property of having firing C-fibers.

The argument is logically valid. (2) is undeniable. Because (3) is supplied by scientific essentialists, we are entitled to accept it. After all, the threat to the original modal argument came from scientific essentialists. So the issue comes down to (1), which seems intuitive. When the rephrasal strategy is applied to (1), we get "It is possible for there to be a population of speakers in an epistemic situation qualitatively identical to ours who would make a true statement by asserting 'There is a being that has pain but lacks parts that have 74,985,263 or more functionally related nonconscious parts'. " But such populations of speakers would mean by this sentence what we mean, as already indicated. Thus, the rephrasal entails the original report. So, given that scientific essentialists are committed to the truth of the rephrasal, they are also committed to the truth of the original report. Hence, they are forced to accept (1) and, in turn, the revised modal argument.

Let us summarize. First, the intuitions needed to extend scientific essentialism from terms like "water" to terms like "pain" are simply missing. Therefore, there is no apparent conflict between pro- and anti-scientific-essentialist intuitions regarding such terms. In view of this, there is no evident requirement to subject the original argument's key modal intuition to the rephrasal strategy. Absent an apparent conflict among our intuitions, the presumption is that the original argument is sound as it stands. Second, even if this assessment is mistaken, the argument can be reformulated so that (1) – its key modal premise – retains its original force even when subjected to the rephrasal strategy. This revised argument withstands the scientific-essentialist critique "twice over."

We thus have a successful modal argument against the thesis that being in pain = having firing C-fibers. Presumably, for any finitely stateable first-order physical state S_i, the argument could be adapted to refute the thesis that being in pain = being in S_i

Despite this result, we have not yet ruled out the thesis that being in pain has an infinitary (or indefinitely long) definition-by-cases. So the following sort of property identity is still in the running: being in pain = being in S_1 or S_2 or S_3 . . . Advocates of the multiple-realizability argument would not be troubled by this prospect, for they are prepared to invoke auxiliary assumptions to exclude this kind of property identity (see section 1). But such auxiliary assumptions are quite problematic.

To refute this sort of property identity, one must turn from the above weak modal argument to a strong modal argument. Notice that the property of having a multiplicity of functionally related nonmental parts is a necessary condition of every physical condition – S_1, S_2, S_3 . . . – of the sort identity theorists would entertain. Suppose the first premise in our weak modal argument is replaced with the following: it is possible for there to be a being who feels pain but does not have a multiplicity of functionally related nonmental parts. The resulting argument is valid, so its correctness comes down to the truth of this premise. Many people – if they set aside philosophical biases – would find this new modal premise intuitive. Moreover, the intuition supporting it survives both stages of the aggressive scientific-essentialist attack. First, there is no contrary twin-Earth intuition to compete with it. So the presumption is that it is immune to scientific-essentialist worries. At the second stage, the intuition also fares well. For, when our report is subjected to the rephrasal strategy, it retains its original force. But it must be admitted that this strong modal premise is not flat out obvious; if we accept it, we do so with hesitation. For this reason, we are not entitled to conclude with conviction that the identity thesis in its full generality is false.

The problem, to repeat, is that the new premise is controversial. Is there any propect of settling whether that premise is false or true? Yes. After all, in the case of the weak modal argument, we were able to establish that it is possible for there to be a being that feels pain but lacks parts that have 74,985,263 or more functionally related nonconscious parts. Virtually everyone (even the identity theorist) has the intuition that this is possible. This intuition is as vivid as those invoked in other successful philosophical arguments (e.g. the intuitions invoked to show that it is possible to have justified true beliefs that are not knowledge or, indeed, those invoked to establish scientific essentialism: twin-Earth, cat-looking robots, gold-appearing compounds, nonidentical qualitative duplicates). Moreover, this intuition retains its original force upon scientific-essentialist rephrasal, so it is the kind of intuition that must be accepted according to scientific-essentialist procedure. It is thus possible for there to be beings (i.e. you and I) who are able to answer a priori the question of whether it is possible for there to be a being that feels pain but lacks parts that have 74,985,263 or more functionally related nonconscious parts. Let us grant, by contrast, that you and I are *not* able to answer a priori the question at issue in the strong modal argument (i.e. the question of whether it is possible for there to be a being that feels pain but lacks a multiplicity of functionally related nonmental parts). Let us also grant that the answer to this question might well differ from the answer to the first question. Nevertheless, the two questions are otherwise quite alike: they each concern the possibility of pain in the absence of certain nonmental properties. Moreover, those properties – and the questions themselves – are expressed in the very same sort of semantically stable vocabulary, which retains its original force upon scientific-essentialist rephrasal. Given that it is possible for there to be beings (you and I) who are able to answer the first question a priori, then unless a specific barrier is identified, uniformity supports the presumption that it should also be possible for there to be beings (though perhaps *wildly* more intelligent than you and I) who are able to answer the second question a priori (by intuition, argument, or theory).

6 The Certainty Argument Reformulated

The previous reformulation of the certainty argument used an instance of the following premise:

> It is possible for some being to know a priori whether or not being *F* = being *G*.

We saw that this premise holds when ⌜*F*⌝ and ⌜*G*⌝ are predicates like "is a computable function" and "is a recursive function." However, if scientific essentialism is right, it fails when ⌜*F*⌝ and ⌜*G*⌝ are predicates like "is water" and "is H_2O." So in view of Boyd's point about the resemblance between "has firing C-fibers" and "is H_2O," scientific essentialists might plausibly challenge the premise when ⌜*F*⌝ is "is in pain" and ⌜*G*⌝ is "has firing C-fibers." Likewise, they might plausibly challenge the premise when ⌜*F*⌝ is "is in pain" and ⌜*G*⌝ is any reasonable first-order physical predicate: "is in S_1," "is in S_2" . . . The discussion in the preceding section suggests, however, that we can get by with a weakened premise that involves just a *necessary condition* for these physical predicates. With this in mind we propose to recast the certainty argument in the following form:

1 It is possible for there to be a being who knows a priori whether or not it is possible for something to be *F* and not *G*.

2 It is possible for there to be a being who knows that he is *F* solely by virtue of the fact that he currently is *F*.

3 *If* it is possible for there to be a being who knows a priori that it is not possible for something to be *F* and not *G*, and it is possible for there to be a being who knows that he is *F* solely by virtue of the fact that he currently is *F*, *then* it is possible for there to be a being who knows that he is *G* solely on the basis of reason and the fact that he currently is *F*.

4 It is *not* possible for there to be a being who knows that he is *G* solely on the basis of reason and the fact that he currently is *F*.

Therefore, it is possible for something to be *F* and not *G*.

This argument is valid. To see why, suppose that it is *not* possible for something to be *F* and not *G*. Then, (1) would imply that it is possible for there to be a being who knows a priori that this is indeed not possible. From this, (2), (3), and *modus ponens*, it follows that it is possible for there to be a being who knows that he is G solely on the basis of reason and the fact that he currently is F. But this contradicts (4). So the supposition is false, and the desired conclusion follows: it *is* possible for something to be F and not G.

If $\ulcorner F \urcorner$ is "is in pain" and $\ulcorner G \urcorner$ is "has a multiplicity of functionally related nonmental parts," this conclusion is just the first premise of the strong modal argument, namely, the premise that it is possible for there to be a being that feels pain but lacks a multiplicity of functionally related nonmental parts. Since the remainder of that argument is unproblematic (even to identity theorists), its conclusion would follow: the identity thesis in its full generality would be false. Thus, the reformulated certainty argument may be thought of as a way of establishing the first premise of the strong modal argument without having to rely on a controversial modal intuition.

Since this reformulated certainty argument is valid, its correctness turns on the truth of the premises. But each one has good reasons supporting it. With $\ulcorner F \urcorner$ and $\ulcorner G \urcorner$ as indicated, (1) is: it is possible for there to be a being who knows a priori whether or not it is possible for a being to be in pain and not have a multiplicity of functionally related nonmental parts. This premise, however, is the point defended at the close of the previous section when we compared the weak and strong modal arguments.[31] The weak modal argument is concerned with the question of whether it is possible for a being to be in pain and not have parts that have 74,985,263 or more functionally related nonconscious parts. The strong modal argument is concerned with the question of whether it is possible for a being to be in pain and not have a multiplicity of functionally related nonmental parts. Given that it is possible for there to be a being (e.g. you or I) who is able to know the answer to the first question a priori, what could block the possibility of a being (perhaps wildly more intelligent) who is able to know the answer to the second question a priori. At present we have no reason to think that there exists a barrier to the possibility of this a priori knowledge.[32] So unless we establish that there exists a barrier we must either accept the possibility of this a priori knowledge or flaunt uniformity considerations and accept an otherwise avoidable mystery.

This leaves us with (2), (3), and (4). But they are substantially the same as premises (2), (3), and (4) in the previous formulation of the certainty argument. Although we have already seen that those premises are acceptable, it would be good to say something about the present premise (4). When in that premise we speak of one's knowing that one has a multiplicity of functionally related nonmental parts on the basis of reason and the fact that one currently is in pain, our intention (as before) is that the person is to have no prior exposure to physical theories, their instruments, or their terminology. Further, our intention is to rule out evidential use of any of the following: sensory facts besides the fact that one is in pain, memories of sensory facts, previously learned empirical theories, testimony of others, and so forth. Understood this way, (4) is compelling: if the evidential resources are restricted in all these ways, the person plainly could not on that slender basis know that he possesses a multiplicity of functionally related nonmental parts. When these restrictions are fully in view, even people in the grip of the identity theory must accept the premise. For its denial is tantamount to holding that, from the sole fact that one is in pain, it is possible to give an otherwise a priori argument for the existence of the external world and one's bodily station in it.[33] This flies in the face of the main lessons of modern epistemology.

The argument therefore seems to go through. We used the weak modal argument to give an a priori defense of the first premise of our certainty argument, namely, it is possible for there to be a being (perhaps wildly more intelligent than ourselves) who is able to know a priori whether pain without a multiplicity of functionally related nonmental parts is possible. This premise, together with the other three premises, yields the conclusion that pain without a multiplicity of functionally related nonmental parts is indeed possible. Because the argument is wholly a priori, it turns out that beings not unlike *ourselves* ought to be able to know a priori that pain without a multiplicity of functionally related nonmental parts is possible.

As indicated, this bit of knowledge is the first premise of the (otherwise uncontroversial) strong modal argument. By thus weaving together the weak modal argument, the certainty argument, and the strong modal argument, we arrive at a refutation of the identity thesis in its full generality.

7 Implications for the Mind–Body Relation

This argument is consistent with certain versions of functionalism which allow for the possibility of pain without a multiplicity of nonmental functional parts. The argument is also consistent with the thesis that there are first-order physical properties that are logically sufficient for mental properties. The Nagel–Jackson knowledge argument is bolder in that, if correct, it would refute both functionalism and the sufficiency thesis. Does the above critique of aggressive scientific essentialism help to salvage the knowledge argument? No. Functionalists may rebut the argument just as before (see note 17). Moreover, even if functionalism were known to be false – say, because certain qualia are totally indistinguishable functionally – knowledge arguments still could not refute the sufficiency thesis. To see why, suppose Mary has experienced one of these qualia P and has a semantically stable expression for it. Suppose there is a creature who also experiences P but who differs significantly from Mary in appearance, behavior, and physiology. Then, presumably, from the physical facts Mary could not infer a priori that the creature experiences P. However, this would not *imply* that the creature's physical properties are not logically sufficient for experiencing P. For there is an alternate explanation: the a priori inference would be possible only if both the mental property P *and* the relevant physical properties were expressible with semantically stable expressions; but, echoing Boyd, scientific essentialism shows that such expressions are not possible for the *physical properties*. (For example, consider a possible world whose matter is structurally and functionally like the matter in the actual world but which differs from the latter in *scale*. Every semantically stable predicate that would apply to "fibers" composed of the one type of matter would apply to "fibers" composed of the other. The problem is that, if functionalism is false, "fibers" composed of the new kind of matter might fail to be sufficient for P.) The fact that scientific essentialism applies to the creature's physical properties could thus explain why Mary cannot know a priori the (supposed) fact that the physical properties are logically sufficient for P. So, *pace* Nagel and Jackson, the existence of unanswerable "open questions" about the "subjective" (even in the presence of all the relevant "objective" knowledge) would not *imply* that physical properties are not logically sufficient for mental properties.

As noted at the outset, prevailing opinion is that the identity thesis is false: mental properties are not identical to first-order physical properties. We found, however, that the currently popular arguments for this opinion are flawed and that to refute the identity thesis one must draw from the history of philosophy, weaving together (cautious reformulations of) the traditional modal and certainty arguments. But the resulting argument goes beyond merely denying the identity thesis; it has some further implications concerning the nature of the mind–body relation.

The first of these implications has to do with a certain version of functionalism which identifies mental states with tokenings of Mentalese sentences in a Belief Box, a Desire Box, etc. (see, e.g. Fodor, 1987). According to the associated functional definitions, it is necessary, for example, that x believes p iff there is a Mentalese sentence S whose content is p and a token s of S is present in x's Belief Box. The idea is that the various expressions on the right-hand side of this biconditional may be characterized functionally in causal terms. What is it for a Mentalese sentence-token to be present in a Belief Box? Recall that Mentalese sentence-tokens are not mental entities akin to, say, sense data or mental images; they are virtually never "in the mind" in the sense of being actual contents of consciousness. In view of this, it is difficult to make sense of the view except in physical terms: for a Mentalese sentence-token s to be present in x's Belief Box, x must have a multiplicity of functionally related physical parts; one of them would be the Belief Box and another, the sentence token *s* somehow physically present there. In turn, it is difficult to see how such sentence-tokens could exist unless they exist in a medium, and it is difficult to see what the medium could be unless it is a physical medium. If this is right, token-in-a-box functionalism would seem to imply that a necessary condition of having mental properties is having a multiplicity of functionally related physical parts. But, if correct, our argument against the identity thesis shows that it is possible for there to be a being that has mental properties but not a multiplicity of functionally related physical parts. So the argument would seem to imply that token-in-a-box functionalism is mistaken.

There is a certain irony here. When the empirical cognitive science which is inspired by this version of functionalism is purged of the latter's metaphysical baggage, it suggests a novel conception of the mind–body relationship. This would go in two steps.

Notice that the argument against the identity thesis apparently would go through if "multiplicity of functionally related nonmental parts" were replaced with simply "nonmental parts." But having nonmental parts is a necessary condition for having a body. The conclusion of the new argument would be that it is possible for there to be beings that feel pain but that have no bodies. Now consider any array of conscious mental properties (intentional as well as purely qualitative) which is sufficient for a being's having a mind. In a variant of the new argument just described, let this array of mental properties take the place of the single qualitative property being in pain. The resulting argument would also seem to go through. Its conclusion would be that it is possible for there to be beings that have minds but no bodies.

For the second step, consider a possible world containing one of these beings (call it *m*). Evidently, there could be an alternate possible world just like the original except that, in addition to *m*, there exists a body *b* with the following characteristics. At a certain level of description, *b* has a functional organization that is isomorphic to *m*'s psychological organization in the following sense: *m* believes *p* iff there is a Mentalese sentence *S* whose content is *p* and a token *s* of *S* is in *b*'s Belief Box; *m* desires *p* iff there is a Mentalese sentence *S* whose content is *p* and a token *s* of *S* is in *b*'s Desire Box; it appears to *m* that *p* iff there is a Mentalese sentence *S* whose content is *p* and a token *s* of *S* is in *b*'s Appearance Box; *m* wills *p* iff there is a Mentalese sentence *S* whose content is *p* and a token *s* of *S* is in *b*'s Volition Box; and so forth. (The intention here is that the constants occurring on the right-hand sides of these biconditionals – "Mentalese sentence," "content," "token," "in," "Belief Box," etc. – are *new technical* terms defined within empirical cognitive science. For example, the "boxes" might be regions of the brain and the "tokens" activated neural nets.) Now suppose that in the envisaged possible world these biconditionals are not just materially true but that they hold as a matter of nomological necessity.[34] If these conditions were fulfilled, it would evidently be correct to say that *m* has a body, namely, *b*. This nomologically necessary relationship would be wholly unlike that of a pilot to a ship or a ghost to a machine. Apparently this is one (but not the only) coherent conception of the mind–body relationship. The irony is that empirical cognitive science, stripped of the metaphysics which happened historically to inspire it, provides the framework for articulating this conception.

Notice, finally, that in the possible world just described the psycho-physical correlations between *m* and *b* were only nomologically necessary; they were not necessary *tout court*. Accordingly, it would seem that there could be another possible world that is a *physical duplicate* of that possible world but in which the indicated psycho-physical correlations do not hold. For example, there could be a world in which a physical duplicate of *b* exists and in which *m* exists but in which *m*'s mental life is quite different from what it is in the world where the psycho-physical correlations do hold. If such a thing is possible, then there can be mental differences without physical differences. If so, at least one popular kind of strong supervenience principle would fail to hold.[35]

Where does this leave us? When we carefully followed scientific-essentialist procedure, we found good intuitive grounds for accepting the possibility of being in pain without 74,985,263 or more functionally related nonconscious parts. It is difficult to deny this. Moreover, it is hard to believe that the epistemic situation would be necessarily different if "74,985,263 or more" were replaced with simply "a multiplicity." Reflections like these led to the conclusion that it should be at least possible for sufficiently intelligent beings to be able to know, without the aid of empirical science, whether or not pain without a multiplicity of functionally related nonmental parts is possible. This in turn led us to conclude (by the reformulated certainty argument) that it is indeed possible for there to be pain without a multiplicity of functionally related nonmental parts. This permitted us to infer (by the strong modal argument) that the identity thesis is false. Each step in this reasoning seems hard to resist. Prevailing opinion about the falsity of the identity thesis thus seems to be sustained. But the argument seems to have further implications concerning the mind–body relation. Rejecting the identity thesis is evidently not the entirely neutral proposition that one might have thought.

Notes

Much of the material in this paper was originally presented in a philosophy of mind seminar which I gave in fall 1983. I presented drafts of the paper at the University of Colorado in fall 1989, the University of Western Washington in spring 1990, and the National Humanities Center in January 1993. For helpful comments, I wish to thank Erik Anderson, Louise Antony, John Bickle, Brad Cohen, Mark Hinchliff, Paul Houda, Norman Kretzmann, Stephen Leeds, Samuel Levey, Joseph Levine, William Lycan, Jennifer Murphy, Michael Peirce, C. D. C. Reeve, William Reinhardt, Georges Rey, Sydney Shoemaker, Gary Stahl, Carol Voeller.

1 I will not discuss the token-identity thesis (the thesis that mental events are identical to first-order physical events). Nor will I discuss the thesis, associated with certain versions of functionalism, that mental properties are identical to second-order physical properties.

2 There is also Donald Davidson's (1970) argument. I will not be able to examine this argument here, but the following remarks will help to locate it within the framework of my discussion. Davidson defends the principle of the anomalism of the mental. As it is intended, this principle does not on its own rule out the property-identity thesis *in its full generality*. For example, as it is intended, it does not on its own rule out the identity between, say, the property of being in pain and a disjunctive property formed from some infinite (or indefinitely large or particularly motley) collection of first-order physical properties. To rule out this and kindred property-identities, one could conjoin the anomalism of the mental and the special auxiliary premises invoked in the multiple-realizability argument. The resulting argument would be valid. But those auxiliary premises turn out to be quite problematic, as we will see in section 1.

3 Possibility in this sense does not imply causal or nomological possibility. "Possible" is used here for the much weaker modality according to which something is possible if and only if it is necessary or contingent.

4 An alternative, very radical response is to deny that modal intuitions have any evidential weight. For criticism of this radical position, see Bealer (1992). A somewhat less radical response to the modal argument is to dismiss dogmatically the particular modal intuition on which it is based. But this intuition is one of a large family of modal intuitions that would drive analogous modal arguments against the identity theory. Given that modal intuitions have prima-facie evidential weight, it is the obligation of the detractor to provide a systematic explanation of why this large family of intuitions is going wrong. Scientific essentialism provides such an explanation. Besides it, no other plausible explanation is known.

5 This is the kind of strong modal premise which Kripke (1980) defends.

6 William Hart (1988) defends this sort of strong modal premise by means of an imaginability argument. But imaginability has questionable evidential weight. For example, Escher drawings of impossible situations are imaginable. What is needed for a successful modal argument is a genuine *intuition*, but one which is immune to the scientific-essentialist worry. See Bealer (1992) for the difference between imagination and intuition.

7 Unlike strong modal arguments, this argument is consistent with a weak materialism according to which: (1) particular first-order physical properties provide sufficient conditions for, e.g., being in pain; and (2) a necessary

condition for, e.g., being in pain is having a body. I should emphasize that the history of the multiple-realizability argument is rather tangled and several distinct versions are alive in contemporary discussions. Some people even seem to equate it with the weak modal argument.

8 What about the following finite "definition": "Hu iff$_{def}$ u is one of the space-time points that *in the actual world* is occupied by a subatomic particle"? The problem is that in the language of our human counterparts in some other possible world these words would not define H because *their* expression "the actual world" would refer to *their* world not ours. The property H would be definable in their words but by means of the sort of infinitary definition indicated in the text. Incidentally, someone might try to hold that H does not express *any* property. But since it seems to, the burden of proof is on the detractor to show otherwise. I can see no non-question-begging way to do so.

9 Instead of relying on a distinction between "natural" and "Cambridge" properties, some nonmodal formulations of the argument rely on a distinction between causal and noncausal properties or between "natural" states and mere "Cambridge" states or between "natural" kinds and mere "Cambridge" classifications. The following articles present nonmodal formulations that, at least implicitly, invoke some such metaphysical distinction: Hilary Putnam (1967, 1975a); Ned Block and Jerry A. Fodor (1972); Jerry A. Fodor (1974). Putnam and Fodor also seem to accept (something like) the following auxiliary premise: if $\ulcorner \ldots F \ldots \urcorner$ qualifies as a good explanation for a certain purpose (e.g. understanding human motivation) and $\ulcorner \ldots G$ or H or $I \ldots \urcorner$ does not, then the property of being $F \neq$ the property of being G or H or I. This premise is based on a fallacy akin to the paradox of analysis. For more on this sort of fallacy, see section 2.

10 See, e.g. Jaegwon Kim (1972). With this point in mind, we should be prepared to take the term "firing C-fibers," not only literally, but also as a dummy for a term that neuroscientists of the future might provide, and we should be prepared to assume that this term successfully picks out a physical basis for pain that is shared by all actually existing species that feel pain.

11 Suppose that the property of being in pain has an adequate definition-by-cases; e.g. the "cases" might be: pain-in-man, pain-in-dogs, etc. Then, in view of the point made earlier, it would make no ontological difference whether the list is finite or infinite.

12 For a recent reformulation of the certainty argument, see George Myro (1993). Certainty arguments are closely related to incorrigibility arguments; see Richard Rorty (1970). A recent reformulation and defense of the latter kind of argument is in Richard Warner (1993).

13 The following present versions of the knowledge argument: Paul E. Meehl (1966); Thomas Nagel (1974); Frank Jackson (1982, 1986), Howard Robinson (1982); Richard Warner (1986); John Foster (1991, esp. pp. 62–79). I owe the point about G. E. Moore to Gary Stahl.

14 Consider an analogy:

The present moment is a time t such that I am now certain that I exist at t.
12:51 p.m. is a time t such that I am not now certain that I exist at t.

Therefore, the present moment $\neq$ 12:51 p.m.

This argument is valid. But in fact the present moment = 12:51 p.m. Given this fact and given the truth of the first premise, it follows that the second premise is false. The point is that, if I am in doubt about whether the present moment = 12:51 p.m., I am in no position to be asserting the second premise.

Paul Churchland (1985) makes analogous criticisms of the Nagel–Jackson argument. But his criticism collapses when it comes to the intensional-abstraction formulation of their argument. Incidentally, in his paper Churchland commits himself to the reducibility of phenomenal qualities to first-order physical properties.

15 This style of criticism evidently applies against George Myro's (1993) variation on the certainty argument, and Richard Warner's (1993) variation on the incorrigibility argument. But our final reformulation and defense of the modal and certainty arguments can, I believe, be successfully adapted for use on behalf of their arguments.

16 See Jackson (1986). Given the structural similarity between the knowledge argument and G. E. Moore's open-question argument, the present connection to the paradox of analysis is predictable.

17 Suppose Mary is told the scientific definitions before her release. She would not *fully understand* them – not the way people with color experience do. But this does not show that there are *two* sets of definitional facts; there is only *one*. This can be seen as follows: if Mary is asked to tell us the definitional facts after her release, she would give *exactly the same* answers she would give if she were asked before her release. Nor would her words have changed their meanings; she would just understand them more fully. With this in mind, identity theorists should put their point thus: anyone who knows with understanding all the physical and definitional facts is in a position to know with understanding *all* the facts.

Functionalists may use these points to rebut the knowledge argument: if Mary knew and understood the relevant functional definitions (i.e. of *this*, experiencing, being like, red), she would be in a position to know all the facts (including the functional-cum-definitional fact that *this* is what it is like to experience red); but it is impossible for her to know and understand these things without first having the relevant experiences.

18 An even more cautious formulation results when "knows" is replaced throughout with the weaker phrase "judges truly and is able to justify."

19 Paul Churchland (1985) claims that people with prior exposure to physiological theory and its terminology could have introspective knowledge of their own brain states. I find this claim incredible. In any case it has no bearing on (4), for as it is intended, (4) rules out such prior exposure.

20 Kripke tells us, "*[I]t could have turned out that P* entails that *P could have been the case*" (1980, pp. 141–2). For ease of exposition, I will slide between ⌜It could have turned out that *P*⌝, ⌜That *P* could have been the case⌝, and ⌜Possibly *P*⌝. No question will be begged, for I could always revert to the first form.

21 "Pain, on the other hand, is not picked out by one of its accidental properties; rather it is picked out by the property of being in pain itself, by its immediate phenomenological quality. Thus pain, unlike heat, is not only rigidly design-

ated by 'pain' but the reference of the designator is determined by an essential property of the referent" (Kripke, 1980, pp. 152–3). See Richard Boyd (1980, p. 84).

22 Michael Levin (1975) tries to make this point with the *topic-neutral* description "what is going on in me when my skin is being damaged." But this description does not apply *uniquely* to pain. To assume that it does would be to beg the question. In my view, the only descriptions that non-question-beggingly apply uniquely to pain must be at least implicitly mentalistic.

In response to the point in the text Kripke might claim that *in the epistemic situation he has in mind* we do not use contingent, accidental properties like these to pick out pain. But he would not be entitled to this reply. Given that he has abandoned first-person authority as to whether his intuitions are descriptive or nondescriptive, he cannot plausibly claim to have first-person authority to the effect that, if his mental contents happen to be descriptive, then those descriptive contents are essential (i.e. rigid) rather than accidental (i.e. non-rigid). A person's first-person authority is not selectively accurate in this way.

23 Recall that the original purpose was to find a rephrasal strategy with two features. First, it *can* be wielded in such a way that our pro-scientific-essentialist intuitions retain their original force and our anti-scientific-essentialist intuitions lose their original force, thereby being rendered consistent with scientific essentialism. Second, the rephrasal strategy *cannot* be wielded in such a way that our anti-scientific-essentialist intuitions retain their original force and our pro-scientific-essentialist intuitions lose their original force, thereby being rendered consistent with traditional anti-scientific-essentialism. If and only if these two conditions are met does the rephrasal strategy successfully break the stalemate. The problem is that the present rephrasal strategy – rephrasal by means of definite description – fails to meet the second condition.

24 The following illustrates this three-step recipe in the case of modal intuitions concerning water. (1) Hold that "water" is synonymous to (something like) "the clear thirst-quenching stuff." (2) Deem the anti-SE intuition expressed by "Possibly, water $\neq H_2O$" to be true, correctly reported, and literally synonymous to the narrow-scope reading of "Possibly, the clear thirst-quenching stuff $\neq H_2O$." (3) Deem the pro-SE intuition uncritically reported with "Possibly, there is a twin-Earth such that . . . the clear thirst-quenching samples on the twin-Earth are not samples of water and, accordingly, water $\neq$ the clear thirst-quenching stuff" to be true but incorrectly reported; it is correctly reported with (something like) "There is a possible but nonactual twin-Earth world such that . . . the stuff that *in the actual world* is clear and thirst-quenching $\neq$ the stuff that *in the possible but nonactual world* is clear and thirst-quenching." This rephrasal is entirely consistent with traditional anti-SE. Note that the description "the stuff that *in the actual world* . . ." is rigid because of its reference to actuality; since its rigidity is independent of scope, there is no conflict with Kripke's cautionary remarks on scope in the Preface to *Naming and Necessity* (1980, pp. 11–14). Now someone already leaning toward scientific essentialism might not find these anti-scientific-essentialist description rephrasals particularly plausible. But, as we have noted, the description rephrasals made by Kripke in defense of scientific essentialism are

not particularly plausible, either. They certainly are not grounded in linguistic behavior or in phenomenology.

25 A caveat is in order. It could be objected that the first rephrasal strategy is overly metalinguistic; e.g. it fails the Langford–Church translation test. No doubt this objection is right. However, scientific essentialists can accept the objection and adopt instead the following object-language version of the rephrasal strategy: the true intuition that we would incorrectly report with ⌜Possibly A⌝ is correctly reported with ⌜It is possible for there to be people in an epistemic situation qualitatively identical to ours such that the thought they have which corresponds to our thought that A would be true⌝. Now in all substantive respects relevant to our discussion this object-language version yields the same results as the original metalinguistic version. Because the metalinguistic version is familiar and because it is so easy to work with, I will take the liberty of using it in the remainder of our discussion. Readers who are uncomfortable with this are invited to substitute the suggested object-language version at appropriate places.

26 Consider the pro-SE intuition reported with "Possibly, there is a twin-Earth such that . . . the clear thirst-quenching samples are not samples of water." Anti-scientific-essentialists must hold that this intuition is true but incorrectly reported; it is correctly reported with "It is possible for there to be a population of speakers in an epistemic situation qualitatively identical to ours who would make a true statement by asserting 'There is a twin-Earth such that . . . the clear thirst-quenching samples are not samples of water' with normal literal intent." But given their internalism, our anti-scientific-essentialists must hold that such a population of speakers would mean what we mean with "The clear thirst-quenching samples are not samples of water." This commits our anti-scientific-essentialists to holding that the rephrasal has the same pro-SE force as the original report. To escape this consequence, our anti-scientific-essentialists might try to hold that, e.g. "thirst-quenching" would mean something different for the envisaged population. But how could it, unless thirst-quenchingness fits into the SE picture? And if thirst-quenchingness fits in, surely water would, too.

27 Some people seem to believe that, whenever something is open to any kind of scientific study, SE automatically holds for it. But this just begs the question in the text. See Bealer (1987) for a theoretical discussion of why and how the scope of SE must be circumscribed. For example, I show there that analogues of the twin-Earth argument fail for functional (as opposed to compositional) terms like "food," "house," etc. Given this, there is certainly no presumption that scientific essentialism holds for mental expressions.

28 Someone might respond that the pain-intuition is missing and the water-intuition is not because we do not seriously accept the pain/C-fiber correlation whereas we do the water/H_2O correlation. But this cannot be the explanation, for we have water-intuitions associated with *hypothetical* correlations which we actually *reject*. For example, we have the intuition that, *if* our chemists had been deceived and all and only water samples here on Earth were really composed of ABC ($\neq H_2O$) and if there were a twin-Earth . . . *then* XYZ ($\neq$ ABC) samples on the twin-Earth would not be samples of water. Clearly, the presence or

absence of a serious acceptance of the relevant empirical theories is not what explains the presence or absence of intuitions regarding these twin-Earth conditionals. My own view (Bealer, 1987) is that, if one's cognitive conditions approximate the ideal, a twin-Earth intuition is present iff an associated general principle holds for relevant underlying semantically stable concepts (i.e. the sort of concepts expressible with terms that would express the very same concept in any population of speakers in a qualitatively identical epistemic situation). If in suitably good cognitive conditions a given twin-Earth intuition is missing (as in the case of twin-Earth intuitions about notions like food or house), this tells us something significant, namely, that the associated general principle does not hold for our underlying semantically stable concepts. I believe that something like this is going on in the case of the missing twin-Earth pain-intuition in the text.

29 When the argument is formulated this way, it counts against David Lewis's version of the identity thesis, at least as I understand it. See Lewis (1966, 1980).

30 Even if these terms meant something different, their meanings would be *very close* to the English (this is all that is needed to construct a possibility that is inconsistent with the thesis that being in pain = having firing C-fibers). The indicated terms are thus fundamentally different from terms like "water," "tree," "vat," "brain"; considerations such as those raised by Hilary Putnam (1981) therefore do not apply.

31 Another defense is to argue that there is no relevant difference between the possibility of the a priori modal knowledge at issue in (1) and the actual a priori modal knowledge associated with scientific essentialism. Another defense is theoretical: the best theory that explains our capacity for a priori knowledge of various uncontroversial possibilities implies, as a corollary, the possibility of the a priori modal knowledge at issue in (1). This view is developed in my forthcoming book *Philosophical Limits of Science*.

32 Epistemology has uncovered only two relevant potential barriers to a priori knowledge of whether a proposition is possible. The first is SE. But we have shown that the terms used to state the proposition at issue in premise (1) are immune to both stages of the SE argument, and so we have no reason to think that SE blocks the possibility of a priori knowledge of whether that proposition is possible. The second kind of potential barrier results from limitations on intelligence: if a being's intelligence is too low, the being will be unable to obtain a priori knowledge of various possibilities. But we have no reason to think that there are necessary limitations on intelligence which block the mere possibility of a being with the a priori knowledge at issue in premise (1). On the one hand, the sort of question at issue (i.e. whether pain without a multiplicity of functionally related nonmental parts is possible) does not seem to be the sort of question which would require infinitary intelligence (e.g. for doing infinitary proofs, infinitary computations, etc.). Some finite level (though perhaps wildly beyond ours) ought to suffice. But, intuitively, for any finite level of intelligence, it is possible for some being to be that intelligent. (This intuition is expressed in semantically stable terms, so SE is committed to accepting it.) On the other hand, even if infinitary intelligence were

required (e.g. for checking proofs with infinitely many premises, etc.), that should not matter, for we have no reason to doubt the possibility of infinitary intelligence. There are no intuitions that go against this possibility; if anything, intuitions support it. And there are no good arguments against it. (It is far weaker than the possibility of an omniscient, omnipotent, benevolent God; so familiar arguments against the existence of God – e.g. the argument from evil – have no bearing.) SE certainly provides no argument against this possibility.

33 Let me elaborate. Using only your rational faculties and the empirical fact that you are currently experiencing pain, would *you* be able to establish that you have a multiplicity of functionally related nonmental parts? Plainly not. The reason is that it is a matter of real controversy whether or not there could be a being who experiences pain but has no body; if your empirical evidence were restricted to your current pain, you would be unable to rule out the proposition that you have no body. Of course, there are several contingent truths which you could establish on this slender evidential basis. For example, using your *logical* faculty, you could derive the contingent truth that you are not in pain only if you are in pain. Using your *intuitive* faculty, you could infer that there exists at least one phenomenal quality of which some conscious being is aware. But it is implausible that, using these two faculties and the fact that you are in pain, you could rule out the proposition that you have no body. Could you construct a *theory* which explains your current pain better than all competitors and which implies that you have a body? Could you construct an *argument* showing that this is a "condition for the very possibility" of your being in pain? There is reason to think that you are unable to do this, namely, the pattern of failure in this connection throughout modern epistemology. Now suppose that you were to become more intelligent. Is it plausible that your situation would be relevantly different? Might there be some formal logical consequence that you had missed which, now that you are more intelligent, would come into view so that you could deduce that you have a body? That is implausible. With your greater intelligence, might you now be able to make an intuitive inference that you have a body? That too is implausible. Perhaps with your greater intelligence you could discover a new theory or argument establishing that you have a body. Although we are not in a position to rule out this prospect with certainty, the pattern of failure in modern epistemology again makes this prospect look dim. Would the situation be different if you became supersmart (e.g. so smart that you could perform infinite computations or derivations or so smart that you could deal with infinitely complex examples)? It does not seem so. For the problem at hand does not seem to be the kind for which such powers would make any difference. Now if, even with such increases in intelligence, it would be impossible for you to establish the desired result using only the indicated evidential basis, then it is implausible that another being could do so. There would be no relevant difference between such a being and you. Surely, these considerations make premise (4) reasonable.

34 On the indicated cognitive science picture, something roughly like the following purely *physical* principles (relevant to sense perception and action) would also

hold as a matter of nomological necessity: if p is a (certain kind of) elementary fact about macroscopic objects in b's immediate vicinity, b's transducers are well-functioning and suitably situated with respect to p, external conditions are normal, and p is S's content, then a token s of S will thereupon come to be inscribed in b's Appearance Box; if p is a (certain kind of) elementary macroscopic proposition about b's nomologically possible behavior, b is in normal well-functioning condition, p is S's content, and a token s of S is inscribed in b's Volition Box, then p will thereupon come to be true.

35 Because "alien" natural properties need not be involved in the envisaged possible world, this evidently is also a counterexample to David Lewis's (1983) weak supervenience principle.

References

Bealer, G. (1987) "The philosophical limits of scientific essentialism," *Philosophical Perspectives* 1, pp. 289–365.

Bealer, G. (1992) "The incoherence of empiricism," *Proceedings of the Aristotelian Society*, suppl. vol. 66, pp. 99–138.

Bealer, G. (forthcoming) *Philosophical Limits of Science*, Oxford: Oxford University Press.

Block, N. and Fodor, J. A. (1972) "What psychological states are not," *Philosophical Review* 81, pp. 159–81.

Boyd, R. (1980) "Materialism without reductionism: what physicalism does not entail," in N. Block (ed.) *Readings in Philosophy of Psychology*, vol. 1, Cambridge, Mass.: Harvard University Press, pp. 67–106.

Churchland, P. M. (1985) "Reduction, qualia, and the direct introspection of brain states," *Journal of Philosophy* 82, pp. 8–28.

Davidson, D. (1970) "Mental events," in L. Foster and J. W. Swanson (eds) *Experience and Theory*, Amherst, Mass.: University of Massachusetts Press, pp. 79–101.

Fodor, J. A. (1965) "Explanations in psychology," in M. Black (ed.) *Philosophy in America*, London: George Allen & Unwin, pp. 161–79.

Fodor, J. A. (1974) "Special sciences, or the disunity of science as a working hypothesis," *Synthese* 28, pp. 97–115.

Fodor, J. A. (1987) *Psychosemantics: the Problem of Meaning in the Philosophy of Mind*, Cambridge, Mass.: Bradford Books/MIT Press.

Foster, J. (1991) *The Immaterial Self: a Defence of the Cartesian Dualist Conception of the Mind*, London: Routledge.

Hart, W. (1988) *Engines of the Soul*, New York: Cambridge University Press.

Jackson, F. (1982) "Epiphenomenal qualia," *Philosophical Quarterly* 32, pp. 127–36.

Jackson, F. (1986) "What Mary didn't know," *Journal of Philosophy* 83, pp. 291–5.

Kim, J. (1972) "Phenomenal properties, psychophysical laws, and the identity theory," *The Monist* 56, pp. 177–92.

Kim, J. (1992) "Multiple realization and the metaphysics of reduction," *Philosophy and Phenomenological Research* 52, pp. 1–26.

Kripke, S. A. (1980) *Naming and Necessity*, Oxford: Blackwell (first published 1972 in D. Davidson and G. Harman (eds) *Semantics of Natural Language*, Dordrecht: Reidel).

Levin, M. (1975) "Kripke's argument against the identity thesis," *Journal of Philosophy* 72, pp. 149–67.

Lewis, D. (1966) "An argument for the identity theory," *Journal of Philosophy* 63, pp. 17–25.

Lewis, D. (1980) "Mad pain and Martian pain," in N. Block (ed.) *Readings in Philosophy of Psychology*, vol. 1, Cambridge, Mass.: Harvard University Press, pp. 216–22.

Lewis, D. (1983) "New work for a theory of universals," *Australasian Journal of Philosophy* 61, pp. 343–77.

Meehl, P. E. (1966) "The compleat autocerebroscopist: a thought-experiment on Professor Feigl's mind–body identity thesis," in P. K. Feyerabend and G. Maxwell (eds) *Mind, Matter, and Method: Essays in Philosophy and Science in Honor of Herbert Feigl*, Minneapolis, Minn.: University of Minnesota Press, pp. 103–80.

Myro, G. (1993) "Thinking," in H. Robinson (ed.) *Objections to Physicalism*, Oxford: Clarendon Press, pp. 27–38.

Nagel, T. (1974) "What is it like to be a bat?" *Philosophical Review* 83, pp. 435–50.

Putnam, H. (1967) "Psychological predicates," in W. H. Capitan and D. D. Merrill (eds) *Art, Mind, and Religion*, Pittsburgh, Pa.: University of Pittsburgh Press, pp. 37–48.

Putnam, H. (1975a) "Philosophy and our mental life," in *Philosophical Papers*, vol. 2, *Mind, Language, and Reality*, Cambridge: Cambridge University Press, pp. 291–303.

Putnam, H. (1975b) "The mental life of some machines," in *Philosophical Papers*, vol. 2, *Mind, Language, and Reality*, Cambridge: Cambridge University Press, pp. 408–28.

Putnam, H. (1981) "Brains in a vat," in *Reason, Truth and History*, Cambridge: Cambridge University Press, pp. 1–21.

Robinson, H. (1982) *Matter and Sense*, Cambridge: Cambridge University Press.

Rorty, R. (1970) "Incorrigibility as the mark of the mental," *Journal of Philosophy* 67, pp. 399–424.

Warner, R. (1986) "A challenge to physicalism," *Australasian Journal of Philosophy* 64, pp. 249–65.

Warner, R. (1993) "Incorrigibility," in H. Robinson (ed.) *Objections to Physicalism*, Oxford: Clarendon Press, pp. 185–205.

Suggestions for Further Reading

1 Introductions and Textbooks

Body and Mind by Keith Campbell (London: Macmillan, 1970; 2nd edn, Notre Dame, Ind. University of Notre Dame Press, 1984) is a very elementary and accessible introduction to the mind–body problem. It discusses the place of this problem in philosophy, how it arises, and such solutions to it as dualism, behaviorism, central-state materialism, a new epiphenomenalism, and functionalism. There is a very good and concise chapter on mind and body in Colin McGinn's *The Character of Mind* (Oxford: Oxford University Press, 1982) in which all main solutions to the problem, from dualism to functionalism, are considered, but without reference to particular philosophers defending them. A less concise and more accessible chapter on the mind–body problem is in a widely used textbook by Paul M. Churchland, *Matter and Consciousness: a Contemporary Introduction to the Philosophy of Mind* (Cambridge, Mass.: Bradford Books MIT Press, 1984; rev. edn, 1988). Churchland discusses the arguments for and against dualism, philosophical behaviorism, reductive materialism (the identity theory), functionalism, and eliminative materialism (which is his favored view). Peter Carruthers in *Introducing Persons: Theories and Arguments in the Philosophy of Mind* (London: Croom Helm, 1986) presents the mind–body problem as deeply interwoven with other questions in philosophy of mind, especially with issues concerning knowledge of mental states and personal identity. He considers two versions of dualism, behaviorism, functionalism, and defends in the end a strong version of materialism according to which each particular conscious state and event is, as a matter of fact, identical with some particular brain-state or event. Peter Smith and O. R. Jones in their *The Philosophy of Mind: an Introduction* (Cambridge: Cambridge University Press, 1986) start from a discussion of dualism and a criticism of several arguments which can be put forward for it. Then they present and defend a broadly functionalist type of physicalism which, according to them, has Aristotelian roots. William Bechtel's *Philosophy of Mind: an Overview for Cognitive Science* (Hillsdale, NJ: Erlbaum, 1988) is an erudite and up-to-date introduction which in large part is devoted to the mind–body problem. It discusses dualism, philosophical behaviorism, type identity theory, eliminative materialism, token-identity theories, and varieties of functionalism. George Graham's *Philosophy of Mind: an Introduction* (Oxford: Blackwell, 1993) is an unconventionally written textbook but some parts of it can be useful for readers interested in the mind–body problem and discussions relevant to it.

2 Anthologies and Collections

The following three anthologies give a very good picture of the mind–body debate as it evolved in the 1960s: J. O'Connor (ed.) *Modern Materialism: Readings on Mind–Body Identity* (New York: Harcourt, Brace & World, 1969); C. V. Borst (ed.) *The Mind–Brain Identity Theory* (London: Macmillan, 1970); D. M. Rosenthal (ed.) *Materialism and the Mind–Body Problem* (Englewood Cliffs, NJ: Prentice-Hall, 1971). *Readings in Philosophy of Psychology*, ed. N. Block (2 vols, Cambridge, Mass.: Harvard University Press, 1980–1) is probably the most widely used anthology in the philosophy of mind. The first volume contains papers on the mind–body problem and has an excellent section on functionalism. *Mind and Cognition: a Reader*, ed. W. G. Lycan (Oxford: Blackwell, 1990) is intended as a sequel to Block collection. It covers all problems in philosophy of mind recently discussed. Two other new anthologies: D. M. Rosenthal (ed.) *The Nature of Mind* (New York: Oxford University Press, 1991) and B. Beakley and P. Ludlow (eds) *The Philosophy of Mind: Classical Problems/Contemporary Issues* (Cambridge, Mass.: MIT Press, 1992), contain a wide selection of texts both historical and recent. Readers who are particularly interested in Davidson's anomalous monism can find the latest stage of the debate on this position in the first part of *Mental Causation*, ed. J. Heil and A. Mele (Oxford: Clarendon Press, 1993). *Objections to Physicalism*, ed. H. Robinson (Oxford: Clarendon Press, 1993) is an interesting collection of original – but fairly advanced – papers criticizing the current physicalist orthodoxy in philosophy of mind.

Bibliography

Achenstein, P. (1977) "The causal relation," *Midwest Studies in Philosophy* 4, pp. 369–86.

Anscombe, G. E. M. (1975) "Causality and determination," in Sosa (ed.) (1975), pp. 63–81.

Armstrong, D. M. (1968a) "The headless woman illusion and the defence of Materialism," *Analysis* 29, pp. 48–9.

Armstrong, D. M. (1968b) *A Materialist Theory of the Mind*, London: Routledge & Kegan Paul.

Armstrong, D. M. (1980a) "The nature of mind," in Block (1980b), pp. 191–9.

Armstrong, D. M. (1980b) *The Nature of Mind and Other Essays*, Brisbane: University of Queensland Press.

Austin, J. L. (1979) "Other minds," in *Philosophical Papers*, ed. J. O. Urmson and G. J. Warnock, 3rd edn, Oxford: Oxford University Press, pp. 76–116.

Barsalou, L. (1987) "The instability of graded structure: implications for the nature of concepts," in U. Neisser (ed.) *Concepts and Conceptual Development: Ecological and Intellectual Factors in Categorization*, Cambridge: Cambridge University Press.

Bartoshuk, L. M. (1978) "Gustatory system," in: R. B. Masterton (ed.) *Handbook of Behavioral Neurobiology*, vol. 1, *Sensory Integration*, New York: Plenum Press, pp. 503–67.

Bealer, G. (1982) *Quality and Concept*, Oxford: Clarendon Press.

Bealer, G. (1987) "The philosophical limits of scientific essentialism," *Philosophical Perspectives* 1, pp. 289–365.

Bealer, G. (1992) "The incoherence of empiricism," *Proceedings of the Aristotelian Society*, suppl. vol. 66, pp. 99–138.

Bealer, G. (forthcoming): *Philosophical Limits of Science*, Oxford: Oxford University Press.

Benacerraf, P. (1973) "Mathematical truth," *Journal of Philosophy* 70, pp. 661–79.

Block, N. (1980a) "Introduction: what is functionalism?", in Block (ed.) (1980b), pp. 171–84.

Block, N. (ed.) (1980b) *Readings in Philosophy of Psychology*, vol. 1, Cambridge, Mass.: Harvard University Press.

Block, N. (ed.) (1981) *Readings in Philosophy of Psychology*, vol. 2, Cambridge, Mass.: Harvard University Press.

Block, N. (1986) "Advertisement for a semantics for psychology," *Midwest Studies in Philosophy* 10, pp. 615–78.

Block, N. and Fodor, J. A. (1972) "What psychological states are not," *Philosophical Review* 81, pp. 159–81.

Boyd, R. (1980) "Materialism without reductionism: what physicalism does not entail," in Block (ed.) (1980b), pp. 67–106.

Brentano, F. (1973) *Psychology from an Empirical Standpoint*, ed. L. McAlister, London: Routledge & Kegan Paul.

Broad, C. D. (1925) *The Mind and its Place in Nature*, London: Routledge & Kegan Paul.

Brueckner, A. L. (1986) "Brains in a vat," *Journal of Philosophy* 83, pp. 148–67.

Burge, T. (1979) "Individualism and the mental," *Midwest Studies in Philosophy* 4, pp. 73–121.

Burge, T. (1982) "Other bodies," in Woodfield (1982), pp. 97–120.

Burge, T. (1988) "Individualism and self-knowledge," *Journal of Philosophy* 85, pp. 649–63.

Burge, T. (1989) "Individuation and causation in psychology," *Pacific Philosophical Quarterly* 70, pp. 303–22.

Cartwright, N. (1983) *How the Laws of Physics Lie*, Oxford: Clarendon Press.

Causey, R. L. (1977) *Unity of Science*, Dordrecht: Reidel.

Caws, P. (1979) *Sartre*, London: Routledge & Kegan Paul.

Chomsky, N. (1975) *Reflections on Language*, New York: Pantheon Press.

Christensen, S. M. and Turner, D. R. (eds) (1993) *Folk Psychology and the Philosophy of Mind*, Hillsdale, NJ: Erlbaum.

Churchland, P. M. (1981) "Eliminative materialism and the propositional attitudes, *Journal of Philosophy* 78, pp. 67–90.

Churchland, P. M. (1984) *Matter and Consciousness: a Contemporary Introduction to the Philosophy of Mind*, Cambridge, Mass.: Bradford Books/MIT Press (rev. edn 1988).

Churchland, P. M. (1985) "Reduction, qualia, and the direct introspection of brain states," *Journal of Philosophy* 82, pp. 8–28.

Churchland, P. M. (1986) "Some reductive strategies in cognitive neurobiology," *Mind* 95, pp. 279–309.

Churchland, P. M. (1988) "Folk psychology and the explanation of human behaviour," *Proceedings of the Aristotelian Society*, suppl. vol. 62, pp. 209–21; reprinted in Christensen and Turner (1993).

Churchland, P. M. (1989) *A Neurocomputational Perspective: the Nature of Mind and the Structure of Science*, Cambridge, Mass.: Bradford Books/MIT Press.

Churchland, P. M. (1993) "Theory, taxonomy and methodology: a reply to Haldane's *Understanding Folk*," *Proceedings of the Aristotelian Society* 93, pp. 313–19.

Churchland, P. M. and Churchland, P. S. (1990) "Could a machine think?", *Scientific American* 262, pp. 32–7.

Churchland, P. S. (1986) *Neurophilosophy: Toward a Unified Understanding of the Mind–Brain*, Cambridge, Mass.: Bradford Books/MIT Press.

Churchland, P. S. (1987) Reply to McGinn, Letters to the Editor, *Times Literary Supplement*, March 13.

Cooper, D. E. (1990) *Existentialism: a Reconstruction*, Oxford: Blackwell.

Crane, T. (1992) "Mental causation and mental reality," *Proceedings of the Aristotelian Society* 92, pp. 185–202.

Cummins, R. (1989) *Meaning and Mental Representation*, Cambridge, Mass.: Bradford Books/MIT Press.

Davidson, D. (1963) "Actions, reasons, and causes," *Journal of Philosophy* 60, pp. 685–700; reprinted in Davidson (1980), pp. 3–19.

Davidson, D. (1970) "Mental events," in L. Foster and J. W. Swanson (eds) *Experience and Theory*, Amherst, Mass.: University of Massachusetts Press, pp. 79–101; reprinted in Davidson (1980), pp. 229–44.

Davidson, D. (1974) "Psychology as Philosophy," in S. C. Brown (ed.) *Philosophy of Psychology*, London: Macmillan, pp. 41–52; reprinted in Davidson (1980).

Davidson, D. (1980) *Essays on Actions and Events*, Oxford: Clarendon Press.

Davidson, D. (1985) "Replies to Essays X–XII," in B. Vermazen and M. B. Hintikka (eds) *Essays on Davidson: Actions and Events*, Oxford: Clarendon Press, pp. 242–52.

Davidson, D. (1986) "A nice derangement of epitaphs," in E. LePore (ed.) *Truth and Interpretation: Perspectives on the Philosophy of Donald Davidson*, Oxford: Blackwell, pp. 433–46.

Davidson, D. (1987) "Knowing one's own mind," *Proceedings and Addresses of the American Philosophical Association* 60, pp. 441–58.

Davidson, D. (1989) "The myth of the subjective," in M. Krausz (ed.) *Relativism: Interpretation and Confrontation*, Notre Dame, Ind.: Notre Dame University Press, pp. 159–72.

Davidson, D. (1993) "Thinking causes," in: Heil and Mele (eds) (1993), pp. 3–17.

Dennett, D. C. (1978) *Brainstorms: Philosophical Essays on Mind and Psychology*, Montgomery, Vt.: Bradford Books/MIT Press.

Dennett, D. C. (1987) *The Intentional Stance*, Cambridge, Mass.: Bradford Books/MIT Press.

Dennett, D. C. (1988) "Quining qualia," in A. J. Marcel and E. Bisiach (eds) *Consciousness in Contemporary Science*, Oxford: Clarendon Press, pp. 42–77.

Dennett, D. C. (1991) *Consciousness Explained*, Boston, Mass.: Little, Brown.

Descartes, R. (1985) *The Philosophical Writings of Descartes*, trans. J. Cottingham, R. Stoothoff, D. Murdoch, A. Kenny, vol. 1, Cambridge: Cambridge University Press.

Descartes, R. (1986) *Meditations on First Philosophy*, trans. J. Cottingham, Cambridge: Cambridge University Press.

Devitt, M. (1990) "A narrow representational theory of the mind," in Lycan (ed.) (1990), pp. 371–98.

Devitt, M. and Sterelny, K. (1987) *Language and Reality: an Introduction to the Philosophy of Language*, Cambridge, Mass.: Bradford Books/MIT Press.

Dretske, F. (1981) *Knowledge and the Flow of Information*, Cambridge, Mass.: Bradford Books/MIT Press.

Dretske, F. (1988) *Explaining Behavior: Reasons in a World of Causes*, Cambridge, Mass.: Bradford Books/MIT Press.

Dretske, F. (1989) "Reasons and causes," *Philosophical Perspectives* 3, pp. 1–15.

Dreyfus, H. (1991) *Being-In-the-World: a Commentary on Heidegger's Being and Time, Division I*, Cambridge, Mass.: MIT Press.

Dreyfus, H. and Hall, H. (eds) (1982) *Husserl, Intentionality, and Cognitive Science*, Cambridge, Mass.: Bradford Books/MIT Press.

Earman, J. (1986) *A Primer on Determinism*, Dordrecht: Reidel.

Edelman, G. (1992) *Bright Air, Brilliant Fire: on the Matter of the Mind*, Harmondsworth: Penguin Books.

Enç, B. (1983) "In defense of the identity theory," *Journal of Philosophy* 80, pp. 279–98.

Falvey, K. and Owens, J. (forthcoming), "Psychological externalism, self-knowledge and skepticism."

Farrell, B. A. (1950) "Experience," *Mind* 59, pp. 170–98.

Feng-hsiung Hsu *et al.* (1990) "A grandmaster chess machine," *Scientific American* 263, pp. 44–50.

Feyerabend, P. K. (1963) "Mental events and the brain," *Journal of Philosophy* 60, pp. 295–6.

Field, H. (1977) "Logic, meaning, and conceptual role," *Journal of Philosophy* 74, pp. 379–409.

Field, H. (1986) "Critical notice: R. Stalnaker, *Inquiry*," *Philosophy of Science* 53, pp. 425–48.

Fodor, J. A. (1965) "Explanations in psychology," in M. Black (ed.) *Philosophy in America*, London: George Allen " Unwin, pp. 161–79.

Fodor, J. A. (1974) "Special Sciences, or: the disunity of science as a working hypothesis," *Synthese* 28, pp. 97–115.

Fodor, J. A. (1975) *The Language of Thought*, New York: Crowell.

Fodor, J. A. (1980) "Methodological solipsism considered as a research strategy in cognitive psychology," *Behavioral and Brain Sciences* 3, pp. 63–73.

Fodor, J. A. (1981a) "Introduction: some notes on what linguistics is about," in Block (ed.) (1981) pp. 197–207.

Fodor, J. A. (1981b) "Propositional attitudes," in Fodor (1981c), pp. 177–203.

Fodor, J. A. (1981c) *Representations: Philosophical Essays on the Foundations of Cognitive Science*, Cambridge, Mass.: MIT Press.

Fodor, J. A. (1981d) "Three cheers for propositional attitudes," in Fodor (1981b), pp. 100–23.

Fodor, J. A. (1982) "Cognitive science and the twin-earth problem," *Notre Dame Journal of Formal Logic* 23, pp. 98–118.

Fodor, J. A. (1983) *The Modularity of Mind: an Essay on Faculty Psychology*, Cambridge, Mass.: Bradford Books/MIT Press.

Fodor, J. A. (1987) *Psychosemantics: the Problem of Meaning in the Philosophy of Mind*, Cambridge, Mass.: Bradford Books/MIT Press.

Fodor, J. A. (1990a) *A Theory of Content and Other Essays*, Cambridge, Mass.: Bradford Books/MIT Press.

Fodor, J. A. (1990b) "Psychosemantics, or where do truth conditions come from?", in Lycan (ed.) (1990), pp. 312–37.

Follesdal, D. (1985) "Causation and explanation: a problem in Davidson's view on action and mind," in LePore and McLaughlin (eds) (1985), pp. 311–23.

Foster, J. (1991) *The Immaterial Self: a Defence of the Cartesian Dualist Conception of the Mind*, London: Routledge.

Fry, D. B. (1979) *The Physics of Speech*, Cambridge: Cambridge University Press.

Gardner, H. (1985) *The Mind's New Science: a History of the Cognitive Revolution*, New York: Basic Books.

Giere, R. N. (1988) *Explaining Science: a Cognitive Approach*, Chicago: University of Chicago Press.

Ginet, C. (1990) *On Action*, Cambridge: Cambridge University Press.

Glymour, C., Kelly, K., Scheines, R., and Sprites, P. (1987) *Discovering Causal Structure: Artificial Intelligence, Philosophy of Science, and Statistical Modeling*, Orlando Fla.: Academic Press.

Goldman, A. I. (1989) "Interpretation psychologized," *Mind and Language* 4, pp. 161–85.

Goodman, N. (1983) *Fact, Fiction, and Forecast*, 4th edn, Cambridge, Mass.: Harvard University Press.

Gordon, R. M. (1986) "Folk psychology as simulation," *Mind and Language* 1, pp. 158–71.

Haldane, J. (1988a) "Folk psychology and the explanation of human behaviour: understanding folk," *Proceedings of the Aristotelian Society*, suppl. vol. 62, pp. 223–54; reprinted in Christensen and Turner (1993).

Haldane, J. (1988b) "Psychoanalysis, cognitive psychology and self-consciousness," in P. Clark and C. Wright (eds) *Mind, Psychoanalysis and Science*, Oxford: Blackwell, pp. 113–39.

Haldane, J. (1989) "Brentano's problem," *Grazer Philosophische Studien* 35.

Haldane, J. (1991) "Incarnational anthropology," in D. Cockburn (ed.) *Human Beings*, Cambridge: Cambridge University Press, pp. 191–211.

Haldane, J. (1993) "Theory, realism and common sense: a reply to Paul Churchland," *Proceedings of the Aristotelian Society* 93, pp. 321–7.

Haldane, J. (forthcoming) "Mind–world identity and the anti-realist challenge," in J. Haldane and C. Wright (eds) *Realism, Reason, and Projection*, New York: Oxford University Press.

Harman, G. (1986) "Wide functionalism," in S. Schiffer and S. Steele (eds) *Cognition and Representation*, Boulder, Colo.: Westview Press, pp. 11–20.

Harman, G. (1990) "The intrinsic quality of experience," *Philosophical Perspectives* 4, pp. 31–52.

Hart, W. (1988) *Engines of the Soul*, New York: Cambridge University Press.

Haugeland, J. (1982) "Weak supervenience," *American Philosophical Quarterly* 19, pp. 93–103.

Heil, J. (1992) *The Nature of True Minds*, Cambridge: Cambridge University Press.

Heil, J. and Mele, A. (1991) "Mental causes," *American Philosophical Quarterly* 28, pp. 61–71.

Heil, J. and Mele, A. (eds) (1993) *Mental Causation*, Oxford: Clarendon Press.

Hellman, G. P. and Thompson, F. W. (1975) "Physicalism: ontology, determination, and reduction," *Journal of Philosophy* 72, pp. 551–64.

Hilbert, D. R. (1987) *Color and Color Perception*. Stanford, Calif.: CSLI.

Honderich, T. (1982) "The argument for anomalous monism," Analysis 42(1), pp. 59–64.

Honderich, T. (1984) "Smith and the champion of mauve," *Analysis* 44(2), pp. 86–9.

Honderich, T. (1988) *A Theory of Determinism: the Mind, Neuroscience, and Life-Hopes*, Oxford: Clarendon Press.

Honderich, T. (1990) *A Theory of Determinism: Mind and Brain*, Oxford: Clarendon Press (paperback edn of first half of Honderich (1988)).

Honderich, T. (1991) "Seeing qualia and positing the world," in A. P. Griffiths (ed.) *A. J. Ayer: Memorial Essays*, Cambridge: Cambridge University Press, pp. 129–51.

Honderich, T. (1993) "The union theory and anti- individualism," in Heil and Mele (eds) (1993), pp. 137–59.

Honderich, T. (1993) *How Free Are You? The Determinism Problem*, Oxford: Oxford University Press.

Honderich, T. (forthcoming) "Seeing things," *Synthese*.

Horgan, T. (1981) "Token physicalism, supervenience, and the generality of physics," *Synthese* 49, pp. 395–413.

Horgan, T. (1982) "Supervenience and microphysics," *Pacific Philosophical Quarterly* 63, pp. 29–43.

Horgan, T. (1984) "Supervenience and cosmic hermeneutics," *Southern Journal of Philosophy* 22, Spindel Conference Supplement, pp. 19–38.

Horgan, T. (1987) "Supervenient qualia," *Philosophical Review* 96, pp. 491–520.

Horgan, T. (1989) "Mental quausation," *Philosophical Perspectives* 3, pp. 47–76.

Horgan, T. (1991) "Actions, reasons, and the explanatory role of content," in B. P. McLaughlin (ed.) *Dretske and His Critics*, Oxford: Blackwell, pp. 73–101.

Horgan, T. (1993) "Nonreductive materialism and the explanatory autonomy of psychology," in Wagner and Warner (eds) (1993).

Horgan, T. and Tienson, J. (1990) "Soft laws," *Midwest Studies in Philosophy* 15, pp. 256–79.

Hume, D. (1978) *A Treatise of Human Nature*, ed. L. A. Selby-Bigge and P. H. Nidditch, 2nd edn, Oxford: Clarendon Press.

Jackson, F. (1982) "Epiphenomenal qualia," *Philosophical Quarterly* 32, pp. 127–36.

Jackson, F. (1986) "What Mary didn't know," *Journal of Philosophy* 83, pp. 291–5.

Jackson, F. and Pettit, P. (1988) "Functionalism and broad content," *Mind* 97, pp. 381–400.

Jackson, F. and Pettit, P. (1990) "In defence of folk psychology," *Philosophical Studies* 59, pp. 31–54.

Johnston, M. (1985) "Why having a mind matters," in LePore and McLaughlin, (eds) (1985), pp. 408–26.

Jones, T., Mulaire, E., and Stich, S. (1991) "Staving off catastrophe: a critical notice of Jerry Fodor's *Psychosemantics*," *Mind and Language* 6, pp. 58–82.

Kalin, N. (1993) "The neurobiology of fear," *Scientific American* 268 (5) (May), pp. 54–60.

Kim, J. (1972) "Phenomenal properties, psychophysical laws, and the identity theory," *The Monist* 56, pp. 177–92.

Kim, J. (1978) "Supervenience and nomological incommensurables," *American Philosophical Quarterly* 15, pp. 149–56.

Kim, J. (1979) "Causality, identity, and supervenience in the mind–body problem," *Midwest Studies in Philosophy* 4, pp. 31–49.

Kim, J. (1982) "Psychophysical supervenience," *Philosophical Studies* 41, pp. 51–70.

Kim, J. (1984a) "Concepts of supervenience," *Philosophy and Phenomenological Research* 45, pp. 153–76.

Kim, J. (1985b) "Epiphenomenal and supervenient causation," *Midwest Studies in Philosophy* 9, pp. 257–70.

Kim, J. (1985) "Psychophysical Laws," in LePore and McLaughlin (eds) (1985), pp. 369–86.

Kim, J. (1987) " 'Strong' and 'Global' supervenience revisited," *Philosophy and Phenomenological Research* 48, pp. 315–26.

Kim, J. (1988) "Supervenience for multiple domains," *Philosophical Topics* 16, pp. 129–50.

Kim, J. (1989) "Mechanism, purpose, and explanatory exclusion," *Philosophical Perspectives* 3, pp. 77–108.

Kim, J. (1992a) "Multiple realization and the metaphysics of reduction," *Philosophy and Phenomenological Research* 52, pp. 1–26.

Kim, J. (1992b) "Supervenience as a philosophical concept," *Metaphilosophy* 21, pp. 1–17.

Kripke, S. A. (1972) "Naming and necessity," in D. Davidson and G. Harman (eds), *Semantics of Natural Language*, Dordrecht: Reidel, pp. 253–355 and 763–9; reprinted 1980 as *Naming and Necessity*, Oxford: Blackwell.

Kripke, S. A. (1979) "A puzzle about belief," in A. Margalit (ed.) *Meaning and Use*, Dordrecht: Reidel, pp. 239–83.

Land, E. (1977) "The retinex theory of color vision," *Scientific American* 237, pp. 108–28.

Langley, P., Simon, H., Bradshaw, G., and Zytkov, J. (1987) *Scientific Discovery: Computational Explorations of the Creative Process*, Cambridge, Mass.: MIT Press.

LePore, E. and Loewer, B. (1987) "Mind matters," *Journal of Philosophy* 84, pp. 630–42.

LePore, E. and Loewer, B. (1989) "More on making mind matter," *Philosophical Topics* 17, pp. 175–91.

LePore, E. and McLaughlin, B. P. (eds) (1985) *Actions and Events: Perspectives on the Philosophy of Donald Davidson*, Oxford: Blackwell.

Levin, M. E. (1975) "Kripke's argument against the identity thesis," *Journal of Philosophy* 72, pp. 149–67.

Lewis, D. (1966) "An argument for the identity theory," *Journal of Philosophy* 63, pp. 17–25; reprinted 1971 in D. M. Rosenthal (ed.) *Materialism and the Mind–Body Problem*, Englewood Cliffs. NJ: Prentice-Hall, pp. 162–71.

Lewis, D. (1972) "Psychophysical and theoretical identifications," *Australiasian Journal of Philosophy* 50, pp. 249–58.

Lewis, D. (1973) *Counterfactuals*, Oxford: Blackwell.

Lewis, D. (1975) "Causation," in Sosa (ed.) (1975), pp. 180–91.

Lewis, D. (1980) "Mad pain and Martian pain," in Block (ed.) (1980b), pp. 216–22.

Lewis, D. (1983) "New work for a theory of universals," *Australian Journal of Philosophy* 61, pp. 343–77.

Loar, B. (1988) "Social content and psychological content," in: R. H.

Loar, B. (1981) *Mind and Meaning*, Cambridge: Cambridge University Press.

Grimm and D. D. Merrill (eds) *Contents of Thought*, Tucson, Ariz: University of Arizona Press, pp. 99–139.

Locke, J. (1975) *An Essay Concerning Human Understanding*, ed. P. H. Nidditch, Oxford: Clarendon Press.

Lockwood, M. (1989) *Mind, Brain, and the Quantum: the Compound "I"*, Oxford: Blackwell.

Loewer, B. (1987) "From information to intentionality," *Synthese* 70, pp. 287–317.

Lowe, E. J. (1991) "Real selves: persons of a substantial kind," sect. 4 in D. Cockburn (ed.) *Human Beings*, Cambridge: Cambridge University Press.

Lycan, W. G. (1988) *Judgement and Justification*, Cambridge: Cambridge University Press.

Lycan, W. G. (ed.) (1990) *Mind and Cognition: a Reader*, Oxford: Blackwell.

Mackie, J. L. (1979) "Mind, brain and causation," *Midwest Studies in Philosophy* 4, pp. 19–29.

Macnamara, J., Govitrikar, V., and Doan, B. (1988) "Actions, laws and scientific psychology," *Cognition* 29, pp. 1–27.

McCloskey, M. (1983) "Naive theories of motion," in D. Gentner and A. L. Stevens (eds), *Mental Models*, Hillsdale, NJ: Erlbaum.

McCloskey, M., Caramazza, A. and Green, B. (1980) "Curvilinear motion in the absence of external forces: naive beliefs about the motion of objects," *Science* 210 (4474), pp. 1139–41.

McGinn, C. (1977) "Charity interpretation and belief," *Journal of Philosophy* 74, pp. 521–35.

McGinn, C. (1982) "The structure of content," in Woodfield (ed.) (1982) pp. 207–58.

McGinn, C. (1989) "Can we solve the mind–body problem?", *Mind* 98, pp. 349–66.

McGinn, C. (1991a) "The hidden structure of consciousness," in McGinn (1991b) pp. 89–125.

McGinn, C. (1991b) *The Problem of Consciousness: Essays Towards Resolution*, Oxford: Blackwell.

McGinn, C. (1993): *Problems in Philosophy*, Oxford: Blackwell.

McLaughlin, B. P. (1984) "Event supervenience and supervenient causation," *Southern Journal of Philosophy*', 22, Spindel Conference Supplement, pp. 71–91.

McLaughlin, B. P. (1985) "Anomalous monism and the irreducibility of the mental," in LePore and McLaughlin (eds), (1985), pp. 331–68.

McLaughlin, B. P. (1989) "Type epiphenomenalism, type dualism and the causal priority of the physical," *Philosophical Perspectives* 3, pp. 109–35.

Malcolm, N. (1968) "The conceivability of mechanism," *Philosophical Review* 77, pp. 45–72.

Marr, D. (1982) *Vision: a Computational Investigation into the Human Representation and Processing of Visual Information*, San Francisco: W. H. Freeman.

Martin, C. B. (forthcoming): "The need for ontology: some alternatives," *Philosophy*.

Martin, C. B. (unpublished): "A new view of the mind."

Martin, C. B. and Pfeifer, K. (1986) "Intentionality and the non- psychological," *Philosophy and Phenomenological Research* 46, pp. 531–54.

Mates, B. (1950) "Synonymity," *University of California Publications in Philosophy* 25.

Maxwell, J. C. (1877) "The kinetic theory of Gases," *Nature* 16, pp. 245–6.

Mele, A. R. (1992) *Springs of Action: Understanding Intentional Behavior*, New York: Oxford University Press.

Menzies, P. (1988) "Against causal reductionism," *Mind* 97, pp. 551–74.

Millikan, R. G. (1984) *Language, Thought and Other Biological Categories: New Foundations for Realism*, Cambridge, Mass.: Bradford Books/MIT Press.

Morgan, C. L. (1923) *Emergent Evolution*, London: Williams " Norgate.

Mulhall, S. (1990) *On Being in the World: Wittgenstein and Heidegger on Seeing Aspects*, London: Routledge.

Murdock, G. P. (1980) *Theories of Illness: a World Survey*, Pittsburgh, Pa.: University of Pittsburgh Press.

Murphy, G. and Medin, D. (1985) "The role of theories in conceptual coherence," *Psychological Review*, 92(3), pp. 289–316.

Myro, G. (1993) "Thinking," in Robinson (ed.) (1993), pp. 27–38.

Nagel, E. (1961) *The Structure of Science*, New York: Harcourt, Brace & World.

Nagel, T. (1974) "What is it like to be a bat?" *Philosophical Review* 83, pp. 435–50; reprinted in Block (1980b), pp. 159–68, and in Nagel 1979, pp. 165–80.

Nagel, T. (1979a) *Mortal Questions*, Cambridge: Cambridge University Press.

Nagel, T. (1979b) "Panpsychism," in Nagel (1979a), pp. 181–95.

Nagel, T. (1979c) "Subjective and objective," in Nagel (1979a), pp. 196–213.

Nagel, T. (1986) *The View from Nowhere*, Oxford and New York: Oxford University Press.

Nersessian, N. J. (1992) "How do scientists think? Capturing the dynamics of conceptual change in science," in R. N. Giere (ed.) *Cognitive Models of Science* (*Minnesota Studies in the Philosophy of Science*, vol. 15), Minneapolis, Minn.: University of Minnesota Press, pp. 3–44.

Nozick, R. (1981) *Philosophical Explanations*, Cambridge, Mass.: Harvard University Press.

Owens, J. (1986) "The failure of Lewis's functionalism," *Philosophical Quarterly* 36, pp. 159–73.

Owens, J. (1987) "In defense of a different doppelganger," *Philosophical Review* 96, pp. 521–54.

Owens, J. (1989) "Contradictory belief and cognitive access," *Midwest Studies in Philosophy* 14, pp. 289–316.

Owens, J. (1990) "Cognitive access and semantic puzzles," in C. A. Anderson and J. Owens (eds), *Propositional Attitudes: the Role of Content in Logic, Language, and Mind*, Stanford, Calif.: CSLI, pp. 147–73.

Owens, J. (1992) "Psychophysical supervenience: its epistemological foundation," *Synthese* 90, pp. 89–117.

Owens, J. (forthcoming): "Content, causation, and psychophysical supervenience," *Philosophy of Science*.

Papineau, D. (1987) *Reality and Representation*, Oxford: Blackwell.

Pattison, M. (1988) *Memoirs of an Oxford Don*, London: Cassell.

Perry, J. (1979) "The problem of the essential indexicals," *Noûs* 13, pp. 3–21.

Petrie, B. (1987) "Global supervenience and reduction," *Philosophy and Phenomenological Research* 48, pp. 119–30.

Pickett, J. M. (1980) *The Sounds of Speech Communication: a Primer of Acoustic Phonetics and Speech Perception*, Baltimore, Md.: University Park Press.

Place, U. T. (1956) "Is consciousness a brain process?", *British Journal of Psychology* 47, pp. 44–50.

Place, U. T. (1988) "Thirty years on: is consciousness still a brain process?", *Australasian Journal of Philosophy* 66, pp. 208–19.

Popper, K. R. and Eccles, J. C. (1978) *The Self and Its Brain*, New York: Springer International.

Post, J. F. (1987) *The Faces of Existence: an Essay in Nonreductive Metaphysics*, Ithaca, NY: Cornell University Press.

Putnam, H. (1961) "Minds and machines," in S. Hook (ed.) *Dimensions of Mind: a Symposium*, New York: Collier, pp. 138–64; reprinted in Putnam (1975b), pp. 362–85.

Putnam, H. (1966) "The mental life of some machines," in H. -N. Castañeda (ed.) *Intentionality, Minds, and Perception*, Detroit, Mich.: Wayne State University Press, pp. 177–200.

Putnam, H. (1967) "Psychological predicates," in W. H. Capitan and D. D. Merrill (eds), *Art, Mind, and Religion*, Pittsburgh, Pa: University of Pittsburgh Press, pp. 37–48; reprinted as "The nature of mental states," in Putnam (1975b), pp. 429–40.

Putnam, H. (1975a) "The meaning of 'Meaning' " in K. Gunderson (ed.) *Language, Mind, and Knowledge* (*Minnesota Studies in the Philosophy of Science*, vol. 7), Minneapolis, Minn.: University of Minnesota Press, pp. 131–93; reprinted in Putnam (1975b), pp. 215–71.

Putnam, H. (1975b) *Philosophical Papers*, vol. 2, *Mind, Language, and Reality*, Cambridge: Cambridge University Press.

Putnam, H. (1975c) "Philosophy and our mental life," in Putnam (1975b), pp. 291–303.

Putnam, H. (1981) *Reason, Truth and History*, Cambridge: Cambridge University Press.

Putnam, H. (1988) *Representation and Reality*, Cambridge, Mass.: Bradford Books/MIT Press.

Pylyshyn, Z. W. (1985) *Computation and Cognition: Toward a Foundation for Cognitive Science*, Cambridge, Mass.: Bradford Books/MIT Press.

Quine, W. V. O. (1960) *Word and Object*, Cambridge, Mass.: MIT Press.

Quine, W. V. O. (1961) "Two dogmas of empiricism," in *From a Logical Point of View: Nine Logico-Philosophical Essays*, New York: Harper " Row, pp. 20–46.

Quine, W. V. O. (1990) *Pursuit of Truth*, Cambridge, Mass.: Harvard University Press.

Ramsey, W., Stich. S., and Garon, J. (1990) "Connectionism, eliminativism and the future of folk psychology," *Philosophical Perspectives* 4, pp. 499–533.

Rey, G. (1983) "A reason for doubting the existence of consciousness," in R. J. Davidson, G. E. Schwartz, and D. Shapiro (eds), *Consciousness and Self-Regulation*, vol. 3, New York: Plenum, pp. 1–39.

Rips, L. (1989) "Similarity, typicality, and categorization," in S. Vosniadou and A. Ortony (eds), *Similarity and Analogical Reasoning*, Cambridge: Cambridge University Press.

Robinson, H. (1982) *Matter and Sense*, Cambridge: Cambridge University Press.

Robinson, H. (ed.) (1993) *Objections to Physicalism*, Oxford: Clarendon Press.

Rorty, R. (1965) "Mind–body identity, privacy and categories," *Review of Metaphysics* 29(1), pp. 24–54.

Rorty, R. (1970) "Incorrigibility as the mark of the mental," *Journal of Philosophy* 67(12) pp. 399–424.

Rorty, R. (1991) "Introduction: antirepresentationalism, ethnocentrism, and liberalism," in *Philosophical Papers*, vol. 1, *Objectivity, Relativism and Truth*, Cambridge: Cambridge University Press, pp. 1–17.

Rorty, R. (1993) "Holism, intrinsicality, and the ambition of transcendence," in B. Dahlbom (ed.) *Dennett and His Critics: Demystifying Mind*, Oxford: Blackwell, pp. 184–202.

Ryle, G. (1949) *The Concept of Mind*, London: Hutchinson.

Scheffler, I. (1967) *Science and Subjectivity*, Indianapolis, Ind.: Bobbs-Merrill.

Seager, W. (1991) *Metaphysics of Consciousness*, London: Routledge.

Searle, J. R. (1980) "Minds, brains, and programs," *Behavioral and Brain Sciences* 3, pp. 417–24.

Searle, J. R. (1983) *Intentionality: an Essay in the Philosophy of Mind*, Cambridge: Cambridge University Press.

Searle, J. R. (1984) *Minds, Brains and Science: the 1984 Reith Lectures*, Cambridge, Mass.: Harvard University Press and Harmondsworth: Penguin Books.

Searle, J. R. "Indeterminancy, empiricism, and the first person," *Journal of Philosophy* 83(3), pp. 123–46.

Searle, J. R. (1990) "Is the brain's mind a computer program?", *Scientific American* 262, pp. 26–31.

Shoemaker, S. (1975) "Functionalism and qualia," *Philosophical Studies* 27, pp. 291–315; reprinted in Shoemaker (1984).

Shoemaker, S. (1982) "The inverted spectrum," *Journal of Philosophy* 79, pp. 357–81; reprinted in Shoemaker (1984).

Shoemaker, S. (1984) *Identity, Cause and Mind: Philosophical Essays*, Cambridge: Cambridge University Press.

Shoemaker, S. (1988) "On knowing one's own mind," *Philosophical Perspectives* 2, pp. 183–209.

Shoemaker, S. (1990) "First-person access," *Philosophical Perspectives* 4, pp. 187–214.

Skillen, A. (1984) "Mind and matter: a problem that refuses dissolution," *Mind* 93, pp. 514–26.

Sklar, L. (1967) "Types of inter-theoretic reduction," *British Journal for the Philosophy of Science* 18, pp. 109–24.

Sklar, L. (1974) *Space, Time, and SpaceTime*, Berkeley, Calif.: University of California Press.

Smith, E. and Medin, D. (1981) *Categories and Concepts*, Cambridge, Mass.: Harvard University Press.

Sober, E. (1984) *The Nature of Selection: Evolutionary Theory in Philosophical Focus*, Cambridge, Mass.: Bradford Books/MIT Press.

Sosa, E. (ed.) (1975) *Causation and Conditionals*, London: Oxford University Press.

Sosa, E. (1984) "Mind–Body interaction and supervenient causation," *Midwest Studies in Philosophy* 9, pp. 271–82.

Stack, M. (1980) "Why I don't believe in beliefs and you shouldn't," paper delivered at annual meeting of the Society for Philosophy and unpublished Psychology.

Stalnaker, R. (1968) "A theory of conditionals," in N. Rescher (ed.) *Studies in Logical Theory*, Oxford: Blackwell, pp. 98–112.

Sterelny, K. (1990) *The Representational Theory of Mind: an Introduction*, Oxford: Blackwell.

Stich, S. (1978) "Autonomous psychology and the belief–desire thesis," *The Monist* 61, pp. 573–91.

Stich, S. (1983) *From Folk Psychology to Cognitive Science: the Case against Belief*, Cambridge, Mass.: Bradford Books/MIT Press.

Stich, S. (1987) Review of J. R. Searle, *Minds, Brains and Science*, *Philosophical Review* 96, pp. 129–33.

Stich, S. (1991) "Do true believers exist?" *Proceedings of the Aristotelian Society*, suppl. vol. 65, pp. 229–44.

Stich, S. and Laurence, S. (in preparation) "Intentionality and naturalism."

Stich, S. and Nichols, S. (forthcoming) "Folk psychology: simulation or tacit theory?", *Mind and Language*.

Stoutland, F. (1976) "The causation of behavior," *Acta Philosophica Fennica* 28 (1–3) (Essays on Wittgenstein in Honour of G. H. von Wright), pp. 286–325.

Strawson, G. (forthcoming) *Mental Reality*, Cambridge, Mass.: Bradford Books/MIT Press.

Strawson, P. F. (1959) *Individuals: an Essay in Descriptive Metaphysics*, London: Methuen.

Swinburne, R. (1986) *The Evolution of the Soul*, Oxford: Clarendon Press.

Taylor, C. (1970) "Mind–body identity, a side issue?", in C. V. Borst (ed.) *The Mind–Brain Identity Theory*, Toronto: Macmillan, pp. 231–41.

Taylor, C. (1985) *Philosophical Papers*, vol. 1, *Human Agency and Language*, Cambridge: Cambridge University Press.

Taylor, C. (1987) "Overcoming epistemology," in K. Baynes, J. Bohman, and T. McCarthy (eds), *After Philosophy: End or Transformation?*, Cambridge, Mass.: MIT Press, pp. 464–88.

Thagard, P. (1988) *Computational Philosophy of Science*, Cambridge, Mass.: Bradford Books/MIT Press.

Tye, M. (1992) "Naturalism and the mental," *Mind* 101(403) (April), pp. 421–41.

Van Gulick, R. (1988) "Metaphysical arguments for internationalism and why they don't work," in S. Silvers (ed.) *Re-representations: Readings in the Philosophy of Mental Representation*, Dordrecht: Reidel.

Vendler, Z. (1984) *The Matter of Minds*, Oxford: Clarendon Press.

Vendler, Z. (1991) "Epiphenomena," in A. P. Martinich and M. J. White (eds) *Certainty and Surface in Epistemology and Philosophical Method: Essays in Honor of Avrum Stroll*, Lewiston, Ut.: Edwin Mellen Press, pp. 101–14.

Wagner, S. and Warner, R. (eds) (1993) *Naturalism: a Critical Appraisal*, South Bend, Ind. University of Notre Dame Press.

Warner, R. (1986) "A challenge to physicalism," *Australasian Journal of Philosophy* 64, pp. 249–65.

Warner, R. (1989) "Why is logic a priori?" *The Monist* 72, pp. 40–51.

Warner, R. (1993a) "Incorrigibility," in Robinson (ed.) (1993), pp. 185–205.

Warner, R. (1993b) "Is the body a physical object?", in Wagner and Warner (1993), pp. 255–71.

Warner, R. (forthcoming) "Incommensurability as a jurisprudential Puzzle," *Chicago-Kent Law Review*.

Weinberg, S. (1992) *Dreams of a Final Theory*, New York: Pantheon Press.

Wilson, G. M. (1989) *The Intentionality of Human Action*, Stanford, Calif.: Stanford University Press.

Wittgenstein, L. (1953) *Philosophical Investigations*, trans. G. E. M. Anscombe, Oxford: Blackwell.

Wittgenstein, L. (1958) *The Blue and Brown Books*, Oxford: Blackwell.

Woodfield, A. (ed.) (1982) *Thought and Object: Essays on Intentionality*, Oxford: Clarendon Press.

Index